# PCI System Architecture

## Third Edition

*MindShare, Inc.*

*Tom Shanley*
*and*
*Don Anderson*

**Addison-Wesley Publishing Company**
Reading, Massachusetts • Menlo Park, California • New York
Don Mills, Ontario • Wokingham, England • Amsterdam
Bonn • Sydney • Singapore • Tokyo • Madrid • San Juan
Paris • Seoul • Milan • Mexico City • Taipei

**Library of Congress Cataloging-in-Publication Data**

ISBN: 0-201-40993-3

Copyright © 1995 by MindShare, Inc.

Sponsoring Editor: Keith Wollman
Project Editor: Eleanor McCarthy
Production Coordinator: Lora L. Ryan
Cover design: Barbara T. Atkinson
Set in 10 point Palatino by MindShare, Inc.

4 5 6 7 8 9 10-MA-9998979695
Fourth printing, November 1995

To Nancy and Sheryl, two very understanding ladies.

# Contents

## About This Book

## Part I: Introduction to the Local Bus Concept

## Chapter 1: The Problem

## Chapter 2: Solutions, VESA and PCI

# PCI System Architecture

# Part II: Revision 2.1 Essentials

## Chapter 3: Intro to PCI Bus Operation

## Chapter 4: Intro to Reflected-Wave Switching

# Contents

## Chapter 5: The Functional Signal Groups

## Chapter 6: PCI Bus Arbitration

# Chapter 7: The Commands

# Contents

# Chapter 8: The Read and Write Transfers

# Chapter 9: Premature Transaction Termination

# Contents

## Chapter 10: Error Detection and Handling

# Contents

## Chapter 12: Shared Resource Acquisition

## Chapter 13: The 64-bit PCI Extension

# Chapter 14: Add-In Cards and Connectors

# Contents

# Part III: Device Configuration in System with a Single PCI Bus

## Chapter 15: Intro to Configuration Address Space

## Chapter 16: Configuration Transactions

# PCI System Architecture

# Chapter 17: Configuration Registers

# Contents

## Chapter 18: Expansion ROMs

## Part IV: PCI-to-PCI Bridge

## Chapter 19: PCI-to-PCI Bridge

# PCI System Architecture

# Contents

# Part V: The PCI BIOS

## Chapter 20: The PCI BIOS

# Part VI: PCI Cache Support

## Chapter 21: PCI Cache Support

# Contents

# Part VII: 66MHz PCI Implementation

## Chapter 22: 66MHz PCI Implementation

# Part VIII: Overview of VLSI Technology VL82C59x Supercore PCI Chipset

## Chapter 23: Overview of VLSI Technology VL82C59x Supercore PCI Chipset

# Contents

# Appendices

# Figures

# PCI System Architecture

# Figures

# Tables

## Acknowledgments

To John Swindle for his tireless attention to detail and his marvelous teaching ability. To the editorial staff at Addison-Wesley for their patience. To the folks at Computer Literacy Bookshops for their collective support in the initial launch of this book series. And finally, to the many hundreds of engineers at Intel, IBM, Compaq, Dell, Hewlett-Packard, Motorola, and other clients, who subject themselves to our teaching on a regular basis.

# Acknowledgments

## The MindShare Architecture Series

The MindShare Architecture book series includes: *ISA System Architecture*, *EISA System Architecture*, *80486 System Architecture*, *PCI System Architecture*, *Pentium System Architecture*, *PCMCIA System Architecture*, *PowerPC System Architecture*, *Plug-and-Play System Architecture*, and *AMD K5 System Architecture*.

Rather than duplicating common information in each book, the series uses the building-block approach. *ISA System Architecture* is the core book upon which the others build. The figure below illustrates the relationship of the books to each other.

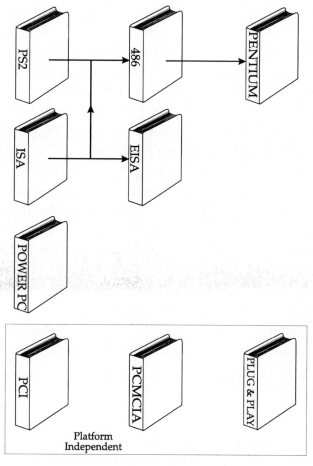

*Series Organization*

## Organization of This Book

The third edition of *PCI System Architecture* has been updated to reflect revision 2.1 of the PCI bus specification. In addition, it has been completely reorganized and expanded to include more detailed discussions of virtually every topic found in the first two editions. The book is divided into eight parts:

- **Part I: Intro to the Local Bus Concept**. Defines the performance problems inherent in PC architecture before the introduction of the local bus. Having defined the problem, the possible solutions are explored.
- **Part II: Revision 2.1 PCI Essentials**. This part of the book provides a detailed explanation of the mainstream aspects of PCI bus operation.
- **Part III: Device Configuration In a System With a Single PCI Bus**. Provides an introduction to the PCI configuration address space, a detailed description of the methods for generating configuration bus transactions, the configuration read and write transactions timing, the configuration registers defined by the specification, and the implementation of expansion ROMs associated with PCI devices.
- **Part IV: The PCI-to-PCI Bridge**. This part provides a detailed discussion of the PCI-to-PCI Bridge specification, a discussion of peer and hierarchical PCI buses, and the accessing of configuration registers in devices residing on subordinate PCI buses.
- **Part V: The PCI BIOS**. This part provides a detailed discussion of the PCI BIOS specification.
- **Part VI: Support for Cacheable PCI Memory**.
- **Part VII: 66MHz PCI Implementation**.
- **Part VIII: Overview of VLSI VL82C59x Supercore Chipset**. This part provides an operational overview of the VLSI chip set.

## Cautionary Note

The reader of this or any other book that covers an evolving hardware technology should be aware that the official specification should be used during the design process. The specification has the final say of what's right and what's wrong. In addition, the reader must realize that the specification for an emerging technology is rapidly evolving. We make every attempt to produce our books on a timely basis, but the next revision of the specification sometimes outruns us.

This version of our PCI book complies with revision 2.1 of the specification, dated 6/1/95.

## Who this Book is For

This book is intended for use by hardware and software design and support personnel. Due to the clear, concise explanatory methods used to describe each subject, personnel outside of the design field may also find the text useful.

## Prerequisite Knowledge

It is highly recommended that the reader have a good knowledge of PC and processor bus architecture prior to reading this book. The MindShare publications entitled *ISA System Architecture* and *80486 System Architecture* provide all of the background necessary for a complete understanding of the subject matter covered in this book. Alternately, the reader may substitute *Pentium System Architecture* or *PowerPC System Architecture* for *80486 System Architecture*.

## Object Size Designations

The following designations are used throughout this book when referring to the size of data objects:

- A **byte** is an 8-bit object.
- A **word** is a 16-bit, or two byte, object.
- A **doubleword** is a 32-bit or four byte, object.
- A **quadword** is a 64-bit, or eight byte, object.
- A **paragraph** is a 128-bit, or 16 byte, object.
- A **page** is a 4K-aligned 4KB area of address space.

## Documentation Conventions

This section defines the typographical convention used throughout this book.

### Hex Notation

All hex numbers are followed by an "h." Examples:

9A4Eh
0100h

### Binary Notation

All binary numbers are followed by a "b." Examples:
0001 0101b
01b

### Decimal Notation

Numbers without any suffix are decimal. When required for clarity, decimal numbers are followed by a "d." The following examples each represent a decimal number:

16
255
256d
128d

### Signal Name Representation

Each signal that assumes the logic low state when asserted is followed by a pound sign (#). As an example, the TRDY# signal is asserted low when the target is ready to complete a data transfer.

Signals that are not followed by a pound sign are asserted when they assume the logic high state. As an example, IDSEL is asserted high to indicate that a PCI device's configuration space is being addressed.

## Identification of Bit Fields (logical groups of bits or signals)

All bit fields are designated in little-endian bit ordering as follows:

[X:Y],

where "X" is the most-significant bit and "Y" is the least-significant bit of the field. As an example, the PCI address/data bus consists of AD[31:0], where AD31 is the most-significant and AD0 the least-significant bit of the field.

## We Want Your Feedback

MindShare values your comments and suggestions. You can contact us via mail, phone, fax or internet email.

**Phone:** (214) 231-2216
**Fax:** (214) 783-4715
**E-mail:** mindshar@interserv.com

To request information on public or private seminars, email your request to: mindshar@interserv.com or call our bulletin board at (214) 705-9604.

## Mailing Address

MindShare, Inc.
2202 Buttercup Drive
Richardson, Texas 75082

# Part I

# Introduction to the Local Bus Concept

# Chapter 1

## In This Chapter

This chapter defines the performance constraints experienced when devices that perform block data transfers are placed on the expansion bus (e.g., the ISA, EISA and Micro Channel buses). It also uses the performance requirements of teleconferencing to highlight the bandwidth requirements of systems requiring fast block transfers between multiple subsystems in order to achieve superior system performance.

## The Next Chapter

The next chapter introduces the concept of the local bus. The VESA VL bus and the PCI bus implementations of the local bus are introduced as solutions to the throughput problem.

## Block-Oriented Devices

In today's operating environments, it is imperative that large block data transfers be accomplished expeditiously. This is especially true in relation to the following types of subsystems:

- Graphics video adapter.
- Full-motion video adapter.
- SCSI host bus adapter.
- FDDI network adapter.

## Graphics Interface Performance Requirements

The Windows, OS/2 and Unix X-Windows user interfaces require extremely fast updates of the graphics image in order to move, resize and update multiple windows without imposing discernible delays on the end-user. Since the screen image is stored in video RAM, this means that the processor must be able to update and/or move large blocks of data within video memory very fast. The same is true for the updating of full-motion video in video ram.

## SCSI Performance Requirements

The SCSI interface is used to move large blocks of data between target I/O devices and system memory. Mass storage devices such as hard disk drives, CD-ROM drives and tape backup subsystems typically reside on the SCSI bus. The time required to read or write files on hard drives or tape, or to read files from CD-ROM can impose delays on the end-user. Anything that can be done to speed up these block data transfers has a significant effect on overall system performance.

## Network Adapter Performance Requirements

When a network adapter is used to transfer entire files of information to or from a server (a print or file server), the rate at which the information can be transferred between system memory and the network adapter detracts from or contributes to overall system performance.

## X-Bus Device Performance Constraints

The devices just described are just some examples of subsystems that benefit significantly from a fast transfer rate. Unfortunately, the majority of subsystems reside on the PC's expansion bus. Depending on the machine's design, this may be the ISA, EISA or Micro Channel expansion bus. As described later in this chapter, all three of these expansion bus architectures suffer from an inadequate data transfer rate.

In many cases, subsystems such as the graphics video adapter have been integrated onto the system board. This would seem to imply that they do not reside on the expansion bus, but this is not the case. Most of the integrated subsystems reside on a buffered version of the expansion bus known as the X-bus (eXtension to the expansion bus; also referred to as the utility bus). This being the case, these subsystems are bound by the mediocre transfer rates achievable when communicating with devices residing on the expansion bus. Figure 1-1 illustrates the relationship of the X-bus to the expansion bus and the system board microprocessor.

When performing memory reads, the microprocessor can communicate with its internal (level one, or L1) cache at its full native speed if the requested information is found in the cache. If the cache is implemented as a write-back cache, memory writes to currently-cached locations may also be completed at full speed. When an L1 cache miss occurs on a memory read or the cache must write information into memory, the processor must use its local bus to communicate with memory. The memory access request is first submitted to the external, level 2 (L2) cache for fulfillment. In the event of an L2 cache miss, the L2 cache performs an access to system DRAM memory. The linkage between the L2 cache and system DRAM memory is typically optimized to allow information transfers to complete as quickly as possible.

When a memory read or write addresses memory other than system DRAM memory or when the processor is performing an I/O read or write, the expansion bus bridge must pass the bus cycle through to the expansion bus. The completion of the bus cycle is bound by the maximum expansion bus speed and the access time of the expansion bus device being accessed. If a large amount of data is to be transferred to or from the target expansion device, performance is bound by the speed of the bus, the access time of the target, and the expansion bus data bus width.

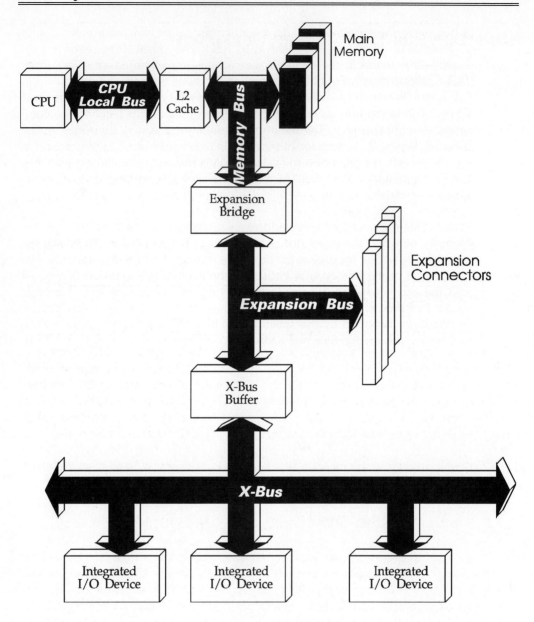

*Figure 1-1. The X-Bus*

## Expansion Bus Transfer Rate Limitations

### ISA Expansion Bus

All transfers performed over the ISA bus are synchronized to an 8MHz (more typically, 8.33MHz) bus clock signal (BCLK). It takes a minimum of two cycles of the bus clock (if the target device is a zero wait state device) to perform a data transfer. This equates to 4.165 million transfers per second. Since the data path on the ISA bus is only 16-bits wide, a maximum of two bytes may be transferred during each transaction. This equates to a theoretical maximum transfer rate of 8.33 MBytes per second.

For more information on the ISA expansion bus, refer to the Addison-Wesley publication entitled *ISA System Architecture*.

### EISA Expansion Bus

Like the ISA bus, all transfers performed over the EISA bus are synchronized to an 8MHz (more typically, 8.33MHz) bus clock signal (BCLK). It takes a minimum of one cycle of the bus clock (if the target device supports EISA burst mode transfers) to perform a data transfer. This equates to 8.33 million transfers per second. Since the data path on the EISA bus is 32-bits wide, a maximum of four bytes may be transferred during each transaction. This equates to a theoretical maximum transfer rate of 33 Mbytes per second.

For more information on the EISA expansion bus, refer to the Addison-Wesley publication entitled *EISA System Architecture*.

### Micro Channel Architecture Expansion Bus

At the current time, the maximum achievable transfer rate on the Micro Channel (as implemented in the PS/2 product line) is 40Mbytes per second (using the 32-bit Streaming Data Procedure). This is based on a 10MHz bus speed with one data transfer taking place during each cycle of the 10MHz clock (10 million transfers per second * four bytes per transfer). Faster transfer rates of 80 and 160Mbytes per second are possible when the 64-bit and enhanced 64-bit Streaming Data Procedures are implemented.

## Teleconferencing Performance Requirements

Figure 1-2 illustrates three PCs linked via a telecommunications network. Each of the three units has the capability to simultaneously merge multiple graphics and video sources onto the screen in real-time. Figure 1-3 illustrates the contents of each screen.

The large portion of the screen (devoted to a graphics image) is utilized to display the document under discussion. In order to successfully emulate an actual face-to-face conferencing situation, the system must be capable of updating this image fast enough to simulate flipping through the pages of a document at the rate of ten pages (or frames) per second. With an image resolution of 1280 x 1024 pixels and color resolution of 16 million colors (three bytes per pixel), the amount of video memory required to store one image is 3.93216Mbytes. To alter the graphics display at the rate of ten frames per second would require a video memory update rate of 39.3216Mbytes per second.

The video preview portion of the screen is used to display a real-time video image of a video source local to the unit. This image has a resolution of 320 x 240 pixels and a color resolution of 256 colors (one byte per pixel). In order to provide full-motion video, the image must be updated at the rate of thirty frames per second. The amount of video memory required to store one image would be 76.8Kbytes. To alter the graphics display at the rate of thirty frames per second would require a video memory update rate of 2.3Mbytes per second.

Each of the two video remote screen areas is used to display a full-motion video image from one of the other two participants. These images each have a resolution of 640 x 480 pixels and a color resolution of 256 colors (one byte per pixel). In order to provide full-motion video, each image must be updated at the rate of thirty frames per second. The amount of video memory required to store one image would be 307.2Kbytes. To alter each of the video remote windows at the rate of thirty frames per second would require a video memory update rate of 9.2Mbytes per second.

Each of the three video images would be transmitted in compressed video image format at the rate of 200Kbytes per second per video stream.

In summary, each host system must supply sufficient bus bandwidth to support the combined transfer rates required to update the images presented in the graphics, preview, remote one and remote two windows, as well as the three 200Kbyte per second compressed video streams. The bus structure must then support the simultaneous transfer rates listed in table 1-1. ISA (8.33Mbytes per second) and the current version of EISA (33Mbytes per second) will not support the combined bandwidth requirement of 60.516Mbytes per second. The Micro Channel (40Mbytes per second) does not currently support the required rate, but the 64-bit Streaming Data Procedures (not supported on the PS/2 product line) are able to achieve transfer rates of 80 to 160Mbytes per second. As described later in this document, the PCI bus currently supports a transfer rate of 132Mbytes per second. If the 64-bit PCI extension is implemented, a transfer rate of 264Mbytes per second can be achieved. Table 1-2 lists the transfer rates for the video and other subsystems.

*Table 1-1. Teleconferencing Transfer Rate Requirements*

| Screen Element | Transfer Rate (Mbytes/second) |
|---|---|
| Graphics Window | 39.216 |
| Preview Window | 2.3 |
| Video Remote One | 9.2 |
| Video Remote Two | 9.2 |
| Preview Compressed Video Stream | .2 |
| Video Remote One Compressed Video Stream | .2 |
| Video Remote Two Compressed Video Stream | .2 |
| Total transfer rate required to support teleconferencing | 60.516 |

*Table 1-2. Required Subsystem Transfer Rates*

| Subsystem | (Mbytes per second) |
|---|---|
| Graphics | 30 to 40 |
| Full-Motion Video | 2 to 9 per window |
| LAN | 15 for FDDI (Fiber Distributed Data Interface) |
| | 3 for Token Ring |
| | 2 for Ethernet |
| Hard Disk | 5 to 20 using SCSI |
| CD-ROM | 2 using SCSI |
| Audio | 1 for CD quality output |

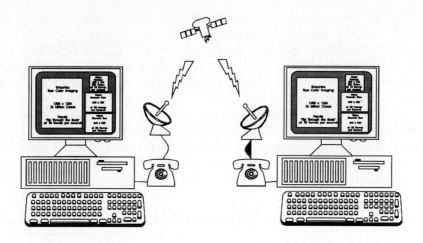

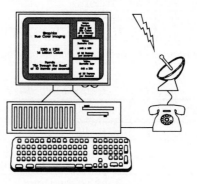

*Figure 1-2. The Teleconference*

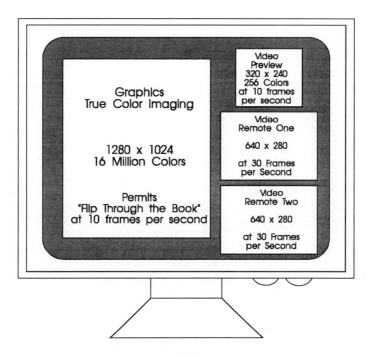

*Figure 1-3. The Teleconference Screen Layout*

# Chapter 2

## The Previous Chapter

The previous chapter discussed the performance constraints placed upon subsystems installed on the expansion bus or integrated onto the system board's X-bus.

## This Chapter

This chapter introduces the concept of the local bus and provides an overview of the two major local bus standards:

- the VESA VL bus
- the PCI bus

## The Next Chapter

The next chapter provides an introduction to the PCI transfer mechanism.

## Graphics Accelerators: Before Local Bus

An interim attempt to improve the performance of video graphics adapters implemented as expansion bus devices involved the enhancement of the adapter's intelligence. Earlier adapters processed very low-level commands issued by the microprocessor. The processor and therefore the programmer had to be intimately involved in every aspect of screen management. Later adapters are frequently based on processors like the Intel i860XR/XP or the Texas Instruments TMS34010/34020 and can handle high-level commands to off-load screen-intensive operations from the microprocessor. As an example, a BITBLT command can be issued to the adapter, causing it to quickly move a window graphic from one area of video memory to another without any further intervention on the microprocessor's part. The video memory is on the expansion adapter card and can therefore be accessed directly by the adapter's local processor at high speed.

## Local Bus Concept

To maximize throughput when performing updates to video graphics memory, many PC vendors have moved the video graphics adapter from the slow expansion bus to the processor's local bus. Figure 2-1 illustrates the processor's local bus. The video adapter is redesigned to connect directly to the processor's local bus and the adapter design is optimized to minimize or eliminate the number of wait states inserted into each bus cycle when the processor accesses video memory and the adapter's I/O registers. In addition, the video graphics adapter typically also incorporates a local processor and can handle high-level commands (as discussed earlier).

## Direct-Connect Approach

There are three basic methods for connecting a device to the microprocessor's local bus. The first scenario is pictured in figure 2-1 and is very straightforward: the device is connected directly to the processor's bus structure. This could be any processor type (such as the 486). As an example, when a 486 performs zero wait-state bus cycles at a bus speed of 33MHz (the actual bus speed is processor implementation-dependent), read burst transfers can be performed at the rate of 132Mbytes per second (if the processor is communicating with video memory that supports burst mode and is cacheable). When performing memory writes to update the video frame buffer in memory, the programmer may specify no more than four bytes to be written to memory per bus cycle. If the video memory supports zero wait-state writes, this would permit a data transfer rate of 66Mbytes/second. The direct-connect approach imposes a number of important design constraints:

- Since the device is connected directly to the processor's local bus, it must be redesigned in order to be used with next generation processors (if the bus structure or protocol are altered).
- Due to the extra loading placed on the local bus, no more than one local bus device may be added.
- Because the local bus is running at a high frequency, the design of the local bus device's bus interface is difficult.
- Although the system may work when it's shipped, it may exhibit aberrant behavior when an Intel Overdrive Processor is installed in the upgrade socket (thereby placing another load on the local bus).
- It does not permit the processor to perform transfers with one device while the local bus device is involved in a transfer with another device.

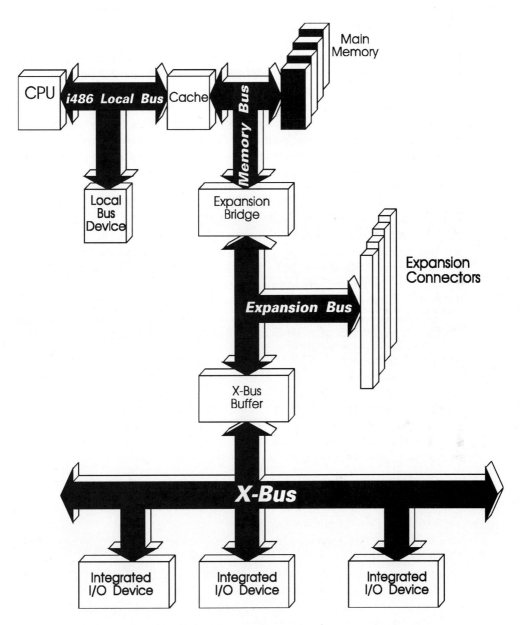

*Figure 2-1. The Direct-Connect Local Bus Approach*

## Buffered Approach

The second approach that can be utilized in connecting a local bus device to the processor's local bus is the buffered approach. Figure 2-2 illustrates this scenario. The buffer/driver redrives all of the local bus signals, thereby permitting fanout to more than one local bus device. Since the buffered local bus is electrically-isolated from the microprocessor's local bus, it only presents one load to the microprocessor's local bus. Typically, a maximum of three local bus devices can be placed on the buffered local bus. This is the only real advantage of this approach over the direct-connect approach.

A major disadvantage of the buffered approach is that the processor's local bus and the buffered local bus are essentially one bus. Any transaction initiated by the processor appears on the local and buffered local buses. Likewise, any bus transaction initiated by a bus master that resides on the buffered local bus appears on both the buffered local bus and the processor's local bus. In other words, either the processor or a local bus master may use the bus, but not both simultaneously. If a local bus master is using the bus and the processor requires the bus to perform a transaction, the processor is stalled until the bus master surrenders ownership of the bus. The reverse situation is also true.

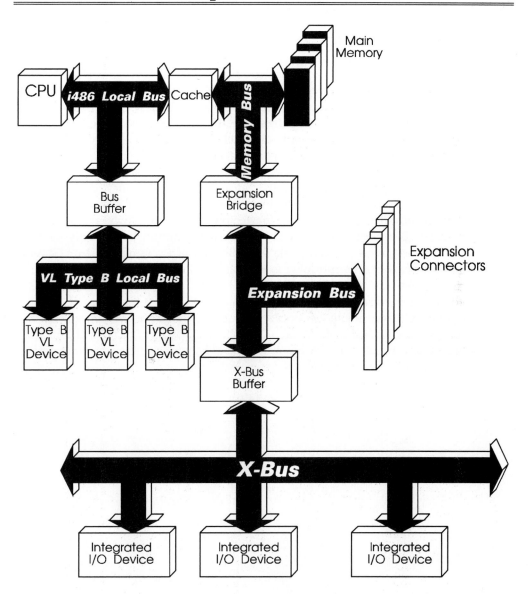

*Figure 2-2. The Buffered Local Bus Approach*

## Workstation Approach

Figure 2-3 illustrates an approach used in many workstation architectures to achieve high performance. The processor's L2 cache controller is combined with a bridge that provides the interface between the processor, main memory and the high-speed I/O bus (in this case, the PCI bus). The devices that reside on the I/O bus may consist only of target devices or a mixture of targets and intelligent peripheral adapters with bus master capability. Via the specially-designed bridge, either the processor (through its L2 cache) or a bus master on the I/O bus (or the expansion bus) can access main memory. Optimally, the processor can continue to fetch information from its L1 or L2 cache while the cache controller provides a bus master on the I/O bus with access to main memory. Bus masters on the I/O bus can also communicate directly with target devices on the I/O bus while the processor is accessing its L1 or L2 cache or while the L2 cache controller is accessing main memory for the processor.

Another very distinct advantage of this approach is that it renders the I/O bus device interface independent of the processor bus. Processor upgrades can be easily implemented without impacting the design of the I/O bus and its associated devices. Only the cache/bridge would require a redesign (to match the new host processor interface).

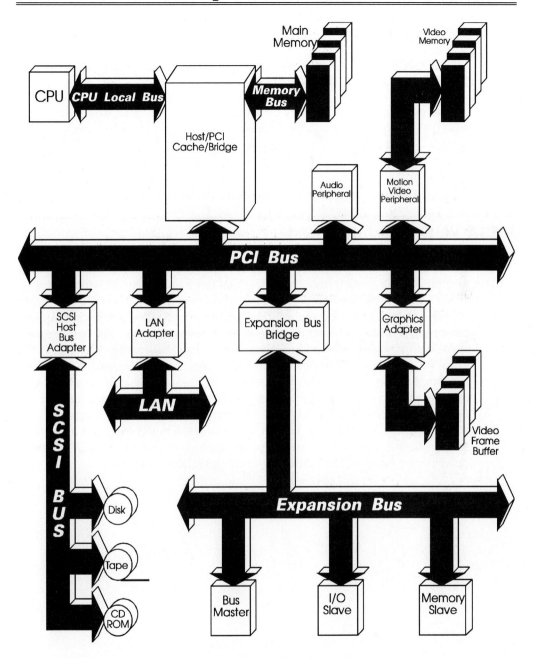

*Figure 2-3. The Workstation Approach*

A variation on this theme would find the processor's L2 cache implemented as a lookaside cache located on the processor's local bus. In this configuration, main memory may be located either on a dedicated memory bus (as shown in figure 2-3) or it may reside on the processor's local bus along with the lookaside L2 cache. If the main memory is located on the processor's local bus, it should be noted that it can only be accessed by the performance of a memory read or write transaction on the processor's local bus. This is true even if a bus master located on the I/O bus is accessing main memory. This could diminish the processor's performance by diminishing the local bus availability. The reverse would also be true: bus masters other than the host processor cannot access main memory while the processor is utilizing its local bus.

## VESA VL Bus Solution

Until several years ago, there existed no standard that defined the interconnection schema used to integrate local bus devices into the PC environment. The Video Electronics Standards Association (VESA), an association of companies involved in the design and manufacturing of video graphics adapters, commissioned the development of a local bus standard. The preliminary specification was completed and refers to the local bus as the VL bus (VESA Local bus). The initial version of the VESA specification, version 1.0, defines two methods of interfacing to the microprocessor's local bus: the direct-connect and the buffered approaches described earlier. The direct-connect approach is referred to as the VL Type "A" bus, while the buffered version is referred to as the VL Type "B" bus. In both cases, the bus is modeled on the 486 bus. Some characteristics of each implementation are listed in table 2-1. A brief description of each of the listed characteristics follows the table.

*Table 2-1. VL Bus Characteristics*

| Characteristics | Type "A" | Type "B" |
|---|---|---|
| logic cost | $0. | Cost of buffering. |
| Performance | At a bus speed of 33MHz, 132Mbytes/second (peak) on burst reads, and 66Mbytes/second on write transfers. | Same as type "A", but the delay imposed by the buffer almost certainly causes wait states to be inserted in each transfer. |
| Longevity | Tied to 386/486 bus structure. | Tied to 386/486 bus structure. |
| Teleconferencing Support | One local bus device. | Three local bus devices. |
| Electrical Integrity | Not defined. | Not defined. |
| Modularity | None. | Three Micro Channel connectors. |
| Auto-Configuration | Supports Auto Configuration (see "Auto-Configuration" section later in this chapter). | Supports Auto-Configuration (see "Auto-Configuration" section later in this chapter). |

## Logic Cost

No additional system board logic is necessary to implement a VL Type "A" local bus device. The device is connected directly to the microprocessor's local bus. In a Type "B" design, the cost of the buffering logic must be taken into account.

## Performance

Using the type "A" and "B" approaches, a peak data transfer rate of 132Mbytes per second may be achieved (at a processor bus speed of 33MHz). It should be noted that the longest burst read performed by the 486 processor occurs during a cache line fill operation. Sixteen bytes (four doublewords) are transferred to the processor during the cache line fill. The first doubleword takes two processor clocks, while the subsequent three doublewords may be transferred back to the microprocessor at the rate of one per processor clock cycle (if the access time of the target device supports this speed).

The 486 processor is only capable of performing burst writes under the following circumstances:

- When it attempts to write two to four bytes (in one bus cycle) to an 8-bit device (BS8# is sampled asserted). An 8-bit device that supports burst mode operation can achieve a transfer rate of 33Mbytes/second (one byte transferred during each processor clock cycle), but it should be noted that this rate can only be sustained for the transfer of up to three successive bytes.

- When it attempts to write two to four bytes (in one bus cycle) to a 16-bit device (BS16# is sampled active). A 16-bit device that supports burst mode operation can achieve a transfer rate of 66Mbytes/second, but it should be noted that this rate can only be sustained for the transfer of one 16-bit object.

When performing 32-bit non-burst write transfers, the 486 microprocessor can achieve a maximum transfer rate of 66Mbytes/second (two processor clock cycles per 32-bit transfer).

It should be noted that the VL bus specification defines bus speeds up to a maximum frequency of 66MHz. All performance estimates quoted in this publication are based on a maximum bus speed of 33MHz because this is the achievable norm at the current time.

## Longevity

Both the type "A" and "B" approaches are short term solutions because they are designed around the and 486 processor bus structure. The interface logic must be redesigned for next generation processors with more advanced bus structures. Bridge logic would be necessary to translate between the new processor bus and the VL bus.

## Teleconferencing Support

The type "A" approach does not offer a teleconferencing solution because it provides support for only one local bus device. At a bare minimum, teleconferencing requires high-speed support for at least two peripheral subsystems: the graphics and full-motion video adapters. The type "B" solution provides minimal teleconferencing support by supporting up to three local bus peripherals.

## Electrical Integrity

The VESA VL 1.0 bus specification provides no electrical design guidelines to ensure the integrity of local bus design. System board designers must design the PCI system board layout from scratch. While this isn't a problem at low bus speeds, buses running at today's accelerated rates present a formidable design challenge.

## Add-in Connectors

Modularity refers to the ability to add new local bus peripherals by installing an option card into a local bus connector. Type "A" solutions are direct-connect and do not provide a connector. Type "B" solutions can support up to three connectors. The VL specification defines a Micro Channel-style connector as the expansion vehicle.

## Auto-Configuration

The VESA VL 1.0 specification states that VL local bus devices must support automatic system configuration. However, the specification does not define the standard automatic configuration support that must be provided in each VL bus-compliant local bus device. The specification also states that VL bus-compliant local bus devices must be transparent to device drivers. In other words, they must respond to the same command set and supply the same status as their non-local bus cousins.

The fact that the VL bus specification does not define the location or format of the local bus devices' configuration registers opens the door for a "tower of Babel" scenario regarding the software interface to these devices.

## Revision 2.0 VL Specification

The rev 2.0 specification adds support for VESA VL bus masters.

## PCI Bus Solution

Intel defined the PCI bus to ensure that the marketplace would not become crowded with various permutations of local bus architectures implemented in a short-sighted fashion. The first release of the specification, version 1.0, became available on 6/22/92. Revision 2.0 became available in April of 1993. The current revision of the specification, 2.1, became available in Q1 of 1995. Intel made the decision not to back the VESA VL standard because the emerging standard did not take a sufficiently long-term approach towards the problems presented at that time and those to be faced in the coming five years. In addition, the VL bus has very limited support for burst transfers, thereby limiting the achievable throughput.

***PCI stands for Peripheral Component Interconnect.*** The PCI bus can be populated with adapters requiring fast accesses to each other and/or system memory and that can be accessed by the host processor at speeds approaching that of the processor's full native bus speed. It is very important to note that all read and write transfers over the PCI bus are burst transfers. The length of the burst is negotiated between the initiator and target devices and may be of any length. ***This is in sharp contrast to the burst capability inherent in the VL bus design.*** Table 2-2 identifies some of PCI's major design goals. The chapters that follow provide a detailed description of the PCI bus and related subjects.

The PCI specification allows system design centered around two of the three approaches discussed earlier: the buffered and workstation approaches. Due to its performance and flexibility advantages, the workstation approach is preferred. Figure 2-4 illustrates the basic relationship of the PCI, expansion, processor and memory buses.

*Table 2-2. Major PCI Revision 2.1 Features*

| Feature | Description |
|---|---|
| Processor Independence | Components designed for the PCI bus are PCI-specific, not processor-specific, thereby isolating device design from processor upgrade treadmill. |
| Support for up to 256 PCI functional devices per PCI bus | Although a typical PCI bus implementation supports approximately ten electrical loads, each PCI device package may contain up to eight separate PCI functions. The PCI bus logically supports up to 32 physical PCI device packages, for a total of 256 possible PCI functions per PCI bus. |
| Support for up to 256 PCI buses | The specification provides support for up to 256 PCI buses. |
| Low-power consumption | A major design goal of the PCI specification is the creation of a system design that draws as little current as possible. |
| Burst used for all read and write transfers | Supports 132Mbytes per second peak transfer rate for both read and write transfers. 264Mbytes per second peak transfer rate for 64-bit PCI transfers. Transfer rates of up to 528Mbytes per second are achievable on a 66MHz PCI bus. |
| Bus speed | Revision 2.0 spec supports PCI bus speeds up to 33MHz. Revision 2.1 adds support for 66MHz bus operation. |
| 64-bit bus width | Full definition of a 64-bit extension. |
| Fast access | As fast as 60ns (at a bus speed of 33MHz when an initiator parked on the PCI bus is writing to a PCI target. |
| Concurrent bus operation | High-end bridges support full bus concurrency with host bus, PCI bus, and the expansion bus simultaneously in use. |
| Bus master support | Full support of PCI bus initiators allows peer-to-peer PCI bus access, as well as access to main memory and expansion bus devices through PCI and expansion bus bridges. In addition, a PCI master can access a target that resides on another PCI bus lower in the bus hierarchy. |
| Hidden bus arbitration | Arbitration for the PCI bus can take place while another bus master is in possession of the PCI bus. This eliminates latency encountered during bus arbitration on buses other than PCI. |
| Low-pin count | Economical use of bus signals allows implementation of a functional PCI target with 47 pins and a functional PCI bus initiator with 49 pins. |
| Transaction integrity check | Parity checking on the address, command and data. |
| Three address spaces | Full definition of memory, I/O and configuration address space. |
| Auto-Configuration | Full bit-level specification of the configuration registers necessary to support automatic peripheral detection and configuration. |
| Software Transparency | Software drivers utilize same command set and status definition when communicating with PCI device or its expansion bus-oriented cousin. |
| Expansion Cards | The specification includes a definition of PCI connectors and add-in cards. |
| Expansion Card Size | The specification defines three card sizes: long, short and variable-height short cards. |

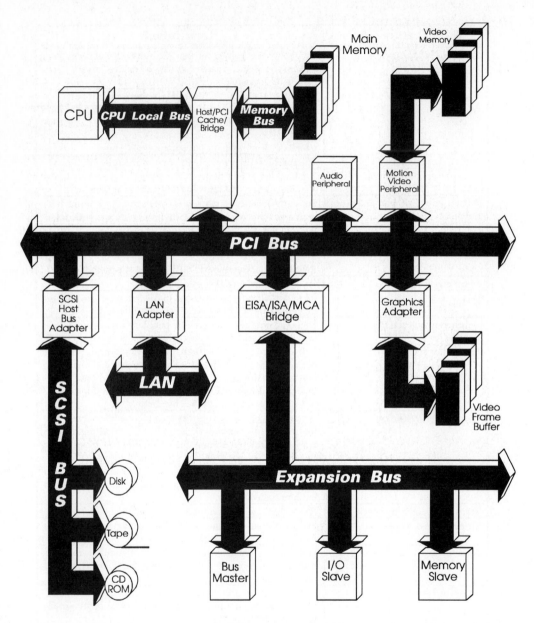

*Figure 2-4. The PCI Bus*

# Chapter 2: Solutions, VESA and PCI

## Market Niche for PCI and VESA VL

Many in the industry are using their crystal balls to predict the outcome of this "bus war," but this will not be a win/lose situation. VL is a good, cost-effective approach for low-end machines that require fast data transfer capability with one subsystem at a time in order to achieve acceptable system performance. Due to the complexity of the PCI chip sets when compared to the logic required by VL 1.0, PCI-based systems are slightly more expensive. Balancing this added cost with PCI's superior performance in supporting bus concurrency, auto-configuration and multiple bus masters, PCI-based machines will dominate the mid and high-end machine market niches.

It should be noted, however, that a machine can be designed without any bridges. All components, including the processor and main memory, would interface directly to the PCI bus. Due to the reduction in logic yielded by the deletion of the bridge logic, this PCI machine would be very price-competitive with a VESA VL-based machine.

## PCI Device

The typical PCI device consists of a complete peripheral adapter encapsulated within an IC package or integrated onto a PCI expansion card. Typical examples would be a network, display or SCSI adapter. During the initial period after the introduction of the PCI specification, many vendors chose to interface pre-existent, non-PCI compliant devices to the PCI bus. This can be easily accomplished using programmable logic arrays (PLAs). Figure 2-5 illustrates ten PCI-compliant devices attached to the PCI bus on the system board. It should also be noted that each PCI-compliant package (VLSI component or add-in card) may contain up to eight PCI functions.

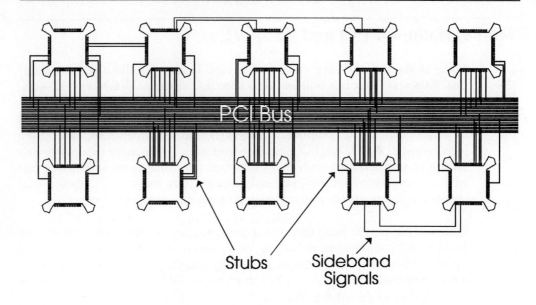

Stubs    Sideband
         Signals

*Figure 2-5. PCI Devices Attached to the PCI Bus*

## Specifications Book is Based On

This book is based on the documents indicated in table 2-3.

*Table 2-3. This Book is Based On*

| Document Title | Revision |
|---|---|
| PCI Local Bus Specification | 2.1 |
| PCI-to-PCI Bridge Specification | 1.0 |
| PCI System Design Guide | 1.0 |
| PCI BIOS Specification | 2.1 |

## Obtaining PCI Bus Specification(s)

The PCI bus specification, version 1.0, was developed by Intel Corporation. The specification is now managed by a consortium of industry partners known as the PCI Special Interest Group (SIG). MindShare, Inc. is a member of the SIG. The specifications are commercially available for purchase. The latest revision of the specification (as of this printing) is 2.1. For information regarding the specifications and/or SIG membership, contact:

**PCI Special Interest Group**
**P.O. Box 14070**
**Portland, OR 97214**
**Tel. (503) 797-4207 (International)**
**Fax (503) 234-6762**
**(800) 433-5177 (in U.S.)**

# Part II

# Revision 2.1 Essentials

# Chapter 3

## The Previous Chapter

The previous chapter introduced the local bus concept, the VESA VL bus and the PCI bus.

## In This Chapter

This chapter provides an introduction to the PCI transfer mechanism, including a definition of the following basic concepts: burst transfers, the initiator, targets, agents, single and multi-function devices, the PCI bus clock, the address phase, claiming the transaction, the data phase, transaction completion and the return of the bus to the idle state.

## The Next Chapter

Unlike most buses, the PCI bus does not incorporate termination resistors at the physical end of the bus to absorb voltage changes and prevent the wavefront caused by the voltage change from being reflected back down the bus. Rather, PCI uses reflections to advantage. The next chapter provides an introduction to reflected-wave switching.

## Burst Transfer

A burst transfer is one consisting of a single address phase followed by two or more data phases. The bus master only has to arbitrate for bus ownership one time. The start address and transaction type are issued during the address phase. The target device latches the start address into an address counter and is responsible for incrementing the address from data phase to data phase.

In the 486, EISA and Micro Channel environments, the ability to perform burst transfers is the product of negotiation between the bus master and the target device. If either or both of them do not support burst mode transfers, the data packet can only be transferred utilizing a series of separate bus transactions. The bus master must arbitrate for ownership of the bus to perform each individual transaction that comprise the series. Another bus master may acquire bus ownership after the master completes any transaction in the series. This can severely impact the bus master's data throughput.

PCI data transfers can be accomplished using burst transfers. Many PCI bus masters and target devices are designed to support burst mode. It should be noted that a PCI target may be designed such that it can only handle single data phase transactions. When a bus master attempts to perform a burst transaction, the target terminates the transaction at the completion of the first data phase. This forces the master to re-arbitrate for the bus to attempt resumption of the burst with the next data item. The target terminates each burst transfer after the first data phase completes. This would yield very poor performance, but may be the correct approach for a device that doesn't require high throughput. Each burst transfer consists of the following basic components:

- The address and transfer type are output during the address phase.
- A data object (up to 32-bits in a 32-bit implementation or 64-bits in a 64-bit implementation) may then be transferred during each subsequent data phase.

Assuming that neither the initiator nor the target device inserts wait states in each data phase, a data object may be transferred on the rising-edge of each PCI clock cycle. At a PCI bus clock frequency of 33MHz, a transfer rate of 132Mbytes/second may be achieved. A transfer rate of 264Mbytes/second may be achieved in a 64-bit implementation when performing 64-bit transfers during each data phase. A 66MHz PCI bus implementation can achieve 264 or 524Mbytes/second transfer rates using 32 or 64-bit transfers. This chapter introduces the burst mechanism used in performing transfers over the PCI bus.

## Initiator, Target and Agents

There are two participants in every PCI burst transfer: the initiator and the target. The initiator, or bus master, is the device that initiates a transfer. The terms bus master and initiator can be used interchangeably, but the PCI specification strictly adheres to the term initiator.

The target, or slave, is the device currently addressed by the initiator for the purpose of performing a data transfer. The terms target and slave can be used interchangeably, but the PCI specification strictly adheres to the term target.

All PCI initiator and target devices are commonly referred to as PCI-compliant agents.

## Single vs. Multi-Function PCI Devices

A PCI physical device package may take the form of a component integrated onto the system board or the form of a PCI add-in card. Each PCI package may incorporate from one to eight separate functions. This is analogous to a multi-function card found in any ISA, EISA or Micro Channel machine. A package containing one function is referred to as a single-function PCI device, while a package containing two or more PCI functions is referred to as a multi-function device.

## PCI Bus Clock

All actions on the PCI bus are synchronized to the PCI CLK signal. The frequency of the CLK signal may be anywhere from 0MHz to 33MHz. The revision 1.0 specification stated that all devices must support operation from 16 to 33MHz, while recommending support for operation down to 0MHz. The revision 2.x PCI specification indicates that **ALL** PCI devices **MUST** support PCI operation within the 0MHz to 33MHz range. Support for operation down to 0MHz provides low-power and static debug capability. The PCI CLK frequency may be changed at any time and may be stopped (but only in the low state). Components integrated onto the system board may operate at a single frequency and may require a policy of no frequency change. Devices on add-in cards must support operation from 0 through 33MHz (because the card must operate in any platform that it may be installed in).

The revision 2.1 specification also defines PCI bus operation at speeds of up to 66MHz. The chapter entitled "66MHz PCI Implementation" describes the operational characteristics of the 66MHz PCI bus, embedded devices and add-in cards.

All PCI bus transactions consist of an address phase followed by one or more data phases. The exception is a transaction wherein the initiator uses 64-bit addressing delivered in two address phases. An address phase is one PCI

CLK in duration. The number of data phases depends on how many data transfers are to take place during the overall burst transfer. Each data phase has a minimum duration of one PCI CLK. Each wait state inserted in a data phase extends it by an additional PCI CLK.

## Address Phase

As stated earlier, every PCI transaction (with the exception of a transaction using 64-bit addressing) starts off with an address phase one PCI CLK period in duration. During the address phase, the initiator identifies the target device and the type of transaction. The target device is identified by driving a start address within its assigned range onto the PCI address/data bus. At the same time, the initiator identifies the type of transaction by driving the command type onto the PCI Command/Byte Enable bus. The initiator asserts the FRAME# signal to indicate the presence of a valid start address and transaction type on the bus. Since the initiator only presents the start address for one PCI clock cycle, it is the responsibility of every PCI target device to latch the address so that it may subsequently be decoded.

By decoding the address latched from the address bus and the command type latched from the Command/Byte Enable bus, a target device can determine if it is being addressed and the type of transaction in progress. It's important to note that the initiator only supplies a start address to the target (during the address phase). Upon completion of the address phase, the address/data bus is then used to transfer data in each of the data phases. It is the responsibility of the target to latch the start address and to auto-increment it to point to the next group of locations during each subsequent data transfer.

## Claiming the Transaction

When a PCI target determines that it is the target of a transaction, it must claim the transaction by asserting DEVSEL# (device select). If the initiator doesn't sample DEVSEL# asserted within a predetermined amount of time, it aborts the transaction.

## Data Phase(s)

The data phase of a transaction is the period during which a data object is transferred between the initiator and the target. The number of data bytes to be transferred during a data phase is determined by the number of Command/Byte Enable signals that are asserted by the initiator during the data phase.

Both the initiator and the target must indicate that they are ready to complete a data phase, or the data phase is extended by a wait state one PCI CLK period in duration. The PCI bus defines ready signal lines used by both the initiator (IRDY#) and the target (TRDY#) for this purpose.

## Transaction Duration

The initiator identifies the overall duration of a burst transfer with the FRAME# signal. FRAME# is asserted at the start of the address phase and remains asserted until the initiator is ready (asserts IRDY#) to complete the final data phase.

## Transaction Completion and Return of Bus to Idle State

The initiator indicates that the last data transfer (of a burst transfer) is in progress by deasserting FRAME# and asserting IRDY#. When the last data transfer has been completed, the initiator returns the PCI bus to the idle state by deasserting its ready line (IRDY#).

If another bus master had previously been granted ownership of the bus by the PCI bus arbiter and were waiting for the current initiator to surrender the bus, it can detect that the bus has returned to the idle state by detecting FRAME# and IRDY# both deasserted.

## "Green" Machine

In keeping with the goal of low power consumption, the specification calls for low-power, CMOS output drivers and receivers to be used by PCI devices.

The next chapter describes the reflected-wave switching used in the PCI bus environment to permit low-power, CMOS drivers to successfully drive the bus.

If the address/data bus signals attached to the CMOS input receivers are permitted to float (around the switching region of input buffers) for extended periods of time, the receiver inputs would oscillate and draw excessive current. To prevent this from happening, it is a rule in PCI that the address/data bus must not be permitted to float for extended periods of time. Since the bus is normally driven most of the time, it may be assumed that the pre-charged bus will retain its state while not being driven for brief periods of time during turnaround cycles (turnaround cycles are described in the chapter entitled "The Read and Write Transfer").

The section entitled "Bus Parking" in the chapter on bus arbitration describes the mechanism utilized to prevent the address/data bus from floating when the bus is idle. The chapter entitled "The Read and Write Transfer" describes the mechanism utilized during data phases with wait states. The chapter entitled "The 64-Bit Extension" describes the mechanism utilized to keep the upper 32 bits of the address/data bus from floating when they are not in use (during a 32-bit transfer).

# Chapter 4

## Prior To This Chapter

The previous chapter provided an introduction to the PCI transfer including definition of the following basic concepts: burst transfers, the initiator, targets, agents, single and multi-function devices, the PCI bus clock, the address phase, claiming the transaction, the data phase, transaction completion and the return of the bus to the idle state.

## In This Chapter

Unlike many buses, the PCI bus does not incorporate termination resistors at the physical end of the bus to absorb voltage changes and prevent the wavefront caused by a voltage change from being reflected back down the bus. Rather, PCI uses reflections to advantage. This chapter provides an introduction to reflected-wave switching.

## The Next Chapter

The next chapter provides an introduction to the signal groups that comprise the PCI bus.

## Each Trace Is a Transmission Line

Consider the case where a signal trace is fed by a driver and is attached to a number of device inputs distributed along the signal trace. In the past, in order to specify the strength of the driver to be used, the system designer would ignore the electrical characteristics of the trace itself and only factor in the electrical characteristics of the devices connected to the trace. This approach was acceptable when the system clock rate was down in the 1MHz range. The designer would add up the capacitance of each input connected to the trace and treat it as a lumped capacitance. This value would be used to select the drive current capability of the driver. In high-frequency environments such as PCI, traces must switch state at rates from 25MHz on up. At these bus speeds, traces act as transmission lines and the electrical characteristics of the trace must also be factored into the equation used to select the characteristics of the output driver.

A transmission line presents impedance to the driver attempting to drive a voltage change onto the trace and also imposes a time delay in the transmission of the voltage change along the trace. The typical trace's impedance ranges from 50 to 110 Ω. The width of the trace and the distance of the trace from a ground plane are the major factors that influence its impedance. A wide trace located close to a ground plane is more capacitive in nature and its impedance is close to 50 Ω. A narrow trace located far from a ground plane is more inductive in nature and its impedance is in the area of 110 Ω. Each device input attached to the trace is largely capacitive in nature. This has the effect of decreasing the overall impedance that the trace offers to a driver.

## Old Method: Incident-Wave Switching

Consider the case where the driver at position one in figure 4-1 must drive the signal line from a logic low to a logic high. Assume that the designer has selected a strong output driver that is capable of driving the signal line from a low to a high at the point of incidence (the point at which it starts to drive). This is referred to as incident-wave switching. As the wavefront propagates down the trace (toward device 10), each device it passes detects a logic low. The amount of time it takes to switch all of the inputs along the trace to a low would be the time it takes the signal to propagate the length of the trace. This would appear to be the best approach because all devices inputs are switched in the quickest possible time (one traversal of the trace).

There are negative effects associated with this approach, however. As mentioned earlier, the capacitance of each input along the trace adds capacitance and thus lowers the overall impedance of the trace. The typical overall impedance of the trace would typically be around 30 Ω. When a 5V device begins to drive a trace, a voltage divider is created between the driver's internal impedance and the impedance of the trace that it is attempting to drive. Assuming that a 20 Ω driver is attempting to drive a 30 Ω trace, two of the five volts is dropped within the driver and a three volt incident voltage is propagated onto the trace. Since current = voltage divided by resistance, the current that must be sourced by the driver = 2 volts/20 Ω, or 100ma.

# Chapter 4: Intro To Reflected-Wave Switching

When considered by itself, this doesn't appear to present a problem. Assume, however, that a device driver must simultaneously drive 32 address traces, four command traces and four other signals. This is not atypical in a 32-bit bus architecture. Assuming that all of the drivers are encapsulated in one driver package, the package must source four amps of current, virtually instantaneously (in as short a period as one nanosecond). This current surge presents a number of problems:

- extremely difficult to decouple.
- causes spikes on internal bond wires.
- increases EMI.
- causes crosstalk inside and outside of the package.

This is the reason that most strong drivers are available in packages that encapsulate only eight drivers. In addition, 20 Ω output drivers consume quite a bit of silicon real-estate and become quite warm at high frequencies.

Another side-effect occurs when the signal wavefront arrives at the physical end of the trace (at device 10 in figure 4-1). If the designer does not incorporate a terminating resistor at the end of the trace, it presents a very high impedance to the signal. Since the signal cannot proceed, it turns around and is reflected back down the bus. During the return passage of the wavefront, this effectively doubles the voltage change seen on the trace at each device's input and at the driver that originated the wavefront. When an incident-wave driver is used (as in this case), the already high voltage it drives onto the trace is doubled. In order to absorb the signal at the physical end of the trace, the system designer frequently includes a terminating resistor.

The usage of incident-wave switching consumes a significant amount of power and violates the green nature of the PCI bus.

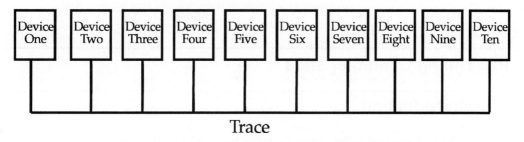

*Figure 4-1. Device Loads Distributed Along a Trace*

## PCI Method: Reflected-Wave Switching

The PCI bus is unterminated and uses wavefront reflection to advantage. A carefully selected, relatively weak output driver is used to drive the signal line halfway to the desired logic state. As an example, the driver would only have to drive the signal line from 0 to 1.5 volts, rather than to 3 volts (as the strong incident-wave driver would). As this wavefront passes each device input along the trace (see figure 4-1), the voltage change is insufficient to register as a logic high.

However, when the wavefront arrives at the unterminated end of the bus, it is reflected back and doubled (to 3 volts). Upon passing each device input again during the wavefront's return trip down the trace, a valid logic one registers at each device. The wavefront is absorbed by the low-impedance within the driver. This method cuts driver size and surge current in half.

In many systems, correct operation of the PCI bus relies on diodes embedded within devices to limit reflections and to successfully meet the specified propagation delay. If a system has long trace runs without connection to a PCI component (e.g., a series of unpopulated add-in connectors), it may be necessary to add diode terminators at that end of the bus to ensure signal quality.

The PCI specification states that devices must only sample their inputs on the rising-edge of the PCI clock signal. The physical layout of the PCI bus traces are very important to ensure that signal propagation is within assigned limits. When a driver asserts or deasserts a signal, the wavefront must propagate to the physical end of the bus, reflect back and make the full passage back down the bus before the signal(s) is sampled on the next rising-edge of the PCI clock. At 33MHz, the propagation delay is specified as 10ns, but may be increased to 11ns by lowering the clock skew from component to component. The specification contains a complete description of trace length and electrical characteristics.

## PCI Timing Characteristics

### Introduction

The sections that follow provide some basic information regarding the timing of PCI signals. For a more detailed description, refer to the specification.

# Chapter 4: Intro To Reflected-Wave Switching

## CLK Signal

As illustrated in figure 4-2, the minimum CLK cycle time is 30ns (at 33MHz; 15ns at 66MHz). The maximum skew on the clock when measured on the CLK pin of any two PCI components is 2ns. The clock frequency can be changed as long as the clock edges remain clean and the T_cyc, T_high and T_low minimums are not violated. The clock may be stopped, but only in the low state.

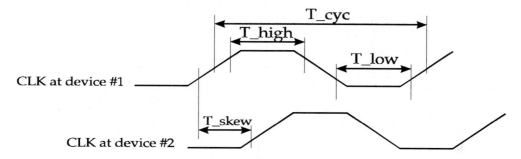

T_cyc is measured from one rising-edge to the next (when CLK crosses the threshold).

  minimum = 30ns (33MHz)
  maximum = $\infty$

T_high is the CLK high time

  minimum = 11ns
  maximum = none

T_low is CLK low time.

  minimum = 11ns
  maximum = none

T_skew represents the delay from the rising-edge of the CLK on one component to another.

  minimum = none
  maximum = 2ns

CLK slew rate (rate of change in volts/ns):
  minimum = 1V/ns
  maximum = 4V/ns

*Figure 4-2. CLK Signal Timing Characteristics*

## Output Timing

Figure 4-3 illustrates the timing characteristics to be met by PCI output drivers. All timings are relative to the point at which the rising-edge of CLK passes the threshold point.

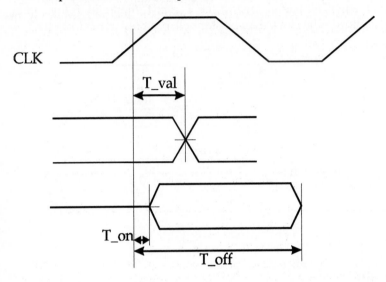

CLK

T_val

T_on

T_off

T_val, for all bussed signals, delay from point when CLK crosses threshold (on rising-edge) to point where signal crosses threshold to new state.

minimum = 2ns
maximum = 11ns

T_on delay from float to point where signal crosses threshold to new state.

minimum = 2ns
maximum = none

T_off delay from float, plus driven period and back to float:

minimum = none
maximum = 28ns

*Figure 4-3. Timing Characteristics of Output Drivers*

## Input Timing

Figure 4-4 illustrates the timing characteristics to be met on PCI input signals. All timings are relative to the point at which the rising-edge of CLK passes the threshold point. The setup times for the REQ# and GNT# signals (these are point-to-point signals; all others are bussed between all devices) deviate from the value illustrated: REQ# setup time is 12ns, while GNT# has a setup time of 10ns. The setup time for all other input signals is 7ns.

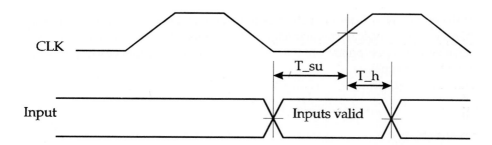

T_su is the setup time. Starts when signal crosses threshold to new state and lasts until the next rising-edge of CLK crosses threshold.

    minimum = 7ns for bussed signals,
                10-12ns for point-to-point signals.
    maximum = none.

T_h is the hold time.

    minimum = 0ns
    maximum = none.

*Figure 4-4. Input Timing Characteristics*

## RST#/REQ64# Timing

The assertion and deassertion of RST# is asynchronous to the PCI clock signal. If desired, a synchronous reset may be implemented, however. RST# must remain asserted for a minimum of 1ms after the power has stabilized. RST# must remain asserted for a minimum of 100 µs after the CLK has stabilized.

When RST# is asserted, all devices must float their output drivers within a maximum of 40ns.

During assertion of RST#, the system board reset logic must assert REQ64# for a minimum of 10 clock cycles. REQ64# may remain asserted for a maximum of 50ns after RST# is deasserted. For a discussion of REQ64# assertion during reset, refer to the chapter entitled "The 64-Bit Extension."

## Slower Clock Permits Longer Bus

If the system board designer chooses to run the PCI clock at a rate slower than 33MHz, the physical characteristics of the bus may be altered while still achieving proper operation (i.e., more loads, more connectors, physically longer trace runs).

# Chapter 5

## The Previous Chapter

The previous chapter provided an introduction to reflected-wave switching.

## This Chapter

This chapter divides the PCI bus signals into functional groups and describes the function of each signal.

## The Next Chapter

When a PCI bus master requires the use of the PCI bus to perform a data transfer, it must request the use of the bus from the PCI bus arbiter. The next chapter provides a detailed discussion of the PCI bus arbitration timing. The PCI specification defines the timing of the request and grant handshaking, but not the procedure used to determine the winner of a competition. The algorithm used by a system's PCI bus arbiter to decide which of the requesting bus masters will be granted use of the PCI bus is system-specific and outside the scope of the specification.

## Introduction

This chapter introduces the signals utilized to interface a PCI-compliant device to the PCI bus. Figures 5-1 and 5-2 illustrate the required and optional signals for master and target PCI devices, respectively. A PCI device that can act as the initiator or target of a transaction would obviously have to incorporate both initiator and target-related signals. In actuality, there is no such thing as a device that is purely a bus master and never a target. At a minimum, a device must act as the target of configuration reads and writes.

Each of the signal groupings are described in the following sections. It should be noted that some of the optional signals are not optional for certain types of

# PCI System Architecture

PCI agents. The sections that follow identify the circumstances where signals must be implemented.

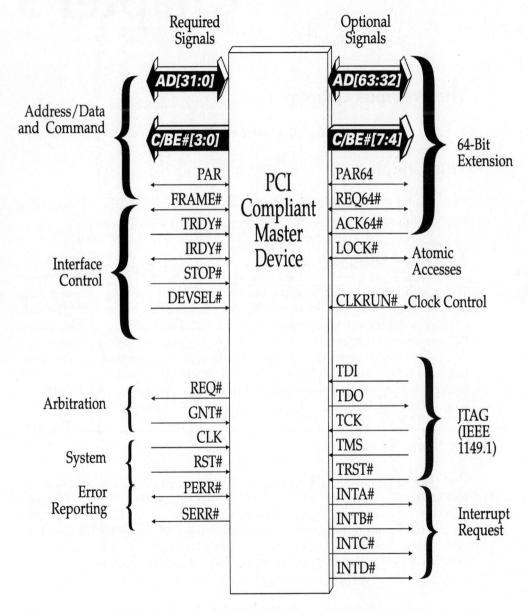

*Figure 5-1. PCI-Compliant Master Device Signals*

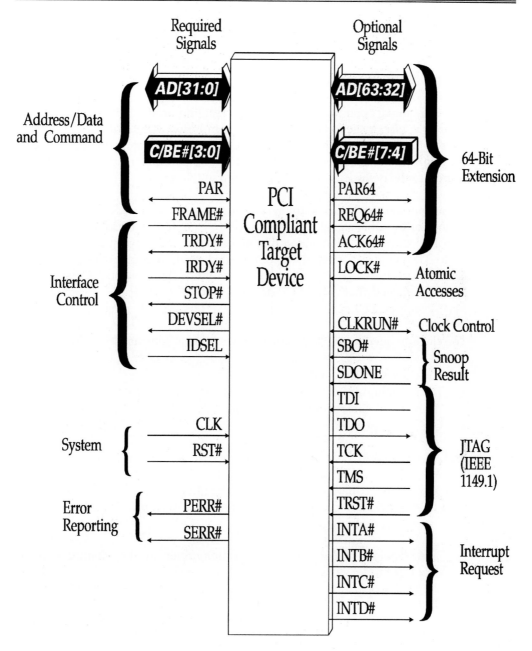

*Figure 5-2. PCI-Compliant Target Device Signals*

## System Signals

### PCI Clock Signal (CLK)

The CLK signal is an input to all devices residing on the PCI bus. It provides timing for all transactions, including bus arbitration. All inputs to PCI devices are sampled on the rising edge of the CLK signal. The state of all input signals are don't-care at all other times. All PCI timing parameters are specified with respect to the rising-edge of the CLK signal.

All actions on the PCI bus are synchronized to the PCI CLK signal. The frequency of the CLK signal may be anywhere from 0MHz to 33MHz. The revision 1.0 PCI specification stated that all devices must support operation from 16 to 33MHz and it strongly recommended support for operation down to 0MHz for static debug and low power operation. The revision 2.x PCI specification indicates that **ALL** PCI devices (with one exception noted below) **MUST** support PCI operation within the 0MHz to 33MHz range.

The clock frequency may be changed at any time as long as:

- The clock edges remain clean.
- The minimum clock high and low times are not violated.
- There are no bus requests outstanding.
- LOCK# is not asserted.

The clock may only be stopped in a low state (to conserve power).

As an exception, components designed to be integrated onto the system board may be designed to operate at a fixed frequency (of up to 33MHz) and may only operate at that frequency.

For a discussion of 66MHz bus operation, refer to the chapter entitled "66MHz PCI Implementation."

# Chapter 5: The Functional Signal Groups

## CLKRUN# Signal

### General

The CLKRUN# signal is optional and is defined for the mobile (i.e., portable) environment. It is not available on the PCI add-in connector. This section provides an introduction to this subject. A more detailed description of the mobile environment and the CLKRUN# signal's role can be found in the document entitled *PCI Mobile Design Guide* (available from the SIG).

Although the PCI specification states that the clock may be stopped or its frequency changed, it does not define a method for determining when to stop (or slow down) the clock, or a method for determining when to restart the clock.

A portable system includes a central resource that includes the PCI clock generation logic. With respect to the clock generation logic, the CLKRUN# signal is a sustained tri-state input/output signal. The clock generation logic keeps CLKRUN# asserted when the clock is running normally. During periods when the clock has been stopped (or slowed), the clock generation logic monitors CLKRUN# to recognize requests from master and target devices for a change to be made in the state of the PCI clock signal. The clock cannot be stopped if the bus is not idle. Before it stops (or slows down) the clock frequency, the clock generation logic deasserts CLKRUN# for one clock to inform PCI devices that the clock is about to be stopped (or slowed). After driving CLKRUN# high (deasserted) for one clock, the clock generation logic tri-states its CLKRUN# output driver. The keeper resistor on CLKRUN# then assumes responsibility for maintaining the deasserted state of CLKRUN# during the period in which the clock is stopped (or slowed).

The clock continues to run unchanged for a minimum of four clocks after the clock generation logic deasserts CLKRUN#. After deassertion of CLKRUN#, the clock generation logic must monitor CLKRUN# for two possible cases:

1. After the clock has been stopped (or slowed), a master (or multiple masters) may require clock restart in order to request use of the bus. Prior to issuing the bus request, the master(s) must first request clock restart. This is accomplished by assertion of CLKRUN#. When the clock generation logic detects the assertion of CLKRUN# by another party, it turns on (or speeds up) the clock and turns on its CLKRUN# output driver to assert CLKRUN#. When the master detects that CLKRUN# has been asserted for

two rising-edges of the PCI CLK signal, the master may then tri-state its CLKRUN# output driver.

2. When the clock generation logic has deasserted CLKRUN#, indicating its intention to stop (or slow) the clock, the clock must continue to run for a minimum of four clocks. During this period of time, a target (or master) that requires continued clock operation (e.g., in order to perform internal housekeeping after the completion of a transaction), may reassert CLKRUN# for two PCI clock cycles to request continued generation of CLK. When the clock generation logic samples CLKRUN# reasserted, it reasserts CLKRUN# and continues to generate the clock (rather than stopping it or slowing it down). The specification doesn't define the period of time that the clock will continue to run after a request for continued operation. The author interprets this as implying that the period is system design-specific.

## Reset Signal (RST#)

When asserted, the reset signal forces all PCI configuration registers, master and target state machines and output drivers to an initialized state. RST# may be asserted or deasserted asynchronously to the PCI CLK edge. The assertion of RST# also initializes other, device-specific functions, but this subject is beyond the scope of the PCI specification. All PCI output signals must be driven to their benign states. In general, this means they must be tri-stated. Exceptions are:

- SERR# is floated.
- If SBO# and SDONE cannot be tri-stated, they will be driven low.
- To prevent the AD bus, the C/BE bus and the PAR signals from floating during reset, they may be driven low by a central resource during reset.

Refer to the chapter entitled "The 64-Bit PCI Extension" for a discussion of the REQ64# signal's behavior during reset.

## Address/Data Bus

The PCI bus uses a time-multiplexed address/data bus. During the address phase of a transaction:

- The **AD bus**, AD[31:0], carries the start address. The resolution of this address is on a doubleword boundary (address divisible by four) during a memory or a configuration transaction, or a byte-specific address during an I/O read or write transaction. Additional information on memory and I/O addressing can be found in the chapter entitled "The Read and Write Transfer." Additional information on configuration addressing can be found in parts III and IV of this book.

- The **Command or Byte Enable bus**, **C/BE#[3:0]**, defines the type of transaction. The chapter entitled "The Commands" defines the transaction types.
- The **Parity signal, PAR**, is driven by the initiator one clock after completion of the address phase or one clock after assertion of IRDY# during each data phase of write transactions. It is driven by the currently-addressed target one clock after the assertion of TRDY# during each data phase of read transactions. One clock after completion of the address phase, the initiator drives PAR either high or low to ensure even parity across the address bus, AD[31:0], and the four Command/Byte Enable lines, C/BE#[3:0]. Refer to the chapter entitled "Error Detection and Handling" for a discussion of parity.

During each data phase:

- The data bus, **AD[31:0]**, is driven by the initiator (during a write) or the currently-addressed target (during a read).
- **PAR** is driven by either the initiator (during a write) or the currently-addressed target (during a read) one clock after the assertion of IRDY# (on a write) or TRDY# (on a read) during each data phase and ensures even parity across AD[31:0] and C/BE#[3:0]. If all four data paths are not being used during a data phase, the agent driving the data bus (the master during a write or the target during a read) must ensure that valid data is being driven onto all data paths (including those not being used to transfer data). This is necessary because PAR must reflect even parity across the entire AD and C/BE buses.
- The Command/Byte Enable bus, **C/BE#[3:0]**, is driven by the initiator to indicate the bytes to be transferred within the currently-addressed doubleword and the data paths to be used to transfer the data. Table 5-1 indicates the mapping of the byte enable signals to the data paths and to the locations within the currently-addressed doubleword. Table 5-2 defines the interpretation of the byte enable signals during each data phase. Any combination of byte enables is considered valid and the byte enables may change from data phase to data phase.

Table 5-1. Byte Enable Mapping To Data Paths and Locations Within the
Currently-Addressed Doubleword

| Byte Enable Signal | Maps To |
|---|---|
| C/BE3# | Data path 3, AD[31:24], and the fourth location in the currently-addressed doubleword. |
| C/BE2# | Data path 2, AD[23:16], and the third location in the currently-addressed doubleword. |
| C/BE1# | Data path 1, AD[15:8], and the second location in the currently-addressed doubleword. |
| C/BE0# | Data path 0, AD[7:0], and the first location in the currently-addressed doubleword. |

Table 5-2. Interpretation of the Byte Enables During a Data Phase

| C/BE3# | C/BE2# | C/BE1# | C/BE0# | Meaning |
|---|---|---|---|---|
| 0 | 0 | 0 | 0 | The initiator intends to transfer all four bytes within the currently-addressed doubleword using all four data paths. |
| 0 | 0 | 0 | 1 | The initiator intends to transfer the upper three bytes within the currently-addressed doubleword using the upper three data paths. |
| 0 | 0 | 1 | 0 | The initiator intends to transfer the upper two bytes and the first byte within the currently-addressed doubleword using the upper two data paths and the first data path. |
| 0 | 0 | 1 | 1 | The initiator intends to transfer the upper two bytes within the currently-addressed doubleword using the upper two data paths. |
| 0 | 1 | 0 | 0 | The initiator intends to transfer the upper byte and the lower two bytes within the currently-addressed doubleword using the upper data path and the lower two data paths. |

| C/BE3# | C/BE2# | C/BE1# | C/BE0# | Meaning |
|--------|--------|--------|--------|---------|
| 0 | 1 | 0 | 1 | The initiator intends to transfer the second and the fourth bytes within the currently-addressed doubleword using the second and fourth data paths. |
| 0 | 1 | 1 | 0 | The initiator intends to transfer the first and the fourth bytes within the currently-addressed doubleword using the first and the fourth data paths. |
| 0 | 1 | 1 | 1 | The initiator intends to transfer the upper byte within the currently-addressed doubleword using the upper data path. |
| 1 | 0 | 0 | 0 | The initiator intends to transfer the lower three bytes within the currently-addressed doubleword using the lower three data paths. |
| 1 | 0 | 0 | 1 | The initiator intends to transfer the middle two bytes within the currently-addressed doubleword using the middle two data paths. |
| 1 | 0 | 1 | 0 | The initiator intends to transfer the first and third bytes within the currently-addressed doubleword using the first and the third data paths. |
| 1 | 0 | 1 | 1 | The initiator intends to transfer the third byte within the currently-addressed doubleword using the third data path. |
| 1 | 1 | 0 | 0 | The initiator intends to transfer the lower two bytes within the currently-addressed doubleword using the lower two data paths. |
| 1 | 1 | 0 | 1 | The initiator intends to transfer the second byte within the currently-addressed doubleword using the second data path. |
| 1 | 1 | 1 | 0 | The initiator intends to transfer the first byte within the currently-addressed doubleword using the first data path. |

| C/BE3# | C/BE2# | C/BE1# | C/BE0# | Meaning |
|--------|--------|--------|--------|---------|
| 1 | 1 | 1 | 1 | The initiator does not intend to transfer any of the four bytes within the currently-addressed doubleword and will not use any of the data paths. This is a null data phase. |

## Preventing Excessive Current Drain

If the inputs to CMOS input receivers are permitted to float for long periods, the receivers tend to oscillate and draw excessive current. In order to prevent this phenomena and preserve the green nature of the PCI bus, several rules are applied:

- When the bus is idle and no bus masters are requesting ownership, either the bus arbiter or a master that has the bus parked on it must enable its AD, C/BE and PAR output drivers and drive a stable pattern onto these signal lines. This issue is discussed in the chapter entitled "PCI Bus Arbitration" under the heading "Bus Parking."
- During a data phase in a write transaction, the initiator must drive a stable pattern onto the AD bus when it is not yet ready to deliver the next set of data bytes. This subject is covered in the chapter entitled "The Read and Write Transfers."
- During a data phase in a read transaction, the target must drive a stable pattern onto the AD bus when it is not yet ready to deliver the next set of data bytes. This subject is covered in the chapter entitled "The Read and Write Transfers."
- A 64-bit card plugged into a 32-bit expansion slot must keep its AD[63:32], C/BE#[7:4] and PAR64 input receivers from floating. This subject is covered in the chapter entitled "The 64-bit PCI Extension."

## Transaction Control Signals

Table 5-3 provides a brief description of each signal used to control a PCI transfer.

*Table 5-3. PCI Interface Control Signals*

| Signal | Master | Target | Description |
|--------|--------|--------|-------------|
| FRAME# | In/Out | In | **Cycle Frame** is driven by the current initiator and indicates the start (when it's first asserted) and duration (the duration of its assertion) of a transaction. In order to determine that bus ownership has been acquired, the master must sample FRAME# and IRDY# both deasserted and GNT# asserted on the same rising-edge of the PCI CLK signal. A transaction may consist of one or more data transfers between the current initiator and the currently-addressed target. FRAME# is deasserted when the initiator is ready to complete the final data phase. |
| TRDY# | In | Out | **Target Ready** is driven by the currently-addressed target. It is asserted when the target is ready to complete the current data phase (data transfer). A data phase is completed when the target is asserting TRDY# and the initiator is asserting IRDY# at the rising-edge of the CLK signal. During a read, TRDY# asserted indicates that the target is driving valid data onto the data bus. During a write, TRDY# asserted indicates that the target is ready to accept data from the master. Wait states are inserted in the current data phase until both TDRY# and IRDY# are sampled asserted. |
| IRDY# | In/Out | In | **Initiator Ready** is driven by the current bus master (the initiator of the transaction). During a write, IRDY# asserted indicates that the initiator is driving valid data onto the data bus. During a read, IRDY# asserted indicates that the initiator is ready to accept data from the currently-addressed target. In order to determine that bus ownership has been acquired, the master must sample FRAME# and IRDY# both deasserted and GNT# asserted on the same rising-edge of the PCI CLK signal. Also refer to the description of TRDY# in this table. |

| Signal | Master | Target | Description |
|--------|--------|--------|-------------|
| STOP# | In | Out | The target asserts **STOP#** to indicate that it wishes the initiator to stop the transaction in progress on the current data phase. |
| IDSEL | In | In | **Initialization Device Select** is an input to the PCI device and is used as a chip select during an access to one of the device's configuration registers. For additional information, refer to the chapter entitled "Configuration Transactions." |
| LOCK# | In/Out | In | Used by the initiator to **lock** the currently-addressed memory target during an atomic transaction series (e.g., during a semaphore read/modify/write operation). Refer to the description (in this chapter) under the heading "Resource Locking" and to the chapter entitled "Shared Resource Acquisition." |
| DEVSEL# | In | Out | **Device Select** is asserted by a target when the target has decoded its address. It acts as an input to the current initiator and the subtractive decoder in the expansion bus bridge. If a master initiates a transfer and does not detect DEVSEL# active within six CLK periods, it must assume that the target cannot respond or that the address is unpopulated. A master-abort results. |

## Arbitration Signals

Each PCI master has a pair of arbitration lines that connect it directly to the PCI bus arbiter. When a master requires the use of the PCI bus, it asserts its device-specific REQ# line to the arbiter. When the arbiter has determined that the requesting master should be granted control of the PCI bus, it asserts the GNT# (grant) line specific to the requesting master. In the PCI environment, bus arbitration can take place while another master is still in control of the bus. This is known as "hidden" arbitration. When a master receives a grant from the bus arbiter, it must wait for the current initiator to complete its transfer before initiating its own transfer. It cannot assume ownership of the PCI bus until FRAME# is sampled deasserted (indicating the start of the last data phase) and IRDY# is then sampled deasserted (indicating the completion of the last data phase). This indicates that the current transaction has been completed and the bus has been returned to the idle state. Bus arbitration is discussed in more detail in the chapter entitled "PCI Bus Arbitration."

While RST# is asserted, all masters must tri-state their REQ# output drivers and must ignore their GNT# inputs. In a system with PCI add-in connectors, the arbiter may require a weak pullup on the REQ# inputs that are wired to the add-in connectors. This will keep them from floating when the connectors are unoccupied.

## Interrupt Request Signals

PCI agents that must generate requests for service can utilize one of the PCI interrupt request lines, INTA#, INTB#, INTC# or INTD#. A description of these signals can be found in the chapter entitled "Interrupt-Related Issues."

## Error Reporting Signals

The sections that follow provide an introduction to the PERR# and SERR# signals. The chapter entitled "Error Detection and Handling" provides a more detailed discussion of error detection and handling.

## Data Parity Error

The **generation of parity information is mandatory for all PCI devices** that drive address or data information onto the AD bus. This is a requirement because the agent driving the AD bus must assume that the agent receiving the data and parity will check the validity of the parity and may either flag an error or even fail the machine if incorrect parity is received.

The **detection and reporting of parity errors by PCI devices is generally required.** The specification is written this way to indicate that, in some cases, the designer may choose to ignore parity errors. An example might be a video frame buffer. The designer may choose not to verify the correctness of the data being written into the video memory by the initiator. In the event that corrupted data is received and written into the frame memory, the only effect will be one or more corrupted video pixels displayed on the screen. Although this may have a deleterious effect on the end user's peace of mind, it will not corrupt programs or the data structures associated with programs.

Implementation of the PERR# pin is required on all add-in PCI cards (and is generally required on system board devices). The data parity error signal, PERR#, may be pulsed by a PCI device under the following circumstances:

- In the event of a data parity error detected by a PCI target during a write data phase, the target must set the DATA PARITY SIGNALED bit in its PCI configuration status register and must assert PERR# (if the PARITY RESPONSE ENABLE bit in its configuration command register is set to one). It may then either continue the transaction or may assert STOP# to terminate the transaction prematurely. During a burst write, the initiator is responsible for monitoring the PERR# signal to ensure that each data item is not corrupted in flight while being written to the target.
- In the event of a data parity error detected by the PCI initiator during a read data phase, the initiator must set the DATA PARITY SIGNALED bit in its PCI configuration status register and must assert PERR# (if the PARITY RESPONSE ENABLE bit in its configuration command register is set to one). The platform designer may include third-party logic that monitors PERR# or may leave error reporting up to the initiator.

To ensure that correct parity is available to any PCI devices that perform parity checking, all PCI devices must generate even parity on AD[31:0], C/BE#[3:0] and PAR for the address and data phases. PERR# is implemented as an output on targets and as both an input and an output on masters. The initiator of a transaction has responsibility for reporting the detection of a data parity error to software. For this reason, it must monitor PERR# during write data phases to determine if the target has detected a data parity error. The action taken by an initiator when a parity error is detected is design-dependent. It may perform retries with the target or may choose to terminate the transaction and generate an interrupt to invoke its device-specific interrupt handler. If the initiator reports the failure to software, it must also set the DATA PARITY REPORTED bit in its PCI configuration status register. PERR# is only driven by one device at time.

A detailed discussion of data parity error detection and handling may be found in the chapter entitled "Error Detection and Handling."

## System Error

The System Error signal, SERR#, may be pulsed by any PCI device to report address parity errors, data parity errors during a special cycle, and critical errors other than parity. SERR# is required on all add-in PCI cards that perform address parity checking or report other serious errors using SERR#. This signal is considered a "last-recourse" for reporting serious errors. Non-catastrophic and correctable errors should be signaled in some other way. In a PC-compatible machine, SERR# typically causes an NMI to the system processor (although the designer is not constrained to have it generate an NMI). In a PowerPC™ PREP-compliant platform, assertion of SERR# is reported to the host processor via assertion of TEA# or MC# and causes a machine check interrupt. This is the functional equivalent of NMI in the Intel world. If the designer of a PCI device does not want an NMI to be initiated, some means other than SERR# should be used to flag an error condition (such as setting a bit in the device's status register and generating an interrupt request). SERR# is an open-drain signal and may be driven by more than one PCI agent at a time. When asserted, the device drives it low for one clock and then tri-states its output driver. The keeper resistor on SERR# is responsible for returning it to the deasserted state.

A detailed discussion of system error detection and handling may be found in the chapter entitled "Error Detection and Handling."

## Cache Support (Snoop Result) Signals

Table 5-4 provides a brief description of the optional PCI cache support signals. The chapter entitled "PCI Cache Support" provides a more detailed explanation of cache support implementation.

Table 5-4. Cache Snoop Result Signals

| Signal | Description |
|--------|-------------|
| SBO# | *Snoop Back Off*. This signal is an output from the PCI cache/bridge and an input to cacheable memory subsystems residing on the PCI bus. It is asserted by the bridge to indicate that the PCI memory access in progress is about to read or update stale information in memory. SBO# is qualified by and only has meaning when the SDONE signal is also asserted by the bridge. When SDONE and SBO# are sampled asserted, the currently-addressed cacheable PCI memory subsystem should respond by signaling a retry to the current initiator. |
| SDONE | *Snoop Done*. This signal is an output from the PCI cache/bridge and an input to cacheable memory subsystems residing on the PCI bus. It is deasserted by the bridge while the processor's cache(s) snoops a memory access started by the current initiator. The bridge asserts SDONE when the snoop has been completed. The results of the snoop are then indicated on the SBO# signal. SBO# sampled deasserted indicates that the PCI initiator is accessing a clean line in memory and the PCI cacheable memory target is permitted to accept or supply the indicated data. SBO# sampled asserted indicates that the PCI initiator is accessing a stale line in memory and should not complete the data access. Instead, the memory target should terminate the access by signaling a retry to the PCI initiator. |

The specification recommends that systems that do not support cacheable memory on the PCI bus should supply pullups on the SDONE and SBO# pins at each add-in connector. Anytime an initiator attempts to access a PCI card with memory, the card will always detect a clean snoop (the system board pullups keep SDONE asserted and SBO# deasserted) and will permit the initiator to access it.

The assertion of RST# at system startup clears the cache line size configuration register to zero. In a system that does not support caching from PCI memory, this register will still contain zero after the configuration software enables the device's memory decoder(s) using the MEMORY ENABLE bit in the device's PCI configuration command register. When this is the case, the memory may ignore the snoop result signals and therefore permit slightly faster access. On the other hand, a non-zero value in this register after the device is enabled indicates that the processor's caches do keep copies of information read from this memory. In this case, the memory target is not permitted to respond (i.e., assert TRDY#) until the snoop result is presented to it by the bridge.

## 64-bit Extension Signals

The PCI specification provides a detailed definition of a 64-bit extension to its baseline 32-bit architecture. Systems that implement the extension support the transfer of up to eight bytes per data phase between a 64-bit initiator and a 64-bit target. The signals involved are defined in table 5-5. A more detailed explanation can be found in the chapter entitled "The 64-Bit PCI Extension."

*Table 5-5. The 64-Bit Extension*

| Signal | Description |
|---|---|
| AD[63:32] | Upper four **data lanes**. In combination with AD[31:0], extends the width of the data bus to 64 bits. These pins aren't used during the address phase of a transfer (unless 64-bit addressing is being used). |
| C/BE#[7:4] | **Byte Enables** for data lanes four-through-seven. Used during the data transfer phase, but not during the address phase (unless 64-bit addressing is being used.) |
| REQ64# | **Request 64-bit Transfer**. Generated by the current initiator to indicate its desire to perform transfers using one or more of the upper four data paths. REQ64# has the same timing as the FRAME# signal. Refer to the chapter entitled "The 64-Bit PCI Extension" for more information. |
| ACK64# | **Acknowledge 64-bit Transfer**. Generated by the currently-addressed target (if it supports 64-bit transfers) in response to a REQ64# assertion by the initiator. ACK64# has the same timing as the DEVSEL# signal. |
| PAR64 | **Parity for the upper doubleword**. This is the even parity bit associated with AD[63:32] and C/BE#[7:4]. For additional information, refer to the chapters entitled "The 64-bit PCI Extension" and "Error Detection and Handling." |

## Resource Locking

The LOCK# signal should be utilized by a PCI initiator that requires exclusive access to a target memory device during two or more separate transactions. The intended use of this function is to support read/modify/write memory semaphore operations. It is **not** intended as a mechanism that permits an initiator to dominate a target device or the bus in general.

If a PCI device implements executable memory or memory that contains system data (managed by the operating system), it must implement the locking function. It is recommended that a host/PCI bridge that has system memory on the host side implement the locking function. Some host bus architectures, however, do not support memory locking (e.g., the 60x bus in PowerPC-based, PReP-compliant platforms). For this reason, the specification recommends but does not require that a host/PCI bridge support locking when acting as the target of a system memory access by a PCI master. Since the device driver associated with a PCI master cannot depend on the ability to lock system memory, the specification recommends that the driver use some type of software protocol (rather than locking) to gain exclusive access to code or data structures shared with other processors in the system.

An initiator requiring exclusive access to a memory target may use the LOCK# signal if it isn't currently being driven by another initiator. When the target device is addressed and LOCK# is deasserted by the initiator during the address phase and then asserted during the data phase, the target device is reserved for as long as the LOCK# signal remains asserted. If the target is subsequently addressed by another initiator while the lock is still in force, the target issues a retry to the initiator. While a target is locked, other bus masters (that don't require exclusive access to a target) are permitted to acquire the bus to access targets other than the locked target.

A more detailed description of the PCI locking capability can be found in the chapter entitled "Shared Resource Acquisition."

## JTAG/Boundary Scan Signals

The designer of a PCI device may optionally implement the IEEE 1149.1 Boundary Scan interface signals to permit in-circuit testing of the PCI device. The related signals are defined in table 5-6. A detailed discussion of boundary scan is beyond the scope of this publication.

*Table 5-6. Boundary Scan Signals*

| Signal | Description |
|--------|-------------|
| TCK | *Test Clock*. Used to clock state information and data into and out of the device during boundary scan. |
| TDI | *Test Input*. Used (in conjunction with TCK) to shift data and instructions into the Test Access Port (TAP) in a serial bit stream. |
| TDO | *Test Output*. Used (in conjunction with TCK) to shift data out of the Test Access Port (TAP) in a serial bit stream. |
| TMS | *Test Mode Select*. Used to control the state of the Test Access Port controller. |
| TRST# | *Test Reset*. Used to force the Test Access Port controller into an initialized state. |

## Interrupt Request Lines

The PCI interrupt request signals (INTA#, INTB#, INTC# and INTD#) are discussed in the chapters entitled "Interrupt-Related Issues" and "The Configuration Registers."

## Sideband Signals

A sideband signal is defined as a signal that is not part of the PCI bus standard and interconnects two or more PCI agents. This signal only has meaning for the agents it interconnects. The following are some examples of sideband signals:

- A PCI bus arbiter could monitor a "busy" signal from a PCI device (such as an EISA or Micro Channel™ expansion bus bridge) to determine if the device is available before granting the PCI bus to a PCI initiator.
- PC compatibility signals like A20GATE, CPU RESET, etc.

## Signal Types

Table 5-7 defines the PCI signal types. The signals that comprise the PCI bus are electrically defined in one of the following fashions:

- **IN** defines a signal as a standard input-only signal.
- **OUT** defines a signal as a standard output-only signal.

# PCI System Architecture

- **T/S** defines a signal as a bi-directional, tri-state input/output signal.
- **S/T/S** defines a signal as a sustained tri-state signal that is driven by only one owner at a time. An agent that drives an s/t/s pin low must actively drive it high for one clock before tri-stating it. A pullup resistor is required to sustain the inactive state until another agent takes ownership of and drives the signal. The resistor is supplied as a central resource in the system design. The next owner of the signal cannot start driving the s/t/s signal any sooner than one clock after it is released by the previous owner.
- **O/D** defines a signal as an open drain. It is wire-ORed with other agents. The signaling agent asserts the signal, but returning the signal to the inactive state is accomplished by a weak pull-up resistor. The deasserted state is maintained by the pullup resistor. The pullup may take two or three PCI clock periods to fully restore the signal to the deasserted state.

*Table 5-7. PCI Signal Types*

| Signal(s) | Type |
|---|---|
| CLK | IN |
| RST# | IN |
| AD[31:0] | T/S |
| C/BE#[3:0] | T/S |
| PAR | T/S |
| FRAME# | S/T/S |
| TRDY# | S/T/S |
| IRDY# | S/T/S |
| STOP# | S/T/S |
| LOCK# | S/T/S |
| IDSEL | IN |
| DEVSEL# | S/T/S |
| REQ# | T/S |
| GNT# | T/S |
| PERR# | S/T/S |
| SERR# | O/D |
| SBO# | IN or OUT |
| SDONE | IN or OUT |
| AD[63:32] | T/S |
| C/BE#[7:4] | T/S |
| REQ64# | S/T/S |
| ACK64# | S/T/S |
| PAR64 | T/S |
| TCK | IN |
| TDI | IN |
| TDO | OUT |
| TMS | IN |
| TRST# | IN |
| INTA# - INTD# | O/D |

# Chapter 5: The Functional Signal Groups

## Central Resource Functions

Any platform that implements the PCI bus must supply a toolbox of support functions necessary for the proper operation of all PCI devices. Some examples would include:

- **PCI bus arbiter**. The arbiter is necessary to support PCI masters. The PCI specification does not define the decision-making process utilized by the PCI bus arbiter. The design of the arbiter is therefore platform-specific.
- **Pullup resistors** on signals that are not always driven to a valid state. This would include: all of the s/t/s signals; AD[63:32]; C/BE#[7:4]; PAR64; and SERR#.
- **Error logic** responsible for converting SERR# to the platform-specific signal (e.g., NMI in an Intel-based platform or TEA# in a PowerPC™-based platform) utilized to alert the host processor that an error has occurred.
- Central resource to **generate** the proper **IDSEL** signal when a PCI device's configuration space is being addressed (this function is typically performed by the host/PCI bridge).
- System board logic to **assert REQ64# during reset**. A detailed description of this function is provided in the chapter entitled "The 64-Bit PCI Extension."
- **Subtractive decoder**. Each PCI target device must implement positive decode. In other words, it must decode any address placed on the PCI bus to determine if it is the target of the current transaction. Only one agent on the PCI bus may implement subtractive decode. This is typically the expansion bus (e.g., EISA, ISA, or Micro Channel) bridge.

## Subtractive Decode

### Background

The expansion bus bridge can claim transactions in one of two fashions:

1. When a transaction is not claimed by any other PCI device within a specified period of time, the PCI/expansion bus bridge may assert DEVSEL# and pass the transaction through to the expansion bus. It can determine that no other PCI device has claimed a transaction by monitoring the state of the DEVSEL# signal generated by the other PCI-compliant devices. If DEVSEL# is not sampled asserted within four clock periods after the ad-

dress phase of a transaction, no other PCI device has claimed the transaction. The expansion bus bridge may then claim the transaction by asserting DEVSEL# during the period between the fifth and sixth clocks of the transaction. This is referred to as subtractive decode. Additional information regarding subtractive decode can be found in the chapter entitled "Premature Transaction Termination" in the section entitled "Master Abort."

2. Since this would result in very poor access time when accessing expansion bus devices, the expansion bus bridge may employ positive address decode. During system configuration, the bridge is configured to recognize certain memory and/or IO address ranges. Upon recognizing an address within this pre-assigned range, the bridge may assert DEVSEL# immediately (without waiting for the DEVSEL# timeout) to claim the transaction. The bridge then passes the transaction through onto the expansion bus.

The ISA bus environment is one that depends heavily on subtractive decoding to claim transactions. Because most ISA bus devices are not plug and play-capable, the configuration software cannot automatically detect their presence and assign address ranges to their address decoders. The ISA bridge uses subtractive decode to claim all transactions that meet the following criteria:

- No other PCI device has claimed the transaction. By definition, all PCI device address decoders are fast (decodes address and asserts DEVSEL# during the clock cell immediately following completion of the address phase), medium (asserts DEVSEL# during the second clock cell after completion of the address phase) or slow (asserts DEVSEL# during the third clock after completion of the address phase). If the ISA bridge does not detect DEVSEL# asserted by any other PCI device (and the target address "makes sense" for the ISA environment), the bridge asserts DEVSEL# during the fourth clock after completion of the address phase. The transaction is then initiated on the ISA bus.

- The target address is one that falls within the overall ISA memory or I/O address ranges. Any memory address below 16MB that goes unclaimed by PCI devices is claimed and passed through to the ISA bus. Any I/O address in the lower 64KB of I/O space that goes unclaimed by PCI devices is claimed and passed through to the ISA bus.

## Tuning Subtractive Decoder

This means that a transaction initiated by the host processor (or any other bus master) does not appear on the ISA bus until four or five clocks after the completion of the address phase on the PCI bus. The processor's performance when accessing ISA devices is therefore substantially degraded. In order to minimize the effect of subtractive decode on performance, the ISA bridge designer can permit the subtractive decoder to be "tuned." During the configuration process, the configuration software reads the configuration status register for every device on the PCI bus. One of the required fields in the status register is the DEVSEL# timing field, indicating whether the device has a fast, medium or slow address decoder. As an example, if every device on the PCI bus indicates that it has a fast decoder, the software can program the subtractive decoder to assert DEVSEL# and claim the transaction during the second clock after the completion of the address phase (if it doesn't detect DEVSEL# asserted during the first clock after the address phase).

## Reading Timing Diagrams

Figure 5-3 illustrates a typical PCI timing diagram. When a PCI signal is asserted or deasserted by a PCI device, the output driver utilized is typically a weak CMOS driver. This being the case, the driver isn't capable of transitioning the signal line past the logic threshold for a logic high or low in one step. The voltage change initiated on the signal line propagates down the trace until it hits the physical end of the trace. As it passes the stub for each PCI device along the way, the wavefront has not yet transitioned past the new logic threshold, so the change isn't detected by any of the devices. When reflected back along the trace, however, the reflection doubles the voltage change on the line, causing it to cross the logic threshold. As the doubled wavefront propagates back down the length of the trace, the signal's new state is detected by each device it passes. The time it takes the signal to travel the length of the bus and reflect back is referred to as the Tprop, or propagation delay. This delay is illustrated in the timing diagrams.

As an example, a master samples FRAME# and IRDY# deasserted (bus idle) and its GNT# asserted on the rising-edge of clock one, indicating that it has bus acquisition. The master initiates the transaction during clock cell one by asserting the FRAME# signal to indicate the start of the transaction. In the timing diagram, FRAME# isn't shown transitioning from high-to-low until sometime after the rising-edge of clock one and before the rising-edge of clock two, thereby illustrating the propagation delay. Coincident with FRAME# assertion, the initiator drives the start address onto the AD bus during clock cell one, but the address change isn't valid until sometime after the rising-edge of clock one and before the rising-edge of clock two.

The address phase ends on the rising-edge of clock two and the initiator begins to turn off its AD bus drivers. The time that it takes the driver to actually cease driving the AD bus is illustrated in the timing diagram (the initiator has not successfully disconnected from the AD bus until sometime during clock cell two).

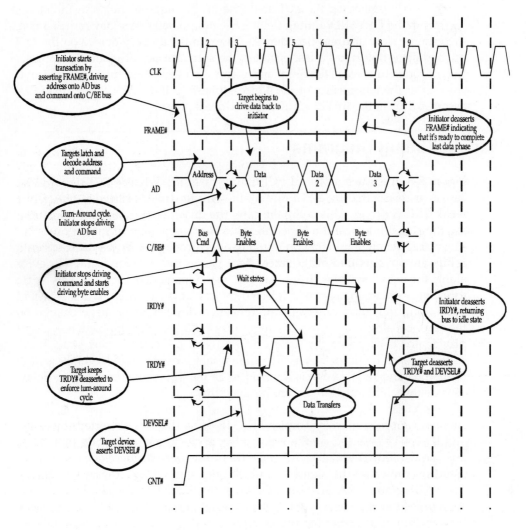

*Figure 5-3. Typical PCI Timing Diagram*

# Chapter 6

## The Previous Chapter

The previous chapter provided a detailed description of the PCI functional signal groups.

## This Chapter

When a PCI bus master requires the use of the PCI bus to perform a data transfer, it must request the use of the bus from the PCI bus arbiter. This chapter provides a detailed discussion of the PCI bus arbitration timing. The PCI specification defines the timing of the request and grant handshaking, but not the procedure used to determine the winner of a competition. The algorithm used by a system's PCI bus arbiter to decide which of the requesting bus masters will be granted use of the PCI bus is system-specific and outside the scope of the specification.

## The Next Chapter

The next chapter describes the transaction types, or commands, that the initiator may utilize when it has successfully acquired PCI bus ownership.

## Arbiter

At a given instant in time, one or more PCI bus master devices may require use of the PCI bus to perform a data transfer with another PCI device. Each requesting master asserts its REQ# output to inform the bus arbiter of its pending request for the use of the bus. Figure 6-1 illustrates the relationship of the PCI masters to the central PCI resource known as the bus arbiter. In this example, there are seven possible masters connected to the PCI bus arbiter in the illustration. Each master is connected to the arbiter via a separate pair of REQ#/GNT# signals. Although the arbiter is shown as a separate component, it usually is integrated into the PCI chip set; specifically, it is typically integrated into the host/PCI or the PCI/expansion bus bridge chip.

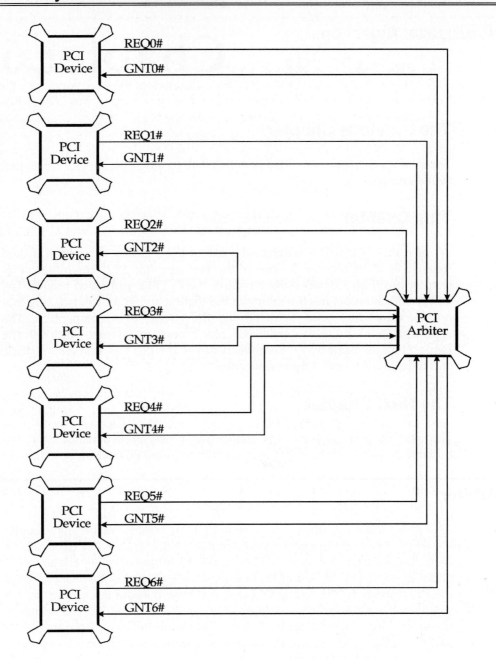

*Figure 6-1. The PCI Bus Arbiter*

# Chapter 6: PCI Bus Arbitration

## Arbitration Algorithm

As stated at the beginning of this chapter, the PCI specification does not define the scheme used by the PCI bus arbiter to decide the winner of the competition when multiple masters simultaneously request bus ownership. The arbiter may utilize any scheme, such as one based on fixed or rotational priority or a combination of the two (rotational between one group of masters and fixed within another group). The 2.1 specification states that the arbiter is required to implement a fairness algorithm to avoid deadlocks. The exact verbiage that is used is:

> The central arbiter is required to implement a fairness algorithm to avoid deadlocks. Fairness means that each potential bus master must be granted access to the bus independent of other requests. However, this does not mean that all agents are required to have equal access to the bus. By requiring a fairness algorithm there are no special conditions to handle when LOCK# is active (assuming a resource lock) or when cacheable memory is located on PCI. A system that uses a fairness algorithm is still considered fair if it implements a complete bus lock instead of a resource lock. However, the arbiter must advance to a new agent if the initial transaction attempting to establish a lock is terminated with retry.

While the statements made regarding lock are clear, the definition of fairness contained in the above text was not clear to the author. Fairness is defined as a policy that ensures that high-priority masters will not dominate the bus to the exclusion of lower-priority masters when they are continually requesting the bus.

The specification contains an example arbiter implementation that does clarify the intent of the specification. The example follows this section.

Ideally, the bus arbiter should be programmable by the system. The startup configuration software can determine the priority to be assigned to each member of the bus master community by reading from the maximum latency (Max_Lat) configuration register associated with each bus master. The bus master designer hardwires this register to indicate, in increments of 250ns, how quickly the master requires access to the bus in order to achieve adequate performance.

In order to grant the PCI bus to a bus master, the arbiter asserts the device's respective GNT# signal. This grants the bus to the master for one transaction (consisting of one or more data phases).

If a master generates a request, is subsequently granted the bus and does not initiate a transaction (assert FRAME#) within 16 PCI clocks after the bus goes idle, the arbiter may assume that the master is malfunctioning. In this case, the action taken by the arbiter would be system design-dependent.

## Example Arbiter with Fairness

A system may divides the overall community of bus masters on a PCI bus into two categories:

1. Bus masters that require fast access to the bus or high throughput in order to achieve good performance. Examples might be the video adapter, an ATM network interface or an FDDI network interface.
2. Bus masters that don't require very fast access to the bus or high throughput in order to achieve good performance. Examples might be a SCSI host bus adapter or a standard expansion bus master.

The arbiter would segregate the REQ#/GNT# signals into two groups with greater precedence given to those in one group. Assume that bus masters A and B are in the group that requires fast access, while masters X, Y and Z are in the other group. The arbiter can be programmed or designed to treat each group as rotational priority within the group and rotational priority between the two groups. This is pictured in figure 6-2.

Assume the following conditions:

- Master A is the next to receive the bus in the first group.
- Master X is the next to receive it in the second group.
- A master in the first group is the next to receive the bus.
- All masters are asserting REQ# and wish to perform multiple transactions (i.e., they keep their respective REQ# asserted after starting a transaction).

The order in which the masters would receive access to the bus is:

1. Master A.
2. Master B.
3. Master X.

4.  Master A.
5.  Master B.
6.  Master Y.
7.  Master A.
8.  Master B.
9.  Master Z.
10. Master A.
11. Master B.
12. Master X, etc.

The masters in the first group are permitted to access the bus more frequently than those that reside in the second group.

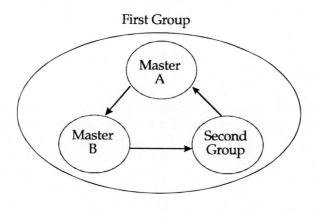

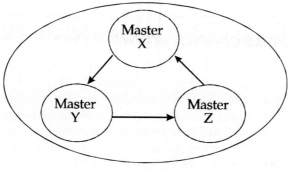

*Figure 6-2. Example Arbitration Scheme*

## Master Wishes To Perform More Than One Transaction

If the master has another burst to perform immediately after the one it just initiated, it should keep its REQ# line asserted after it asserts FRAME# to begin the current transaction. This informs the arbiter of its desire to maintain ownership of the bus after completion of the current transaction. Depending on other pending requests, the arbiter may or may not permit the master to maintain bus ownership after the completion of the current transaction. In the event that ownership is not maintained, the master should keep its REQ# asserted until it is successful in acquiring bus ownership again.

At a given instant in time, only one bus master may use the bus. This means that no more than one GNT# line will be asserted by the arbiter during any PCI clock cycle.

## Hidden Bus Arbitration

Unlike some arbitration schemes, the PCI scheme allows bus arbitration to take place while the current initiator is performing a data transfer. If the arbiter decides to grant ownership of the bus for the next transaction to a master other than the initiator of the current transaction, it removes the GNT# from the current initiator (i.e., it preempts it) and issues GNT# to the next owner of the bus. The next owner cannot assume bus ownership, however, until the bus is idled by the current initiator. No bus time is wasted on a dedicated period of time to perform an arbitration bus cycle. This is referred to as hidden arbitration.

## Bus Parking

A master must only assert its REQ# output to signal a current need for the bus. In other words, a master must not use its REQ# output to "park" the bus on itself. If a system designer implements a bus parking scheme, the bus arbiter design should indicate a default bus owner by asserting the device's GNT# signal when no request from any bus masters are currently pending. In this manner, a REQ# from the default bus master is granted immediately (if no other bus masters require the use of the PCI bus).

If the bus arbiter is designed to implement bus parking, it asserts GNT# to a default bus master when none of the REQ# lines are active. In this manner, the bus is immediately available to the default bus master if it should require the use of the bus (and no other higher-priority request is pending). If the master that the bus is parked on subsequently requires access to the PCI bus, it needn't assert its REQ#. Upon sampling bus idle (FRAME# and IRDY# deasserted) and its GNT# asserted, it can immediately initiate a transaction. The choice of which master to park the bus on is defined by the designer of the bus arbiter. Any process may be used, such as the last bus master to use the bus or a predefined default bus master.

There are two possible scenarios regarding the method utilized when implementing bus parking:

1. The arbiter may monitor FRAME# and IRDY# to determine if the bus is busy before parking the bus. Assume that a master requests the bus, receives its GNT# and starts a multiple data phase burst transaction. If it doesn't have another transaction to run after this one completes, it deasserts its REQ# when it asserts FRAME#. In this case, the arbiter may be designed to recognize that the bus is busy and, as a result, will not deassert the current master's grant to park the bus on another master.
2. The arbiter may not monitor for bus idle. Assume that a master requests the bus, receives its GNT# and starts a multiple data phase burst transaction. If it doesn't have another transaction to run after this one completes, it deasserts its REQ# when it asserts FRAME#. In this case, the arbiter may, in the absence of any requests from other masters, take away GNT# from the current master and issue GNT# to the master it intends to park the bus on. When the current master has exhausted its master latency timer and determines that it has lost its grant, it is forced to relinquish the bus, wait two clocks, and then rearbitrate for it again to resume the transaction at the point where it left off.

The specification recommends that the bus be parked on the last master that acquired the bus. In case two, then, the arbiter would continue to issue GNT# to the burst master and it can continue its transaction until either it is completed or until a request is received from another master.

When the arbiter parks the bus on a master (by asserting its grant) and the bus is idle, that master becomes responsible for keeping the AD bus, C/BE bus and PAR from floating (to keep the CMOS input buffers on all devices from oscillating and drawing excessive current). The master must enable its AD[31:0], C/BE#[3:0], and (one clock later) its PAR output drivers. The master doesn't have to turn on all of its output drivers in a single clock (it may take up to eight clocks, but two to three clocks is recommended). This procedure ensures that the bus doesn't float during bus idle periods. If the arbiter is not designed to park the bus, the arbiter itself should drive the AD bus, C/BE# lines and PAR during periods when the bus is idle.

## Request/Grant Timing

When the arbiter determines that it is a master's turn to use the bus, it asserts the master's GNT# line. The arbiter may deassert a master's GNT# on any PCI clock. A master must ensure that its GNT# is asserted on the rising clock edge on which it wishes to start a transaction. If GNT# is deasserted, the transaction must not proceed. Once asserted by the arbiter, GNT# may be deasserted under the following circumstances:

- If GNT# is deasserted and FRAME# is asserted the transfer is valid and will continue. The deassertion of GNT# by the arbiter indicates that the master will no longer own the bus at the completion of the transaction currently in progress. The master keeps FRAME# asserted while the current transaction is still in progress. It deasserts FRAME# when it is ready to complete the final data phase.
- The GNT# to one master can be deasserted simultaneously with the assertion of another master's GNT# **if the bus isn't in the idle state**. The idle state is defined as a clock cycle during which both FRAME# and IRDY# are deasserted. If the bus appears to be idle, the master whose GNT# is being removed may be using stepping to drive the bus (even though it hasn't asserted FRAME# yet; stepping is covered in the chapter entitled "The Read and Write Transfers"). The coincidental deassertion of its GNT# along with the assertion of another master's GNT# could result in contention on the AD bus. The other master could immediately start a transaction (because the bus is technically idle). The problem is prevented by delaying grant to the other master by one cycle. Table 6-1 defines the bus state as indicated by the current state of FRAME# and IRDY#.
- GNT# may be deasserted during the final data phase (FRAME# is deasserted) in response to the current bus master's REQ# being deasserted.

*Table 6-1. Bus State*

| FRAME# | IRDY# | Description |
|--------|-------|-------------|
| deasserted | deasserted | Bus Idle. |
| deasserted | asserted | Initiator is ready to complete the last data transfer of a transaction, but it has not yet completed. |
| asserted | deasserted | A transaction is in progress and the initiator is not ready to complete the current data phase. |
| asserted | asserted | A transaction is in progress and the initiator is ready to complete the current data phase. |

## Example of Arbitration Between Two Masters

Figure 6-3 illustrates bus usage between two masters arbitrating for access to the PCI bus. The following assumptions must be made in order to interpret this example correctly:

- Bus master **A** requires the bus to perform two transactions. The first consists of a three data phase write and the second transaction type is a single data phase write.
- The arbitration scheme is fixed and bus master **B** has a higher priority than bus master **A**, or the scheme is rotational and it is **B's** turn next.
- Bus master **B** only requires the bus to execute a single transaction consisting of one data phase.

It is important to remember that all PCI signals are sampled on the rising-edge of the PCI CLK signal. If the current owner of the bus requires the bus to perform additional transactions upon completion of the current transaction, it should keep its REQ# line asserted after assertion of FRAME# for the current transaction. If no other bus masters are requesting the use of the bus or the current bus master has the highest priority, the bus arbiter will continue to grant the bus to the current bus master at the conclusion of the current transaction.

The sample arbitration sequence pictured in figure 6-3 proceeds as follows:

1. Prior to clock edge one, bus master **A** asserts its REQ# to request access to the PCI bus. The arbiter samples its REQ# active at the rising-edge of clock one. At this point, bus master **B** doesn't yet require the bus. During clock cell one, the arbiter asserts GNT# to bus master **A**, granting it

ownership of the bus. During the same clock period, bus master **B** asserts its REQ#, indicating its desire to execute a transaction.

2. Bus master **A** samples its GNT# asserted on the rising-edge of clock two. In addition, it also samples IRDY# and FRAME# deasserted, indicating that the bus is in the idle state. In response, bus master **A** initiates the first of its two transactions. It asserts FRAME# and begins to drive the start address onto AD[31:0] and the command onto the Command/Byte Enable bus. If master **A** did not have another transaction to perform after this one, it would deassert its REQ# line during clock cell two. In this example, it does have another transaction to perform, so it keeps its REQ# line asserted.

3. The PCI bus arbiter samples the requests from bus masters **A** and **B** asserted at the rising-edge of clock two and begins the arbitration process to determine the next bus master.

4. During clock cell two, the arbiter removes the GNT# from master **A**. On the rising-edge of clock three, master **A** determines that it has been preempted, but continues its transaction because its LT timer has not yet expired (the LT timer is covered later in this chapter).

5. During clock cell three, the arbiter asserts bus master **B's** GNT#. On the rising-edge of clock four, master **B** samples its GNT# asserted, indicating that it may be the next owner of the bus. It must continue to sample its GNT# on each subsequent rising-edge of the clock until it has bus acquisition. This is necessary because the arbiter may remove its grant and grant the bus to another party with a higher priority before the bus goes idle. Master **B** cannot begin to use the bus until the bus returns to the idle state.

6. Master **A** begins to drive the first data item onto the AD bus (this is a write transaction) during clock cell three, asserts the appropriate Command/Byte Enables (to indicate the data lanes to be used for the transfer) and asserts IRDY# to indicate to the target that the data is present on the bus. At the rising-edge of clock four, IRDY# and TRDY# are sampled asserted and the first data transfer takes place.

7. At the rising-edge of clock five, IRDY# and TRDY# are sampled asserted and the second data transfer takes place.

8. During clock cell five, master **A** keeps IRDY# asserted and deasserts FRAME#, indicating that the final data phase is in progress. At the rising-edge of clock six, IRDY# and TRDY# are sampled asserted and the third and final data transfer is completed.

9. During clock cell six, bus master **A** deasserts IRDY#, returning the bus to the idle state.

10. On the rising-edge of clock seven, master **B** samples FRAME# and IRDY# both deasserted and determines that the bus is now idle. It also samples its GNT# still asserted, indicating that it has bus acquisition. In response, it starts its transaction and turns off its REQ# line during clock cell seven (because it only requires the bus to perform this one transaction).

11. When it asserts FRAME# during clock cell seven, master **B** also begins driving the address onto the AD bus and the command onto Command/Byte Enable bus.

12. At the rising-edge of clock eight, the arbiter samples master **B**'s REQ# deasserted and master **A**'s REQ# still asserted. In response, the arbiter deasserts master **B**'s GNT# and asserts master **A**'s GNT# during clock cell eight. Master **A** had kept its REQ# line asserted because it wanted to use the bus for another transaction. Master **A** now samples IRDY# and FRAME# on the rising-edge of each clock until the bus is sensed idle. At that time, it can begin its next transaction.

13. During clock cell eight, master **B** deasserts FRAME#, indicating that its first (and only) data phase is in progress. It also begins to drive the write data onto the AD bus and the appropriate setting onto the Command/Byte Enable bus during clock cell eight. It asserts IRDY# to indicate to the target that the data is present on the AD bus.

14. At the rising-edge of clock nine, IRDY# and TRDY# are sampled asserted and the data transfer takes place.

15. The initiator, master **B**, then deasserts IRDY# (during clock cell nine) to return the bus to the idle state.

16. Master **A** samples the bus idle and its GNT# asserted at the rising-edge of clock ten and initiates its second transaction during clock cell ten. It also deasserts its REQ# when its asserts FRAME#, indicating to the arbiter that it does not require the bus again upon completion of this transaction.

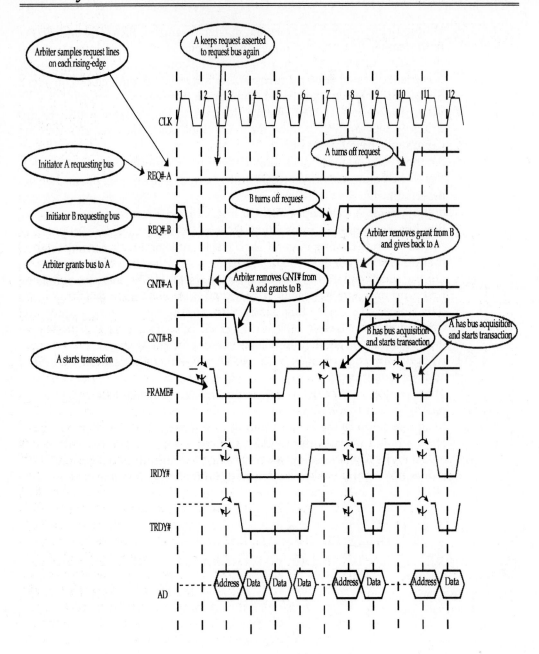

*Figure 6-3. PCI Bus Arbitration Between Two Masters*

# Chapter 6: PCI Bus Arbitration

## Bus Access Latency

When a bus master wishes to transfer a block of data between itself and a target PCI device, it must request the use of the bus from the bus arbiter. Bus access latency is defined as the amount of time that expires from the moment a bus master requests the use of the PCI bus until it completes the first data transfer of the transaction. Figure 6-4 illustrates the different components of the access latency experienced by a PCI bus master. Table 6-2 describes each latency component.

*Table 6-2. Access Latency Components*

| Component | Description |
|---|---|
| Bus Access Latency | Defined as the amount of time that expires from the moment a bus master requests the use of the PCI bus until it completes the first data transfer of the transaction. In other words, it is the sum of arbitration, bus acquisition and target latency. |
| Arbitration Latency | Defined as the period of time from the bus master's assertion of REQ# until the bus arbiter asserts the bus master's GNT#. This period is a function of the arbitration algorithm, the master's priority and whether any other masters are requesting access to the bus. |
| Bus Acquisition Latency | Defined as the period time from the reception of GNT# by the requesting bus master until the current bus master surrenders the bus. The requesting bus master can then initiate its transaction by asserting FRAME#. The duration of this period is a function of how long the current bus master's transaction-in-progress takes to complete. This parameter is the larger of either the current master's LT value (in other words, its timeslice) or the longest latency to first data phase completion in the system (which is limited to a maximum of 16 clocks). |
| Target Latency | Defined as the period of time from the start of a transaction until the currently-addressed target is ready to complete the first data transfer of the transaction. This period is a function of the access time for the currently-addressed target device (and is limited to a maximum of 16 clocks). |

# PCI System Architecture

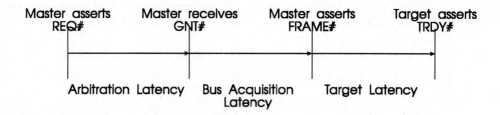

*Figure 6-4. Access Latency Components*

PCI bus masters should always use burst transfers to transfer blocks of data between themselves and a target PCI device (some poorly-designed masters use a series of single-data phase transactions to transfer a block of data). The transfer may consist of anywhere from one to an unlimited number of bytes. A bus master that has requested and has been granted the use of the bus (its GNT# is asserted by the arbiter) cannot begin a transaction until the current bus master completes its transaction-in-progress. If the current master were permitted to own the bus until its entire transfer were completed, it would be possible for the current bus master to lock out other bus masters from using the bus for extended periods of time. The extensive delay incurred could cause other bus masters (and/or the application programs they serve) to experience poor performance or even to malfunction (buffer overflows or starvation may be experienced).

As an example, a bus master could have a buffer full condition and is requesting the use of the bus in order to off-load its buffer contents to system memory. If it experiences an extended delay (latency) in acquiring the bus to begin the transfer, it may experience a data overrun condition as it receives more data from its associated device (such as a network) to be placed into its buffer.

In order to insure that the designers of bus masters are dealing with a predictable and manageable amount of bus latency, the PCI specification defines two mechanisms:

- Master Latency Timer.
- Target-Initiated Termination.

## Master Latency Timer: Prevents Master From Monopolizing Bus

### Location and Purpose of Master Latency Timer

The master latency timer, or LT, is implemented as a PCI configuration register in the bus master's configuration space. It is either initialized by the configuration software at startup time, or contains a hardwired value. The value contained in the LT defines the minimum amount of time (in PCI clock periods) that the bus master is permitted to retain ownership of the bus whenever it acquires bus ownership and initiates a transaction.

### How LT Works

When the bus master detects bus idle (FRAME# and IRDY# deasserted) and its GNT# asserted, it has bus acquisition and may initiate a transaction. Upon initiation of the transaction, the master's LT is initialized to the value written to the LT by the configuration software at startup time (or its hardwired value). Starting on the next rising-edge of the PCI clock and on every subsequent rising-edge, the master decrements its LT by one.

If the master is in the midst of a burst transaction and the arbiter removes its GNT#, this indicates that the arbiter has detected a request from another master and is granting ownership of the bus for the next transaction to the other master. In other words, the current master has been preempted.

If the current master's LT has not yet been exhausted (decremented all the way down), it has not yet used up its timeslice and may retain ownership of the bus until either:

- it completes its burst transaction or
- its LT expires,

whichever comes first. If it is able to complete its burst before expiration of its LT, the other master that has its GNT# may assume bus ownership when it detects that the current master has returned the bus to the idle state. If the current master is not able to complete its burst transfer before expiration of its LT, it is permitted to complete one more data transfer and must then yield the bus.

If the current master has exhausted its LT, still has its GNT# and has not yet completed it burst transfer, it may retain ownership of the bus and continue to burst data until either:

- it completes its overall burst transfer or
- its GNT# is removed by the arbiter.

In the latter case, the current master is permitted to complete one more data transfer and must then yield the bus.

It should be noted that, when forced to prematurely terminate a data transfer, the bus master must "remember" where it was in the transfer. After a brief period, it may then reassert its REQ# to request bus ownership again so that it may continue where it left off. This topic is covered in the chapter entitled "Premature Transaction Termination."

## Is Implementation of LT Register Mandatory?

It must be implemented as a read/writable register by any master that performs more than two data phases per transaction. This implies that the register is optional and may therefore be hardwired to zero. If you do this, be aware that your master has a timeslice of zero! In other words, if you initiate a transaction and the arbiter immediately removes your GNT# (because another master is requesting the bus), your master can perform one (and only one) data phase and must relinquish the bus.

## Can LT Value Be Hardwired (read-only)?

Yes, for a master that performs one or two data phases per transaction, but the hardwired value may not exceed 16. Please refer to the previous sections regarding the implication if you choose to hardwire a value of zero.

## How Does Configuration Software Determine Timeslice To Be Allocated To Master?

The bus master designer implements a read-only register referred to as the minimum grant (Min_Gnt) register. A better name for this register might be the Timeslice Request register. This register is found in the bus master's configuration space. A value of zero indicates that the bus master has no specific requirements regarding the setting assigned to its LT. A non-zero value indicates, in increments of 250ns, how long a timeslice the master requires in order to achieve adequate performance. The value hardwired into this register by the bus master designer assumes a bus speed of 33MHz.

The BIOS determines the timeslice to load into a master's LT register by using the value from the MIN_GNT register in conjunction with the BIOS's knowledge of the PCI bus speed. These factors are used to compute the duration of the requested timeslice (as a number of PCI clock ticks). The timeslice requests from all masters on the bus are evaluated to determine the actual timeslice allocated to each master.

## Treatment of Memory Write and Invalidate Command

Any master performing a memory write and invalidate command (see the chapters entitled "The Commands" and "PCI Cache Support") should not terminate its transfer until it reaches a cache line boundary (even if its LT has expired and it has been preempted) unless STOP# is asserted by the target. If it reaches a cache line boundary with its LT expired and its GNT# has been removed by the arbiter, the initiator *must* terminate the transaction. If a memory write and invalidate command is terminated by the target (STOP# asserted by a non-cacheable memory target), the master should complete the line update in memory using the memory write command as soon as it can. Cacheable memory targets must not disconnect a memory write and invalidate command except at cache line boundaries, even if caching is currently disabled. For this reason, the snooper (i.e., the host/PCI bridge) can always assume that the memory write and invalidate command will complete without disconnection if the access is within a memory range designated as cacheable.

If FRAME# is still asserted (i.e., it's not the last data phase of the transaction) when the master's LT expires (it's timeslice has just expired), *and* the command is a memory write and invalidate, *and* the current data phase is transferring the final doubleword of the current cache line when GNT# is deasserted, the master must terminate the transaction at the end of the next cache line. This is necessary because the master, by keeping FRAME# asserted, committed to transfer at least one more doubleword to the target (and that is the first doubleword of the next line).

## Limit on Master's Latency

Is a rule that the initiator may not keep IRDY# deasserted for more than eight PCI clocks during any data phase. If the initiator has no buffer space available to store read data, it must delay requesting the bus until is has room for the data. On a write transaction, the initiator must have the data available before it asks for the bus.

## Preventing Target From Monopolizing Bus

### General

The problem of a bus master hogging the bus is solved by:

1. The inclusion of the LT associated with each master.
2. The rule that requires the initiator to keep IRDY# deasserted for no longer than eight PCI clocks during any data phase.

It is also possible, however, for a target with a very slow access time to monopolize the bus while a data item is being transferred between itself and the current master. The target does not assert target ready signal, TRDY#, until it is ready to complete the transfer of the data item. This problem is addressed in the PCI specification by requiring slow targets to terminate a transfer prematurely if it will tie up the bus for long periods. There are four possible cases:

1. If the **time to complete** the **first data phase** will be **greater than 16 PCI CLKs** (from the assertion of FRAME#), the target **must** (the revision 2.0 specification used the word "should" rather than "must") immediately issue a **retry** to the master. This rule applies to all new devices. There are only two exceptions: memory reads performed at startup time to copy an expansion ROM image into RAM; and configuration accesses during startup (configuration accesses performed after startup must adhere to the 16 PCI clock limit). A host/PCI bridge that is snooping is permitted to exceed the 16 clock limit, but may never exceed 32 clocks. An example would be a target with an empty buffer that must access a slow device to get the requested data. This forces the master to terminate the transaction with no data transferred, thus freeing up the bus for other masters to use. After two PCI clocks have elapsed, the master that received the retry can reassert its request and, when it receives its GNT#, reinitiate its transaction again. The start address it issues is the address of the data item that was retried.
2. If it will take **more than eight PCI clocks to complete a data phase** other than the first (referred to as the **subsequent latency timeout**) and it is not the final data phase (FRAME# is still asserted), the target issues one of the

following on or before the eighth clock: a **disconnect C; or a target abort**. Use of disconnect C results in the data item not being transferred. The master terminates the transaction and may choose to resume it later at the doubleword that wasn't transferred (if it was prefetching, it may choose not to resume the transaction). In the author's opinion, target abort is less preferred.

3. Alternately, if the **target can transfer the current data item within eight clocks but knows in advance that the next data item will take more than eight clocks**, it must issue a disconnect A or B during the current data phase. The current data item is transferred and the master terminates the transaction, "remembers" the point of disconnection and may resume the transaction later at the next doubleword. After two PCI clocks have elapsed, the master that received the disconnect can reassert its request and, when it receives its GNT#, reinitiate its transaction again at the next data item.

4. If an attempt to communicate with a target results in a **collision on a busy resource** (e.g., a PCI master is attempting a transfer with an EISA target, but the EISA bridge recognizes that an EISA master currently owns the EISA bus), the target should immediately issue a **retry** to the master. This forces the PCI master to terminate the transaction with no data transferred, thus freeing up the PCI bus for other masters to use. After two PCI clocks have elapsed, the master that received the retry must reassert its request and reinitiate its transaction again. The start address it issues is the address of the data item that was retried.

For more information on termination and re-initiation, refer to the chapter entitled "Premature Transaction Termination."

The subsequent latency timeout is completely independent of the master's LT. The target has no visibility to the master's LT (and visa versa) and therefore cannot tell whether it has timed out or not. This means that slow access targets always (before or after LT expiration) disconnect from the master, thereby fragmenting the overall burst transaction into a series of single data phase transactions. Two examples of devices that might perform disconnects are:

- Targets that are very slow all of the time (virtually all ISA bus devices would fall into this category).
- A target that exhibits very slow access sometimes (perhaps because of a buffer full condition or the need for mechanical movement) and would therefore tie up the PCI bus.

## Target Latency on First Data Phase

The following rule was stated earlier: If the time to complete the first data phase will be greater than 16 PCI CLKs, the target must (the revision 2.0 specification used the word "should" rather than "must") immediately issue a retry to the master. This rule applies to all new devices.

A master cannot depend on targets responding to the first data phase within 16 clocks because this rule only affects new devices. Target devices designed prior to the revision 2.1 specification can take longer than 16 clocks to respond.

## Options for Achieving Maximum 16 Clock Latency

The target can use any of the following three methods to meet the 16 clock requirement:

1.  The simplest case is one where the target can always respond within 16 clocks. No special action is necessary.
2.  In the second case, a target may occasionally not be able to meet the 16 clock limit due to a busy resource (e.g., a video frame buffer is being refreshed). In this case, the target simply issues a retry to the master. More than likely, the busy condition will have been cleared by the time the master retries the transaction. It is possible, however, that the master may have to make several attempts before succeeding. A target is only permitted to use this option if there is a high probability that it will be able to complete the transfer the first time that the master retries it. Otherwise, it must use option three.
3.  In the third case (option three), the target has to access a slow medium to fetch the requested data and it will take longer than 16 clocks. In this case, the target latches the address, command and the first set of byte enables (and the data, if a write) and then issues a retry to the initiator. The initiator is thereby forced to end the transaction with no data transferred and is required to retry the transaction again later using precisely the same address, command and byte enables (and data, if a write). The target, meanwhile, proceeds to fetch the requested data and set it up in a buffer for the master to read later when it retries the transaction. When the target sees the master retry the transaction, it attempts to match the second request with the initial request by comparing the start address, command and initial byte enables (and the data, if a write) to those latched earlier. If they match, the requested data is transferred to the

master. If they aren't an exact match, the target interprets this as a new request (for data other than that in its buffer) and issues a retry to the master again. To summarize, if the master doesn't duplicate the transaction exactly each time it retries the transaction, it will never have its read request fulfilled. The target is not required to service retries from its buffered data that aren't exact matches. Option three is referred to as a delayed transaction. It can also be used for a write transaction (e.g., where the bus master is not permitted to proceed with other activities until it accomplishes the write). In this case, the target latches the address, command, byte enables and the first data item and issues the retry. It then proceeds to write the data item to the slow destination. Each time that the master retries the write transaction it will receive a retry until the target device has acknowledge receipt of the data. When the target is ready to permit the transfer and the master next attempts the access, the target compares the address, command, byte enables and the write data to determine if this is the same master that initially requested the write transfer.

## Different Master Attempts Access To Device With Previously-Latched Request

If a different master attempts to access the target and the target can only deal with one latched request at a time, it must issue a retry to the master without latching its transaction information.

## Special Cycle Monitoring While Processing Request

If the target is designed to monitor for special cycles, it must be able to process a special cycle during the same period of time that is processing a previously latched read or write request.

## Delayed Request and Delayed Completion

A delayed transaction consists of two parts: the request phase and the completion phase. The request phase occurs when the target latches the request and issues retry to the master. This is referred to as the delayed request transaction. Once the transaction has been latched, the target (typically, but not necessarily, a bridge to a slow expansion bus) begins the transaction on the target bus. When the transfer completes on the target bus, this is referred to as the delayed completion. This is the start of the completion phase. A delayed transaction must complete on the target bus before it is permitted to complete on the initiating bus. The master is required to periodically re-attempt the transfer until the target finally asserts TRDY# and allows the data to be transferred. This ends the completion phase of the delayed transaction.

## Discard of Delayed Requests

A device that has "memorized" a delayed request and issued a retry to the initiator is permitted to discard the request any time prior to its initiation of the request on the destination bus. This is permitted because the master will retry the transaction again, thereby giving the device the opportunity to "re-memorize" the transaction.

## Multiple Delayed Requests from Same Master

A master may be designed to stall on the repeating of a retried transaction until it completes successfully (before proceeding on to another transaction). Alternately, the master may be designed to present additional requests, each of which may receive retries. The master must continue to retry all of these transactions until they each complete. The specification contains the following statement:

> The repeating of the requests is not required to be equal, but is required to be fair.

The author is not sure if this is a fragment of the Equal Opportunities Act or is actually part of the specification (in other words, I don't know how to interpret it).

## Discard of Delayed Completions

Once a delayed request has been completed on the destination bus, it may be discarded under two cirumstances:

- it is a read within a memory region that the bridge knows is prefetchable, or the command was a memory read line or memory read multiple (both of which imply that the originating master "knows" that the memory region is prefetchable).
- the originating master has not retried the transaction within $2^{15}$ clocks. When this timer (referred to as the discard timer) expires, the device is required to discard the data.

When the delayed completion is discarded along with read data, the device may take one of two actions:

- When the data was read from a prefetchable region, the specification recommends that the error be ignored (because the data is still correct in the memory location from which it orginated).
- When the data was read from a non-prefetchable memory region (e.g., memory-mapped I/O), it is recommended that the error be reported to the device driver.

## Handling Multiple Data Phases

When the master is successful in completing the first data phase, it may proceed with more data phases. The target may issue a disconnect on any data phase after the first. In this case, the master is not required to resume the transaction later. Both the master and the target consider the original request fulfilled.

## Master or Target Abort Handling

A delayed transaction is also considered completed if it receives a master abort or a target abort rather than a retry on a re-attempt of the retried transaction. The target compares to ensure that the master is the one that originated the request before it issues the master or target abort to it. This means that the transaction on the target bus ended in a master abort because no target responded or in a target abort because of a broken target. In both of these cases, the master is not required to repeat the transaction.

## Deadlock Condition

Assume that a system has two PCI buses connected by a PCI-to-PCI bridge. Two masters (referred to as bus master A and bus master B) reside on bus zero and a target is on bus one. The target is designed to revision 2.1 and implements delayed transaction capability, but can only handle one request at a time. If it should detect another transaction before it has completed the delayed request it is currently processing, it issues retry to the initiating master. The bridge doesn't implement delayed transaction capability. Now assume that the following sequence of events takes place:

1. Bus master A initiates a memory read from the target.
2. The bridge claims the transaction and propagates it to bus one.

3. The target memorizes the transaction and issues a retry to the bridge. The
4. The bridge passes the retry back to bus master A.
5. Bus master B initiates a memory write to the same memory target.
6. The bridge posts the write and bus master B completes its write.
7. Bus master A retries its read.
8. The bridge is required to flush its posted-write buffer before it can retry the read on bus one. When the bridge initiates the memory write, the target issues a retry to it (because it cannot handle another transaction until the delayed read request has been completed).
9. A deadlock now exists. The bridge cannot retry the read until it is successful in completing its posted writes and the target will not accept the writes.

The solution is that the *2.1 target is required to accept a write during the period before it has completed the previously-latched delayed request.*

## Commands That Can Use Delayed Transactions

All transactions that must complete on the destination bus before they can complete on the originating bus may be handled as delayed transactions. This would include:

- Interrupt Acknowledge.
- I/O read.
- I/O write.
- Memory read.
- Memory read line.
- Memory read multiple.
- Configuration read.
- Configuration write.

The memory write and the memory write and invalidate commands can be completed on the originating bus before they complete on the destination bus if they are in a prefetchable memory region and are posted in the bridge.

## What Is Prefetchable Memory?

Memory is defined as prefetchable if it exhibits the following characteristics:

- no side effects on reads (contents of memory not altered).
- returns all bytes on reads irrespective of the byte enable settings.

- bridges can merge writes within this area without causing errors.

In a nutshell, regular memory is prefetchable while memory-mapped I/O (or any other badly-behaved memory region) is not.

## Delayed Read Prefetch

A delayed read can result in the reading of more data than indicated in the master's initial data phase if the target knows that prefetching data doesn't alter the contents of memory locations (as it would in memory-mapped I/O ports). The target can prefetch more data than initially requested under the following circumstances:

- The master has used the memory read line or memory read multiple command, thereby indicating that it knows the target is prefetchable memory.
- The master used a memory read command, but the bridge that accepted the delayed transaction request recognizes that the address falls within a range defined as prefetchable.

In all other cases, the target (i.e., the bridge) cannot perform anything other than the single data phase indicated by the originating master.

## Request Queuing and Ordering Rules

A target device (typically a bridge) can be designed to latch and process multiple delayed requests. The device must, however, ensure that the transactions are performed in the proper order. Table 6-3 defines the rules that the device must observe in order to ensure that posted memory writes and delayed transactions are performed in the proper order. The table was extracted from the specification. The following abbreviations are used in the table:

- **PMW = posted memory write**. The master is permitted to end a memory write immediately if the device posts it (i.e., it memorizes the address, command, byte enables and the write data).
- **DRR = delayed read request**. A delayed read request occurs when the target latches the address, command and byte enables and issues a retry to the master. It is then the responsibility of the target to perform the read on the target bus to fetch the requested data.

- **DWR = delayed write request**. A delayed write request occurs when the target latches the address, command, byte enables and write data and issues a retry to the master. It is then the responsibility of the target to perform the write on the target bus.
- **DRC = delayed read completion**. A delayed read completion occurs when the device that latched a read request completes reading the requested data on the target bus and has the data ready to deliver to the master that originated the request. The device is now waiting for the originating master to retry its read so that it may deliver the data to the master.
- **DWC = delayed write completion**. A delayed write completion occurs when the device that latched a write request completes writing the data on the target bus for the master that originated the write. The device is now waiting for the originating master to retry its write so that it may confirm the delivery of the write data.

The table is formatted as follows:

- The first column represents a posted write or a delayed transaction request or completion that has just been latched.
- The second column indicates whether the transaction just latched can pass through the bridge before a previously-posted memory write is performed.
- The third column indicates whether the transaction just latched can pass through the bridge before a previously-latched delayed read request is performed.
- The fourth column indicates whether the transaction just latched can pass through the bridge before a previously-latched delayed write request is performed.
- The fifth column indicates whether the transaction just latched can pass through the bridge before a previously-latched delayed read completion is delivered to the master that initiated the read.
- The sixth column indicates whether the transaction just latched can pass through the bridge before a previously-latched delayed write completion is delivered to the master that initiated the write.

As an example, the table indicates that a delayed read request cannot be performed on the destination bus before previously-posted memory writes are performed on that bus. If it did and one (or more) of the writes were to the same area of memory, the read could fetch stale data.

*Table 6-3. Ordering Rules*

| Transaction just latched | PMW | Delayed Request | | Delayed Completion | |
|---|---|---|---|---|---|
| | | DRR | DWR | DRC | DWC |
| PMW | No | Yes | Yes | Yes | Yes |
| DRR | No | Yes/No | Yes/No | Yes/No | Yes/No |
| DWR | No | Yes/No | Yes/No | Yes/No | Yes/No |
| DRC | No | Yes/No | Yes/No | Yes/No | Yes/No |
| DWC | Yes/No | Yes/No | Yes/No | Yes/No | Yes/No |

The primary rule is that all device accesses must complete in order from the programmer's perspective. The specification contains a detailed explanation of the ordering rules in section 3.3.3.3.6 and in Appendix E.

### Locking, Delayed Transactions and Posted Writes

A locked transaction can be completed using a delayed transaction. All of the locking rules apply (see the chapter entitled "Shared Resource Acquisition"), except that the target must lock itslef when it accepts the request (even though it hasn't completed the semaphore read from memory yet). The target must not accept any additional delayed requests while it is locked. In essence, it must mimic the target that lives behind it. It must only accept requests from the locking master. LOCK# must be latched and used in the compare to determine if it's the locking master.

## Fast Back-to-Back Transactions

Assertion of its grant by the PCI bus arbiter gives a PCI bus master access to the bus for a single transaction. If a bus master desires another access, it should continue to assert its REQ# after it has asserted FRAME# for the first transaction. If the arbiter continues to assert its GNT# at the end of the first transaction, the master may then immediately initiate a second transaction. However, a bus master attempting to perform two, back-to-back transactions usually must insert an idle cycle between the two transactions. This is illustrated in figure 6-5. When it doesn't have to insert the idle cycle between the two bus transactions, this is referred to as fast back-to-back transactions. This can only occur if there is a guarantee that there will not be contention (on any signal lines) between the masters and/or targets involved in the two transactions. There are two scenarios where this is the case.

1.  In the first case, the master guarantees that there will be no contention.
2.  In the second case, the master and the community of PCI targets collectively provide the guarantee.

The sections that follow describe these two scenarios.

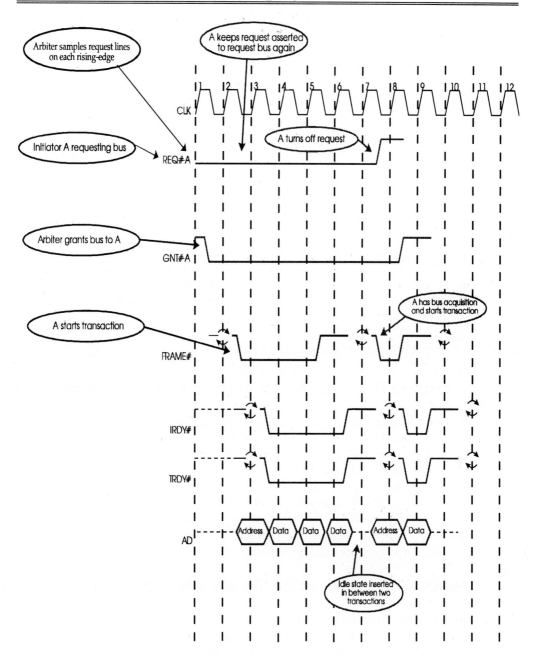

*Figure 6-5. Back-to-Back Transactions With an Idle State In-Between*

## Decision to Implement Fast Back-to-Back Capability

The subsequent two sections describe the rules that permit deletion of the idle state between two transactions. Since they represent a fairly constraining set of rules, the designer of a bus master should make an informed decision as to whether or not it's worth the additional logic it would take to implement it.

Assume that the nature of a particular bus master is such that it typically performs long burst transfers whenever it acquires bus ownership. In this case, including the extra logic to support fast back-to-back transactions would not make a great deal of sense. Percentage-wise, you're only saving one clock tick of latency in between each pair of long transfers.

Assume that the nature of another master is such that it typically performs lots of small data bursts. In this case, inclusion of the extra logic may result in a measurable increase in performance. Since each of the small transactions typically only consists of a few clock ticks and the master performs lots of these small transactions in rapid succession, the savings of one clock tick in between each transaction pair can amount to the removal of a fair percentage of overhead normally spent in bus idle time.

## Scenario One: Master Guarantees Lack of Contention

In this scenario (defined in revision 1.0 of the specification and still true in revision 2.x), the master must ensure that, when it performs two back-to-back transactions with no idle state in between the two, there is no contention on any of the signals driven by the bus master or on those driven by the target. An idle cycle is required whenever AD[31:0], C/BE#[3:0], FRAME#, PAR and IRDY# are driven by different masters from one clock cycle to the next. The idle cycle allows one cycle for the master currently driving these signals to surrender control (cease driving) before the next bus master begins to drive the bus. This prevents bus contention.

### How Collision Avoided On Signals Driven By Master

The master must ensure that the same set of output drivers are driving the master-related signals at the end of the first transaction and the start of the second. This means that the master must ensure that it is driving the bus at the end of the first transaction and at the start of the second.

To meet this criteria, the first transaction must be a write transaction and the second transaction can be either a read or a write but must be initiated by the same master. Refer to figure 6-6. When the master acquires bus ownership and starts the first transaction (clock edge one), it asserts FRAME# and continues to assert its REQ# line to request the bus again after the completion of the current transaction. When the address phase is completed (clock edge two), the master drives the first set of data bytes onto the AD bus and sets the byte enables to indicate which data paths contain valid data bytes. At the conclusion of the first (clock edge three) and any subsequent data phases, the bus master is driving the AD bus and the byte enables. Furthermore, the bus master is asserting IRDY# during the final data phase. On the rising-edge of the PCI clock where the final data item is transferred (clock edge three), FRAME# has already been deasserted and IRDY# asserted (along with TRDY# and DEVSEL#). If, on this same clock edge (clock edge three) the master samples its GNT# still asserted by the arbiter, this indicates that it has retained bus ownership for the next transaction.

In the clock cell immediately following this clock edge (clock edge three), the master can immediately reassert FRAME# and drive a new start address and command onto the bus. There isn't a collision on the FRAME# signal because the same output driver that was driving FRAME# deasserted at the end of the first transaction begins to assert FRAME# at the start of the second transaction. There isn't a collision on the AD bus or the C/BE bus because the same master's drivers that were driving the final data item and byte enables at the end of the first transaction are driving the start address and command at the start of the second transaction.

At the end of the address phase of the second transaction (clock edge four), the same master that was deasserting IRDY# at the end of the first transaction begins to reassert it (so there is no collision between two different IRDY# drivers).

## How Collision Avoided On Signals Driven By Target

The signals asserted by the target of the first transaction at the completion of the final data phase (clock edge three) are TRDY# and DEVSEL# (and, possibly, STOP#). Two clocks after the end of the data phase, the target may also drive PERR#. Since it is a rule in this scenario that the same target must be addressed in the second transaction, the same target again drives these signals. Even if the target has a fast address decoder and begins to assert DEVSEL# (and TRDY# if it is a write) during clock cell four in the second transaction, the fact that it is the same target ensures that there is not a collision on TRDY# and DEVSEL# (and possibly STOP# and PERR#) between output drivers associated with two different targets.

## How Targets Recognize New Transaction Has Begun

It is a rule that all PCI targets must recognize either of the following conditions as the start of a new transaction:

- Bus idle (FRAME# and IRDY# deasserted) on a rising-edge of the PCI clock followed on the next rising-edge by address phase in progress (FRAME# asserted and IRDY# deasserted).
- Final data phase in progress (FRAME# deasserted and IRDY# asserted) on a rising-edge of the PCI clock, followed on the next rising-edge by address phase in progress (FRAME# asserted and IRDY# deasserted).

Implementation of support for this type of fast back-to-back capability is optional for an initiator, but all targets must be able to decode them.

## Fast Back-to-Back and Master Abort

When a master experiences a master abort on a transaction during a fast back-to-back series, it may continue performing fast transactions (as long as it still has its GNT#). No target responded to the aborted transaction, thereby ensuring that there will not be a collision on the target-related signals. If the transaction that ended with a master abort was a special cycle, the target(s) that received the message were already given sufficient time (by the master) to process the message and should be prepared to recognize another transaction.

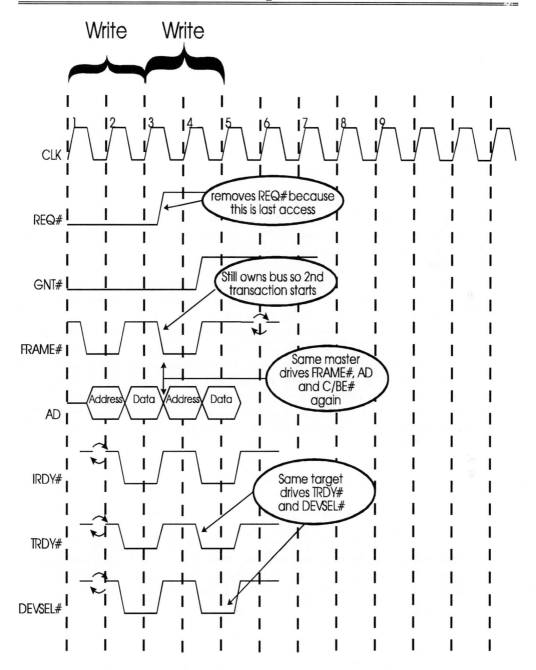

*Figure 6-6. Arbitration For Fast Back-To-Back Accesses*

## Scenario Two: Targets Guarantee Lack of Contention

In the second scenario (defined in revision 2.0 of the specification and still true in revision 2.1), the entire community of PCI targets that reside on the PCI bus and the bus master collectively guarantee lack of contention during fast back-to-back transactions. A constraint incurred when using the master-guaranteed method (defined in revision 1.0 of the specification) is that the master can only perform fast back-to-back transactions if both transactions access the same target and the first transaction is a write.

The reason that scenario one states that the target of the first and second transactions must be the same target is to prevent the possibility of a collision on the target-related signals: TRDY#, DEVSEL# and STOP# (and, possibly, PERR#). This possibility can be avoided if:

1. All targets have medium or slow address decoders and
2. All targets are capable of discerning that a new transaction has begun without a transition through the bus idle state and are capable of latching the address and command associated with the second transaction.

If the full suite of targets on a PCI bus meet these requirements, then any bus master that is fast back-to-back capable can perform fast back-to-back transactions with different targets in the first and second transactions. The first transaction must still be a write, however, and the second transaction must be performed by the same master (to prevent collisions on master-related signals).

The previous statement implies that there is a method to determine if all targets support this feature. During system configuration (at power-up), software polls each device's configuration status register and checks the state of its FAST BACK-TO-BACK CAPABLE bit. The designer of a device hardwires this read-only bit to zero if the device doesn't support this feature, while hardwiring it to a one indicates that it does. If all devices indicate support for this capability, then the configuration software can set each bus master's FAST BACK-TO-BACK ENABLE bit in its configuration command register (this bit, and therefore this capability is optional for a bus master). When this bit is set, a master is enabled to perform fast back-to-back transactions with different targets in the first and second transactions.

A target supports this capability if it meets the following criteria:

- Normally a target recognizes a bus idle condition by sampling FRAME# and IRDY# deasserted. It then expects and recognizes the start of the next transaction by sampling FRAME# asserted and IRDY# deasserted. At that point, it latches the address and command and begins address decode. To support the feature under discussion, it must recognize the completion of the final data phase of one transaction by sampling FRAME# deasserted and IRDY# and TRDY# asserted. This would then be immediately followed by the start of the next transaction, as indicated by sampling FRAME# asserted and IRDY# deasserted on the next rising-edge of the PCI clock.

- The target must ensure that there isn't contention on TRDY#, DEVSEL# and STOP# (and, possibly, PERR#). If the target has a medium or slow address decoder, this provides the guarantee. If the target has a fast address decoder, it must delay assertion of these three signals by one clock to prevent contention. Note that this does not affect the DEVSEL# timing field in the device's configuration status register. The setting in this field is used by the bus's subtractive decoder to adjust when it asserts DEVSEL# to claim transactions unclaimed by PCI devices. During the second transaction of a fast back-to-back transaction pair, the subtractive decoder must delay its assertion of DEVSEL# if it normally claims during the medium or slow time slot (otherwise, a collision may occur on DEVSEL#, TRDY#, and STOP# (and, possibly, PERR#).

- There are two circumstances when a target with a fast address decoder doesn't have to insert this one clock delay:

1. The current transaction was preceded by a bus idle state (FRAME# and IRDY# deasserted).
2. The currently-addressed target was also addressed in the previous transaction. This ensures a lack of contention on TRDY#, STOP# and DEVSEL# (because it was driving these signals during the previous transaction).

## State of REQ# and GNT# During RST#

While RST# is asserted, all masters must tri-state their REQ# output drivers and must ignore their GNT# inputs.

## Pullups On REQ# From Add-In Connectors

In a system with PCI add-in connectors, the arbiter may require a weak pullup on the REQ# inputs that are wired to the add-in connectors. This will keep them from floating when the connectors are unoccupied.

## Broken Master

The arbiter may assume that a master is broken if the arbiter has issued GNT# to the master, the bus has been idle for 16 clocks, and the master has not asserted FRAME# to start its transaction. The arbiter is permitted to ignore all further requests from the broken master and may optionally report the failure to the operating system (in a device-specific fashion).

# Chapter 7

## The Previous Chapter

The previous chapter provided a description of PCI bus arbitration.

## In This Chapter

This chapter defines the types of commands, or transaction types, that a bus master may initiate when it has acquired ownership of the PCI bus.

## The Next Chapter

The next chapter provides a detailed analysis of the PCI transfer, utilizing timing diagrams and a description of each step involved in the transfer.

## Introduction

When a bus master acquires ownership of the PCI bus, it may initiate one of the types of transactions listed in table 7-1. During the address phase of a transaction, the Command/Byte Enable bus, C/BE#[3:0], is used to indicate the command, or transaction, type. Table 7-1 provides the setting that the initiator places on the Command/Byte Enable lines during the address phase of the transaction to indicate the type of transaction in progress. The following sections provide a description of each of the command types.

Table 7-1. PCI Command Types

| C/BE3# | C/BE2# | C/BE1# | C/BE0# | Command Type |
|--------|--------|--------|--------|--------------|
| 0 | 0 | 0 | 0 | Interrupt Acknowledge |
| 0 | 0 | 0 | 1 | Special Cycle |
| 0 | 0 | 1 | 0 | I/O Read |
| 0 | 0 | 1 | 1 | I/O Write |
| 0 | 1 | 0 | 0 | Reserved |
| 0 | 1 | 0 | 1 | Reserved |
| 0 | 1 | 1 | 0 | Memory Read |
| 0 | 1 | 1 | 1 | Memory Write |
| 1 | 0 | 0 | 0 | Reserved |
| 1 | 0 | 0 | 1 | Reserved |
| 1 | 0 | 1 | 0 | Configuration Read |
| 1 | 0 | 1 | 1 | Configuration Write |
| 1 | 1 | 0 | 0 | Memory Read Multiple |
| 1 | 1 | 0 | 1 | Dual-Address Cycle |
| 1 | 1 | 1 | 0 | Memory Read Line |
| 1 | 1 | 1 | 1 | Memory Write and Invalidate |

## Interrupt Acknowledge Command

### Introduction

In response to an interrupt request, an Intel x86 processor issues two interrupt acknowledge transactions to read the interrupt vector from the interrupt controller. The interrupt vector tells the processor which interrupt service routine to execute.

### Background

In an Intel x86-based system, the host processor is usually the device that services interrupt requests received from subsystems that require servicing. In a PC-compatible system, the subsystem requiring service issues a request by asserting one of the system interrupt request signals, IRQ0 through IRQ15. When the IRQ is detected by the interrupt controller, it asserts INTR to the host processor. Assuming that the host processor is enabled to recognize interrupt requests (the interrupt flag bit in the EFLAGS register is set to one), the processor responds by requesting the interrupt vector from the interrupt controller. This is accomplished by the processor stepping through the following sequence:

1. **Processor generates an interrupt acknowledge bus cycle.** No address is output by the processor because the address of the target device, the interrupt controller, is implicit in the bus cycle type. The purpose of this bus cycle is to **command the interrupt controller to prioritize** its **currently-pending requests** and select the request to be processed. The processor doesn't expect any data to be returned by the interrupt controller during this bus cycle.

2. **Processor generates a second interrupt acknowledge bus cycle to request the interrupt vector** from the interrupt controller. BE0# is asserted by the processor, indicating that an 8-bit vector is expected to be returned on the lower data path, D[7:0]. To state this more plainly, the processor requests that the interrupt controller return the index into the interrupt table in memory. This tells the processor which table entry to read. The table entry contains the start address of the device-specific interrupt service routine in memory. In response to the second interrupt acknowledge bus cycle, the interrupt controller must drive the interrupt table index, or vector, associated with the highest-priority request currently pending back to the processor over the lower data path, D[7:0], and assert BRDY# to the processor to indicate the presence of the vector. In response, the processor reads the vector from the bus and uses it to determine the start address of the interrupt service routine that it must execute.

## Host/PCI Bridge Handling of Interrupt Acknowledge Sequence

When the host/PCI bridge detects the start of an interrupt acknowledge sequence on the host side, it can handle it one of two ways:

1. It filters out (does not pass to the PCI bus) the first interrupt acknowledge bus cycle. BRDY# is asserted to the processor to terminate the first interrupt acknowledge bus cycle. When the processor initiates the second interrupt acknowledge bus cycle, the bridge acquires the PCI bus and initiates a PCI interrupt acknowledge transaction. This transaction is illustrated in figure 7-1 and is described in the next section. When the PCI target that contains the interrupt controller detects the interrupt acknowledge transaction, it asserts DEVSEL# to claim the transaction. It then internally generates two, back-to-back interrupt acknowledge pulses to the

8259A interrupt controller, thereby emulating the double interrupt acknowledge generated by an Intel x86 processor. In response, the interrupt controller drives the interrupt vector onto the lower data path and asserts TRDY# to indicate the presence of the vector to the initiator (the host/PCI bridge). When the host/PCI bridge samples TRDY# and IRDY# asserted, it reads the vector from the lower data path and terminates the PCI interrupt acknowledge transaction. During this period, the bridge was inserting wait states into the host processor's second interrupt acknowledge bus cycle. It then drives the 8-bit interrupt vector onto the processor's lower data path and asserts BRDY# to the processor. When the processor samples BRDY# asserted, it reads the vector from the bus and uses it to index into the memory-based interrupt table to get the start address of the interrupt service routine to execute.

2.  Instead of filtering out the first of the processor's interrupt acknowledge bus cycles, the bridge could pass it onto the PCI bus. Rather than waiting for the completion of the PCI transaction, however, the bridge would immediately assert BRDY# to the processor, permitting it to end the first interrupt acknowledge bus cycle and begin the second. This would permit the interrupt controller to claim the transaction earlier and therefore return the vector sooner. When the interrupt controller returns the vector, it is passed directly back to the processor and BRDY# is asserted, permitting the processor to read the vector and terminate the second bus cycle.

## PCI Interrupt Acknowledge Transaction

Figure 7-1 illustrates the PCI interrupt acknowledge transaction. The bridge does not drive an address onto the AD bus during the address phase, but must drive stable data onto the AD bus along with correct parity on the PAR line. The C/BE bus contains the interrupt acknowledge command during the address phase. During the data phase, the target holds off the assertion of TRDY# and DEVSEL# to enforce the turnaround cycle. This is necessary to permit the bridge sufficient time to turn off its AD bus output drivers before the target (the interrupt controller) begins to drive the requested interrupt vector back to the bridge on the AD bus. The target then drives the vector onto the data path(s) indicated by the byte enable settings on the C/BE bus (just BE0# asserted in an ix86 environment) and asserts TRDY# to indicate the presence of the requested vector. The byte enables are a duplicate of the byte enables asserted by the host processor during its second interrupt acknowledge bus cycle. When the bridge samples IRDY# and TRDY# asserted, it reads the vector from the AD bus and terminates the PCI interrupt acknowledge transaction. It then passes the vector back to the host processor and asserts

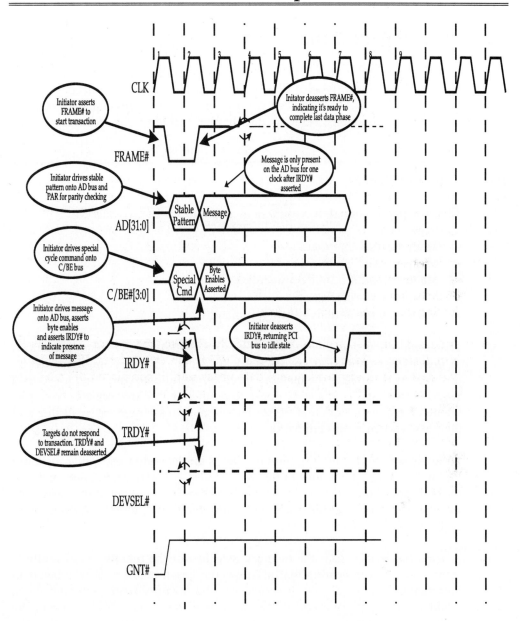

*Figure 7-2. The Special Cycle Transaction*

## I/O Read and Write Commands

The I/O read and write commands are used to transfer data between the initiator and the currently-addressed I/O target. The target must decode the entire 32-bit address. For a detailed description of I/O addressing and I/O read and write transactions, refer to the chapter entitled "The Read and Write Transfers."

## Accessing Memory

The PCI specification defines five commands utilized to access memory:

- Memory read command.
- Memory read line command.
- Memory read multiple command.
- Memory write command.
- Memory write and invalidate command.

The specification says that the cache line size configuration register (described in the chapter entitled "Configuration Registers") must be implemented by bus masters that utilize the memory write and invalidate command (described later in this chapter). It also strongly recommends that this register be implemented for bus masters that utilize the memory read, memory read line and memory read multiple commands.

If the cache line size configuration register is implemented, the initiator should follow the usage guidelines outlined in table 7-3 when performing memory reads. If an initiator accesses memory and does not implement the cache line size configuration register, it should follow the same guidelines, assuming a cache line size of 16 or 32 bytes.

When a bus master uses the memory read line or the memory read multiple commands, it is indicating that it knows the target memory is well-behaved (not memory-mapped I/O). It should use the memory read command when reading from memory-mapped I/O. If the read traverses a bridge, use of the bulk read commands gives the bridge permission to prefetch data within the addresses area. This would permit the bridge to establish a buffered link through the bridge between the initiator and the target, with the bridge loading the prefetch buffer from the memory on the destination bus and the initiator reading the data from the other end of the buffer on the initiating bus. This would result in a dramatic improvement in performance.

The specification strongly recommends that the bulk read/write commands be used when transferring large blocks of data to or from memory. These commands are memory write and invalidate, memory read line and memory read multiple.

*Table 7-3. Preferred Use of Read Commands*

| Read Command Type | To Be Used When |
|---|---|
| Memory Read | Reading data from non-prefetchable memory (e.g., memory-mapped I/O) or reading a single doubleword. |
| Memory Read Line | Reading more than one doubleword but no more than a cache line in prefetchable memory space. |
| Memory Read Multiple | Read crosses a cache line boundary in a prefetchable memory range. |

# Writing Memory

The initiator may use the memory write or the memory write and invalidate command to update data in memory.

## Memory Write Command

This command is used to transfer one or more data objects to memory. When the target asserts TRDY#, it has assumed responsibility for maintaining the coherency of the data. This can be done by ensuring that any software-transparent posting buffer is flushed prior to synchronization events such as interrupts, or the updating of an I/O status register or memory flag being passed through the device that contains the posted-write buffer (i.e., a bridge).

## Memory Write and Invalidate Command

### Problem

Assume that a PCI master is performing a memory write and the processor's write back cache(s) is snooping the transaction. It experiences a snoop hit on a modified line. This means that the initiator is about to update a stale line in memory. Assuming that the cache is not capable of data snarfing (latching the data from the AD bus) to keep the cache line updated, it could invalidate the cache line. This, however, would be a mistake. The fact that the line is marked modified indicates that some or all of the information in the line is more current than the corresponding line in memory. The memory write being performed by the current initiator is updating some subset of the memory line. Trashing the line from the cache would quite probably trash some data that is more current than that in the memory line.

If the cache permits the initiator to complete the memory write and then flushes the cache line to memory, the data just written by the initiator is over-written by the stale data in the cache line. The correct action would be to force the initiator that is attempting the write to get off the bus (abort the transaction). The cache then acquires the bus and performs a memory write to transfer, or flush, the modified cache line to memory. In the cache directory, the cache line is then invalidated because the initiator will subsequently update a subset of the memory line immediately after the cache line is flushed to memory. The cache then removes the back off, permitting the initiator to reinitiate the memory write. The memory line now contains the most current data. The cache snoops this transaction as well, but it now results in a cache miss (because the cache line was invalidated after it was deposited in memory). The cache does not interfere in the memory write this time.

### Description of Memory Write and Invalidate Command

The memory write and invalidate command is identical to the memory write command except that it guarantees the transfer of a complete cache line (or multiple cache lines) during the current transaction. This implies that the cache line size configuration register must be implemented in the initiator so that it can make the termination that an entire cache line will be written.

If, when snooping, the write-back cache detects a memory write and invalidate initiated and experiences a snoop hit on a modified line, the cache can just invalidate the line and doesn't need to back off the initiator in order to perform the flush to memory. This is possible because the initiator has indicated that it is updating the entire memory line and all of the data in the modified cache line is therefore stale and can be invalidated. This increases performance by eliminating the requirement for the back off and line flush.

It is a requirement that the initiator must assert all of the byte enable signals during each data phase of the memory write and invalidate transaction. It is also required that linear addressing be used. For information on the byte enables and on linear addressing, refer to the chapter entitled "The Read and Write Transfer."

## More Information On Memory Transfers

For a detailed description of read and write transactions, refer to the chapter entitled "The Read and Write Transfers."

## Configuration Read and Write Commands

Each PCI device may implement up to 64 doublewords of configuration registers that are used during system initialization to configure the PCI device for proper operation in the system. To access a PCI agent's configuration registers, a configuration read or write command must be initiated and the agent must sense its IDSEL input asserted during the address phase. IDSEL acts as a chip-select, AD[10:8] select the function (i.e., the logical device) within the package and the contents of AD[7:2] (during the address phase) are used to select one of the target logical device's 64 doublewords of configuration space.

The x86 processor family implements two address spaces: memory and I/O. PCI requires the implementation of a third address space: configuration space. The mechanism used to generate configuration transactions is described in the chapter entitled "Configuration Transactions."

## Dual-Address Cycle

The initiator uses the dual-address cycle command to indicate that it is using 64-bit addressing. This subject is covered in the chapter entitled "The 64-Bit PCI Extension."

## Reserved Bus Commands

Targets must not respond (assert DEVSEL#) to reserved bus commands. This means that use of a reserved bus command will result in the initiator experiencing a master abort.

# Chapter 8

## The Previous Chapter

The previous chapter introduced the types of commands, or transactions, that an initiator may perform once it has acquired ownership of the PCI bus.

## In This Chapter

This chapter provides a detailed description of the basic PCI data transfer, using timing diagrams to illustrate the exact sequence and timing of events during the transfer.

## The Next Chapter

The next chapter describes the circumstances under which the initiator or target may need to abort a transaction and the mechanisms provided to accomplish the abort.

## Some Basic Rules

The ready signal from the device sourcing the data must be asserted when it is driving valid data onto the data bus. The PCI agent receiving the data can keep its ready line deasserted until it is ready to receive the data. Once a device's ready signal is asserted, it must remain so until the end of the current data phase.

An agent may not alter its control line settings once it has indicated that it is ready to complete the current data phase. Once the initiator has asserted IRDY#, it may not change the state of IRDY# or FRAME# regardless of the state of TRDY#. Once a target has asserted TRDY# or STOP#, it may not change TRDY#, STOP# or DEVSEL# until the current data phase completes.

# PCI System Architecture

## Parity

Parity generation, checking, error reporting and timing is not discussed in this chapter. This subject is covered in detail in the chapter entitled "Error Detection and Handling."

## Read Transaction

### Description

During the following description of the read transaction, refer to figure 8-1.

Each clock cycle is numbered for easy reference and begins and ends on the rising-edge. It is assumed that the bus master has already arbitrated for and been granted access to the bus. The bus master then must wait for the bus to become idle. This is accomplished by sampling the state of FRAME# and IRDY# on the rising-edge of each clock (along with GNT#). When both are sampled deasserted (clock edge one), the bus is idle and a transaction may be initiated by the bus master.

At the start of clock one, the initiator asserts FRAME#, indicating that the transaction has begun and that a valid start address and command are on the bus. FRAME# must remain asserted until the initiator is ready to complete the last data phase. At the same time that the initiator asserts FRAME#, it drives the start address onto the AD bus and the transaction type onto the Command/Byte Enable lines, C/BE[3:0]#. The address and transaction type are driven onto the bus for the duration of clock one.

A turn-around cycle (i.e., a dead cycle) is required on all signals that may be driven by more than one PCI bus agent. This period is required to avoid a collision when one agent is in the process of turning off its output drivers and another agent begins driving the same signal(s). During clock one, IRDY#, TRDY# and DEVSEL# are not driven (in preparation for takeover by the new initiator and target). They are kept in the deasserted state by keeper resistors on the system board (required system board resource).

At the start of clock two, the initiator ceases driving the AD bus. This will allow the target to take control of the AD bus to drive the first requested data item (between one and four bytes) back to the initiator. During a read, clock two is defined as the turn-around cycle because ownership of the AD bus is changing from the initiator to the addressed target. **It is the responsibility of the addressed target to keep TRDY# deasserted to enforce this period.**

Also at the start of clock two, the initiator ceases to drive the command onto the Command/Byte Enable lines and uses them to indicate the bytes to be transferred in the currently-addressed doubleword (as well as the data paths to be used during the data transfer). Typically, the initiator will assert all of the byte enables during a read.

The initiator also asserts IRDY# to indicate that it is ready to receive the first data item from the target . Upon asserting IRDY#, the initiator does not deassert FRAME#, thereby indicating that this is not the final data phase of the example transaction. If this were the final data phase, the initiator would assert IRDY# and deassert FRAME# simultaneously to indicate that it is ready to complete the final data phase.

It should be noted that the initiator does not have to assert IRDY# immediately upon entering a data phase. It may require some time before it's ready to receive the first data item (e.g., it has a buffer full condition). However, the initiator may not keep IRDY# deasserted for more than eight PCI clocks during any data phase. This rule has been added in version 2.1 of the specification.

During clock cell three, the target:

- asserts DEVSEL# to indicate that it has recognized its address and will participate in the transaction.
- begins to drive the first data item (between one and four bytes, as requested by the setting of the C/BE lines) onto the AD bus and asserts TRDY# to indicate the presence of the requested data.

When the initiator and the currently-addressed target sample TRDY# and IRDY# both asserted at the rising-edge of clock four, the first data item is read from the bus by the initiator, completing the first data phase. The first data phase consisted of clock cell two and the wait state (turnaround cycle) inserted by the target (clock cell three). At the start of the second data phase (clock edge four), the initiator sets the byte enables to indicate the bytes to be transferred within the next doubleword.

It is a rule that the initiator must immediately output the byte enables for a data phase upon entry to the data phase. If for some reason the initiator doesn't know what the byte enable setting will be for the next data phase, it should keep IRDY# deasserted and not let the current data phase end until it knows what they will be.

In this example, the initiator keeps IRDY# asserted upon entry into the second data phase, but does not deassert FRAME#. This indicates that the initiator is ready to read the second data item, but this is not the final data phase.

In a multiple-data phase transaction, it is the responsibility of the target (if it supprts bursting) to latch the start address into an address counter and to manage the address from data phase to data phase. As an example, upon completion of one data phase, the target would increment the latched address by four to point to the next doubleword. It then examines the initiator's byte enable settings to determine the bytes to be transferred within the currently-addressed doubleword. This subject is covered in more detail later in this chapter.

In this example, the target is going to need some time to fetch the second data item requested, so it deasserts TRDY# to insert a wait state (clock cell five) into the second data phase. In order to keep the data paths from floating, the target must continue to drive a stable data pattern, usually consisting of the last data item, onto the AD bus until it has acquired and is presenting the second requested data item. This is illustrated in clock four. It is necessary to keep the AD bus from floating in order to prevent all of the CMOS input buffers connected to the AD bus from oscillating and drawing excessive current. Mentioned earlier in the book, this is one of the measures taken to achieve the green nature of the PCI bus.

At the rising-edge of clock five, the initiator samples TRDY# deasserted and, recognizing that the target is requesting more time for the transfer of the second data item, it inserts a wait state into the second data phase (clock cell five).

During the wait state, the target begins to drive the second data item onto the AD bus and asserts TRDY# to indicate its presence. When the initiator samples both IRDY# and TRDY# asserted at the rising-edge of clock six, it reads the second data item from the bus. This completes the second data phase. The second data phase consisted of clock cells four and five.

At the start of the third data phase, the initiator sets the byte enables to indicate the bytes to be transferred in the next doubleword. It also deasserts

IRDY#, indicating that it requires more than one clock cell before it will be ready to receive the data.

During clock cell six, the target keeps TRDY# asserted, indicating that it is driving the third requested data item onto the AD bus. In this example, however, the initiator requires more time before it will be able to read the data item (probably because it has a temporary buffer full condition). This causes a wait state to be inserted into data phase three. The target must continue to drive the third data item onto the AD bus during the wait state (clock cell seven).

During clock cell seven, the initiator asserts IRDY#, indicating its willingness to accept the third data item on the next rising clock edge. It also deasserts FRAME#, indicating that this is the final data phase. Sampling both IRDY# and TRDY# asserted at the rising-edge of clock eight, the initiator reads the third data item from the bus. The third data phase consisted of clocks six and seven. Sampling FRAME# deasserted instructs the target that this is the final data item.

The overall burst transfer consisting of three data phases has been completed. The initiator deasserts IRDY#, returning the bus to the idle state (on the rising-edge of clock nine), and the target deasserts TRDY# and DEVSEL#.

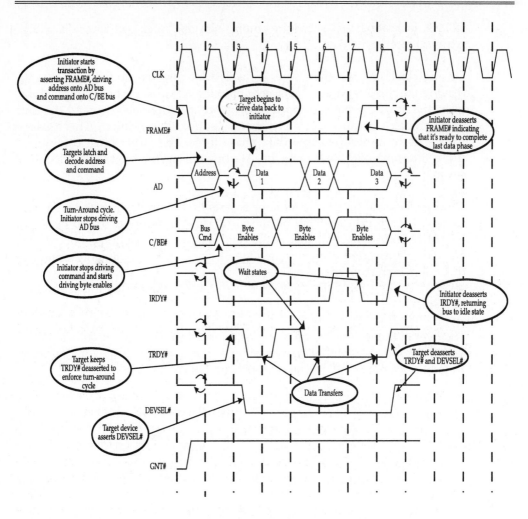

*Figure 8-1. The Read Transaction*

## Treatment of Byte Enables During Read or Write

### Byte Enable Settings May Vary from Data Phase to Data Phase

PCI permits burst transactions where the byte enables change from one data phase to the next. Furthermore, the initiator may use any byte enable setting, consisting of contiguous or non-contiguous byte enables. During a read transaction, the initiator will typically assert all of the byte enables during each data phase, but it may use any combination.

It should be noted that all targets may not be capable of handling non-contiguous byte enables. An example would be an PCI/ISA bridge. In this case, the target could take one of the following actions:

- assert SERR#.
- break the transaction into two 16-bit transfers.

## Data Phase with No Byte Enables Asserted

As stated in the previous paragraph, any combination of byte enables is valid in any data phase. This includes a data phase with no byte enables asserted (a null data phase). This can occur for a number of reasons. Some examples would be:

- During a burst transfer, the **programmer may wish to "skip" a double-word**. This would be accomplished by keeping all byte enables deasserted during that data phase.
- At the initiation of a **64-bit transfer**, the initiator does not yet know whether the target device is a 64 or a 32-bit device. In certain cases, if a 32-bit device responds, this can result in the first data phase being null. This case is described in the chapter entitled "The 64-bit PCI Extension."
- There are cases where the **last data phase** of a block transfer may not have any of the byte enables asserted. Assume that an expansion bus master (EISA or Micro Channel) has initiated a series of accesses with a PCI target. The bridge between the expansion and PCI buses will frequently packetize this series of bus master accesses into a PCI burst transfer. When the expansion bus master has completed its last data transfer, the bridge signals this to the target by deasserting FRAME#. This informs the target that the last data transfer is in progress. Since the bus master has already transferred all of the data, however, the bridge will not assert any of the byte enables during this last data phase.

When none of the byte enables are asserted, the target must react as follows:

- **On a read**: the target must ensure that no data or status is destroyed or altered as a result of this data transfer. The target must supply a stable pattern on all data paths and must generate the proper parity (for the AD and C/BE buses) on the PAR bit.

- **On a write**: the target must not store any data and the initiator must supply a stable pattern on all data paths and ensure that PAR is valid for the AD and C/BE buses.

## Target with Limited Byte Enable Support

I/O and memory targets may support restricted byte enable settings and may respond with target abort (see the chapter entitled "Premature Transaction Termination") for any other pattern. All devices must support any byte enable combination during configuration transactions.

## Rule for Sampling of Byte Enables

If the target requires sampling of the byte enables (in order to precisely determine which bytes are to be transferred within the currently-addressed doubleword) during each data transfer, it must wait for the byte enables to be valid during each data phase before completing the transfer. An example of a device that requires sampling of byte enables would be a memory-mapped I/O device. It should not accept a write to or a read from 8-bit ports within the currently-addressed doubleword until it has verified (via the byte enables) that the initiator is in fact addressing those ports.

If a target does not require examination of the byte enables on a read, the target must supply all four bytes. An example of a device that would not have to wait to sample the byte enables would be a typical memory target. Memory typically yields the same data from a location no matter how many times the location is read from. In other words, performing a speculative read from the memory does not alter the data stored in the location. This type of memory target can be designed to supply all four bytes in every data phase of a read burst. The initiator only take the bytes it's addressing and ignores the others.

## Cases Where Byte Enables Can Be Ignored

If the target **memory is cacheable** (its cache line size configuration register contains a non-zero value), it should ignore the byte enable settings during each data phase (except for parity generation) and return all four bytes bytes (or eight bytes, if it's a 64-bit transfer).

If the target **memory is prefetchable**, it returns all four bytes (or eight bytes, if it's a 64-bit transfer) during each read data phase.

## Performance During Read Transactions

As described earlier, a turn-around cycle must be included in the first data transfer of a read transaction. This being the case, a single data phase read from a target consists of at least three cycles of the PCI clock (one clock cell for the address phase and two clock cells for the data phase). At a clock rate of 33MHz, a read transaction consisting of a single data transfer would take 90ns to complete. An idle cycle (at 33MHz, 30ns in duration) must be included between transactions, resulting in 120ns per transaction. Using back-to-back single data phase read transfers, the data throughput would be 8.33 million transfers per second. If each transfer involved four bytes, the resultant transfer rate would be 33.33Mbytes per second.

In actual practice, though, most read transactions involve a burst transfer of multiple objects between the initiator and the currently-addressed target. The read transaction involving multiple data phases only requires the turn-around cycle during the first data phase. The second through the last data phases can each be accomplished in a single clock cycle (if both the initiator and the currently-addressed target are capable of zero wait state transfers). The achievable transfer rate during the second through the last data phases is thus one transfer every 30ns (at a PCI bus speed of 33MHz), or 33 million transfers per second. If each data phase involves the transfer of four bytes, the resultant data transfer rate is 132Mbytes per second. Figure 8-2 illustrates a read transaction consisting of three data phases, two of which complete with zero wait states.

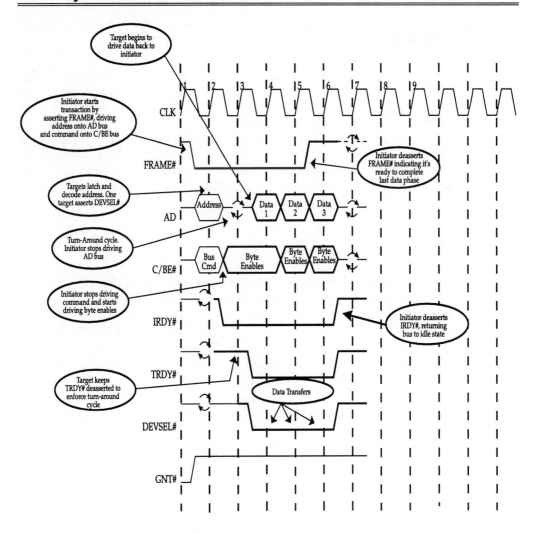

*Figure 8-2. Optimized Read Transaction (no wait states)*

# Chapter 8: The Read and Write Transfers

## Write Transaction

### Description

During the following description of the write transaction, refer to figure 8-3.

It is assumed that the bus master has already arbitrated for and been granted access to the bus (GNT# asserted). The bus master then must wait for the bus to become idle. This is accomplished by sampling the state of FRAME# and IRDY# (and GNT#) on the rising-edge of each clock. When both are sampled deasserted (on the rising-edge of clock one), the bus is idle and a transaction may be initiated by the bus master whose grant signal is currently asserted by the bus arbiter.

At the start of clock cell one, the initiator asserts FRAME# to indicate that the transaction has begun and that a valid start address and command are present on the bus. FRAME# remains asserted until the initiator is ready to complete the last data phase. At the same time that the initiator asserts FRAME#, it drives the start address onto the AD bus and the transaction type onto the Command/Byte Enable bus. The address and transaction type are driven onto the bus for the duration of clock one.

A turn-around cycle is required on all signals that may be driven by more than one PCI bus agent. This period is required to avoid the collision that would occur if a device turned on its output drivers at the same time that another device's output drivers are disconnecting from the signal(s). During clock cell one, IRDY#, TRDY# and DEVSEL# are not driven (in preparation for takeover by the new initiator and target).

At the start of clock cell two, the initiator changes the information that it is presenting to the target over the AD bus. During a write transaction, the initiator is driving the AD bus during both the address and data phases. Since it doesn't have to hand off control of the AD bus to the target, as it does during a read, a turn-around cycle is unnecessary. The initiator may begin to drive the first data item onto the AD bus at the start of clock cell two. In addition, during clock cell two the initiator uses the Command/Byte Enable lines to indicate the bytes to be transferred to the currently-addressed doubleword and the data paths to be used during the first data phase.

At the start of clock cell two, the initiator drives the write data onto the AD bus and asserts the respective byte enables to indicate the data paths that carry valid data. It also asserts IRDY# to indicate the presence of the data on the bus. The initiator doesn't deassert FRAME# when it asserts IRDY# (because this is not the final data phase).

It should be noted that the initiator does not have to assert IRDY# immediately upon entering a data phase. It may require some time before it's ready to source the first data item (e.g., it has a buffer empty condition). However, the initiator may not keep IRDY# deasserted for more than eight PCI clocks during any data phase. **This rule has been added in version 2.1 of the specification.**

During clock cell two, the target decodes the address and command and asserts DEVSEL# to claim the transaction. In addition, it asserts TRDY#, indicating its readiness to accept the first data item.

At the rising-edge of clock three, the initiator and the currently-addressed target sample both TRDY# and IRDY# asserted, indicating that they are both ready to complete the first data phase. This is a zero wait state transfer. The target accepts the first data item from the bus on the rising-edge of clock three (and samples the byte enables in order to determine which bytes are being written), completing the first data phase.

During clock cell three, the initiator drives the second data item onto the AD bus and sets the byte enables to indicate the bytes to be transferred and the data paths to be used during the second data phase. It also keeps IRDY# asserted and does not deassert FRAME#, thereby indicating that it is ready to complete the second data phase and that this is not the final data phase. Assertion of IRDY# indicates that the write data is present on the bus.

At the rising-edge of clock four, the initiator and the currently-addressed target sample both TRDY# and IRDY# asserted, indicating that they are both ready to complete the second data phase. This is a zero wait state data phase. The target accepts the second data item from the bus on the rising-edge of clock four (and samples the byte enables), completing the second data phase.

The initiator requires more time before beginning to drive the next data item onto the AD bus (it has a buffer empty condition). It inserts a wait state into the third data phase by deasserting IRDY# at the start of clock cell four. This allows the initiator to delay presentation of the new data by one clock, but it must set the byte enables to the proper setting for the third data phase at the start of clock cell four.

In this example, the target also requires more time before it will be ready to accept the third data item. To indicate the requirement for more time, the target deasserts TRDY# during clock cell four. When the initiator and target sample IRDY# and TRDY# deasserted at the rising-edge of clock five, they insert a wait state (clock cell five) into the third data phase.

During clock cell four, although the initiator does not yet have the third data item available to drive, it must drive a stable pattern onto the data paths rather than let the AD bus float (remember the rule about PCI being green). The specification doesn't dictate the pattern to be driven during this period. It is usually accomplished by continuing to drive the previous data item. The target will not accept the data being presented to it for two reasons:

- By deasserting TRDY#, it has indicated that it isn't ready to accept data.
- By deasserting IRDY#, the initiator has indicated that it is not yet presenting the next data item to the target.

During clock cell five, the initiator asserts IRDY# and drives the final data item onto the AD bus. It also deasserts FRAME# to indicate that this is the final data phase. The target keeps TRDY# deasserted, indicating that it is not yet ready to accept the third data item.

At the rising-edge of clock six, the initiator samples IRDY# asserted, indicating that it is presenting the data, but TRDY# is still deasserted (because the target is not yet ready to accept the data item). The target also samples FRAME# deasserted, indicating that the final data phase is in progress. The only thing impeding the completion of the final data phase now is the target (by keeping TRDY# deasserted until it is ready to accept the final data item).

In response to sampling TRDY# deasserted on clock edge six, the target and initiator insert a second wait state (clock cell six) into the third data phase. During the second wait state, the initiator continues to drive the third data item onto the AD bus and maintains the setting on the byte enables. The target keeps TRDY# deasserted, indicating that is not ready yet.

At the rising-edge of clock seven, the target and initiator sample IRDY# asserted, indicating that the initiator is still presenting the data, but TRDY# is still deasserted. In response, the target and initiator insert a third wait state (clock cell seven) into the third data phase. During the third wait state, the initiator continues to drive the third data item onto the AD bus and maintains the setting on the byte enables. The target asserts TRDY#, indicating that it is ready to complete the final data phase.

At the rising-edge of clock eight, the target and initiator sample both IRDY# and TRDY# asserted, indicating that both the initiator and the target are ready to end the third and final data phase. In response, the third data phase is completed on the rising-edge of clock eight. The target accepts the third data item from the AD bus. The third data phase consisted of four clock periods (the first clock cell of the data phase, clock cell four, plus three wait states).

During clock cell eight, the initiator ceases to drive the data onto the AD bus, stops driving the C/BE bus, and deasserts IRDY# (returning the bus to the idle state). The target deasserts TRDY# and DEVSEL#.

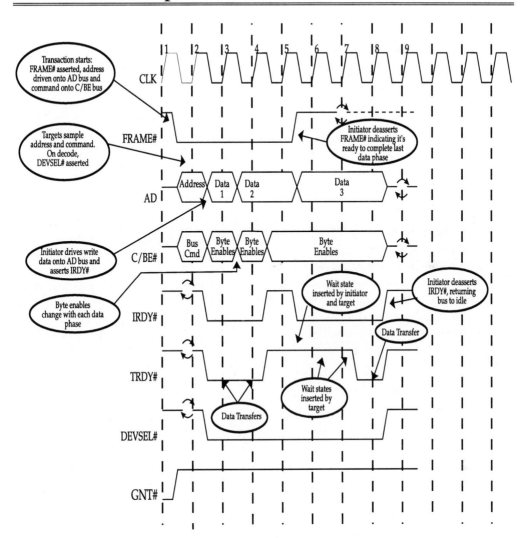

*Figure 8-3. The PCI Write Transaction*

## Performance During Write Transactions

Transactions wherein an initiator performs a single data phase write to a target consist of at least two cycles of the PCI clock (the address phase and a one clock data phase). An idle cycle (at 33MHz, 30ns in duration) must be included between transactions. At a clock rate of 33MHz, then, a single data phase write transaction takes 90ns to complete. Using back-to-back single data phase write transfers, the data throughput would be 11.11 million transfers per second. If each transfer involved four bytes, the resulting transfer rate would be 44.44Mbytes per second.

The second through the last data transfer of a write transaction involving multiple data phases can each be accomplished in a single clock cycle (if both the initiator and the currently-addressed target are capable of zero wait state data phases). The achievable transaction rate during the second through the last data phases is thus one transaction every 30ns (at a PCI bus speed of 33MHz), or 33 million transfers per second. If each transfer involves the transfer of four bytes, the data transfer rate is 132Mbytes per second. Figure 8-4 illustrates a write transaction consisting of three zero wait state data phases.

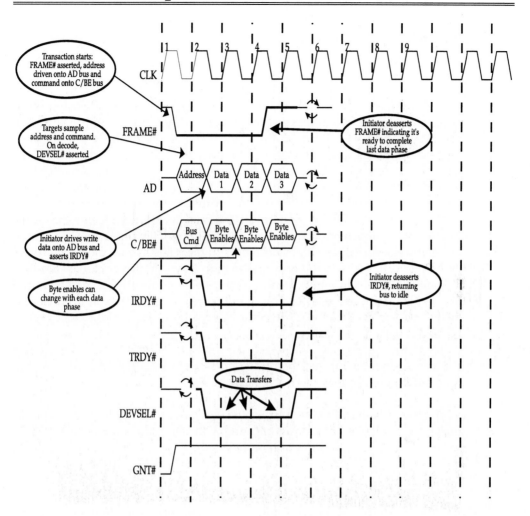

*Figure 8-4. Optimized Write Transaction (no wait states)*

## Posted-Write Buffer

### General

A bridge (PCI-to-PCI bridge or host/PCI) may incorporate a posted-write buffer that allows a bus master to complete a memory write quickly. The transaction and the write data are latched within the bridge's posted-write buffer and the master is permitted to complete the transaction. When a bridge implements a posted-write buffer, a potential problem exists. Another bus master (or the same one) may initiate a memory read from the target of the posted write before the data is actually written to the memory target. If this were permitted, the master performing the read would not receive the freshest copy of the information. In order to prevent this from occurring, the bridge designer must first flush all posted writes to their destination memory targets before permitting a read to occur on the bus. A device driver can ensure that all memory data has been written to its device by performing a read from the device. This will force the flushing of all posted write buffers in bridges that reside between the processor executing the read and the target device before the read is permitted to complete.

It is also a requirement that the bridge must perform all posted writes in the same order in which they were originally posted.

A bridge is only permitted to post writes to regular memory targets. Software must be assured real-time communication with I/O and memory-mapped I/O devices, as well as with configuration registers.

### Combining

A bridge may combine posted memory writes to successive doublewords into a single burst memory write transaction using linear addressing. This feature is recommended to improve performance. The doublewords must be written in the same order in which they were posted. This means that writes posted to doublewords 0, 1 and 2 (they were posted in that order) can be combined into a linear burst write, while writes posted to doublewords 2, 1, 0 cannot. Instead, these three writes would have to be performed as three separate single data phase memory write transactions. Writes posted to doublewords 0, 1, and 3 (in that order) can be combined into a linear burst write with no byte enables asserted in the third data phase. The specification recommends that bridges that permit combining include a control bit to allow this feature to be disabled.

## Byte Merging

A bridge may combine writes to a single doubleword within one entry in the posted-write buffer. This feature is recommended to improve performance and is only permitted in memory address ranges that are prefetchable (for more information on prefetchable memory, refer to the base address register section in the chapter entitled "Configuration Registers" and to the chapter entitled "PCI-to-PCI Bridge"). As an example, assume that a bus master performs two memory writes: the first writes to locations 00000100h and 00000101h and the second writes to locations 00000102h and 00000103h. These four locations reside within the same doubleword. The bridge could absorb the first two-byte write into a doubleword buffer entry and then absorb the second two byte write into the same doubleword buffer entry. When the bridge performs the memory write, it can complete it in a single data phase. It is a violation of the specification, however, for a bridge to combine separate byte writes to the same location into a single write on the destination bus. As an example, assume that a bus master performs four separate memory writes to the same doubleword: the first writes to location zero in the doubleword, the second to location zero again, the third to location one and the fourth to location two. When the bridge performs the posted writes, it has to perform a single data phase transaction to write the first byte to location zero. It then performs a second single data phase memory write to locations zero (the second byte written to it by the bus master), one and two.

## Collapsing Is Forbidden

Multiple writes to the same location(s) cannot be performed as a single write on the other side of the bridge. This is referred to as collapsing multiple writes to the same location into one write of the last write's data to the location. Two sequential writes to the same doubleword where at least one of the byte enables was asserted in both transactions must be performed as two separate transactions on the other bus. Collapsing of writes is forbidden for any type of write transactions.

The specification states that a bridge may allow collapsing within a specific range when a device driver indicates that this will not cause operational problems. How the device driver would indicate this to a bridge is outside the scope of the specification.

### Cache Line Merging

The bridge may perform cache line merging within an area of memory that the bridge knows is cacheable or when it uses combining and/or byte merging to create a burst write of a cache line. It captures (i.e., it posts) individual memory writes performed by bus masters on one PCI bus to build a cache line to be written on the other bus using a memory write and invalidate transaction or a linear memory write transaction. The author would like to note that the specification doesn't specifically state that a memory write and invalidate command would be used.

# Addressing Sequence During Memory Burst

## Linear and Cacheline Wrap Addressing

The start address issued during any form of memory transaction is a double-word-aligned address presented on AD[31:2] during the address phase. The following discussion assumes that the memory target supports bursting. The memory target latches this address into an address counter and uses it for the first data phase. Upon completion of the first data phase and assuming that it's not a single data phase transaction, the memory target must update its address counter to point to the next doubleword to be transferred.

On a memory access, a memory target must check the state of address bits one and zero (AD[1:0]) to determine the policy to use when updating its address counter at the conclusion of each data phase. Table 8-1 defines the addressing sequences defined in the revision 2.1 specification and encoded in the first two address bits. Only two addressing sequences are currently defined:

- **Linear, or sequential, address mode**. All memory devices that support multiple data phase transfers must implement support of linear, or sequential, addressing. The memory write and invalidate command must use linear addressing. At the completion of each data phase, the memory target increments its address counter by four to point to the next sequential doubleword for the next data phase.
- **Cacheline wrap mode**. Support for cacheline wrap mode is optional and is only used for memory reads. At the start of each data phase of the burst read, the memory target increments the doubleword address in its address counter. When the end of the cache line is encountered and assuming that the transfer did not start at the first doubleword of the cache line,

the target wraps to the start address of the cacheline and continues incrementing the address in each data phase until the entire cache line has been transferred. If the burst continues past the point where the entire cache line has been transferred, the target starts the transfer of the next cache line at the same address that the transfer of the previous line started at.

Implementation of the cacheline wrap mode is optional for memory and meaningless for I/O and configuration targets. The addressing sequence used during a cache line fill is established at the start of the transfer based on the start memory address and the length of the transfer. This implies that the memory target must know that a cache line fill is in progress (wrap mode indicated) and the size of a cache line (established at startup when the platform-specific configuration program writes the system cache line size to the memory target's cache line size configuration register).

The 486 processor's internal cache has a line size of sixteen bytes (four doublewords) and has a 32-bit data bus. It must therefore perform four 32-bit transfers to fill a cache line. The first doubleword address output by the processor is the one that resulted in an internal cache miss. This could be any of the four doublewords within the line. For a detailed description of the 486 cache line fill addressing sequence, refer to the Addison-Wesley publication entitled *80486 System Architecture*. For that used by the Pentium processor, refer to the Addison-Wesley publication entitled *Pentium Processor System Architecture*. For that used by the PowerPC 60x processors, refer to the Addison-Wesley publication entitled *PowerPC System Architecture*. The x86 processors do not use wrap addressing (they use toggle mode addressing--described in the 486 and Pentium MindShare books). The PowerPC 601 processor also doesn't use wrap addressing (see the MindShare PowerPC book for an explanation). The PowerPC 603 and 604 processors both use wrap addressing.

As an example, assume that the cache line size is 16 bytes and the start doubleword address issued by the master is 00000104h. This doubleword resides within the 16-byte aligned cache line that occupies memory locations 00000100h through 0000010Fh. The sequence of the doubleword transfers would be 00000104h, 00000108h, 0000010Ch and 00000100h. If the burst continues past this point, the next series of doublewords transferred would be 00000114h, 00000118h, 0000011Ch and 00000110h.

If the target does not implement the cache line size register, the target must issue a disconnect A or B on the first data phase or a disconnect C on the second one (it can't handle wrap mode because it doesn't know the line size).

If the master wants to use a different sequence after the first line has been read, it must end the transaction and begin a new one indicating linear addressing.

*Table 8-1. Memory Burst Address Sequence*

| AD1 | AD0 | Addressing Sequence |
|:---:|:---:|---|
| 0 | 0 | **Linear**, or sequential, addressing sequence during the burst. |
| 0 | 1 | **Reserved**. Prior to revision 2.1, this indicated toggle-mode addressing. When detected, the memory target should signal a disconnect A or B during the first data phase or a disconnect C on the second data phase. |
| 1 | 0 | **Cacheline wrap** mode. Newly defined in revision 2.1. |
| 1 | 1 | **Reserved**. When detected, the memory target should signal a disconnect A or B during the first data phase or a disconnect C on the second data phase. |

## Target Response to Reserved Setting on AD[1:0]

Assuming that the initiator has started a multi-data phase memory transaction and that it has placed a reserved pattern on AD[1:0] in the address phase (01b or 11b pattern), the revision 2.x-compliant memory target must either issue a disconnect A or B on the transfer of the first data item, or a disconnect C during the second data phase. This is necessary because the initiator is indicating an addressing sequence the target is unfamiliar with (because it is reserved in the revision 2.1 specification).

## Do Not Merge Processor I/O Writes into Single Burst

To ensure that I/O devices function correctly, bridges must never combine sequential I/O accesses into a single (merging byte accesses performed by the processor into a single-doubleword transfer) or a multi-data phase transaction. Each individual I/O transaction generated by the host processor must be performed on the PCI bus as it appears on the host bus. This rule includes both regular and memory-mapped I/O accesses.

## PCI I/O Addressing

### General

The start I/O address placed on the AD bus during the address phase has the following format:

- AD[31:2] identify the target doubleword of I/O space.
- AD[1:0] identify the least-significant byte within the target doubleword that the initiator wishes to perform a transfer with (00b = byte 0, 01b = byte 1, etc.).

At the end of the address phase, all I/O targets latch the start address and the I/O read or write command and begin the address decode. An I/O target claims the transaction based on the byte-specific start address that it latched. If that 8-bit I/O port is implemented in the target, the target asserts DEVSEL# and claims the transaction. If the target "owns" the entire target doubleword, only AD[31:2] must be decoded to identify the target doubleword and assert DEVSEL#.

The byte enables asserted during the data phase identify the least-significant byte within the doubleword (the same one indicated by the setting of AD[1:0]) as well as any additional bytes (within the addressed doubleword) that the initiator wishes to transfer. The initiating bus master may start an I/O burst with a null data phase (no byte enables asserted) to skip the first doubleword.

It is illegal (and makes no sense) for the initiator to assert any byte enables of lesser significance than the one indicated by the AD[1:0] setting. If the initiator does assert any of the illegal byte enable patterns, the target must terminate the transaction with a target abort. Table 8-2 contains some examples of I/O addressing.

*Table 8-2. Examples of I/O Addressing*

| AD[31:0] | C/BE3# | C/BE2# | C/BE1# | C/BE0# | Description |
|----------|--------|--------|--------|--------|-------------|
| 00001000h | 1 | 1 | 1 | 0 | just location 1000h |
| 000095A2h | 0 | 0 | 1 | 1 | 95A2 and 95A3h |
| 00001510h | 0 | 0 | 0 | 0 | 1510h-1513h |
| 1267AE21h | 0 | 0 | 0 | 1 | 1267AE21h-1267AE23h |

## Situation Resulting in Target-Abort

If an I/O target claims a transaction (asserts DEVSEL#) based on the byte-specific start address issued during the address phase, then subsequently examines the byte enables (issued during the data phase) and determines that it cannot fulfill the initiator's request, the target must respond by indicating a target-abort (STOP# asserted, TRDY# and DEVSEL# deasserted) to the initiator. The target-abort is covered in the chapter entitled "Premature Transaction Termination." A typical example wherein the target must abort the transaction could result from the following x86 instruction:

```
IN    AX, 60 ;read two bytes from I/O starting at address 60h
```

When executed by a 486 processor, doubleword address 00000060h is driven onto the host bus during the resultant I/O read transaction and the processor asserts BE0# and BE1#, but not BE2# and BE3#. This indicates to the host/PCI bridge that the processor is addressing locations 00000060h and 00000061h within I/O doubleword starting at port 00000060h. Assuming that the host/PCI bridge doesn't incorporate either of these I/O port addresses, it arbitrates for and receives ownership of the PCI bus and initiates an I/O read transaction.

During the address phase, the host/PCI bridge drives the address of the least-significant I/O port to be read by the processor, 00000060h, onto the AD bus. The bridge determines this is the least-significant port to be read by examining the processor's byte enable setting and testing for the least-significant byte enable asserted by the processor. In this case, it is BE0#, corresponding to the first location in the currently-addressed doubleword, 00000060h.

In a PC-compatible machine, this is the address of the keyboard data port. Assuming that the keyboard controller resides on the PCI bus (e.g., embedded within or closely-associated with the PCI/ISA bridge), the keyboard controller would assert DEVSEL# to claim the transaction. Subsequently, when the processor's byte enables are presented during the data phase and are sampled by the target, BE0# and BE1# are asserted. This identifies I/O addresses 60h and 61h as the target locations.

Since port 61h has nothing to do with the keyboard interface (it is system control port B, a general I/O status port on the system board), the keyboard interface cannot service the entire request. It must therefore issue a target-abort to the initiator (STOP# asserted, TRDY# and DEVSEL# deasserted) and terminate the transaction with no data transferred. As a result, the initiator sets its TARGET-ABORT DETECTED status bit and the target sets its SIGNALED TARGET-ABORT status bit (in their respective PCI configuration status registers). The initiator reports this error back to the software in a device-specific fashion (e.g., by generating an interrupt request).

An ISA expansion bus bridge doesn't have specific knowledge regarding all of the I/O ports that exists on the ISA bus. It therefore claims I/O transactions that remain unclaimed by PCI I/O devices. Since it doesn't "know" what I/O ports exists behind it, it can not judge whether to target abort the transaction based on the byte enable settings.

## I/O Address Management

As in any PCI read/write transaction, it is the responsibility of the I/O target to latch the start address delivered by the initiator. It then assumes responsibility for managing the address for each subsequent data phase that follows the first data phase. Unlike memory address management, in PCI there is no explicit or implicit I/O address sequencing from one data phase to the next. The initiator and the target must both understand and utilize the same I/O address management. Two examples would be:

- Both the initiator and the target understand that the doubleword address (on AD[31:2]) delivered by the initiator is to be incremented by four at the completion of each data phase. In other words, the read or write transaction proceeds sequentially through the target's I/O address space a doubleword at a time.
- Both the initiator and the target understand that the target doesn't increment the doubleword address for each subsequent data phase. This is how a designer would implement a FIFO port.

At the time of this writing, the author is unaware of any currently-existing processor that is capable of performing burst I/O write transactions. It's easy to assume that the Intel x86 INS (input string) and OUTS (output string) instructions cause the processor to generate a burst I/O read or write series, but this isn't so. When an INS instruction is executed by the x86 processor, it results in a series of back-to-back I/O read and memory write bus cycles. The OUTS instruction results in a string of back-to-back memory read and I/O write bus cycles.

# When I/O Target Doesn't Support Multi-Data Phase Transactions

Many PCI I/O targets are not designed to handle multi-data phase transactions. A target can determine that the initiator intends to perform a second data phase upon completion of the first by checking the state of FRAME# when IRDY# is sampled asserted in the first data phase. If IRDY# has been asserted by the initiator and it still has FRAME# asserted, this indicates that this is not the final data phase in the transaction.

If an I/O target doesn't support multi-data phase transactions and the initiator indicates that a second data phase is forthcoming, the target must respond in one of two ways:

- When it's ready to transfer the first data item, **terminate the first data phase with a disconnect A or B** (STOP#, TRDY# and DEVSEL# asserted). The first data item is transferred successfully, but the initiator is forced to terminate the transaction at that point. It must then re-arbitrate for bus ownership and re-address the target using a byte-specific start address within the next I/O doubleword.
- **Terminate the second data phase with a disconnect C** (STOP# and DEVSEL# asserted, TRDY# deasserted). The first data phase completes normally. The initiator is then forced to terminate the transaction during the second data phase without transferring any additional data. The initiator then re-arbitrates for bus ownership and re-addresses the target using a byte-specific start address within the same I/O doubleword.

# Address/Data Stepping

## Advantages: Diminished Current Drain and Crosstalk

Turning on a large number of signal drivers simultaneously (e.g., driving a 32-bit address onto the AD bus) can result in:

- a large spike of current drain.
- a significant amount of crosstalk within the driver chip and on adjacent external signal lines.

# Chapter 8: The Read and Write Transfers

The designer could choose to alleviate both of these problems by turning on the drivers associated with non-adjacent signal drivers in groups over a number of steps, or clock periods.

As an example, assume that the system board designer lays out the 32 AD lines as adjacent signal traces in bit sequential order. By simultaneously driving all 32 lines, crosstalk would be generated on the traces (and within the driver chip). Now assume that there are four 8-bit groups of signal drivers connected as follows:

- driver group one is connected to AD lines 0, 4, 8, 12, 16, 20, 24, 28.
- driver group two is connected to AD lines 1, 5, 9, 13, 17, 21, 25, 29.
- driver group three is connected to AD lines 2, 6, 10, 14, 18, 22, 26, 30.
- driver group four is connected to AD lines 3, 7, 11, 15, 19, 23, 27, 31.

The initiator could turn on the first driver group in clock cell one of a transaction, followed by group two in clock cell two, group three in clock cell three, and group four in clock cell four. Using this sequence, non-adjacent signal lines are being switched during each clock cell, reducing the interaction and crosstalk.

## Why Targets Don't Latch Address During Stepping Process

Since the entire address is not present on the bus until clock cell four, the initiator must delay assertion of the FRAME# signal until clock cell four when the final group driver is switched on. Because the assertion of FRAME# qualifies the address as being valid, no targets latch and use the address until FRAME# is sampled asserted.

## Data Stepping

The data presented by the initiator during each data phase of a write transaction is qualified by the assertion of the IRDY# signal by the initiator. The data presented by the target during each data phase of a read transaction is qualified by the assertion of the TRDY# signal by the target. In other words, data can be stepped onto the bus, as well as address.

## How Device Indicates Ability to Use Stepping

A device indicates its ability to perform stepping via the WAIT CYCLE CONTROL bit in its configuration command register. There are three possible cases:

- If the device is not capable of stepping, the bit is hardwired to zero.
- If the device always using stepping, the bit is hardwired to one.
- If the device's ability to use stepping can be enabled and disabled via software, the bit is implemented as a read/writable bit. If the bit is read/writable, reset sets it to one.

## Designer May Step Address, Data, PAR (and PAR64) and IDSEL

The address may be stepped onto the AD bus (including the 64-bit extension) because it is qualified by FRAME#. PAR (and PAR64) may also be stepped because they are guaranteed qualified one clock after the end of the address phase and one clock after the assertion of IRDY# or TRDY# during each data phase. IDSEL can be stepped because it is qualified by the FRAME# signal (refer to the section entitled "Resistively-Coupled IDSEL Is Slow" in the chapter entitled "Configuration Transactions"). Data can be stepped onto the AD bus during each data phase because it is qualified by the assertion of IRDY# (on a write) or TRDY# (on a read).

Table 8-3 defines the relationship of the AD bus, PAR, PAR64, IDSEL and DEVSEL# and the conditions that qualify them as valid.

*Table 8-3. Qualification Requirements*

| Signal(s) | Qualifier |
|---|---|
| AD bus during address phase | Qualified when FRAME# signal sampled asserted at the end of the address phase. |
| AD bus during data phase on read | Qualified when TRDY# signal sampled asserted on a rising clock edge during the data phase. |
| AD bus during data phase on write | Qualified when IRDY# signal sampled asserted on a rising clock edge during the data phase. |
| PAR and PAR64 | Implicitly qualified on rising clock edge after address phase, or one clock after IRDY# and TRDY# (data phase). |
| IDSEL | Qualified when FRAME# sampled asserted at the end of the address phase and a type zero configuration command is present on the C/BE bus (with AD[1:0] =00b). |

## Continuous and Discrete Stepping

The initiator (or the target) may use one of two methods to step a valid address or data onto the AD bus, or a valid level onto the PAR and PAR64 signal lines, or IDSEL:

- If the device driving the AD bus and the parity pins or IDSEL, either initiator or target, **uses very weak output drivers**, it may take several clocks for it to drive a valid level onto these bus signals (i.e., the propagation delay may be lengthy because it may take several reflections, with the resultant voltage-doubling effect, before the address (or data) is in the correct state on the bus). This is known as **continuous stepping**. See note in the next section.
- The device driving the AD bus and the parity pins or IDSEL, either initiator or target, may have **strong output drivers** and may drive a subset of them on each of several clock edges until all of them have been driven. This is known as **discrete stepping**.

## Disadvantages of Stepping

There are two disadvantages associated with stepping:

- Due to the prolonged period it takes to set up the address or data on the bus, there is a performance penalty associated in any address or data phase where stepping is used.
- In the midst of stepping the address onto the bus, the arbiter may remove the grant from the stepping master. This subject is covered in the next section.

The specification strongly discourages the use of continuous stepping because it results in poor performance and also because it creates violations of the input setup time at all inputs.

## Preemption While Stepping in Progress

When the PCI bus arbiter grants the bus to a bus master, the master then waits for bus idle before initiating its transaction. If, during this period of time, the arbiter detects a request from a higher priority master, it can remove the grant from the first master before it begins a transaction (i.e., before it asserts FRAME#).

Assuming that this doesn't occur, the master retains its grant and awaits bus idle. Upon detection of the bus idle state, the master begins to step the address onto the AD bus, but delays the assertion of FRAME# for several clocks until the address is fully driven. During this period of time, the arbiter may still remove the grant from the master. The arbiter hasn't detected FRAME# asserted and may therefore assume that the master hasn't yet started a transaction (even though the arbiter can see that the bus is idle). If the arbiter receives a request from a higher-priority master, it may remove the grant from the master that is currently engaged in stepping an address onto the AD bus. In response to the loss of grant, the stepping master must immediately tri-state its output drivers.

It is a rule that the arbiter cannot deassert one master's grant and assert grant to another master during the same clock cell if the bus is idle. The bus may not, in fact, be idle. A master may not have asserted FRAME# yet because it is in the act of stepping the address onto the AD bus.

# Chapter 8: The Read and Write Transfers

If the arbiter were to simultaneously remove the stepping master's GNT# and issue GNT# to another master, the following problem would result. On the next rising-edge of the clock, the stepping master detects removal of its GNT# and begins to turn off its address drivers (which takes time). At the same time, the other master detects its GNT# and bus idle (because the stepping master had not yet asserted FRAME#) and initiates a transaction. This results in a collision on the AD bus.

When the bus appears to be idle, the arbiter must remove the grant from one master, wait one clock cell, and then assert grant to the other master. This provides a one clock cell buffer zone for the stepping master to disconnect completely before the other master detects its grant plus bus idle and starts its transaction.

It is permissible for the arbiter to simultaneously remove one master's grant and assert another's during the same clock cell if the bus isn't idle (i.e., a transaction is in progress). There is no danger of a collision because the master that has just received the grant cannot start driving the bus until the current master idles the bus.

## Broken Master

The arbiter may assume that a master is broken if the arbiter has issued GNT# to the master, the bus has been idle for 16 clocks, and the master has not asserted FRAME# to start its transaction. The arbiter is permitted to ignore all further requests from the broken master and may optionally report the failure to the operating system (in a device-specific fashion).

## Stepping Example

Figure 8-5 provides an example of an initiator using stepping over a period of three clocks to drive the address onto the AD bus. The initiator can start the transaction on clock three (GNT# sampled asserted and bus idle: FRAME# and IRDY# sampled deasserted). It then begins to drive the address onto the AD bus and the command onto the C/BE bus. During the clock cell four, it continues to drive the address onto the AD bus. During the clock cell five, it finalizes the driving of the address and asserts FRAME#, indicating the presence of the address and command. When the targets sample FRAME# asserted on the rising-edge of clock six (the end of the address phase), they latch the address and command and begin the address decode. Since this is an example of a write transaction, the initiator begins to drive the data onto the AD bus at the start of the data phase (clock six). Once again, it uses stepping, asserting the write data over a period of two clocks. It withholds the assertion of IRDY# until the data has been fully driven.

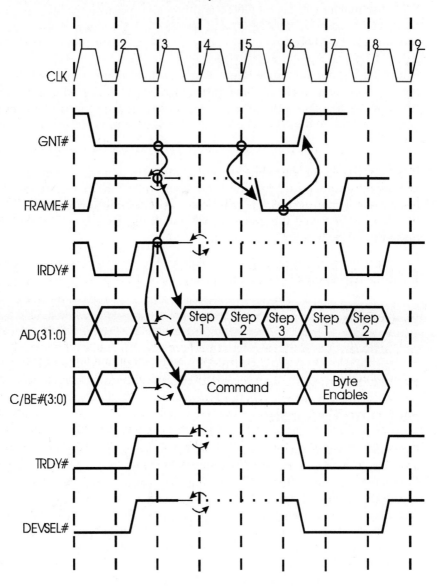

*Figure 8-5. Example of Address Stepping*

## When Not to Use Stepping

Stepping must not be utilized when using 64-bit addressing because targets that respond to 64-bit addressing expect the upper 32 bits of the address to be presented one tick after FRAME# is sampled asserted.

## Who Must Support Stepping?

All PCI devices must be able to handle address and data stepping performed by the other party in a transaction. The ability to use stepping, however, is optional.

## Response to Illegal Behavior

The 2.1 specification does not encourage the device designer to actively check for protocol violations. If a device does detect a violation, however, the following policy is advised.

Upon detection of illegal use of bus protocol, all PCI devices should be designed to gracefully return to the idle state (i.e., cease driving all bus signals) as quickly as possible. The specification is understandably vague on this point. It depends on the nature of the protocol violation as to whether the devices can gracefully return to their idle states and still function properly. As an example, the specification cites the case where the initiator simultaneously deasserts FRAME# and IRDY#. In this case, when the target detects this illegal end to the transaction, it is suggested that the target deassert all target-related signals and return its state machine to the idle state. In the event that a protocol violation leaves a target device questioning its ability to function correctly in the future, it can respond to all future access attempts with a target abort. If the target thinks that the protocol violation has not impaired its ability to function correctly, it just surrenders all signals, returns to the idle state, and does not indicate any type of error.

# Chapter 9

## The Previous Chapter

The previous chapter described the read and write burst transfers.

## In This Chapter

This chapter describes the circumstances under which the initiator or target may need to abort a transaction and the mechanisms provided to accomplish the abort.

## The Next Chapter

The next chapter describes error detection, reporting and handling.

## Introduction

In certain circumstances, a transaction must be prematurely terminated. Either the initiator or the target makes the determination to prematurely terminate a transaction. The following sections define the circumstances requiring termination and the mechanisms used to accomplish it. The first half of this chapter discusses situations wherein the master makes the decision to prematurely terminate a transaction. The second half discusses situations wherein the target makes the decision.

## Master-Initiated Termination

The initiator terminates a transaction for one of three reasons:

- The **transaction has completed normally**. All data involved in the transaction has been transferred to or from the target. This is not a premature transaction termination.

- The **initiator has been preempted** by another bus master. The initiator's Latency Timer has expired and the arbiter has removed the initiator's bus grant signal (GNT#).
- The initiator has aborted the transaction because **no target has responded** to the address. This is referred to as a master abort.

Normal transaction termination is described in the chapter entitled "The Read and Write Transfers." The second and third scenarios are described in this chapter.

## Master Preempted

Figure 9-1 illustrates two cases of a preemption. In the first case (the upper part of the diagram), the arbiter removes GNT# from the initiator, but the initiator's LT has not yet expired, indicating that its timeslice has not yet been exhausted. It may therefore continue to use the bus either until it has completed its transfer, or until its timeslice is exhausted, whichever comes first.

In the second case, the initiator has already used up its timeslice but has not yet lost its GNT#. It may therefore continue bus ownership until it has completed its transfer, or until its GNT# is removed, whichever comes first. The following two sections provide a detailed description of the two scenarios illustrated.

### Preemption During Timeslice

In the upper example in figure 9-1, the current initiator is preempted on clock one (GNT# has been removed by the arbiter), indicating that the arbiter has detected a request from another master and is instructing the current master to finish its transaction and surrender the bus. At the point of preemption (clock one), however, the initiator's LT timer has not yet expired (i.e., its timeslice has not been exhausted). The initiator may therefore retain bus ownership until it has either completed its overall transfer or until its timeslice is exhausted, which ever comes first.

Data transfers occur on clocks two through five and the initiator also decrements its LT on the rising-edge of each clock. On the rising-edge of clock five, a data item is transferred and the initiator's timeslice expires (its LT is exhausted). The rule is that the initiator can perform one final data phase and must then surrender ownership of the bus.

# Chapter 9: Premature Transaction Termination

In clock five, the initiator keeps IRDY# asserted and deasserts FRAME#, indicating that it's ready to complete the final data phase. The target realizes that this is the final data phase because it samples FRAME# deasserted and IRDY# asserted on clock six. The final data item is transferred on clock six. The initiator then deasserts IRDY#, returning the bus to the idle state on clock seven. The master that has its GNT# and has been testing for bus idle on each clock can now assume bus ownership on clock seven.

## Timeslice Expiration Followed by Preemption

The lower half of figure 9-1 illustrates another preemption case. The initiator determines that its LT has expired at the rising-edge of clock one, and a data transfer occurs at the same time (IRDY# and TRDY# sampled asserted). The initiator doesn't have to yield the bus yet because the arbiter hasn't removed its GNT#. It may therefore retain bus ownership until it either completes its overall data transfer or until its GNT# is removed by the arbiter, which occurs first.

Data transfers take place on clocks one, two, four and five. On clock five, the initiator detects that its GNT# has been removed by the arbiter, indicating that it must surrender bus ownership after performing one more data phase.

In clock five, the initiator keeps IRDY# asserted and removes FRAME#, indicating that the final data phase is in progress. The final data item is transferred on clock six. The initiator then deasserts IRDY# in clock six, returning the bus to the idle state. The master that has its GNT# and has been testing for bus idle on each clock can now assume bus ownership on clock seven.

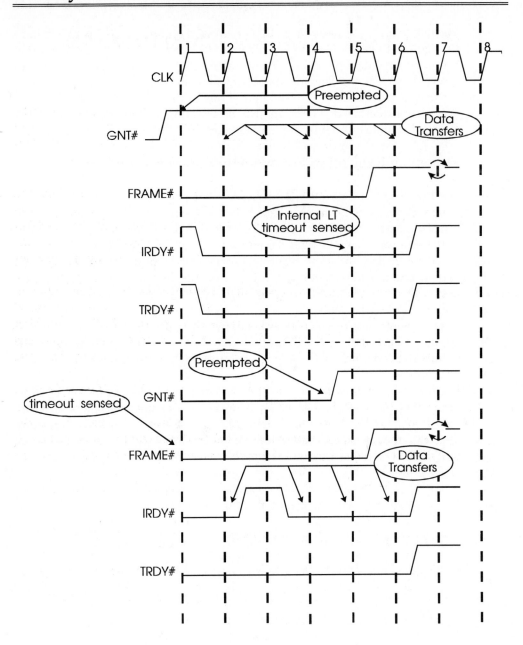

*Figure 9-1. Master-Initiated Termination Due to Preemption and Master Latency Timer Expiration*

# Chapter 9: Premature Transaction Termination

## Master Abort: Target Doesn't Claim Transaction

### Introduction

An initiator performs a master-abort for one of several reasons. Generally speaking, master abort occurs when the transaction is not claimed by a target (DEVSEL# is not sampled asserted within a pre-defined period of time). This could occur for a number of reasons. The following are some examples:

- **No device resides at the address** driven onto the bus by the initiator. When this is the case, no target will assert DEVSEL# to claim the transaction. This is considered to be an error. The master must set the MASTER ABORT DETECTED bit in its configuration status register. It should then alert software that a problem has been encountered (usually, by generating an interrupt).
- When the initiator has started a **special cycle** to broadcast a message to multiple targets simultaneously, no target asserts DEVSEL# in response. If multiple targets recognized the message and responded to the transaction by asserting DEVSEL#, the DEVSEL# line would be in contention between multiple drivers. Master abort is the normal termination of a special cycle and is not considered to be an error.
- When a **configuration access** is attempted by the host/PCI bridge **with a non-existent target**, DEVSEL# isn't sampled asserted. When this occurs on a configuration read, the host/PCI bridge must return all ones to the processor. On a configuration write, the processor write is permitted to terminate normally (e.g., BRDY# asserted to the Intel x86, or TA# asserted to the PowerPC).
- When a bus master initiates a transaction **using a reserved command**, no target responds and the result is a master abort.

There are two possible cases to consider:

- The initiator starts a single data phase transaction and aborts it due to no response. This case is illustrated in figure 9-2.
- The initiator starts a multi-data phase transaction and aborts it due to no response. This case is illustrated in figure 9-3.

## Master Abort on Single Data Phase Transaction

Refer to figure 9-2. The initiator starts the transaction at the start of clock one by asserting FRAME# and driving the address onto the AD bus and the command type onto the Command/Byte Enable lines. During the first and only data phase of this transaction, the initiator asserts IRDY# (during clock three in this example) to indicate its readiness to complete the transfer. At the same time, it deasserts FRAME#, indicating to the target that this is the final data phase.

During the data phase, the initiator samples DEVSEL# on clocks three through five to determine if a PCI target with a fast, medium or slow decoder claims the transaction. In this example, DEVSEL# is sampled deasserted each time. The initiator then samples DEVSEL# a final time on clock six to determine if the subtractive decoder in the PCI/expansion bus bridge has claimed the transaction. In the example, the transaction has not been claimed by any target, so the initiator must abort the transaction and return the bus to the idle state in an orderly fashion. This is accomplished by deasserting IRDY# during clock six. The bus is idle on clock seven and is available for use by another master.

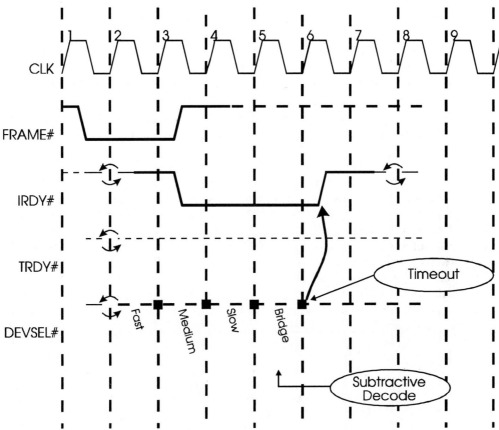

*Figure 9-2. Example of Master-Abort on Single-Data Phase Transaction*
*(note: this is not a special cycle)*

## Master Abort on Multi-Data Phase Transaction

Figure 9-3 illustrates an example of a multi-data phase transaction that results in a master abort. During the data phase, the initiator asserts IRDY# (during clock three in this example; it could be asserted earlier or later) when it is ready to complete the first data phase, but keeps FRAME# asserted to indicate its intention to perform a second data phase upon the completion of this one.

The initiator samples DEVSEL# on clocks three through five to determine if a PCI target with a fast, medium or slow decoder has claimed the transaction. In this example, DEVSEL# is sampled deasserted each time. The initiator then samples DEVSEL# a final time on clock six to determine if the subtractive decoder in the PCI/expansion bus bridge has claimed the transaction. In the example, the transaction has not been claimed by any target, so the initiator must abort the transaction and return the bus to the idle state in an orderly fashion. This is accomplished by deasserting FRAME# in clock six and then IRDY# in clock seven. This returns the bus to the idle state on clock eight.

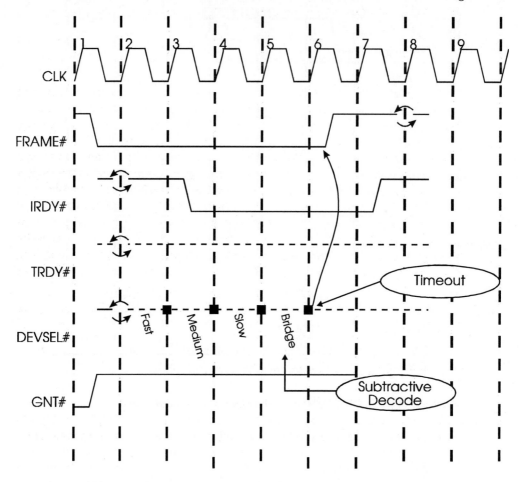

*Figure 9-3. Example of Master-Abort on Multiple Data Phase Transaction*

# Chapter 9: Premature Transaction Termination

### Action Taken by Master in Response to Master Abort

#### General

When the initiator experiences a master-abort, it must set its MASTER ABORT DETECTED bit in its configuration status register and report the error back to the device driver (typically, via an interrupt request).

#### Special Cycle and Configuration Access

The status bit should not be set, however, if the abort was experienced during a special cycle or a configuration access. Regarding the special cycle case, no target is expected to respond (assert DEVSEL#) during a special cycle. With reference to the configuration access, it is entirely possible that the programmer will stimulate the host/PCI bridge to attempt a configuration read from a device that doesn't exist. At power up time, the configuration software performs a series of configuration reads to determine the presence or absence of devices on the PCI bus. The host/PCI bridge must be designed to return all ones (hex Fs) to the host processor when a master abort results from a configuration read attempt. If a master abort results from a configuration write attempt, the data driven to the non-existent PCI target falls on the floor (i.e., no one cares). With respect to the host processor, the host/PCI bridge acts as if the write completed normally.

# Target-Initiated Termination

# STOP# Signal

A target may use the STOP# signal to instruct the initiator to prematurely end the transaction on the current data phase. Using the DEVSEL# and TRDY# signals in conjunction with STOP#, the target can indicate one of the following to the initiator:

- Disconnect upon completion of the current data phase (the current doubleword is transferred). There are two variants: **disconnect A and B**. The initiator may choose to continue the transfer (starting with the next doubleword) at a later time, or may choose not to resume the transaction (this might occur if it were prefetching and did not really need the data).
- Disconnect during the current data phase without transferring the current doubleword. This is referred to as **disconnect C**. The initiator may choose

to continue the transfer (starting with the current doubleword) at a later time, or may choose not to resume the transaction (this might occur if it were prefetching and did not really need the data).

- Issue a **retry** during the first data phase. No data is transferred during the transaction and the initiator is obliged to retry the transaction later.
- **Target abort** the transaction and do not retry (no data is transferred).

## Disconnect

### Disconnect A and B

Disconnect A or B is indicated to the initiator by asserting TRDY# and STOP# while keeping DEVSEL# asserted. This tells the initiator that the target is ready to transfer the current data item (TRDY# asserted) and then stop the transfer (STOP# asserted). DEVSEL# remaining asserted gives the initiator permission to resume the transaction at a later time (if so desired; resumption is not mandatory) at the point that it left off (on the doubleword that would have been transferred in the next data phase).

Disconnect A and B are differentiated from each other by the state of IRDY# at the point where the disconnect is indicated. It is a disconnect A if IRDY# is not asserted when STOP# and TRDY# are asserted. See clock two in figure 9 - 4. In this case, the current doubleword cannot be transferred until the initiator asserts IRDY#. When IRDY# is asserted (on clock three), the initiator also deasserts FRAME#, indicating that this is the final data phase. The current doubleword is transferred and the transaction ends. The target deasserts STOP#, TRDY# and DEVSEL# in clock three.

It is a disconnect B if IRDY# is asserted when STOP# and TRDY# are asserted. In this case, the current doubleword is transferred on that clock (clock two) and no more data is transferred. FRAME# is still asserted. Normally, the initiator deasserts FRAME# when it asserts IRDY# for the last data phase, but in this case the initiator did not know this was the last data phase when it asserted IRDY#. For this reason, in clock two the initiator keeps IRDY# asserted and deasserts FRAME#, indicating that it is ready to complete the final data phase. Both the initiator and the target know that no data will be transferred in this "null" data phase, however. The target deasserts TRDY# to enforce this fact. In clock three, IRDY# is deasserted to return the bus to the idle state. The target deasserts STOP# and DEVSEL# (the target is not permitted to deassert them until it samples FRAME# deasserted).

# Chapter 9: Premature Transaction Termination

Assuming that the master decides to resume the transfer, after keeping its REQ# deasserted for two PCI clocks, the master should then reassert its REQ# and re-arbitrate for bus ownership. When it has successfully re-acquired bus ownership, the initiator should re-initiate the transaction using the double-word address of the next data item that would have been transferred if the disconnect had not occurred. In other words, the initiator should resume the transfer where it left off. This implies that the master must "remember" the address to resume at.

A master that experiences a disconnect has transferred at least one data item. The master is not required to resume the transaction later (because it may have been prefetching).

Some targets only support single data phase transactions. When a master attempts a multiple data phase transaction, the target asserts STOP# along with TRDY# during the first data phase of the burst. This informs the master that the target is ready to transfer the current data item, but is also instructing the master to disconnect from it after the transfer has taken place. The master terminates the transaction as instructed. If the master intends to continue the data transfer, it arbitrates for the bus again and then reinitiates the burst starting with the next doubleword.

Cacheable memory target are not permitted to disconnect a memory write and invalidate transaction except at cache line boundaries. This is necessary because the snooper (the host/PCI bridge) may have already eliminated a modified copy of the line based on the master's promise to overwrite the entire line in memory).

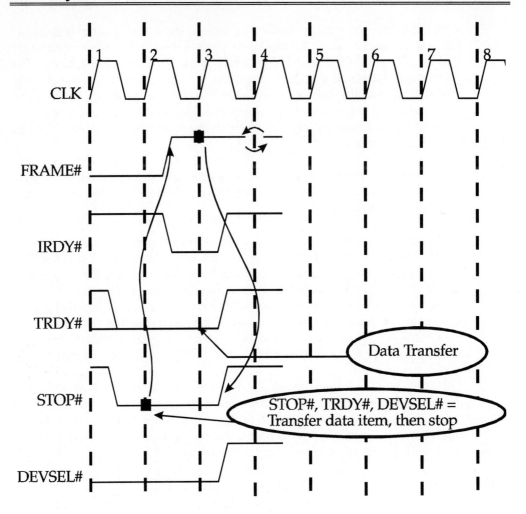

*Figure 9-4. Type "A" Disconnect*

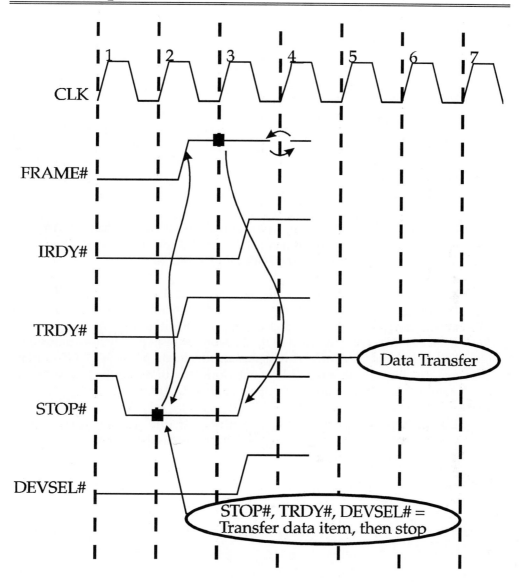

*Figure 9-5. Type "B" Disconnect*

## Disconnect C

Refer to figure 9 - 6. Assume that at least one data phase has completed (on clock one) and at least one doubleword has therefore been transferred. When the initiator completed the previous data phase and entered the current one (in clock one), it kept IRDY# asserted to indicate that it is ready to complete the current data phase. It did not, however, deassert FRAME# because this isn't the final data phase. In this data phase, the target asserts STOP# (during clock one) and deasserts TRDY#, indicating that it wants the initiator to terminate the transaction on this data phase with no data transferred. In response, the initiator keeps IRDY# asserted (in clock two) and deasserts FRAME#, indicating that the final data phase in progress. No data is transferred in this last data phase, however, because the target has TRDY# deasserted. In clock three, the initiator deasserts IRDY#, returning the bus to the idle state. The target deasserts STOP# and DEVSEL#.

Figure 9 - 7 also illustrates a disconnect C, but the initiator has deasserted IRDY# upon entry to the current data phase. When the initiator discovers (on the rising-edge of clock two) that the target wants it to stop on this data phase without transferring the current doubleword, it responds by asserting IRDY# and deasserting FRAME#. This signals the final data phase (a null data transfer). The initiator deasserts IRDY# one clock later to return the bus to the idle state and the target deasserts STOP# and DEVSEL#.

Upon receipt of a disconnect C, the initiator has the option of resuming the transaction later or not. If it was prefetching data that wasn't explicitly required, it may choose not to.

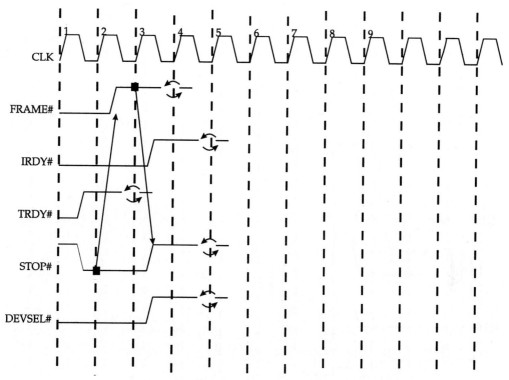

*Figure 9 - 6. Disconnect C Issued with IRDY# Asserted*

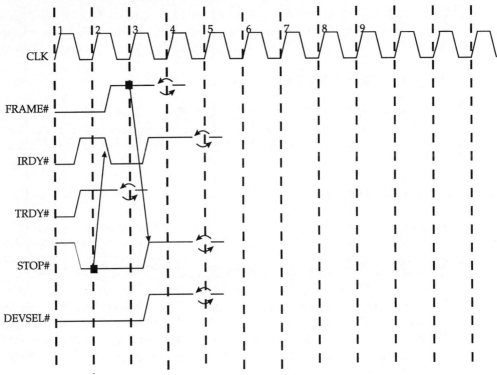

*Figure 9 - 7. Disconnect C Issued without IRDY# Deasserted*

## Reasons Target Issues Disconnect

### Target Slow to Complete Data Phase

Assume that the target determines that the **latency to complete any data phase** (including the first) will be **longer than eight PCI clocks and the initiator intends to perform another data phase (FRAME# is still asserted)**. The target must issue a disconnect C to the initiator on or before the eighth clock of the current data phase. *It should be noted that this rule is new in revision 2.1 of the specification. The target used to be permitted to take as long as it needed to transfer a data item and would then issue a disconnect A or B to the initiator. In essence, the old wording of this rule permitted a target to tie up the bus for long periods of time.*

# Chapter 9: Premature Transaction Termination

This rule ensures that a slow target will not tie up the bus for extended periods of time. This subject is covered in the chapter entitled "PCI Bus Arbitration" in the section entitled "Preventing Target From Monopolizing Bus."

### Target Doesn't Support Burst Mode

If a target doesn't support burst mode and it detects that the master intends to perform a second data phase (FRAME# is still asserted), it must issue a disconnect A or B to the initiator during the first data phase. Alternately, it may issue a disconnect C in the second data phase.

### Memory Target Doesn't Understand Addressing Sequence

If a **memory target doesn't understand the addressing sequence** indicated by the initiator via AD[1:0] during the address phase, the target must issue a disconnect A or B to the initiator when it is ready to complete the first data phase, or, as an alternative, may issue a disconnect C during the second data phase. This forces the initiator to fragment a burst transaction into single data phase transactions that the target can handle. The initiator may be using an AD[1:0] pattern defined in a later revision of the specification than the target was designed to. This subject is covered in the chapter entitled "The Read and Write Transfers" in the section entitled "Addressing Sequence During Memory Burst".

### Transfer Crosses Over Target's Address Boundary

If a target determines during the current data phase that the initiator intends to perform another data phase (FRAME# is still asserted) and that the **current data item is the last within its address boundaries**, it must issue a **disconnect A or B** when it is ready to complete the current data phase. This forces the master to terminate the transaction upon transferring the last data item in this target's space. Alternately, the target could issue a **disconnect C** in the data phase after the target's last doubleword is transferred. The master then waits two PCI clocks and reasserts its REQ# to request ownership of the bus again. When it has re-acquired bus ownership, it resumes its transaction using the next doubleword address. This gives an opportunity to another target that implements the next sequential doubleword address to claim the transaction, thereby permitting the transfer to continue across target boundaries.

### Burst Memory Transfer Crosses Cache Line Boundary

During a memory burst transaction, a cacheable PCI memory target detects that the initiator intends to perform another data phase (FRAME# is still asserted) after completion of the current data phase and is transferring the last doubleword within the current cache line in the current data phase. In order to force the bus master to generate the start address of the next cache line to be snooped by the host/PCI bridge, the target must issue a disconnect A or B when it is ready to transfer the last doubleword of the current line. This forces the bus master to yield bus ownership, re-arbitrate for ownership again, and then initiate a new memory transaction starting at the first doubleword of the next cache line. This permits the snooper (the host/PCI bridge) to snoop the next line address in the processor's L1 and L2 caches.

# Retry

A target only issues retry to the initiator if cannot permit any data to be transferred during the current transaction. In other words, it is a rule that if a target is going to issue a retry to the initiator, it must do it on the first data phase. The signaling for a retry is identical as that for a disconnect C except that it occurs in the first data phase. Unlike the disconnect C, however, the initiator is required to re-attempt the transaction at a later time when it receives a retry.

Retry is indicated to the initiator (by the target) by asserting STOP# and deasserting TRDY# while keeping DEVSEL# asserted. This tells the initiator that the target does not intend to transfer the current data item (TRDY# deasserted) and that the initiator must stop the transaction on this data phase (STOP# asserted). The continued assertion of DEVSEL# indicates that the initiator must retry the transaction at a later time. Furthermore, it must use the exact same address, command and byte enables. If it's a write, it must use exactly the same data in the first data phase. This rule is unconditional. The access must be retried as many times as it takes to complete the transfer. If the master also has target capability, it must respond to accesses by other masters that occur in between its attempts to retry the transaction.

The specification cites the example of a multi-function device with three functions. More than one function in a multi-function device may have bus master capability. Assume that the device has three functions all having bus master capability. Such a device only has one pair of REQ#/GNT# signals, however. Assume that function zero initiates a transaction and receives a retry. It must try the transaction again later. If the GNT# line is still asserted, function one can perform a transaction, and, when it's finished, function three can perform a transaction. Assume that function one's transaction completes, but function two's transaction receives a retry. Both function zero and function two must periodically re-attempt their retried transactions until they are able to complete them.

Figures 9 - 8 and 9 - 9 illustrate two variants on the retry. In figure 9 - 8 the initiator has already asserted IRDY# when the target issues the retry. When the retry is received, the initiator responds by keeping IRDY# asserted (in clock two) and deasserting FRAME#. One clock later it deasserts IRDY# to return the bus to the idle state. The target deasserts STOP# and DEVSEL#. In figure 9 - 9 the initiator has not yet asserted IRDY# when it receives the retry from the target. In response, the initiator asserts IRDY# (in clock two) and deasserts FRAME#. One clock later, it deasserts IRDY# to return the bus to the idle state. The target deasserts STOP# and DEVSEL#.

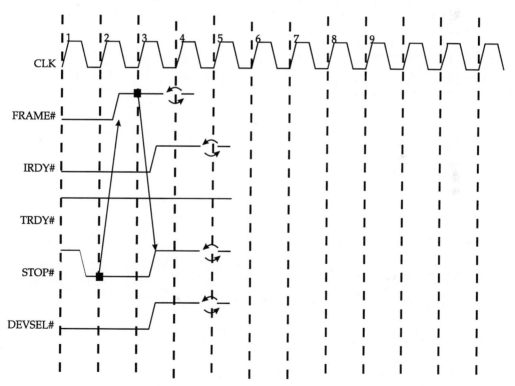

*Figure 9 - 8. Retry Received with IRDY# Asserted*

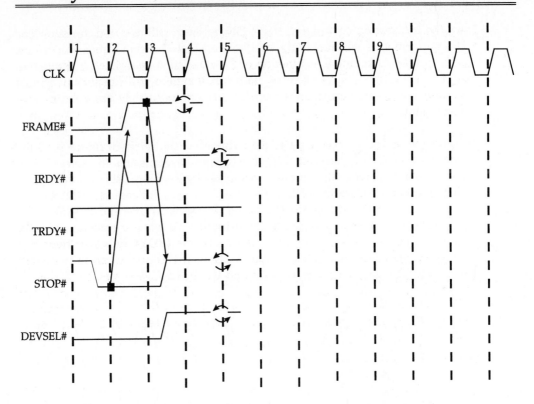

*Figure 9 - 9. Rertry Received without IRDY# Deasserted*

## Reasons Target Issues Retry

### Target Very Slow to Complete First Data Phase

If the latency to first data phase completion will be longer than 16 PCI clocks, the target must issue a retry to the initiator. This rule prevents a target with a very long latency to first data phase completion from monopolizing the bus. This subject is covered in the chapter entitled "PCI Bus Arbitration" in the section entitled "Preventing Target From Monopolizing Bus."

### Snoop Hit on Modified Cache Line

A cacheable PCI memory target is not permitted to accept or supply data (i.e., it may not assert TRDY#) until the snoop result is presented (on SDONE and SBO#) by the snooper. If a cacheable PCI memory target determines that the snooper (the processor's L1 or L2 cache) experienced a snoop hit on a modi-

# Chapter 9: Premature Transaction Termination

fied line (SDONE and SBO# asserted), the target must retry the initiator. The cache then arbitrates for bus ownership and writes the modified cache line into the cacheable PCI memory target. The snooper then either eliminates the the line from its cache (if snooping a memory write by the master), or marks its copy clean (if snooping a memory read by the master). The retried master then re-attempts its access. The transaction is snooped again, resulting in a clean snoop this time (SDONE asserted and SBO# deasserted). The target asserts TRDY# and accepts data from or supplies data to the master. This subject is covered in the chapter entitled "PCI Cache Support."

### Resource Busy

If a target recognizes that a necessary resource is currently busy, it should immediately issue a retry to the initiator. An example would be an attempt by a PCI master to access an EISA target while the EISA bus is currently owned by an EISA bus master. In that case, the PCI/EISA bridge should immediately issue a retry to the PCI master to force it to free the PCI bus for use by other masters. This subject is covered in the chapter entitled "PCI Bus Arbitration" in the section entitled "Preventing Target From Monopolizing Bus."

### Memory Target Locked

A locked memory target must issue a retry when a master other than the one that locked it attempts to access it. This subject is covered in the chapter entitled "Shared Resource Acquisition."

## Host Bridge Retry Counter

The specification recommends (not a requirement) that the host/PCI bridge implement a retry counter. The counter is initialized whenever the bridge successfully transfers data during a transaction. Each time that the bridge experiences a retry during a data transfer, the counter is decremented (or incremented). When the retry count limit (implementation-specific) has been reached, the bridge should discontinue retries of the transaction and should permit the host processor to complete the transaction in progress. On a read, the bridge should supply dummy data to the processor. On a write, the bridge should pretend that the write completed with no problems. After permitting the processor to complete the transaction, the bridge would then generate an interrupt to alert the processor that a problem exists.

This recommendation exists for the following reason. Assume that the host processor initiates a host bus transaction to perform a read from a PCI target device. The bridge arbitrates for ownership of the PCI bus and initiates the transaction. In response, the addressed target issues a retry, causing the bridge to terminate the PCI transaction without transferring the requested data to the processor. After two PCI clocks, the bridge re-arbitrates for ownership of the PCI bus, retries the read transaction and again receives a retry in response.

The bridge keeps inserting wait states into the host processor's bus transaction while it awaits the requested data. If the target continues to issue retries for an extended period, the host processor cannot recognize an external interrupt that is awaiting servicing during this period (the interrupt the host/PCI bridge generates to signal the excessive retry condition). The processor cannot recognize the interrupt and use its bus to fetch and execute the interrupt service routine until the current bus cycle is permitted to complete.

## Target Abort

### Description

If a target detects a fatal error or will never be able to respond to the transaction, it may signal a target-abort. This instructs the initiator to end the transaction and indicates that the target does not want the transaction resumed. It also means that any data already transferred during this transaction may be corrupted. The initiator should set the TARGET-ABORT DETECTED bit in its configuration status register and the target should set the SIGNALED TARGET-ABORT bit in its configuration status register.

Target abort is indicated to the initiator by asserting STOP#, deasserting TRDY# and deasserting DEVSEL# early. This tells the initiator that the target will not transfer the current data item (TRDY# deasserted) and that the initiator must stop the transaction on the current data phase (STOP# asserted). The early deassertion of DEVSEL# instructs the initiator not to re-attempt the transaction.

# Chapter 9: Premature Transaction Termination

## Reasons Target Issues Target Abort

### Broken Target

If a target is broken and unable to transfer data, it may indicate this by issuing a target abort to the master.

### I/O Addressing Error

I/O address error. This subject is covered in the chapter entitled "The Read and Write Transfers" in the section entitled "Situation Resulting In Target Abort."

### Address Phase Parity Error

One of the ways a target can respond to a parity error detected at the completion of the address phase (in addition to its assertion of SERR#) is to issue a target abort to the initiator.

### Master Abort on Other Side of PCI-to-PCI Bridge

When a PCI-to-PCI bridge passes a transaction through the bridge for an initiator and the transaction is not claimed by a target on the other bus, the bridge master aborts the unclaimed transaction on the destination bus and target aborts the transaction on the initiating bus.

## Master's Response to Target Abort

In response to a target abort, the initiator takes one of the following actions:

- Generates an **interrupt** to alert its related device driver to check its status.
- Generates **SERR#** (assuming the master's SERR ENABLED bit is set to one in its PCI configuration command register). For more information on SERR#, refer to the chapter entitled "Error Detection and Handling."

## Target Abort Example

Figure 9-10 illustrates a target signaling a target-abort. To indicate that it wishes to abort the transaction, the target asserts STOP# and deasserts TRDY# (if it wasn't already deasserted) and DEVSEL#. This instructs the initiator to stop on the current data phase (STOP# asserted) with no data transferred

(TRDY# deasserted) and not to retry the transaction again (DEVSEL# deasserted early).

The initiator samples the state of STOP#, TRDY# and DEVSEL# at the rising-edge of clock two and responds by deasserting FRAME# and asserting IRDY# (if it wasn't already asserted) during clock cell two. This indicates that the initiator is ready to complete the final data phase (a null data phase). During clock three, the target deasserts STOP# (in response to sampling FRAME# deasserted). At the same time, the initiator deasserts IRDY#, returning the bus to the idle state on clock four.

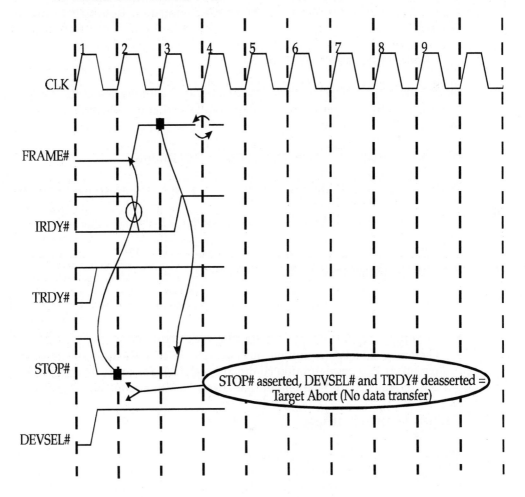

*Figure 9-10. Target-Abort Example*

# Chapter 9: Premature Transaction Termination

## How Soon Does Initiator Attempt to Re-Establish Transfer After Retry or Disconnect?

In the event of a target-initiated retry, the initiator must repeat the transaction again. Resumption of a transaction terminated with a disconnect (A, B or C) is optional. The initiator must deassert its REQ# line for a minimum of two PCI clocks: one when the bus goes idle (FRAME# and IRDY# deasserted) and another either the clock immediately before or after the return to idle. This provides lower-priority bus masters with an opportunity to gain bus ownership. If the initiator intends to complete the data transfer that was disconnected or retried, it must reassert its REQ# again after its two clock deassertion (or it may experience starvation).

## Target-Initiated Termination Summary

Table 9-1 summarizes the three cases of target-initiated termination.

*Table 9-1. Target-Initiated Termination Summary*

| Termination Type | TRDY# | STOP# | DEVSEL# | Data Transfer? | Comments |
|---|---|---|---|---|---|
| Disconnect **A** or **B** | asserted | asserted | asserted | some data transferred, including current doubleword | If master wants to transfer more data, transaction will be re-initiated on next doubleword address. |
| Disconnect **C** | deasserted | asserted | asserted | some data transferred, but not current doubleword | Occurs in a data phase other than the first. The master may resume the transaction or not. If resumed, it will start on the same doubleword. |
| Retry | deasserted | asserted | asserted | no | Occurs in first data phase. Master is obliged to retry the transaction. |
| Target Abort | deasserted | asserted | deasserted | perhaps | Fatal error; no retry. |

# Chapter 10

## Prior To This Chapter

The previous chapter described circumstances under which the initiator or target may need to abort a transaction and the mechanisms provided to accomplish the abort.

## In This Chapter

The PCI bus architecture provides two error reporting mechanisms: one for reporting data parity errors and the other for reporting more serious system errors. This chapter provides a discussion of error detection, reporting and handling using these two mechanisms.

## The Next Chapter

The next chapter provides a discussion of interrupt-related issues.

## Introduction to PCI Parity

The PCI bus is parity-protected during both the address and data phases of a transaction. A single parity bit, PAR, protects AD[31:0] and C/BE#[3:0]. If a 64-bit data transfer is in progress, an additional parity bit, PAR64, protects AD[63:32] and C/BE#[7:4]. 64-bit parity has the same timing as 32-bit parity and is discussed in the chapter entitled "The 64-Bit PCI Extension."

The PCI device driving the AD bus during the address phase or any data phase of a transaction must always drive a full 32-bit pattern onto the AD bus (because parity is based on the full content of the AD bus and the C/BE bus). This includes:

- Special and interrupt acknowledge transactions where the address bus doesn't contain a valid address, and during type zero configuration transactions where AD[31:11] do not contain valid information.
- Data phases where the device supplying data isn't supplying all four bytes (because all four byte enables are not asserted).

The PCI device driving the AD bus during the address phase or any data phase of a transaction is responsible for calculating and supplying the parity bit for the phase one clock after the address or data is first driven onto the bus (when TRDY# is asserted during a read data phase to indicate the presence of the read data on the bus, or IRDY# is asserted during a write data phase to indicate the presence of the write data on the bus). Even parity is used. The computed parity bit supplied on PAR must be set (or cleared) so that the 37-bit field consisting of AD[31:0], C/BE#[3:0] and PAR contains an even number of one bits.

During the PCI clock cycle immediately following the conclusion of the address phase or any data phase of a transaction, the PCI agent receiving the address or data computes expected parity based on the information latched from AD[31:0] and C/BE#[3:0]. The agent supplying the parity bit must present it on the rising clock edge that immediately follows the conclusion of the address phase or one clock after presentation of data during a data phase. The device(s) receiving the address or data expect the parity to be present and stable at that point. The computed parity bit is then compared to the parity bit actually received on PAR to determine if address or data corruption has occurred. If the parity is correct, no action is taken. If the parity is incorrect, the error must be reported. This subject is covered in the sections that follow.

During a read transaction where the initiator is inserting wait states by delaying assertion of IRDY#, the initiator can be designed to sample the target's data (when TRDY# is sampled asserted), calculate expected parity, sample actual parity (on the clock edge after TRDY# sampled asserted) and assert PERR# (if the parity is incorrect). In this case, the initiator must keep PERR# asserted until two clocks after the completion of the data phase.

During a write transaction where the target is inserting wait states by delaying assertion of TRDY#, the target can be designed to sample the initiator's data (when IRDY# is sampled asserted), calculate expected parity, sample actual parity (on the clock edge after IRDY# sampled asserted) and assert PERR# (if the parity is incorrect). In this case, the target must keep PERR# asserted until two clocks after the completion of the data phase.

# Chapter 10: Error Detection and Handling

## PERR# Signal

PERR# is a sustained tri-state signal used to signal the detection of a parity error related to a data phase. There is one exception to this rule: a parity error detected on a data phase during a special cycle is reported using SERR# rather than PERR#. This subject is covered later in this chapter in the section entitled "Special Case: Data Parity Error During Special Cycle."

PERR# is implemented as an output on targets and as an input/output on masters. Although PERR# is bussed to all PCI devices, it is guaranteed to be driven by only one device at a time (the initiator on a read, or the target on a write). Additional detail on the usage and timing of the PERR# signal can be found under the heading "Data Parity" later in this chapter.

## Data Parity

### Data Parity Generation and Checking on Read

#### Introduction

During each data phase of a read transaction, the target drives data onto the AD bus. It is therefore the target's responsibility to supply correct parity to the initiator on PAR during the clock immediately following the assertion of TRDY#. At the conclusion of each data phase, it is the initiator's responsibility to latch the contents of AD[31:0] and C/BE#[3:0] and to calculate the expected parity during the clock cycle immediately following the conclusion of the data phase. The initiator then latches the parity bit supplied by the target from the PAR signal on the next rising-edge of the PCI clock and compares computed vs. actual parity. If a miscompare occurs, the initiator then asserts PERR# during the next clock. The assertion of PERR# lags the conclusion of each data phase by two PCI clock cycles.

The platform design may or may not include logic that monitors PERR# during a read and takes some system-specific action when it is asserted by a PCI master that has received corrupted data. The master may also take other actions in addition to the assertion of PERR#. The section (in this chapter) entitled "Data Parity Reporting" provides a detailed discussion of the actions taken by a bus master upon receipt of bad data.

## Example Burst Read

Refer to the read burst transaction illustrated in figure 10-1 during this discussion. The initiator drives the address and command onto the bus during the address phase (clock one). The targets latch the address and command on clock two and begin address decode. In this example, the target has a fast address decoder and asserts DEVSEL# during clock two. In addition, the following occurs during clock two:

- All targets that latched the address and command compute the expected parity based on the information latched from AD[31:0] and C/BE#[3:0].
- The initiator sets the parity signal, PAR, to the appropriate value to force even parity.
- The target keeps TRDY# deasserted to insert the wait state necessary for the turnaround cycle on the AD bus.

On clock three, the targets latch the PAR bit and compare it to the expected parity computed during clock two. If any of the targets have a miscompare, they assert SERR# (if the PARITY ERROR RESPONSE and SERR# ENABLE bits in their respective configuration command registers are set to one) within two clocks (recommended) after the error was detected. This subject is covered in the section in this chapter entitled "Address Parity."

During clock three, the target begins to drive the first data item onto the AD bus and asserts TRDY# to indicate its presence. The initiator latches the data on clock four (IRDY# and TRDY# are sampled asserted).

During clock four, the target drives the PAR signal to the appropriate state for first data phase parity. The initiator computes the expected parity. The initiator latches PAR on clock five and compares it to the expected parity. If the parity is incorrect, the initiator asserts PERR# during clock five.

The second data phase begins during clock four. The target drives the second data item onto the bus and keeps TRDY# asserted to indicate its presence. The initiator latches the data on clock five (IRDY# and TRDY# sampled asserted). During clock five, the initiator computes the expected parity. The actual parity is latched from PAR on clock six and checked against the expected parity. If an error is detected, the initiator asserts PERR# during clock six.

The third data phase begins on clock five. The target drives the third data item onto the AD bus and keeps TRDY# asserted to indicate its presence. The initiator deasserts IRDY# to indicate that it is not yet ready to accept the third data item (e.g., it has a buffer full condition). When the initiator samples TRDY# asserted on clock six, this qualifies the presence of the third data item on the bus. The initiator can be designed to submit the data (along with the byte enables) to its parity generator at this point. Assuming that it is designed this way, the initiator can latch the PAR bit from the bus on clock seven (it's a rule that the target must present PAR one clock after presenting the data). At the earliest, then, the initiator could detect a parity miscompare during clock seven and assert PERR#. It must keep PERR# asserted until two clocks after completion of the data phase. During the third data phase, the initiator re-asserts IRDY# during clock seven and deasserts FRAME# to indicate that it is ready to complete the final data phase. The final data phase completes on clock eight when IRDY# and TRDY# are sampled asserted. The initiator reads the final data item from the bus at that point. At the latest (if early parity check wasn't performed), the initiator must sample PAR one clock afterwards, on clock nine, and, in the event of an error, must assert PERR# during clock nine.

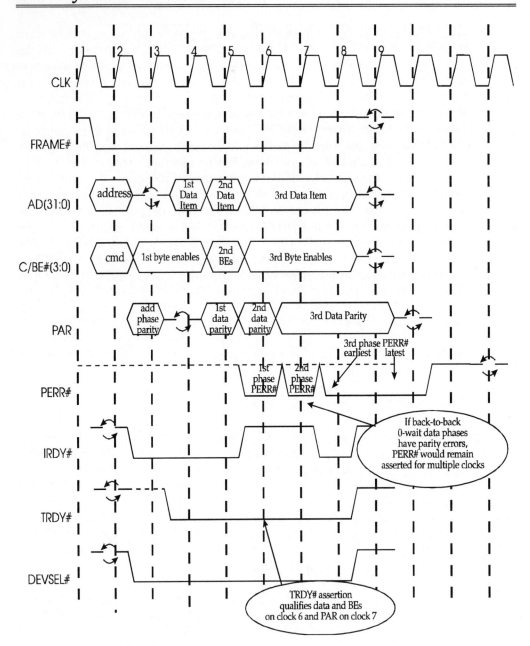

*Figure 10-1. Parity on Read Transaction*

## Data Parity Generation and Checking on Write

### Introduction

During each data phase of a write transaction, the initiator drives data onto the AD bus. It is therefore the initiator's responsibility to supply correct parity to the target on PAR during the clock immediately following the assertion of IRDY#. At the conclusion of each data phase, it is the target's responsibility to latch the contents of AD[31:0] and C/BE#[3:0] and to calculate the expected parity during the clock cycle immediately following the conclusion of the data phase. The target then latches the parity bit supplied by the initiator from the PAR signal on the next rising-edge of the PCI clock and compares computed vs. actual parity. If a miscompare occurs, the target then asserts PERR# during the next clock. The assertion of PERR# lags the conclusion of each data phase by two PCI clock cycles. During a burst write, it is the initiator's responsibility to sample the state of the PERR# signal on the second rising-edge of the PCI clock after the conclusion of each data phase. If it samples PERR# asserted by the target, this indicates that the last data item written to the target was corrupted in flight. The section (in this chapter) entitled "Data Parity Reporting" provides a detailed discussion of the actions taken by a bus master upon detection of a data phase parity error.

### Example Burst Write

Refer to the write burst transaction illustrated in figure 10-2 during the following discussion. The address phase completes on clock two. All targets latch the address and command. During clock two, all targets compute the expected parity. During clock two, the initiator supplies the parity bit on the PAR signal. All targets latch PAR on clock three. They then compare expected vs. actual parity. If an error were detected, the target(s) that detected the miscompare would assert SERR# (if the PARITY ERROR RESPONSE and SERR# ENABLE bits in their respective configuration command registers are set to one) within two clocks (recommended).

The first data phase starts during clock two. The initiator supplies the first data item on the AD bus and asserts IRDY# to indicate its presence. The first data item is latched by the target on clock two (IRDY# and TRDY# sampled asserted). During clock three, the initiator supplies the parity bit on PAR. The target computes the expected parity. The actual parity is latched on clock four and is compared to the expected parity. In the event of an error, the target asserts PERR# in clock four (if the PARITY ERROR RESPONSE bit in its configuration command register is set to one) back to the initiator to indicate that the first data item was corrupted in flight. The initiator samples PERR# on clock five to determine if the first data item transferred with no errors.

The second data phase starts during clock three. The initiator drives the second data item onto the AD bus and the second set of byte enables onto the C/BE bus. The target latches the data and byte enables on clock four (IRDY# and TRDY# sampled asserted). During clock four, the target computes the expected parity. The actual parity is latched on clock five and is compared to the expected parity. In the event of an error, the target, if enabled to report parity errors, asserts PERR# (in clock five) back to the initiator to indicate that the second data item was corrupted in flight. The initiator samples PERR# on clock six to determine if the second data item transferred with no errors.

The third data phase starts during clock four. The initiator drives the third data item onto the AD bus and the third set of byte enables onto the C/BE bus. The target deasserts TRDY#, indicating that it isn't yet ready to accept the third data item (e.g., it has a buffer full condition). The initiator keeps IRDY# asserted and deasserts FRAME#, indicating that it is ready to complete the final data transfer. The target asserts TRDY# and latches the data and byte enables on clock four (IRDY# and TRDY# sampled asserted).

The target could be designed to check parity and report a parity error while its inserting wait states in the data phase. In this example, the target latches the data and byte enables on clock five (because IRDY# is asserted, indicating that the data is present) and submits them to its parity generator to compute the expected parity during clock five. Also during clock five, the initiator begins to drive the parity bit onto PAR. The target then latches PAR on clock six and compares the actual parity to the expected parity. In the event of an error, the target asserts PERR# during clock six. It must keep PERR# asserted until two clocks after completion of the data phase. During the third data phase, the target re-asserts TRDY# during clock six to indicate that it is ready to complete the data phase. The final data phase completes on clock seven when IRDY# and TRDY# are sampled asserted. The target latches the final data item from the bus at that point. At the latest (if early parity check wasn't performed), the target must sample PAR one clock afterwards, on clock eight, and, in the event of an error, must assert PERR# during clock eight.

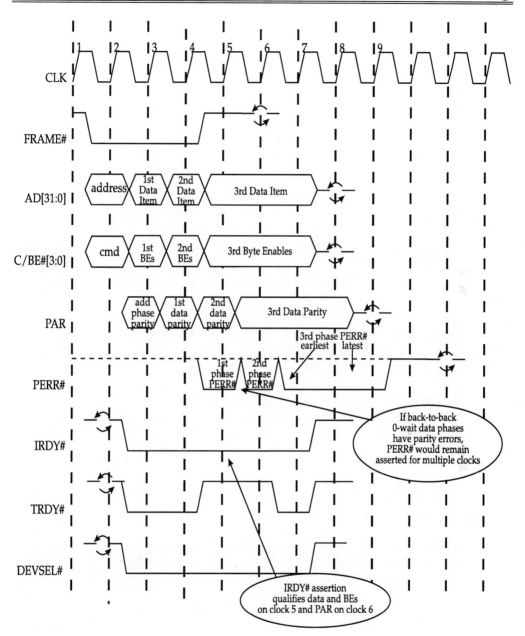

*Figure 10-2. Parity on Write Transaction*

## Data Parity Reporting

### General

Upon detection of a data phase parity error, the device that checked the parity is responsible for asserting the DETECTED PARITY ERROR bit in its PCI configuration status register. It also asserts PERR# if the PARITY ERROR RESPONSE bit in its PCI configuration command register is set to one. Only two categories of devices are excluded from the requirement to implement the PERR# signal and the PARITY ERROR RESPONSE bit. They are described in the section entitled "Devices Excluded From PERR# Requirement" later in this chapter.

If a data phase parity error is detected, PERR# must be asserted (at the latest) in the second clock after completion of the data phase (i.e., one clock after PAR is latched). Once PERR# is asserted, it must not be deasserted until during the third clock after the data phase completes. Figures 10-1 and 10-2 both illustrate examples where the devices receiving the data checked parity and asserted PERR# before the completion of the data phase.

### Parity Error During Read

During a read transaction, the target sources the data and the parity. The initiator receives the data and parity and checks the parity for correctness. If the data is incorrect, the initiator must set the DETECTED PARITY ERROR bit in its PCI configuration status register (irrespective of the state of its PARITY ERROR RESPONSE bit). Assuming that the initiator's PARITY ERROR RESPONSE bit is set to one, the initiator asserts PERR# in the second clock immediately following completion of the data phase and sets the DATA PARITY REPORTED bit in its configuration status register.

Whether or not the bus master continues the transaction or terminates it is master design-dependent. The specification recommends that the transaction be continued to completion. In addition to the assertion of PERR#, the bus master is required to report the parity error to the system software. The specification recommends utilization of an interrupt or the setting of a bit in a status register that is polled by the device driver. Alternately, the designer can assert SERR#, but this approach should not be used lightly. It will more than likely result in a system shutdown. In a particular platform design, the chip set logic may convert any assertion of PERR# into SERR#.

# Chapter 10: Error Detection and Handling

## Parity Error During Write

During a write transaction, the initiator sources the data and the parity. The target receives the data and parity and checks the parity for correctness. If the data is incorrect, the target must set its DETECTED PARITY ERROR bit to one (irrespective of the state of its PARITY ERROR RESPONSE bit). Assuming that the target's PARITY ERROR RESPONSE bit is set to one, the target asserts PERR# in the second clock immediately following completion of the data phase. The initiator samples PERR# on the second clock after completion of the data phase. If PERR# has been asserted by the target, the initiator sets the DATA PARITY REPORTED bit in its PCI configuration status register. Targets never set this bit because only the bus master reports the error to software.

Whether or not the bus master continues the transaction or terminates it is master design-dependent. The specification recommends that the transaction be continued to completion. In addition to the assertion of PERR#, the bus master is required to report the parity error to the system software. The specification recommends utilization of an interrupt or the setting of a bit in a status register that is polled by the device driver. Alternately, the designer can assert SERR#, but this approach should not be used lightly. It will more than likely result in a system shutdown. In a particular platform design, the chip set logic may convert any assertion of PERR# into SERR#.

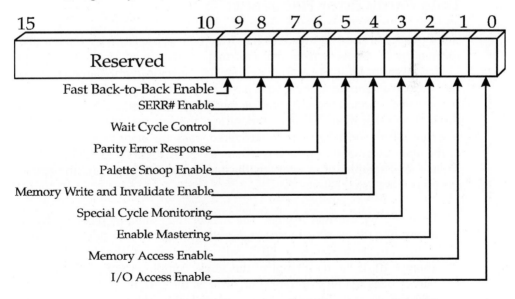

*Figure 10-3. PCI Device's Configuration Command Register*

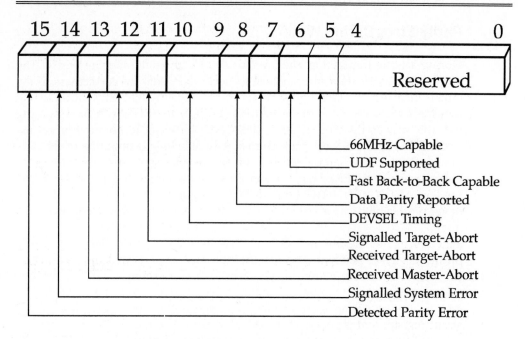

*Figure 10-4. PCI Device's Configuration Status Register*

## Data Parity Error Recovery

The PCI specification permits recovery from data phase parity errors but does not require it. Recovery from the error may be attempted by the master, the device driver or by the operating system. The specification recommends that recovery be attempted at the lowest possible level (i.e., by the bus master). Error recovery cannot be attempted if the device reports the error by some mechanism other than PERR# assertion (e.g., the error is reported via SERR# assertion). If the error can not be recovered from, the error must be reported to the operating system (if the bus master's DATA PARITY RESPONSE bit is set to one). Examples of recovery by the master, device driver and the operating system are listed below:

- **Recovery by the bus master**. The master may attempt recovery by re-attempting the transaction if it knows that it will have no side effects (e.g., if the target device is a FIFO buffer, the access should not be re-attempted). If the re-attempt of the access completes with no errors, the master does not have to report an error to the system. If the attempt (or, perhaps, several attempts) is unsuccessful, then the master must report the error. If there is a device driver associated with the master, the master alerts the driver to the error by generating an interrupt, setting a status bit, or some similar method. If there isn't a device driver associated with the master, the master may report the error by asserting SERR#.

- **Recovery by the device driver**. Assuming that the bus master reported the error to its device driver, the driver may instruct the bus master to re-attempt the transaction (once again, the driver must know that the re-attempt will not cause side effects). If the access completes with no errors, the device driver does not have to report the error to the operating system. If the access error cannot be recovered from, the driver must report the error to the operating system.
- **Recovery by the operating system**. How the operating system responds to the report of a data parity error is operating system-specific.

## Special Case: Data Parity Error During Special Cycle

The initiator uses a special cycle to broadcast a message (during the data phase) to the entire community of targets. In the event that any of the target(s) detects a parity error related to the data phase, this indicates that the message was corrupted in flight. Since messages are used to issue instructions to sub-systems, a corrupted message might place a subsystem in a state never intended. The PCI specification considers this to be a destabilizing event (like an address phase parity error). SERR# is used as the reporting mechanism.

The target(s) that detected the error must assert SERR# if:

- the SERR# ENABLE bit in its PCI configuration command register is set to one,
- and the PARITY ERROR RESPONSE bit is also set to one in its command register.

The target(s) must set the DETECTED PARITY ERROR bit in their configuration status registers. Any PCI device that signals SERR# is required to set the SIGNALED SYSTEM ERROR bit in its PCI configuration status register.

## Devices Excluded from PERR# Requirement

The PCI specification excludes two types of devices from the requirement to implement the PERR# signal and the PARITY ERROR RESPONSE bit in the configuration command register. The following two sections describe these device categories.

## Chipsets

In a PC, the chip set is embedded on the system board and typically consists of the host/PCI bridge and the PCI/expansion bus bridge. These two entities can be designed not to implement the PERR# pin. Consider the following example.

When the host/PCI bridge initiates a PCI read transaction for the host processor, it receives a data item from the target at the completion of each data phase. One clock after the receipt of each data item it latches the parity bit(s) (PAR and possibly PAR64) and compares the received parity to that it computed. If the expected vs. received parity miscompares, the host/PCI bridge doesn't have to generate PERR# (because the bridge is usually the device that monitors PERR# and reports them to the operating system). Instead, it can alert the processor that a parity error was received in a host bus-specific fashion. For example, in a PowerPC-based system, it could generate machine check to the processor.

Assume that a machine has been designed as a completely embedded environment: all devices are integrated onto the PCI bus and there are no PCI expansion slots. Also assume that none of the embedded devices checks the integrity of data written to them over the PCI bus. In this case, no device will ever assert PERR# upon receipt of a corrupted data item. There is therefore no requirement for PERR# implemented as an input pin on the host/PCI bridge.

## Devices That Don't Deal with OS/Application Program or Data

An ideal example would be a video frame buffer. It is legal to build a video frame buffer that doesn't check the integrity of data written into its memory buffer. In the event that one or more data items are corrupted while being written into the buffer, the only effect is "wild and crazy" pictures on the screen. While this may be destabilizing to the end user's state of mind, it is not corrupting programs or data in memory or on permanent storage (e.g., hard drives).

# Chapter 10: Error Detection and Handling

## SERR# Signal

SERR# is an output from all PCI devices and is an input to the platform support logic (i.e., the chip set). A PCI device is not permitted to assert SERR# unless the SERR# ENABLE bit in its configuration command register is set to one. SERR# is implemented as an open-drain, shared signal because multiple PCI devices may assert SERR# simultaneously. The system designer provides a pull-up resistor on the SERR# signal line. When any (or all) PCI devices that are asserting SERR# cease driving it, the pull-up has the responsibility to return SERR# to the deasserted state. This can take several PCI clocks.

When asserted, SERR# is asserted on the rising-edge of the PCI clock and is asserted for one clock and then tri-stated. It may be asserted at any time (i.e., its assertion is not tied to any type or phase of a PCI transaction). The specification suggests that SERR# should be asserted as quickly as possible (within two clocks of detecting an error condition is recommended).

The SERR# signal is used to signal the following types of conditions:

- parity error on the address phase of a transaction.
- parity error on the data phase of a special cycle transaction.
- problems other than parity detected by a PCI device.
- critical system failures detected by system board logic.

Before deciding to assert SERR# for an error, the designer should always consider that assertion of SERR# is considered an indication of a very serious problem. As examples, upon detection of SERR# assertion the platform logic may assert NMI in an Intel system or TEA# or MC# in a PowerPC system. The NMI or machine check interrupt handler is invoked and may halt the machine. The PCI specification does not dictate the action to be taken by the system logic when SERR# assertion is detected. As indicated earlier, it could result in a high-priority interrupt, or in the setting of a status bit to be polled by system software, etc.

Once system logic detects SERR# asserted, it must sample SERR# deasserted on two successive clock edges before assuming that it has been deasserted. This requirement is because open-drain signaling cannot guarantee stable signals on every clock edge.

The sections that follow contain additional discussion of SERR# usage.

## Address Parity

### Address Parity Generation and Checking

Refer to figure 10-5 during the following discussion. Every PCI transaction starts with the address phase (clock one in the figure). During the address phase, the initiator drives the start address onto AD[31:0] and the command (transaction type) onto C/BE#[3:0]. It also asserts FRAME# to indicate the presence of a valid start address and transaction type on the bus. At the end of the address phase (on the rising-edge of clock two), the community of targets latch the address, command and the state of the FRAME# signal. Sampling FRAME# asserted at this point qualifies the address and command as valid. All targets then begin address decode during clock two.

In addition, the following actions are also taken during clock two:

- The targets calculate the expected parity to determine the value they expect to latch from the PAR signal on clock three.
- The initiator drives PAR to either a one or a zero to force even parity on the 37-bit field consisting of AD[31:0], C/BE#[3:0] and PAR.

On the rising-edge of clock three, the targets latch the state of the PAR signal. During clock three the targets compare the expected parity they computed to the actual parity bit supplied by the initiator on the PAR signal. If it results in a good compare, the targets take no action.

If, however, it results in a miscompare by any (or all) of the targets, the address and/or command were corrupted in flight. This is considered to be a destabilizing event in the PCI environment. The initiator is reaching out and touching someone it never meant to touch or is touching them in a way it never meant to. SERR# is the reporting mechanism. The next section describes error reporting of address phase parity errors.

### Address Parity Error Reporting

Each target that detects an address phase parity miscompare must assert SERR# for one clock (if the device's SERR# ENABLE bit is set to one in its configuration command register). Any devices that assert SERR# must also set the SIGNALED SYSTEM ERROR bit in their configuration status registers to one. The device's DETECTED PARITY ERROR bit must also be set to one

# Chapter 10: Error Detection and Handling

(even if SERR# isn't signaled by a device due to the state of its SERR# EN-ABLE bit). The PCI configuration command register is pictured in figure 10-3. The status register is pictured in figure 10-4.

As stated earlier, the specification recommends that SERR# be asserted within two PCI clocks of error detection. The earliest that SERR# would therefore be asserted would be during clock three of fig 10-5, but it could be during clock four, five, or later (although not recommended).

In addition to the assertion of SERR#, the target device that is apparently addressed in a corrupted address phase can react in one of the following ways:

- assert DEVSEL# and complete the transaction normally.
- assert DEVSEL# and terminate the transaction with a target abort.
- not assert DEVSEL# and let the master time out and execute a master abort.

The target is not permitted to terminate the transaction with a retry or a disconnect.

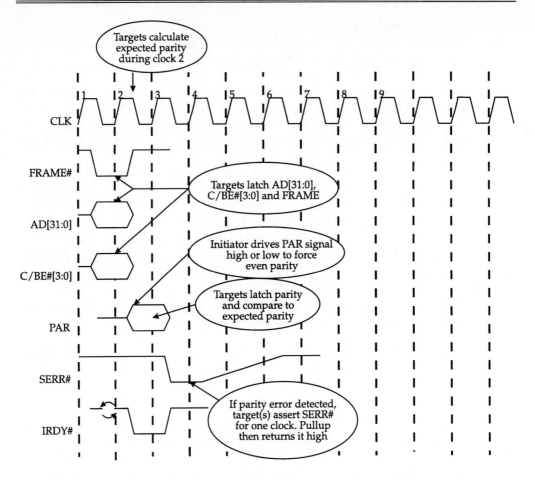

*Figure 10-5. Address Parity Generation/Checking*

# System Errors

## General

The following sections outline the various causes of SERR# assertion. In all cases, a device is not enabled to assert SERR# unless the SERR# ENABLE bit in its configuration command register is set to one.

# Chapter 10: Error Detection and Handling

## Address Phase Parity Error

This subject is discussed under the heading "Address Parity" in this chapter.

## Data Parity Error During Special Cycle

This subject is discussed under the heading "Special Case: Data Parity Error During Data Phase of a Special Cycle" earlier in this chapter.

## Target Abort Detection

A master that doesn't have a mechanism (such as an interrupt line) to report a target abort to system software, may assert SERR# to alert system software. The master must also set the RECEIVED TARGET ABORT bit in its status register.

## Other Possible Causes of System Error

When any PCI device suffers a serious failure that impairs its ability to operate correctly, it may assert SERR# (if its SERR# ENABLE bit is set to one) to inform system software of the failure. It must also set the SIGNALED SYSTEM ERROR status bit in its configuration status register.

## Devices Excluded from SERR# Requirement

The exceptions stated for PERR# implementation in the section entitled "Devices Excluded From PERR# Requirement" are also exceptions for SERR#.

# Chapter 11

## Prior To This Chapter

The previous chapter described error detection, reporting and handling.

## In This Chapter

This chapter provides a discussion of issues related to interrupt routing, generation and servicing.

## The Next Chapter

The next chapter provides a discussion of memory target locking. Locking is useful in multiprocessing environments.

## Single-Function PCI Device

A single-function PCI device is a physical package (add-in board or a component embedded on the PCI bus) that embodies one and only one functional (i.e., logical) device. If this device generates interrupt requests to request servicing from the system software, the designer should bond the device's interrupt request signal to the INTA# pin on the package (component or add-in board). A single-function PCI device must only use INTA# (never INTB#, INTC# or INTD#). In addition, the designer must hardwire this bonding information within the device's read-only, interrupt pin configuration register. Table 11-1 indicates the value to be hardwired into this register (01h for INTA# for a single-function PCI device). The interrupt pin register resides in the second byte of configuration doubleword number 15d in the device's configuration header space. The configuration header space (the first 16 doublewords of its configuration space) for the device is illustrated in figure 11-1. It should be stressed that the format illustrated is for PCI device's other than PCI-to-PCI bridge devices. The layout of the header space for this type of bridge can be found in the chapter entitled "PCI-to-PCI Bridge."

Table 11-1. Value To Be Hardwired Into Interrupt Pin Register

| Interrupt Signal Bonded To | Value Hardwired In Pin Register |
|---|---|
| INTA# pin | 01h |
| INTB# pin | 02h |
| INTC# pin | 03h |
| INTD# pin | 04h |

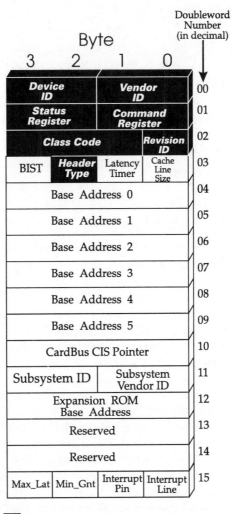

Figure 11-1. PCI Device's Configuration Header Space Format

# Chapter 11: Interrupt-Related Issues

## Multi-Function PCI Device

A multi-function PCI device is a physical package (add-in board or a component embedded on the PCI bus) that embodies between two and eight PCI functional devices. An example might be a card with a high-speed communications port and a parallel port implemented in the same package. There is no conceptual difference between a multi-function PCI device and a multi-function ISA, EISA or Micro Channel card.

The device designer may implement up to four interrupt pins on a package: INTA#, INTB#, INTC# and INTD#. Each function within the package is only permitted to use one of these interrupt pins to generate requests. Each functional device's interrupt pin register indicates which of the package's INTx# pins the device's interrupt request signal is bonded to (refer to table 11-1).

If a package implements one pin, it must be called INTA#. If it implements two pins, they must be called INTA# and INTB#, etc. All functions embodied within a package may be bonded to the same pin, INTA#, or each may be bonded to a dedicated pin (this would be true for a package with up to four functions embodied within it).

Groups of functional devices within the package may share the same pin. As an example, a package embodying eight functions could bond their interrupt request signals in any of the following combinations:

- all eight bonded to the INTA# pin.
- four bonded to INTA# and four to INTB#.
- two bonded to INTA#, two to INTB#, two to INTC# and two to INTD#.
- seven to INTA# and one to INTB#.
- etc.

## Connection of INTx# Lines To System Board Traces

The temptation is great to imagine that the INTA# pin on every PCI package is connected to a trace on the system board called INTA#, and that the INTB# pin on every PCI package is connected to a trace on the system board called INTB#, etc. While this may be true in a particular system design, it's only one of many different scenarios permitted by the specification.

The system board designer may route the PCI interrupt pins on the various PCI packages to the system board interrupt controller in any fashion. As examples:

- They may all be tied to one trace on the system board that is hardwired to one input on the system interrupt controller.
- They may each be connected to a separate trace on the system board and each of these traces may be hardwired to a separate input on the system interrupt controller.
- They may each be connected to a separate trace on the motherboard. Each of these traces may be connected to a separate input of a programmable interrupt routing device. This device can be programmed at startup time to route each individual PCI interrupt trace to a selected input of the system interrupt controller.
- All of the INTA# pins can be tied together on one trace. All of the INTB# pins can be tied together on another trace, etc. Each of these traces can, in turn, be hardwired to a separate input on the system interrupt controller or may be hardwired to separate inputs on a programmable routing device.
- Etc.

The exact verbiage used in this section of the specification is:

"The system vendor is free to combine the various INTx# signals from PCI connector(s) in any way to connect them to the interrupt controller. They may be wire-ORed or electronically switched under program control, or any combination thereof."

## Interrupt Routing

### General

Ideally, the system configuration software should have maximum flexibility in choosing how to distribute the interrupt requests issued by various devices. The best scenario is pictured in figure 11-2. In this example, each of the individual PCI interrupt lines is provided to the programmable router as a separate input. In addition, the ISA interrupt request lines are completely segregated from the PCI lines. The ISA lines are connected to the master and slave interrupt controllers. In turn, the interrupt request output of the master interrupt controller is connected to one of the inputs on the programmable interrupt routing device. The router could be implemented using an Intel APIC I/O module. The APIC I/O module can be programmed to assign a separate interrupt vector (interrupt table entry number) for each of the PCI interrupt request lines. It can also be programmed so that it realizes that one of its inputs is connected to an Intel 8259A interrupt controller.

Whenever any of the PCI interrupts are asserted, the APIC I/O module supplies the vector associated with that input to the processor's embedded local APIC module. Whenever the 8259A master interrupt controller generates a request, the APIC I/O informs the processor that it must poll the 8259As to get the vector. In response, the Intel P54C processor generates two back-to-back interrupt acknowledge bus cycles. The first forces the 8259As to prioritize their pending ISA requests. The second requests that the interrupt controller send the vector to the processor. For a detailed discussion of APIC operation, refer to the MindShare architecture series book entitled *Pentium Processor System Architecture*.

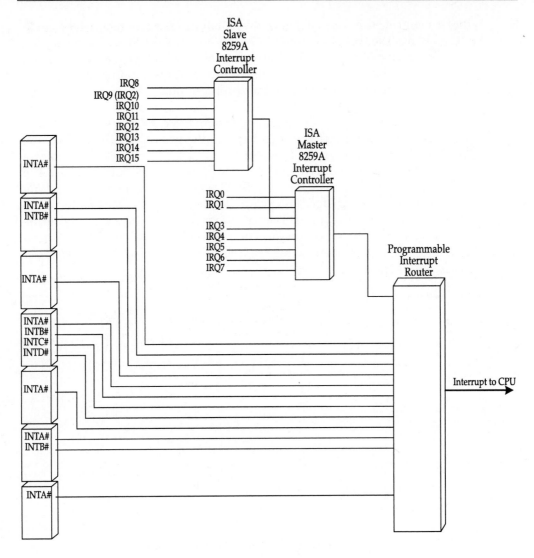

*Figure 11-2. Preferred Interrupt Design*

Figure 11-3 illustrates another approach. Each of the PCI interrupt request lines are connected to a separate input of the programmable router. The router is programmed at startup time to route each of the PCI interrupt request onto selected ISA interrupt request lines. This is a more limiting approach because ISA interrupt request lines are positive edge-triggered and are not shareable.

# Chapter 11: Interrupt-Related Issues

The PCI interrupts can only be routed onto ISA interrupt request lines that are not in use by ISA devices.

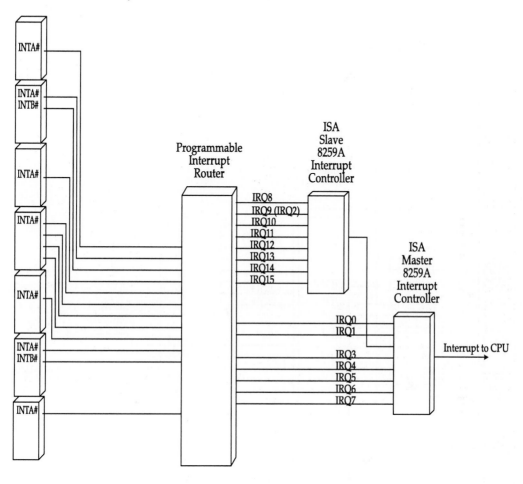

*Figure 11-3. Alternative Interrupt Layout*

Figures 11-4 and 11-5 illustrate typical designs for platforms implemented in the 1993/1994 timeframe using the available chip sets. Of these two designs, figure 11-5 would be preferred over 11-4. The programmable router is built into the PCI/ISA bridge chip and provides four inputs to connect PCI interrupt request signal lines to. The router can be programmed to route each PCI interrupt request signal to any of the ISA interrupt request lines. Once again, ISA interrupt request lines are positive edge-triggered and are not shareable. The PCI interrupts can only be routed onto ISA interrupt request lines not being used by ISA devices. As you can see in figure 11-4, the INTA# request line is heavily-weighted (seven devices) in this scenario. By laying out the PCI interrupt traces as illustrated in figure 11-5, the interrupts are spread more evenly (only three devices per line) across the four inputs of the router.

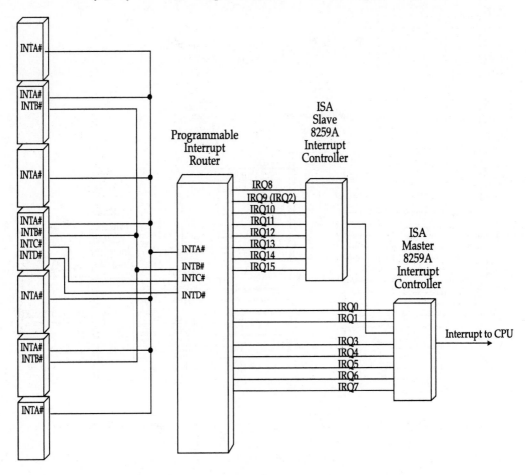

*Figure 11-4. Typical Design In Current Machines (1993/1994)*

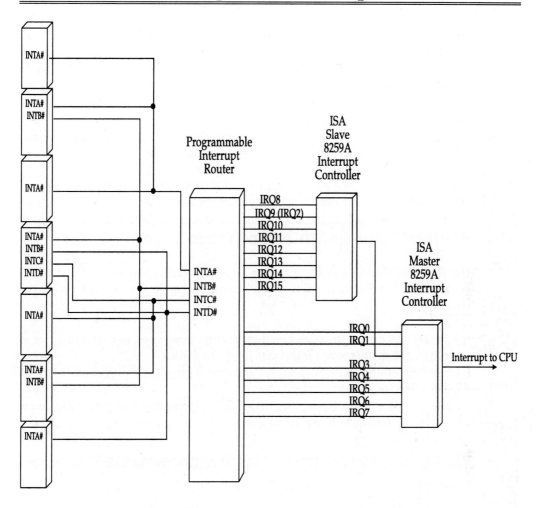

*Figure 11-5. Another Typical Design In Current Machines (1993/1994)*

## Routing Recommendation In 2.1 Specification

In many of today's PC systems, the programmable router embedded within the PCI/ISA bridge has four inputs for connection to PCI interrupt traces. In addition, most current PCI devices are single-function devices. If they are interrupt-driven, they must therefore use the INTA# pin on the package. Recognizing that it would be best to "spread" the interrupts from the various single-function devices across the interrupt router's four inputs, the specification writers recommend (in section 2.2.6) the interconnect of the INTA# outputs to the system board traces and the interconnect to the router's four inputs such that they are evenly spread across the four pins.

## Platform "Knows" Interrupt Trace Layout

The platform startup software is platform-specific and "knows" how the PCI interrupt traces are connected on the motherboard. As an example, it might know that:

- the INTA# pin on the SCSI host bus adapter integrated onto the PCI bus is physically connected to input pin 13 on the router.
- the INTA# pin on PCI expansion slot one is physically connected to input pin 14 on the router.
- the INTB# pin on the embedded Ethernet controller is physically connected to input pin 15 on the router.

## Well-Designed Platform Has Programmable Interrupt Router

A well-designed platform incorporates a software-programmable interrupt routing device. The startup configuration software attempts to program the router to distribute the PCI interrupts in an optimal fashion. Using figure 11-4 as an example, the startup configuration software can program the router to route each of these PCI interrupts to unused ISA IRQ lines.

Each IRQ input of the interrupt controller that is connected to a single ISA device is programmed for positive-edge triggered, non-shareable operation, while those connected to PCI interrupt lines must be programmed as active low, level-sensitive, shareable inputs.

# Chapter 11: Interrupt-Related Issues

It must be recognized that the startup configuration software is typically not very intelligent and may not make the best possible decisions. The router can be reprogrammed after system startup by a user running a configuration utility and making more informed selections. The section in this chapter entitled "PCI Interrupts Are Shareable" provides a detailed discussion of the issues related to interrupt routing and performance implications.

## Interrupt Routing Information

Once the startup configuration software has programmed the router, the routing information (the system IRQ line the device's PCI interrupt pin is routed to) must then be saved in the interrupt line register in the PCI device's configuration header space (refer to figure 11-1). The definition of the routing information is machine architecture-specific. The specification dictates the definition for x86-based PCs. Table 11-2 indicates the values to be written into the interrupt line register in an Intel x86-based PC. The values 16d - 254 are reserved, while the value 255d indicates routing "unknown" or "no connection." Although it doesn't state this in the specification, it is the author's opinion that RST# should initialize the interrupt line register to a value of FFh, thereby indicating that a system IRQ line has not yet been assigned to the device's interrupt pin.

*Table 11-2. Interrupt Line Register Values*

| System IRQ Line Interrupt Routed To | Value To Be Written In Line Register |
|:---:|:---:|
| IRQ0 | 0d |
| IRQ1 | 1d |
| IRQ2 | 2d |
| IRQ3 | 3d |
| IRQ4 | 4d |
| IRQ5 | 5d |
| IRQ6 | 6d |
| IRQ7 | 7d |
| IRQ8 | 8d |
| IRQ9 | 9d |
| IRQ10 | 10d |
| IRQ11 | 11d |
| IRQ12 | 12d |
| IRQ13 | 13d |
| IRQ14 | 14d |
| IRQ15 | 15d |

## PCI Interrupts Are Shareable

The PCI interrupt request signals are open-drain. Multiple devices connected to the same PCI interrupt request signal line can assert it simultaneously without damage. The net result is that the line is driven low. The system board designer provides a pullup resistor on each of the lines, so that their native state (when no device is asserting a request) is deasserted.

## "Hooking" the Interrupt

After the system startup configuration software executes (typically from firmware), the system initialization begins. The system or the operating system must provide a device-specific interrupt service routine for each interrupt-driven device in the system. Furthermore, the startup and operating system software must build an interrupt jump table in memory. Each entry in the interrupt table must contain the start address (i.e., the entry point) of the device-specific interrupt service routine associated with a particular device.

When the system is first powered up, system DRAM memory contains junk. Since the interrupt table resides in DRAM in a PC, the interrupt table must be built prior to enabling interrupt-driven devices to generate interrupt requests. Placing the start address of a device's interrupt service routine into the correct entry in the interrupt table is commonly referred to as "hooking" the interrupt. The next section provides a detailed discussion of how the interrupt table is built during system startup in a PC environment.

## Interrupt Chaining

### General

As stated earlier, when the system first starts up, the processor has interrupt recognition disabled and the interrupt table has not yet been built in memory. There are basically two categories of interrupt-driven devices that will have to have entries made in the interrupt table:

- embedded devices that the system already knows about.
- devices discovered during the startup and auto-config process.

The interrupt handlers for each interrupt driven device exists in one of three places:

- within the system BIOS ROM. The interrupt handlers for some or all of the embedded devices (embedded on the PCI bus and/or the X bus) are found within the system BIOS ROM. The startup POST/BIOS code knows the entry points of these handlers and the entries in the interrupt table that they are associated with.
- within a device ROM associated with the interrupt-driven device itself. These device ROMs are "discovered" during the bus scan process at startup and the initialization code within them is automatically executed upon discovery.
- within a loadable device driver loaded by the operating system during the operating system load and initialization process. As the operating system loads each loadable driver into memory, it calls the initialization code within the driver. The initialization code probes the bus for its associated device. If found and the device is interrupt-driven, the driver contains the device's interrupt handler. The driver initialization code is responsible for placing the start address of the interrupt handler into the proper entry within the interrupt table.

The following sections provide an example of the sequence of actions taken to build the interrupt table in memory.

## Step One: Initialize All Entries In Table To Null Value

Initially, the interrupt table in DRAM memory contains junk. The startup firmware sets each entry to point to the start address of a dummy interrupt service routine. This routine consists of only an IRET instruction in an Intel x86 machine, or an RFI instruction in a PowerPC machine.

## Step Two: Initialize All Entries For Embedded Devices

As stated earlier, the system designer usually includes the interrupt handlers for embedded devices in the system POST/BIOS firmware. These devices are already hardwired to pre-defined interrupt request lines and each of these lines is associated with a pre-defined vector, or entry, in the interrupt table. For each embedded device, the startup firmware stores the start address of the embedded device's handler into the associated table entry in memory.

## Step Three: Hook Entries For Embedded Device BIOS Routines

The system firmware usually contains a series of BIOS routines used to communicate with I/O devices. In an Intel x86 machine, the INT instruction is used to call a BIOS routine. The parameter supplied with the INT instruction is the interrupt table entry that contains the pointer to the routine to be called. As an example, INT 21h causes the processor to call the interrupt service routine pointed to by entry 21h in the interrupt table.

During system startup, the system firmware stores the pointers to these routines into the appropriate entries in the table (after first saving the pointers previously stored in those entries).

## Step Four: Perform Expansion Bus ROM Scan

After completing the PCI bus scan, the system firmware then scans the expansion bus for expansion ROMs associated with devices residing on that bus. At 2KB intervals starting at memory address 00C0000h and proceeding through memory address 00DFFFFh, the first two bytes are read. A value of 55h in the first location and AAh in the second is the signature of a device ROM. When a device ROM is discovered, the system firmware calls the device's initialization code within the ROM just discovered.

ISA bus device's typically have their interrupt lines assigned via DIP switches on the card. Assuming that a device is interrupt-driven, the device's initialization code hooks the appropriate entry in the interrupt table. Since ISA IRQ lines are not shared with other devices, it does this by storing the start address of its own interrupt handler routine in the entry. When the device's initialization routine completes execution, it returns control to the system firmware. The system firmware then continues scanning the 00C0000h through 00DFFFFh ( or 00EFFFFh in some systems) memory range (on 2KB address boundaries) for more ROMs.

## Step Five: Perform PCI Device Scan

The firmware-based configuration software attempts to read the vendor ID from function zero at each physical PCI device position on the PCI bus. Any position that returns a vendor ID of FFFFh is unoccupied. Those that return values other than FFFFh are occupied by a single or a multi-function device. For each occupied position, the firmware takes the following actions:

1.  Reads functional device zero's configuration header registers to determine the needs and requirements of the device.
2.  Allocates memory space to the device's memory address decoder(s), I/O space to its I/O address decoder(s), etc.
3.  Reads from the device's interrupt pin register to determine if it's interrupt driven. A value of zero indicates that it isn't, while a value of 01h, 02h, 03h, or 04h indicates that it is and which of the device's PCI interrupt pins the device uses to generate interrupt requests.
4.  Programs the interrupt router to route interrupts generated by the device to a specific system interrupt line (IRQ line).
5.  Writes the routing information into the device's interrupt line (routing) register. As an example, if it is routed to IRQ3, the value 03h is written to its interrupt line register.
6.  Probes the device's expansion ROM base address configuration register to determine if the device has an embedded device ROM. If it does, the ROM base address register is programmed with a start memory address and its memory address decoder is enabled.
7.  The ROM code image is copied into system DRAM (it's a rule in PCI that ROM code is never executed in place). The ROM address decoder is disabled.
8.  The system firmware than calls the initialization routine embedded in the ROM code image. If the device is interrupt driven and the device-specific handler is embedded within the ROM image, the interrupt line register is read to determine the routing information. This is used to determine the entry in the interrupt table to be hooked. This entry may have already been utilized to point to an embedded device's interrupt handler. The current contents of the entry is saved in the body of the device's handler and the start address of the device's handler is stored in the entry. In this way, the interrupt table entry now points to this device's handler and the handler "remembers" the pointer to the previous device's handler.
9.  If the ROM image contains a device-specific BIOS routine, the start address of the routine is stored in the appropriate interrupt table entry (after first saving the pointer previously stored in that entry).
10. Upon completion of the device ROM's initialization code, program execution passes back to the system firmware which then continues scanning the PCI bus. It checks bit seven of the header type configuration register to determine if this is a multi-function device. If cleared to zero, the device is

a single function device. The next physical device position is probed on the PCI bus to determine if it's occupied.

11. If bit seven is set to one, this is a multi-function device. The software then probes functions one through seven within the physical device to determine which are implemented. The process described above is then repeated for each device discovered.

## Step Six: Load Operating System

After both the PCI and expansion bus scans have been completed, the system firmware begins to read the operating system startup code into memory and then cedes control to it. The actions taken by the operating system are specific to that operating system. The discussion that follows is generic in nature.

At some point, the operating system initialization code processes the CONFIG.SYS file (or its equivalent, such as the Windows 95 Registry). Each time that a "DEVICE=" statement is encountered, the following actions are taken:

1. The indicated device driver is loaded into memory and the operating system calls its initialization code.
2. The device driver's initialization code determines if its associated device is present in the machine. For a device driver associated with an ISA device, this is accomplished by probing I/O ports associated with the device to see if it's present. For a driver associated with a PCI device, this is accomplished by issuing a PCI BIOS call (or a HAL call in Windows™ NT), supplying the device's vendor and device ID as search parameters. The BIOS checks CMOS RAM or walks the PCI bus to determine if the device is present. If present, the driver's initialization code then reads the interrupt line register to obtain the interrupt routing information. In the case of an ISA device, the interrupt line is supplied as a parameter on the "DEVICE=" command line in CONFIG.SYS.
3. Having determined the interrupt line associated with the device, the driver first reads and saves the pointer previously residing in the interrupt table entry. It then replaces it with the pointer to the device-specific interrupt service routine embedded within the device driver body. The driver's initialization code then returns control to the operating system initialization code which then continues processing CONFIG.SYS.

# Chapter 11: Interrupt-Related Issues

## Linked-List Has Been Built for Each Interrupt Level

The operating system load process has now completed and the machine is operational. The interrupt table has been completely initialized. The interrupt service routine currently pointed to by an interrupt table entry is associated with the last device "discovered" during the bus scan and OS load process that uses that interrupt level.

In turn, that interrupt service routine "remembers" the start address of the interrupt service routine associated with the device that had previously hooked the same interrupt. In turn, the previous device's interrupt service routine "remembers" the start address of the interrupt service routine associated with the device that hooked the same interrupt before it had, etc. A linked list has been established for each interrupt level.

## Servicing Shared Interrupts

### Example Scenario

Refer to fig 11-6 during the discussion that follows. This figure illustrates two devices, an Ethernet controller and communications port two, that both generate interrupt requests using the same PCI interrupt request line (e.g., two functional devices in the same package that both share INTA#, or two devices in separate packages that share the same interrupt request signal trace on the system board). Assume that the COM port hooked the interrupt first, followed by the Ethernet controller.

Each device has an open-collector driver that it uses to assert an interrupt request. This is accomplished when the device's logic asserts its internal IRQ# signal, providing an enable to the driver. This creates a path to ground and the external request line is driven low. The interrupt signal trace on the system board has a pullup resistor on it, thereby keeping the request line deasserted when none of the devices connected to that line are generating a request. If more than one device is generating a request, the external interrupt request line is low. In other words, a low on the request line indicates to the interrupt controller that one or more devices are generating a request.

In addition to driving the request line low, a device also sets an interrupt pending bit in a device-specific I/O status port known to its interrupt service routine.

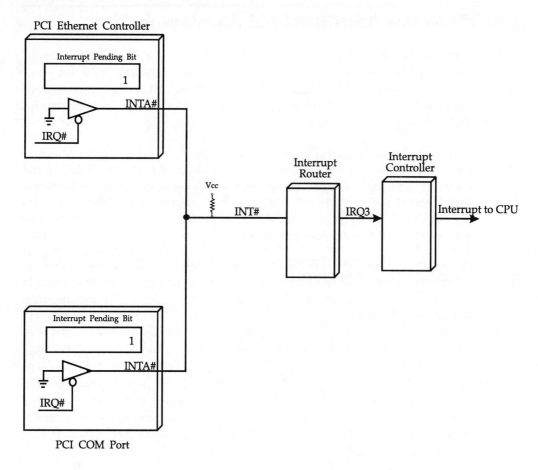

PCI Ethernet Controller

Interrupt Pending Bit

1

INTA#

IRQ#

Vcc

INT#

Interrupt
Router

IRQ3

Interrupt
Controller

Interrupt to CPU

Interrupt Pending Bit

1

INTA#

IRQ#

PCI COM Port

*Figure 11-6. Shared Interrupt Model*

## Both Devices Simultaneously Generate Requests

Referring to figure 11-6, both devices sharing the same interrupt request signal (the Ethernet controller and the COM port) assert a request. Each of them sets their respective interrupt pending bits to one and both turn on their respective request output drivers, setting the interrupt request line low (asserted). In this example, assume that the interrupt routing device routes the PCI interrupt request line onto system interrupt line IRQ3.

# Chapter 11: Interrupt-Related Issues

## Processor Interrupted and Requests Vector

The interrupt controller asserts interrupt request to the processor. Assuming that the processor is enabled to recognize external interrupts (IE bit set to one in the x86's EFLAGS register, or EE bit set to one in a PowerPC processor's MSR register), the processor recognizes the interrupt on the next instruction boundary.

The processor automatically saves its place in the interrupted program. Assuming that it's an Intel x86 processor, this is accomplished by pushing the contents of the CS, IP and FLAG registers into stack memory. The processor then generates two, back-to-back interrupt acknowledge bus cycles. The first is to command the interrupt controller to prioritize its pending requests. The second is to request the vector associated with the highest-priority interrupt currently pending. In this case, assuming that IRQ3 is the highest pending request, the processor receives the vector associated with IRQ3. The vectors are programmed into the interrupt controller during startup time and are listed in table 11-3. The vector, or table entry, for IRQ3 is 0Bh. When the processor receives the vector, 0Bh, it multiplies it by four (if in real mode; by eight if in protected mode) because each entry in the interrupt table contains the four byte start address of an interrupt service routine. This yields the start memory address of the table entry, 0000002Ch. The processor then reads the contents of memory locations 0000002Ch through 0000002Fh to obtain the start address of the interrupt service routine to execute.

Table 11-3. ISA Interrupt Vectors

| IRQ Number | Vector (Table Entry) |
|------------|----------------------|
| IRQ0 | 08h |
| IRQ1 | 09h |
| IRQ2 | 0Ah |
| IRQ3 | 0Bh |
| IRQ4 | 0Ch |
| IRQ5 | 0Dh |
| IRQ6 | 0Eh |
| IRQ7 | 0Fh |
| IRQ8 | 70h |
| IRQ9 | 71h |
| IRQ10 | 72h |
| IRQ11 | 73h |
| IRQ12 | 74h |
| IRQ13 | 75h |
| IRQ14 | 76h |
| IRQ15 | 77h |

## First Handler Executed

In this example, the COM port had hooked the interrupt first, followed by the Ethernet controller. This means that entry 0Bh in the table currently points to the Ethernet controller's interrupt service routine and the entry point of the COM port's interrupt service routine is known to the Ethernet controller's routine.

The processor jumps to the Ethernet controller's interrupt service routine. At the front end of this routine, the programmer reads the Ethernet controller's interrupt pending bit from an I/O status port implemented in the Ethernet controller to determine if the Ethernet controller is currently generating a request. In this case, it is. The body of the Ethernet controller's interrupt service routine is therefore executed and its request is serviced. The act of servicing the interrupt should clear the interrupt in the device. The Ethernet controller clears its interrupt pending bit and deasserts its local IRQ# signal. This disables the open-collector driver and removes the path to ground from the external interrupt request signal line. The line remains low, however, because the COM port is still generating a request.

## Return to Interrupted Program, Followed by Second Interrupt

At the completion of the Ethernet controller's interrupt service routine, an IRET instruction is executed to return the processor to its interrupted program flow. The processor resumes execution at the instruction it would have executed if it had not been interrupted. It is immediately interrupted again, however, because the interrupt controller is still generating a request for the COM port interrupt.

## First Handler Executed Again, Passes Control to Second

The processor jumps to the Ethernet Controller's interrupt service routine again and the Ethernet controller is again checked to determine if it has a request pending. Since its interrupt pending bit was cleared, the body of its interrupt service routine isn't executed. Rather, the Ethernet controller's interrupt service routine jumps to the entry point of the COM port's interrupt service routine. The device-specific COM port interrupt service routine checks the COM port's interrupt pending bit to determine if it requires servicing. Since its bit is set to one, the body of the interrupt service routine is executed. Once, again, the act of servicing an interrupt clears the request. The COM port clears its interrupt pending bit and disables its open-collector driver, removing the path to ground from the external interrupt request signal line. The pullup resistor on the line automatically desasserts it. All interrupts on that line have been serviced.

## Implied Priority Scheme

Any architecture (e.g., PCI, EISA, and Micro Channel) that utilizes a shared interrupt scheme has an explicit and an implicit interrupt priority scheme. In EISA, ISA and Micro Channel, the interrupt controllers are programmed at startup time to use an explicit fixed-priority scheme (see table 11-4).

Table 11-4. Interrupt Priority Scheme

| PC Interrupt Priority (highest to lowest) |
|:---:|
| IRQ0 |
| IRQ1 |
| IRQ8 |
| IRQ9 |
| IRQ10 |
| IRQ11 |
| IRQ12 |
| IRQ13 |
| IRQ14 |
| IRQ15 |
| IRQ3 |
| IRQ4 |
| IRQ5 |
| IRQ6 |
| IRQ7 |

If an interrupt line is shared by multiple devices, as they are in PCI, there is also an implied priority scheme among the devices that share an interrupt request line. In the Ethernet, COM port example covered earlier, whenever an interrupt occurs on IRQ3, the processor always jumps to the Ethernet controller's interrupt service routine first. Control is only passed to the COM port's interrupt service routine by the Ethernet controller's interrupt service routine if the Ethernet controller isn't currently generating a request. If the Ethernet controller were to generate interrupt requests at a high frequency, the COM port might starve to death while awaiting servicing.

Assuming that both devices have loadable device drivers, a fix for this problem would be to change the order of the "DEVICE=" statements in CONFIG.SYS to change the order in which the interrupt table entry is hooked by the two devices.

## Interrupts and PCI-to-PCI Bridges

Refer to the chapter entitled "PCI-to-PCI Bridge" for a description of interrupts and PCI-to-PCI bridges.

# Chapter 12

## The Previous Chapter

The previous chapter provided a discussion of interrupt-related issues.

## In This Chapter

The intended usage of the lock function is to permit masters to perform the read/modify/write of a memory semaphore as an atomic transaction series. It is a clear violation of the intent of the specification for a master to use the locking function to lock out other masters from memory so as to attain better performance. This chapter describes a scenario wherein a master must perform multiple accesses to a memory target with the assurance that no other master will access the device in between its accesses. It then describes the mechanism for implementing this function in the PCI environment.

## The Next Chapter

The next chapter provides a detailed discussion of the 64-bit extension capabilities.

## Using Semaphore to Gain Exclusive Ownership of Resource

### Memory Semaphore Definition

In some circumstances a master must perform a series of accesses to a particular memory target with the assurance that no other master will access the same target until the master's series of accesses have been completed. This is often referred to as an atomic series of transactions.

The following is an example of a situation that would require this ability to lock out other masters from accessing a particular target. Assume that the host system is executing multiple tasks under a multiprocessing operating system (such as OS/2, Unix, or Windows NT). A memory location is used to indicate the availability of a central resource, such as the page table in memory. A memory location that is used to reflect the availability or unavailability of a shared resource is referred to as a memory semaphore. When a task executing on a processor needs to access the page table, it must first determine that the page table isn't currently owned by another task.

To ascertain the availability of the page table, the task must first read from the memory semaphore associated with the page table and check the state of the semaphore byte to determine the page table's availability. If the byte is zero, this indicates that the page table is available. The task then sets the byte to a non-zero value and writes the byte back into the memory semaphore. In this manner, the task has acquired exclusive ownership of the page table and may initiate a series of one or more page table accesses without fear that another task will attempt to access the page table during this period. If any other task should check the state of the respective memory semaphore during this period, the state of the semaphore (i.e., non-zero) informs it that the page table is currently unavailable. When the current table owner has completed its series of page table accesses, it writes a zero into the memory semaphore, thereby marking the page table available again.

## Synchronization Problem

Assume that one task is executing on processor **A** and another task is executing on processor **B**. The task on processor **A** must access the page table in memory. Using the bus to communicate with memory, processor **A** first initiates and completes a memory read bus cycle to read the page table's memory semaphore. The state of the semaphore is zero, indicating that the page table is available. The task sets the semaphore to a non-zero value in processor **A**'s register (to mark the page table unavailable to other tasks) and processor **A** then requests the use of the bus to perform the memory write bus cycle to update the semaphore in memory.

At this time, processor **B** is also requesting the use of the bus and is granted access to the bus before processor **A** (because it has higher priority or is next in line for a bus access). Upon acquiring bus ownership, processor **B** then initiates a memory read bus cycle to read the page table's semaphore and determine the availability of the page table. When the task on processor **B** completes its memory read and is then testing the state of the semaphore, processor **A** gains access to the bus and performs the memory write to change the semaphore to a non-zero value. Upon completion of the write, the task on processor **A** believes that it now has gained exclusive ownership of the page table.

Meanwhile, the task on processor **B** determines that the current state of the semaphore is zero. It has no knowledge that processor **A** has already updated the semaphore in memory. Thinking that the semaphore is still zero, it initiates a memory write to write a non-zero value into the same semaphore. When processor **A** has completed the memory write to update the semaphore, processor **B** then acquires bus ownership and also writes a non-zero value into the same semaphore.

The tasks on processors **A** and **B** now each believe that the page table belongs solely to them. This situation would be prevented if processor **A** were able to perform the semaphore read, modification and update as an atomic, indivisible operation with the assurance that no other master can access the same memory semaphore until the atomic transaction series has been completed.

## PCI Solutions: Bus and Resource Locking

### LOCK# Signal

The PCI bus locking mechanism is implemented via the PCI LOCK# signal. There is only one LOCK# signal and only one master can use it at a time. This means that only one master may perform a locked transaction series during a given period of time. The LOCK# signal is a sustained tri-state signal. As with all PCI sustained tri-state signals, the system board designer is required to provide a pullup resistor on the LOCK# signal. When not in use, the state of LOCK# is therefore deasserted.

### Bus Lock: Permissible but Not Preferred

If a bus master could instruct the PCI bus arbiter to lock the bus when the semaphore is read from memory and not grant the bus to any other master until so instructed by the bus master, the synchronization problem described earlier would be solved. This is referred to as a bus lock.

PCI permits this implementation wherein LOCK# is sampled by the arbiter. The PCI master initiates the memory read and asserts LOCK#. When the PCI bus arbiter samples LOCK# asserted by the current initiator, it recognizes this as a request for exclusive bus ownership. Assuming that the first data phase of the memory read transaction completes normally (no target abort or retry issued by the target), the initiator may assume that no other bus master will be able to access the memory target until it completes the update of the semaphore. After completion of the read and while the master is internally testing the state of the semaphore, the master continues to assert the LOCK# signal (even though it's not currently using the bus).

While LOCK# remains asserted, the arbiter ignores PCI bus requests from all masters other than the one that established the lock. The arbiter knows which master established the lock because each master has a dedicated REQ#/GNT# signal pair and it knows which master asserted LOCK# when it was granted bus ownership.

When the master that established the lock later requests ownership of the PCI bus again to perform the memory write to update the semaphore, the arbiter grants it the bus. The master performs the memory write and then releases the LOCK# signal. This instructs the arbiter to cease the bus lock. It also instructs the locked memory target to unlock itself. A PCI memory target that is locked unlocks itself whenever it detects FRAME# deasserted with LOCK# deasserted.

In the event that the master reads the semaphore and determines that it has already been set to a non-zero value by another master, it just ceases to assert the LOCK# signal (and the target unlocks itself when it detects FRAME# and LOCK# deasserted).

The bus lock implementation impedes other masters from accessing any PCI targets just to prevent anyone from accessing the small area of the memory target that the semaphore resides in. For this reason, this approach is considered to be less than optimal. The next section describes the preferred approach, resource locking.

# Resource Lock: Preferred Solution

## Introduction

The PCI bus implements a signal, LOCK#, that a master can use to prevent the synchronization problem described earlier. It allows a master to reserve a particular memory target (or a portion of it) for its sole use until it completes a series of accesses to the target. When the final access of the atomic transaction series has been completed, the master indicates that it no longer requires exclusive ownership of the target. PCI permits other masters to use the bus to access targets other than the locked target during the period that a master has exclusive ownership of a particular target.

## Determining Lock Mechanism Availability

There is only one PCI LOCK# signal line and it may only be used by one master at a time. If a master wishes to use the LOCK# signal to reserve a target for exclusive access, it must first determine that the LOCK# signal is not already in use by another master. This is accomplished in the following manner:

- Do not assert REQ# if LOCK# is currently asserted.
- If FRAME# and LOCK# are sampled deasserted, the locking resource is not busy. The master may assert its REQ#.
- While waiting for GNT#, the master must continue to monitor LOCK#. If LOCK# is sampled asserted, the master deasserts its REQ# (because another master has already started using LOCK#).
- When the master samples bus idle (FRAME# and IRDY# deasserted) and LOCK# deasserted, it has acquisition of the bus and of the LOCK# signal. It may start the memory read transaction to read the semaphore from memory for testing.

The same rules apply for establishing a bus lock.

## Establishing Lock on Memory Target

Figure 12-1 illustrates the process of gaining exclusive ownership of a memory target. The access that establishes the lock on the memory target must be a memory read (to read the semaphore). The specification states that the master may only access the target that it has locked (no other targets) for the duration of the exclusive transaction series. This rule exists to ensure that the master accomplishes the read/modify/write of the semaphore in an expeditious fashion so as to have minimal impact on other masters that may need to access the memory target (or any other target, if the system implements bus locking).

Assume that a master wishes to acquire exclusive ownership of a memory target to perform a semaphore read/modify/write operation. When the master has established that the LOCK# signal is not currently in use (see previous section) by another master, it asserts REQ# to the arbiter to request access to the bus. While waiting for the grant (GNT#), the master must continue to monitor the LOCK# signal. If LOCK# is sampled asserted, another master has gained ownership of LOCK# and the master must deassert REQ# until LOCK# is available.

1. Assuming that the master has acquired the bus (its GNT# is asserted and the bus is idle), the master initiates the transfer at the start of clock one by asserting FRAME#, leaving LOCK# deasserted to request the lock (this sounds contradictory, but continue reading), and driving the address and command type (memory read) onto the AD bus and the Command/Byte Enable lines, respectively.
2. The target latches the address and command and samples LOCK# deasserted at the rising-edge of clock two. It proceeds with the address decode.
3. The master asserts LOCK# during clock two to instruct the target to stay locked after this transaction completes.
4. The target decodes the address and asserts DEVSEL# and TRDY# during clock three (medium speed decoder). It also "remembers" that LOCK# was sampled deasserted at the end of the address phase. This instructs the target to lock itself. In fact, the target will only lock itself if the first data phase of the transaction completes successfully (the lock is formally established at the completion of the first data phase). If the first data phase doesn't complete (for example, the target issues a retry because it cannot complete the access yet), the master has not gained exclusive ownership of the target. It must terminate the transaction, release LOCK#, and try again later.
5. The master asserts LOCK# at the rising-edge of clock two to maintain the lock past the end of this transaction. FRAME# is deasserted because the last (and only) data phase is in progress.
6. At the rising-edge of clock four, the first (and only) data item is available for transfer (IRDY# and TRDY# are asserted) and the master reads the data (the semaphore) from the target. The successful completion of the data phase formally establishes the target lock. In this example, the master was only transferring one data item, so the transaction is terminated during clock four (IRDY#, DEVSEL# and TRDY# are deasserted).
7. The master continues to assert LOCK# to indicate that LOCK# is now in use. The target samples LOCK# asserted and FRAME# deasserted on the rising-edge of clock five. This target (or a portion of it) is now locked and cannot be accessed by any other master. The target remains locked until it samples LOCK# and FRAME# deasserted on a rising-edge of the clock.

# Chapter 12: Shared Resource Acquisition

At a minimum, the memory target locks the 16 byte-aligned memory block, also referred to as a paragraph, that the memory semaphore resides within. A memory target can be designed to lock anything from the paragraph that contains the semaphore up to the entire memory target. The optimum would be to lock just the paragraph. Other masters that don't require the locking mechanism could then successfully access locations outside the bounds of the locked paragraph while the lock is still in force.

When a target (or a portion of it) has been locked, the target must only permit the master that established the lock to access to the locked area. Any attempt by any other master to access the locked area must result in a retry to the master. If the memory is multi-ported, the lock also precludes any memory accesses by entities within the device itself until the lock is removed.

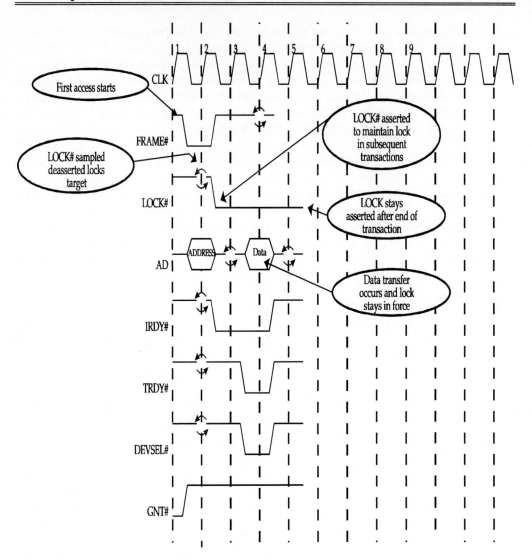

*Figure 12-1. Establishing the Lock to Read the Semaphore*

# Chapter 12: Shared Resource Acquisition

## Unlocked Targets May Be Accessed by any Master

During the period of time that a target is locked, masters that don't require use of the locking signal (to perform an atomic transaction series) can successfully acquire the bus and perform transfers with unlocked targets (including unlocked portions of the memory target that contains the locked area). A locked target refuses (retries) access attempts within its locked area that are initiated by other masters, but permits access attempts by the master that locked it.

## Access to Locked Target by Master Other than Owner: Retry

Figure 12-2 illustrates an attempt by a master other than the one who locked it to access a locked target. The master performing this bus transaction is not performing an atomic transaction series, so it is not required to sample LOCK# prior to assuming bus ownership. The illustration shows the LOCK# signal being held asserted by the master that locked the target.

1. The current master initiates the transfer attempt at the start of clock one by asserting FRAME# and driving the address and the command onto the AD and Command/Byte Enable buses, respectively. The LOCK# signal is still asserted by the master that read the semaphore from memory at an earlier point in time.
2. The target latches the address, command and the state of the LOCK# signal at the rising-edge of clock two and begins the address decode.
3. The initiator deasserts FRAME# during clock two, indicating that the last (and only) data phase is in progress.
4. When the target decodes its address, it asserts DEVSEL# in clock three to claim the transaction. It has also determined that the master attempting to access it is not the one that locked it. The master that locked it would have demonstrated its control of the LOCK# signal by deasserting LOCK# during the address phase. The locked memory target must therefore reject the access by issuing a retry to the current master. STOP# is asserted along with DEVSEL#, and TRDY# stays deasserted. This combination indicates that the initiator is to stop the transaction on the current data phase (STOP# asserted) with no data transferred (TRDY# deasserted) and that the initiator is to retry the transaction again later (DEVSEL# asserted).
5. When the initiator samples STOP# and DEVSEL# asserted and TRDY# deasserted at the rising-edge of clock four, it terminates the transaction without a data transfer and will re-attempt the access later. For more information on retry, refer to the chapter entitled "Premature Transaction

Termination." The initiator then deasserts IRDY#, returning the bus to the idle state. The target deasserts STOP# and DEVSEL#.

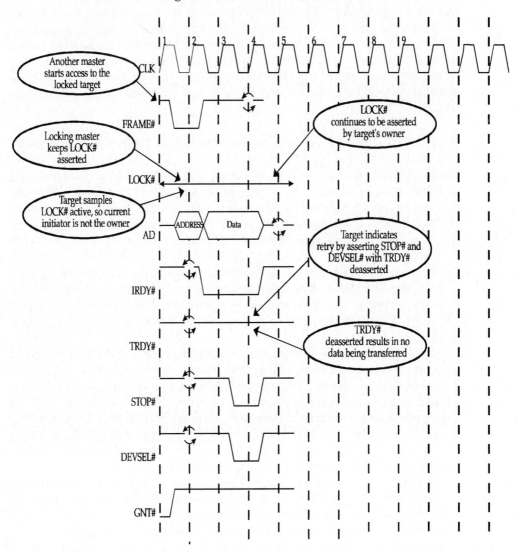

*Figure 12-2. Attempted Access to a Locked Memory Target*

# Chapter 12: Shared Resource Acquisition

## Continuation and/or End of Locked Transaction Series

Figure 12-3 illustrates the continuation and/or the end of an exclusive access series. In this example, the master had accessed the target earlier (to read the memory semaphore) and locked it for its exclusive use (LOCK# was left asserted by the master when it ended the earlier access). When the locking master gains bus ownership again (GNT# asserted by the arbiter and the bus is idle), it starts the next access in the locked series (the memory write to update the memory semaphore).

1. At the start of the transaction (the rising-edge of clock one), the initiator asserts FRAME# and deasserts LOCK#. It deasserts LOCK# to reestablish its lock on the target and identify itself as the target's owner.
2. The target latches the address, command and the state of the LOCK# signal at the end of the address phase (on the rising-edge of clock two) and begins the address decode.
3. Upon decoding the address and asserting DEVSEL#, the target locks itself again (because LOCK# was sampled deasserted at the end of the address phase).
4. During clock two, the initiator reasserts LOCK# to continue the lock through the end of this transaction. If the initiator left LOCK# deasserted during the transaction and the target were to issue a retry for some reason, the master has lost control of the target. In other words, after the master terminated the transaction (due to the retry), the target would sample FRAME# and LOCK# deasserted, instructing the target to unlock itself.
5. The data is written into the memory semaphore at the rising-edge of clock three when TRDY# and IRDY# are both sampled active. The initiator and target release IRDY# and TRDY#, respectively. If the master must maintain the lock on the target for one or more additional accesses, it continues to assert LOCK# after the end of the transaction. If, on the other hand, the master has completed its exclusive series of accesses to the target, it releases LOCK# at the end of the current transaction. When the target samples FRAME# and LOCK# both deasserted (on clock four in the example), it clears its lock.

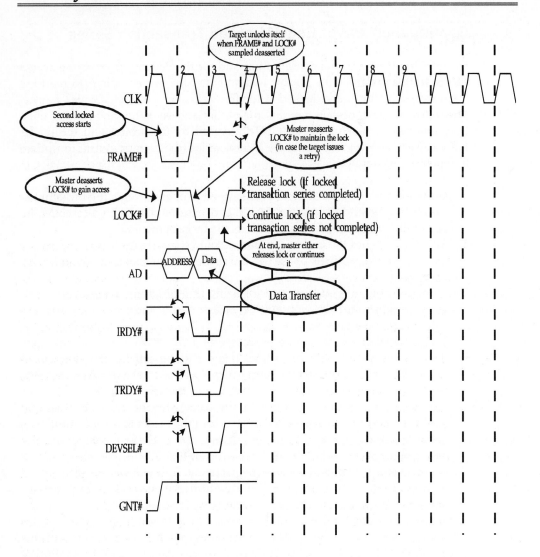

*Figure 12-3. The Update of the Memory Semaphore and Release of Lock*

# Chapter 12: Shared Resource Acquisition

## Potential Deadlock Condition

### Assumptions

The following assumptions are made for this discussion:

1. The system implements a write-back cache that can contain lines that have been modified by the host processor but have not yet been written back to memory.
2. The system supports cacheable memory targets on the PCI bus. In other words, the host processor's L1 and L2 caches are permitted to cache information from PCI memory targets.
3. When a PCI bus master is performing a burst memory access to/from a cacheable PCI memory target, the host/PCI bridge is capable of automatically generating new snoop addresses when the burst crosses a line boundary and submits the new address to the L2 cache for a lookup.
4. A cacheable memory target is designed so that it locks its entire memory address range when a master instructs it to lock itself. In this example, the memory target's start address is 00000000h.
5. The host processor has a cache line size of 32 bytes (e.g., the Pentium or the PowerPC 604 processor). Lines therefore start on addresses divisible by 32 (e.g., 00000000h, 00000020h, 00000040h, etc.).
6. At some point prior in time, the processor has read the cache line that starts at memory address 00000020h into its L1 and L2 caches and then subsequently made at least one modification (a memory write) within this line. The line is therefore marked modified in the L2 cache. Because the L2 is a write-back cache, however, the modification has not been propagated through to the PCI memory target. The memory target therefore contains stale data within the line starting at memory location 00000020h.
7. It is a rule in PCI that cacheable memory targets residing on the PCI bus are not permitted to accept data from or supply data to a master until the results of the snoop becomes available. The target must keep TRDY# deasserted until the snoop result becomes available on SDONE and SBO#. If the snoop result is clean (SDONE asserted and SBO# deasserted), the target can assert TRDY# and accept or supply data. If the snoop results in a hit on a modified line (SDONE and SBO# asserted), the target must issue a retry to the bus master. This is necessary because the master is attempting to transfer data to or from a stale line in memory. After the master terminates its transfer (due to the retry), the host/PCI bridge arbitrates for bus ownership to write the modified line into the cacheable memory tar-

get. Upon completion of the push-back of the modified line to memory, the L2 cache transitions the state of its line (from modified to clean if the master was attempting a memory read; from modified to invalid if the master was attempting a memory write). The PCI master that was retried then re-initiates its memory access. The host/PCI bridge snoops the transaction again, this time resulting in a clean snoop (SDONE asserted and SBO# deasserted). The memory target therefore asserts TRDY# and permits the transfer.

## Problem Scenario

A bus master now initiates a read burst from the memory target starting at address 00000000h and instructs the target to lock itself. The read burst consists of multiple data phases and will cross over the line boundary into the line that starts at location 00000020h. The cacheable memory target asserts DEVSEL# to claim the transaction, but keeps TRDY# deasserted until it detects the snoop result. When the master initiated the transaction, the host/PCI bridge latched the address and submits it to the L1/L2 caches for a snoop. Either because the line starting at memory location 00000000h isn't in the cache or has not been modified by the processor since being read from the memory target, the snoop result is clean (SDONE asserted and SBO# deasserted). The target therefore asserts TRDY# to permit the first data item to be transferred. Upon the successful completion of the first data phase, the target locks its entire address range (not just the 16 byte block that the first data item resides within).

When the burst crosses over the line boundary into the next line, the host/PCI bridge submits this new line address to the L2 cache for a lookup. The target keeps TRDY# deasserted until the snoop result is presented. Because the line that starts at memory address 00000020h is marked modified in the processor's L1 or L2 cache, the snoop results in a hit on a modified line (SDONE and SBO# asserted). The bridge will continually indicate a snoop hit on a modified line (SDONE and SBO# asserted) until it is successful in performing the write-back of the modified line to the cacheable PCI memory target. This means that any further attempts by any PCI master to access any cacheable memory target will result in retry.

The snoop result causes the memory target to issue a retry to the master. The master terminates the transfer without transferring the first data item within the line starting at location 00000020h. The target remains locked, however, because the first data phase of the transaction had completed without a retry.

# Chapter 12: Shared Resource Acquisition

The master will not reassert its REQ# to reattempt the access for two PCI clocks. This opens a window of opportunity for another master to get the bus. The master is, however, still asserting LOCK# to keep the memory target locked.

The instant that the host/PCI bridge experienced the hit on the modified line, it asserted its REQ# to use the bus to perform the snoop push-back of the modified line to the memory target. When it starts its memory write transaction to deposit the line in the memory target, the memory target issues a retry (because the target is marked locked and the bridge did not demonstrate control of the LOCK# signal by deasserting it during the address phase). The bridge is therefore forced off the bus and will request the bus again in two PCI clocks to reattempt its memory update.

The master that initially received a retry (because of the snoop hit during its burst) now gets the bus and re-initiates its burst at the point where it received a retry. The start address it puts on the bus is 00000020h. This once again results in a snoop hit on a modified line and the master receives another retry.

## Solution

A deadlock condition now exists: the master and the bridge continually perform interleaved access attempts to the target and always receive a retry. The PCI specification handles this case as follows. PCI cacheable memory targets that lock their entire range and support write-back caching are required to accept snoop push-backs from the bridge even when they are locked.

The bridge indicates that it is attempting to perform the write-back by starting the transaction indicating a hit on a modified line and then transitioning the indication to a clean snoop during the address phase. When a locked cacheable memory target detects SDONE and SBO# asserted (hit on modified line) on the edge where a transaction is started and then detects SDONE asserted and SBO# deasserted (clean snoop) at the end of the address phase, the target is required to assert TRDY# and accept the complete line of data being written back to its memory. It is not permitted to issue a retry or a disconnect during the line write.

Optionally, the locked, cacheable target may also be designed to accept write-backs of modified lines to memory that are being performed by the bridge because the modified line is being cast out of the processor's caches to make room for a new line. The target can tell that this is the case if it detects a tran-

sition during the address phase from standby (SDONE deasserted, SBO# don't care) to clean (SDONE asserted and SBO# deasserted).

This potential for a deadlock also exists when bus lock, rather than target locking, is implemented. An arbiter that supports bus locking must be designed to grant the bus to the bridge to perform the write-back.

## Devices that Must Implement Lock Support

The use of LOCK# is not recommended for target devices other than bridges or memory controllers that support system memory (i.e., executable memory). Some host bus architectures (e.g., the PowerPC PReP architecture), however, do support memory locking. For this reason, the specification recommends but does not require that a host/PCI bridge support locking when acting as the target of a system memory access by a PCI master. If the host/PCI bridge implements LOCK# support, it should permit a PCI master to lock system memory and, optionally, may implement the ability to lock PCI memory targets. Since the device driver associated with a PCI master cannot depend on the ability to lock system memory, the specification recommends that the driver use some method other than locking (some type of software protocol) to gain exclusive access to code or data structures shared with other processors in the system.

All PCI masters that must have the ability to gain exclusive ownership of a block of memory must implement locking capability.

## Use of LOCK# with 64-bit Addressing

Locking works the same with dual-address phase transactions as those that use a single address phase. LOCK# is deasserted during the first address phase and asserted during the second.

## Summary of Locking Rules

### Implementation Rules for Masters

Any master that implements locking capability must adhere to the following rules:

1.  The master may only access a single target for the duration of the lock. This rule exists to force masters to expeditiously return a locked resource to the available state.
2.  A lock cannot straddle device boundaries. The 16 byte block (minimum) to be locked must reside completely within one memory target.
3.  The maximum memory area that a master can count on locking is a 16 byte block (aligned on a 16 byte boundary). In fact, a target may lock a larger area (up to and including the entire memory target), but a master has no way of knowing this. An access anywhere within a 16 byte block locks the entire 16 byte block.
4.  The first transaction of a locked transactions series must be a memory read (to read the semaphore from memory).
5.  Lock must be asserted during the clock immediately following the address phase and must be kept asserted after the transaction has concluded (in order to keep the target locked).
6.  The LOCK# signal must be deasserted if the first data phase ends in a retry. In this case, the master has not locked the target. Other masters can successfully access it.
7.  LOCK# must be deasserted whenever a transaction is terminated by a target abort (in any data phase). This basically indicates that the target is broken or can never complete the access.
8.  LOCK# must also be deasserted if the transaction is terminated by a master abort (no target has responded).
9.  LOCK# must be deasserted for at least one idle cycle between consecutive locked transaction series.

## Implementation Rules for Targets

PCI memory targets that support locking must adhere to the following rules:

1.  The target of a transaction locks itself when LOCK# is sampled deasserted at the end of the address phase.
2.  Once a target is locked, the target must remain locked until it samples both FRAME# and LOCK# deasserted or until it issues a target abort to the initiator.
3.  The target must, at a minimum, lock the 16 byte aligned area of memory that the first data item of the read resides within. It may, however, lock a larger area, up to and including the entire target.
4.  Cacheable PCI memory targets that support a write-back cache associated with the host processor must permit the host/PCI bridge to perform a write-back to memory even when the target is locked.

# Chapter 13

## The Previous Chapter

The previous chapter described a scenario wherein a master must perform multiple accesses to a target with the assurance that no other master will access the device in between its accesses. It then described the mechanism for implementing this function in the PCI environment.

## In This Chapter

This chapter describes the 64-bit extension that permits masters and targets to perform eight byte transfers during each data phase. It also describes 64-bit addressing used to address memory targets that reside above the 4GB boundary.

## The Next Chapter

The next chapter provides an introduction to the PCI expansion card and connector definition. It covers card and connector types, 5V and 3.3V operability, shared slots, and pinout definition. This chapter concludes part II of the book, "Revision 2.1 Essentials."

## 64-bit Data Transfers and 64-bit Addressing: Separate Capabilities

The PCI specification provides a mechanism that permits a 64-bit bus master to perform 64-bit data transfers with a 64-bit target. At the beginning of a transaction, the 64-bit bus master automatically senses if the responding target is a 64-bit or a 32-bit device. If it's a 64-bit device, up to eight bytes may be transferred during each data phase. Assuming a series of 0-wait state data phases, throughput of 264Mbytes/second can be achieved at a bus speed of 33MHz (8 bytes/transfer x 33 million transfers/second). If the responding target is a 32-bit device, the bus master automatically senses this and steers all data to or from the target over the lower four data paths (AD[31:0]).

The specification also defines 64-bit addressing capability. This capability is only used to address memory targets that reside above the 4GB address boundary. Both 32 and 64-bit bus masters can perform 64-bit addressing. In addition, memory targets that respond to 64-bit addressing (that reside over the 4GB address boundary) can be implemented as either 32 or 64-bit targets.

It is important to note that 64-bit addressing and 64-bit data transfer capability are two features, separate and distinct from each other. A device may support one, the other, both, or neither.

In order to support the 64-bit data transfer capability, the PCI bus implements an additional thirty-nine pins:

- **REQ64#** is asserted by a 64-bit bus master to indicate that it would like to perform 64-bit data transfers. REQ64# has the same timing and duration as the FRAME# signal. The REQ64# signal line must be supplied with a pullup resistor on the system board. REQ64# cannot be permitted to float when a 32-bit bus master is performing a transaction.
- **ACK64#** is asserted by a target in response to REQ64# assertion by the master (if the target supports 64-bit data transfers). Like DEVSEL#, ACK64# is a function of address decode and has the same timing and duration as DEVSEL# (but ACK64# must not be asserted unless REQ64# is asserted by the initiator). Like REQ64#, the ACK64# signal line must also be supplied with a pullup resistor on the system board. ACK64# cannot be permitted to float when a 32-bit device is the target of a transaction.
- **AD[63:32]** comprise the upper four address/data paths.
- **C/BE#[7:4]** comprise the upper four command/byte enable signals.
- **PAR64** is the parity bit that provides even parity for the upper four AD paths and the upper four C/BE signal lines.

The following sections provide a detailed discussion of 64-bit data transfer and addressing capability.

## 64-bit Cards in 32-bit Add-in Connectors

A 64-bit card installed in a 32-bit expansion slot automatically only uses the lower half of the bus to perform transfers. This is true because the system board designer connects the REQ64# output pin and the ACK64# input pin on the connector to individual pullups on the system board and to nothing else.

# Chapter 13: The 64-bit PCI Extension

When a 64-bit bus master is installed in a 32-bit card slot and it initiates a transaction, its assertion of REQ64# is not visible to any of the targets. In addition, its ACK64# input is always sampled deasserted (because it's pulled up on the system board). This forces the bus master to use only the lower part of the bus during the transfer. Furthermore, if the target addressed in the transaction is a 64-bit target, it samples REQ64# deasserted (because it's pulled up on the system board), forcing it to only utilize the lower half of the bus during the transaction and disable its ACK64# output.

In addition, the 64-bit extension signal lines on the card itself cannot be permitted to float when they are not in use. This would violate the "green" aspect of the specification. When the card is installed in a 32-bit slot, it cannot use the upper half of the bus. The manner in which the card detects the type of slot (REQ64# sampled deasserted at startup time) is described in the next section.

## Pullups Prevent 64-bit Extension from Floating When Not in Use

If the 64-bit extension signals (AD[63:32], C/BE#[7:4] and PAR64) are permitted to float when not in use, input buffers that they are connected to will oscillate and draw excessive current. This violates the "green" nature of the PCI bus environment. In order to prevent the extension from floating when not in use, the system board designer is required to include pullup resistors on the extension signals to keep them from floating. Because these pullups are guaranteed to keep the extension from floating when not in use, 64-bit devices that are embedded on the system board and 64-bit cards installed in 64-bit PCI add-in connectors don't need to take any special action to keep the extension from floating when they are not using it.

The 64-bit extension is not in use under the following circumstances:

1. The PCI bus is idle.
2. A 32-bit bus master is performing a transaction with a 32-bit target.
3. A 32-bit bus master is performing a transaction with a 64-bit target. Upon detecting REQ64# deasserted at the start of the transaction, the target will not use the upper half of the bus.
4. A 64-bit bus master addresses a target to perform 32-bit data transfers (REQ64# deasserted) and the target resides below the 4GB address boundary (the upper half of the bus is not used during the address phase). Whether the target is a 32-bit or a 64-bit target, the upper half of the bus isn't used during the data phases (because REQ64# is deasserted).
5. A 64-bit bus master attempts a 64-bit data transfer (REQ64# asserted) with a 32-bit memory target that resides below the 4GB boundary. In this case, the

initiator only uses the lower half of the bus during the address phase (because it's only generating a 32-bit address). When it discovers that the currently-addressed target is a 32-bit target (ACK64# not asserted when DEVSEL# asserted), the initiator ceases to use the upper half of the bus.

## Problem: 64-bit Cards Inserted in 32-bit PCI Connectors

Installation of a 64-bit card in a 32-bit card connector is permitted. The main (32-bit) portion of the connector contains all of the 32-bit PCI signals, while an extension to the connector contains the 64-bit extension signals (with the exception of REQ64# and ACK64# which are located on the 32-bit portion of the connector).

When a 64-bit device is installed in a 32-bit PCI expansion slot, the system board pullups on AD[63:32], C/BE#[7:4] and PAR64 are not available to the add-in card. This means that the add-in card's input buffers that are connected to the extension signal pins will float.

The specification states that the add-in card designer must not solve this problem by supplying pullup resistors on the extension lines on the add-in card. Using this approach would cause problems when the card is installed in a 64-bit expansion slot. There would then be two sets of pullup resistors on these signal lines (the ones on the card plus the ones on the system board). If all designers solved the problem in this manner, a machine with multiple 64-bit cards inserted in 64-bit card connectors would have multiple pullups on the extension signals, resulting in pullup current overload.

The specification provides a method for a 64-bit card to determine at startup time whether its installed in a 32-bit or a 64-bit connector. If the card detects that it is plugged into a 64-bit connector, the pullups on the system board are connected to the extension. The card need not take any action to keep the extension from floating when the extension is not in use. On the other hand, if a 64-bit card detects that it is installed in a 32-bit card connector, the logic on the card must keep the extension input signals on the card from floating. The specification states that an approach similar to one of the following should be used:

- Biasing the input buffer.
- Actively driving the outputs continually (since they aren't connected to anything).

## How 64-bit Card Determines Type of Slot Installed In

When the system is powered up, the reset signal is automatically asserted. During this period of time, the logic on the system board is responsible for asserting the

REQ64# signal. This signal line has a single pullup resistor on it and is connected to the REQ64# signal on all 64-bit devices integrated onto the system board and on all 64-bit PCI expansion slots. The specification states that the REQ64# signal line on each 32-bit PCI expansion slot (REQ64# and ACK64# are located on the 32-bit portion of the connector), however, each has its own independent pullup resistor. Refer to figure 13-1.

During reset time, the system board reset logic initially asserts the PCI RST# signal while the POWERGOOD signal from the power supply is deasserted. During the assertion of RST#, the system board logic asserts REQ64# and keeps it asserted until after it removes the RST# signal. When POWERGOOD is asserted by the power supply logic, the system board reset logic deasserts the PCI RST# signal. On the trailing-edge of RST# assertion, all 64-bit devices are required to sample the state of the REQ64# signal.

All 64-bit devices that are embedded on the PCI bus or are installed in 64-bit expansion slots sample REQ64# asserted on the trailing-edge of RST#. This informs them that they are connected to the extension pullups on the system board and need take no special action to keep the extension from floating when not using it.

All 64-bit devices that are installed in 32-bit card slots, however, detect REQ64# deasserted on the trailing-edge of RST#. This informs them that they are not connected to the system board-resident pullups on the extension signals. The card logic must therefore take responsibility for the state of its own on-card 64-bit extension signal lines. The card must therefore use one of the methods cited in the previous section to prevent floatation of the on-card 64-bit extension.

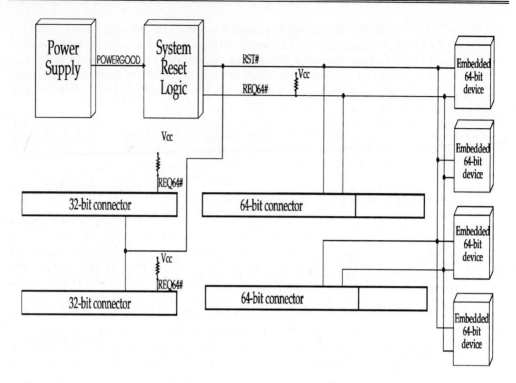

*Figure 13-1. REQ64# Signal Routing*

## 64-bit Data Transfer Capability

The agreement to perform 64-bit transfers is established by a handshake between the initiator and the target. When the initiator supports 64-bit transfers and wishes to perform a 64-bit transfer, it asserts REQ64# along with FRAME# during the address phase. If the currently-addressed target supports 64-bit data transfers, it replies with ACK64#. Because they are both pulled high, the quiescent state of REQ64# and ACK64# is deasserted. If either the master or the target, or both, do not support 64-bit data transfers, 32-bit data transfers are used instead.

During 64-bit transfers, all transfer timing during data phases is identical to that used during 32-bit data transfers. One to eight bytes may be transferred between the initiator and the target during each data phase and all combinations of byte enables are valid (including none asserted; an example is provided later in this chapter). The setting on the byte enable lines may be changed with each data phase. The following sections provide examples of:

- 64-bit initiator performing a transfer with a 64-bit target.
- 64-bit initiator performing a transfer with a 32-bit target.
- 32-bit initiator performing a transfer with a 64-bit target.

## Only Memory Commands May Use 64-bit Transfers

Only memory commands may utilize 64-bit data transfer capability. The specification provides the following arguments for not implementing support for 64-bit data transfers for the other types of commands:

- During the special cycle transaction, no target responds with DEVSEL#. ACK64#, therefore, is also not asserted.
- Configuration transactions do not require the level of throughput achievable with 64-bit data transfers and therefore do not justify the added complexity and cost necessary to support 64-bit data transfer capability. The author has heard arguments from some designers that devices that require large streams of configuration information would benefit from 64-bit configuration support.
- As with configuration transactions, I/O transactions do not require a high level of throughput and therefore do not justify the added complexity and cost necessary to support 64-bit data transfer capability.
- By definition, the interrupt acknowledge command only performs a single data phase consisting of a one, two, three or four byte transfer.

## Start Address Quadword-Aligned

When a bus master starts a transfer and asserts REQ64#, the start address it issues is quadword, not doubleword, aligned (e.g., address 00000100h, 00000108h, 00000110h, etc.). This means that AD[2] must be set to zero.

## 64-bit Target's Interpretation of Address

Assuming that the target supports 64-bit data transfers (it asserts ACK64#), the target latches the start quadword address into its address counter (if it supports burst mode). If the addressing sequence indicated by the bus master on AD[1:0] is sequential, or linear, addressing, the target increments the address in its address counter by eight at the completion of each data phase to point to the next sequential quadword. The target samples the eight byte enables, C/BE#[7:0], during each data phase to determine which of the eight bytes within the currently-addressed quadword is to be transferred and which of the eight data paths are to be used.

## 32-bit Target's Interpretation of Address

If the target that responds to the transaction is a 32-bit target (ACK64# not as-serted), it treats the start address as a doubleword-aligned address and latches it into its address counter. If the addressing sequence indicated by the bus master on AD[1:0] is sequential, or linear, addressing, the target increments the address in its address counter by four at the completion of each data phase to point to the next sequential doubleword. The target samples the four lower byte enables, C/BE#[3:0], during each data phase to determine which of the four bytes within the currently-addressed doubleword is to be transferred and which of the four data paths (on the AD[31:0] portion of the bus) are to be used.

## 64-bit Initiator and 64-bit Target

Figure 13-2 illustrates a 64-bit master performing a 64-bit read data transfer with a 64-bit memory target. The master is not using 64-bit addressing (it's not necessary because the target in the example does not reside over the 4GB address boundary). The following numbered sequence describes this transaction.

1.  On the rising-edge of clock one, the initiator asserts FRAME# to indicate the start of the transfer and REQ64# to indicate its desire to perform 64-bit trans-fers. It also drives the quadword-aligned start address onto the AD bus and sets C/BE#[3:0] to indicate that it is performing a memory read transaction. AD[63:32] and C/BE#[7:4] aren't used during the address phase. The system board designer is required to include pullups on AD[63:32], C/BE#[7:4] and PAR64 so that these signal lines do not float when they aren't in use (e.g., during the address phase of this transaction). Additional information regard-ing the pullup requirement can be found in the section in this chapter entitled "Preventing Flotation of 64-Bit Extension."

2.  The targets latch the address, command and REQ64# on the rising-edge of clock two and begin the decode process. The initiator ceases to drive the AD bus so that the target can begin to drive the first requested data onto the AD bus. The initiator also ceases to drive the read command onto the C/BE bus and sets C/BE#[7:0] to indicate which bytes are to be transferred within the first quadword and which data paths are to be used during the first data phase. The initiator asserts IRDY# to indicate that is ready to receive the first data item. It also keeps FRAME# asserted, indicating that this is not the final data phase.

3.  During clock two, the target asserts DEVSEL# to claim the transaction. It also asserts ACK64#, indicating that it is capable of using all eight data paths. The target leaves TRDY# deasserted to enforce the turn-around cycle.

4. During clock three, the target asserts TRDY# to indicate the presence of the first data item on the AD bus and it begins to drive the requested data onto AD[63:0].

5. At the rising-edge of clock four, TRDY# and IRDY# are sampled asserted and the first data is transferred. This completes the first data phase.

6. The second data phase starts during clock four. The target increments its address counter by eight (assuming that linear addressing was indicated during the address phase). The initiator drives the next data request onto the byte enables. It keeps IRDY# asserted and does not deassert FRAME#, indicating that it is ready to complete the second data phase and that it is not the final data phase.

7. Also during clock four, the target deasserts TRDY#, indicating that it requires a wait state inserted into data phase two in order to fetch the next requested data item.

8. On the rising-edge of clock five, TRDY# is sampled deasserted, resulting in a delay of the second data transfer and the conversion of clock five into a wait state.

9. During the wait state (clock five), the target begins to drive the requested data onto the data bus and asserts TRDY# to indicate its presence on the bus.

10. On the rising-edge of clock six, IRDY# and TRDY# are sampled asserted and the requested data is transferred, completing the second data phase.

11. The third data phase begins during clock six. The initiator drives the next data request onto the byte enables, but deasserts IRDY#, indicating that it isn't ready to accept the third data item yet (e.g., it has a buffer full condition). In other words, the initiator requires a wait state inserted into data phase three.

12. During clock six, the target increments its address counter by eight to point to the next quadword and begins to drive the requested data onto the data bus.

13. On the rising-edge of clock seven, IRDY# is sampled deasserted, resulting in a delay of the third data transfer and the conversion of clock seven into a wait state.

14. During clock seven (the wait state), the initiator asserts IRDY# to indicate that it is now ready to accept the data. It also deasserts FRAME# and REQ64# to indicate that the last data phase is in progress.

15. On the rising-edge of clock eight, IRDY# and TRDY# are sampled asserted and the last data is transferred.

16. During clock eight, the initiator deasserts IRDY#, indicating the conclusion of the last data phase. The bus returns to the idle state on clock nine.

17. During clock eight, the target deasserts TRDY#, DEVSEL# and ACK64# and ceases to drive the last data item onto the data bus. The initiator ceases to drive the byte enables.

# PCI System Architecture

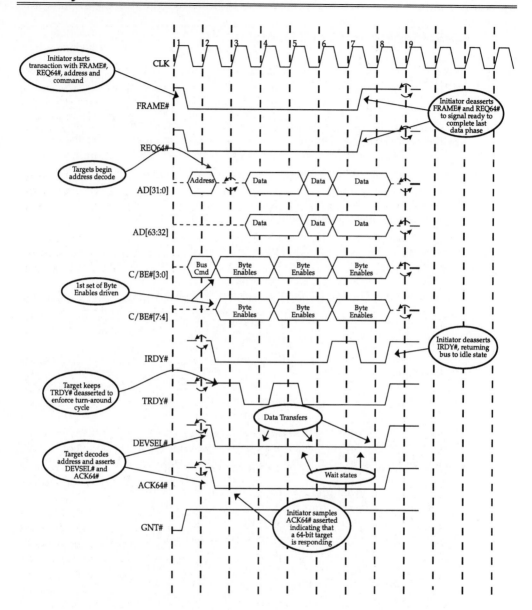

*Figure 13-2. Transfer Between a 64-bit Initiator and 64-bit Target*

# Chapter 13: The 64-bit PCI Extension

## 64-bit Initiator and 32-bit Target

Figure 13-3 illustrates a 64-bit PCI initiator performing a 64-bit write data transfer with a 32-bit PCI target. The start address is 00000100h, linear addressing is indicated (AD[1:0] are set to 00b), and the initiator will attempt to transfer eight bytes per data phase (all eight byte enables will be asserted in the first data phase and eight bytes will be driven onto AD[63:0]]). The following numbered sequence describes this data transfer.

1. On the rising-edge of clock one, the initiator starts the transaction by asserting FRAME# and REQ64#. It drives the quadword-aligned address, 00000100h, onto the AD bus and the memory write command onto C/BE#[3:0]. C/BE#[7:4] are not driven during the address phase.
2. On the rising-edge of clock two, the targets sample the address, command and REQ64# and begin the address decode. The 32-bit target treats the start address, 00000100h, as a doubleword-aligned address identifying the block of four locations from 00000100h through 00000103h.
3. During clock two, the initiator begins to drive eight bytes of write data onto the eight data paths and asserts the all eight byte enables, C/BE#[7:0]. It asserts IRDY# to indicate the presence of the data on the bus. It does not deassert FRAME#, thereby indicating that this is not the final data phase.
4. The addressed target does a fast address decode during clock two and asserts DEVSEL# to claim the transaction. It simultaneously asserts TRDY#, indicating that it is ready to receive the first data item. It does not assert ACK64#, indicating that it can only perform data transfers over the lower four data paths (and that it is not connected to C/BE#[7:4]).
5. On the rising-edge of clock three, the initiator samples DEVSEL#, IRDY# and TRDY# asserted and ACK64# deasserted. DEVSEL# asserted indicates that the addressed target has claimed the transaction. The deasserted state of ACK64# indicates that the target can only transfer data over the lower four data paths and cannot see the C/BE#[7:4] lines.
6. IRDY# and TRDY# asserted indicates that the initiator is presenting the data (eight bytes) and the target is ready to accept it (four bytes), but only over the lower four data paths. The target latches the four bytes destined for memory locations 00000100h through 00000103h from the lower four data paths. The fact that this is a 32-bit target means that the start address that it latched into its address counter during the address phase, 00000100h, is treated as a doubleword-aligned address, not quadword-aligned. Upon completion of the first data phase on clock three, the target increments its address counter by four to point to the next doubleword, 00000104h.
7. At the start of the second data phase (during clock four), the initiator copies the settings on the upper byte enables, C/BE#[7:4], to the lower byte enables, C/BE#[3:0], and copies the data that had been driven onto the upper four data paths (destined for memory locations 00000104h through 00000107h) onto the

lower four data paths. The initiator ceases to drive C/BE#[7:4] and AD[63:32], but these signal lines are prevented from floating by the required pullups on the system board.

8. The initiator keeps IRDY# asserted, indicating the presence of the next four bytes on the lower part of the data bus. It does not deassert FRAME#, indicating that this is not the final data phase.

9. On the rising-edge of clock four, IRDY# and TRDY# are sampled asserted and the four bytes on the lower four data paths are written into memory locations 00000104h through 00000107h. This completes the second data phase.

10. During clock four, the initiator asserts all four of the lower four byte enables, but deasserts IRDY# to indicate that it is not yet ready to drive the third data item onto the data paths (e.g., it has a buffer dry condition). Although it's not yet ready to deliver the third data item, the initiator is responsible for keeping the AD bus driven with a stable pattern. The designer typically just continues to drive the previous data item until ready to start driving the new one.

11. Also during clock four, the target increments its address counter to point to doubleword-aligned address 00000108h, but deasserts TRDY# to indicate that it is not yet ready to accept data.

12. On the rising-edge of clock five, IRDY# and TRDY# are sampled deasserted, forcing clock five to become a wait state in the third data phase. During clock five (the wait state), the initiator then asserts IRDY# and begins to drive the data onto the data bus. At the same time, the initiator deasserts FRAME# and REQ64#, indicating that the last data transfer is in progress.

13. TRDY# is sampled deasserted on the rising-edge of clocks six and seven, indicating that the target is not yet ready to accept the last data item. Clocks six and seven are therefore wait states in data phase three. The initiator must continue to drive the byte enables and the data until the target accepts the data.

14. During clock seven, the target asserts TRDY# to indicate that it is ready to accept the last data item.

15. On the rising-edge of clock eight, TRDY# and IRDY# are sampled asserted and the last data item is transferred. The four bytes on AD[31:0] are written into memory locations 00000108h through 0000010Bh. The initiator then ceases to drive the AD and C/BE buses and IRDY#, returning the bus to the idle state. The target deasserts TRDY# and DEVSEL#.

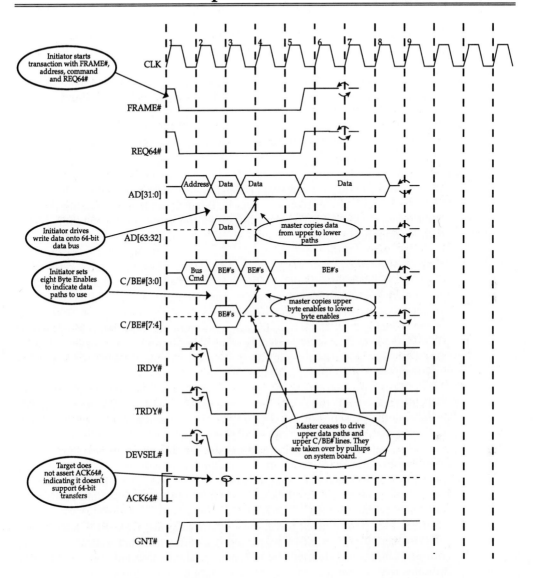

*Figure 13-3. Transfer Between a 64-bit Initiator and a 32-bit Target*

## Null Data Phase Example

In the previous section, the 64-bit bus master attempted to perform a burst write with a 32-bit target. It started the transaction on a quadword-aligned address (00000100h) and wanted to transfer eight bytes in the first and all subsequent data phases.

Now consider the case where the master starts the transfer on a misaligned address (not a quadword-aligned address). In this example, the master starts the transfer with the last four bytes in the first quadword, 00000104h through 00000107h, but wants to transfer eight bytes in every subsequent data phase. The start address issued is 00000100h, but only C/BE#[7:4] are asserted during the first data phase (not C/BE#[3:0]). This example uses the same timing diagram as the previous section (figure 13-3).

1. On the rising-edge of clock one, the initiator starts the transaction by asserting FRAME# and REQ64#. It drives the quadword-aligned address, 00000100h, onto the AD bus and the memory write command onto C/BE#[3:0]. C/BE#[7:4] are not driven during the address phase.
2. On the rising-edge of clock two, the targets sample the address, command and REQ64# and begin the address decode. The 32-bit target treats the start address, 00000100h, as a doubleword-aligned address identifying the block of four locations from 00000100h through 00000103h.
3. During clock two, the initiator begins to drive four bytes of write data onto AD[63:32] and asserts the upper four byte enables, C/BE#[7:4]. It asserts IRDY# to indicate the presence of the data on the bus. It does not deassert FRAME#, indicating that this is not the final data phase.
4. The addressed target does a fast address decode during clock two and asserts DEVSEL# to claim the transaction. It simultaneously asserts TRDY#, indicating that it is ready to receive the first data item. It does not assert ACK64#, indicating that it can only perform data transfers over the lower four data paths (and that it is not connected to C/BE#[7:4]).
5. On the rising-edge of clock three, the initiator samples DEVSEL#, IRDY# and TRDY# asserted and ACK64# deasserted. DEVSEL# asserted indicates that the addressed target has claimed the transaction. The deasserted state of ACK64# indicates that the target can only transfer data over the lower four data paths and cannot see the C/BE#[7:4] lines.
6. IRDY# and TRDY# asserted indicates that the initiator is ready to complete the write (of the upper four bytes) and the target is ready to accept write data, but only over the lower four data paths. Because none of the lower four byte enables, C/BE#[3:0], are asserted, the target treats this as a null data phase and doesn't latch any data. The fact that this is a 32-bit target means that the start address that it latched into its address counter during the address phase, 00000100h, is treated as a doubleword-aligned address, not quadword-aligned.

Upon completion of the null data phase on clock three, the target increments its address counter by four to point to the next doubleword, 00000104h.

7. At the start of the second data phase (during clock four), the initiator copies the settings on the upper byte enables, C/BE#[7:4], to the lower byte enables, C/BE#[3:0], and copies the data that had been driven onto the upper four data paths (destined for memory locations 00000104h through 00000107h) onto the lower four data paths. The initiator ceases to drive C/BE#[7:4] and AD[63:32], but these signal lines are prevented from floating by the required pullups on the system board.

8. The initiator keeps IRDY# asserted, indicating the presence of the next four bytes on the lower part of the data bus. It does not deassert FRAME#, indicating that this is not the final data phase.

9. On the rising-edge of clock four, IRDY# and TRDY# are sampled asserted and the four bytes on the lower four data paths are written into memory locations 00000104h through 00000107h. This completes the second data phase.

10. During clock four, the initiator asserts all four of the lower four byte enables, but deasserts IRDY# to indicate that it is not yet ready to drive the third data item onto the data paths (e.g., it has a buffer dry condition). Although it's not yet ready to deliver the third data item, the initiator is responsible for keeping the AD bus driven with a stable pattern. The designer typically just continues to drive the previous data item until ready to start driving the new one.

11. Also during clock four, the target increments its address counter to point to doubleword-aligned address 00000108h, but deasserts TRDY# to indicate that it is not yet ready to accept data.

12. On the rising-edge of clock five, IRDY# and TRDY# are sampled deasserted, forcing clock five to become a wait state in the third data phase. During clock five (the wait state), the initiator then asserts IRDY# and begins to drive the data onto the data bus. At the same time, the initiator deasserts FRAME# and REQ64#, indicating that the last data transfer is in progress.

13. TRDY# is sampled deasserted on the rising-edge of clocks six and seven, indicating that the target is not yet ready to accept the last data item. Clocks six and seven are therefore wait states in data phase three. The initiator must continue to drive the byte enables and the data until the target accepts the data.

14. During clock seven, the target asserts TRDY# to indicate that it is ready to accept the last data item.

15. On the rising-edge of clock eight, TRDY# and IRDY# are sampled asserted and the last data item is transferred. The four bytes on AD[31:0] are written into memory locations 00000108h through 0000010Bh. The initiator ceases to drive the AD and C/BE buses and IRDY#, returning the bus to the idle state. The target deasserts TRDY# and DEVSEL#.

## 32-bit Initiator and 64-bit Target

If the initiator is a 32-bit bus master, it never asserts REQ64# when it starts a transaction (it's not even connected to REQ64#). When it addresses a 64-bit target during the transaction, the target does not assert ACK64# along with DEVSEL# when it decodes the address. Because the initiator does not assert REQ64#, the target recognizes that the initiator is a 32-bit bus master. It therefore recognizes that the start address is doubleword-aligned and that it should increment by four rather than by eight.

## Performing One 64-bit Transfer

The specification contains the following statement: "Using a single data phase with 64-bit transfers may not be very effective." The discussion that follows illustrates the rationale for this statement.

Assume that an initiator starts a transaction in order to perform a write consisting of eight bytes (one quadword). Assuming that an initiator wants to write one quadword-aligned group of eight bytes, it cannot be assumed that this will result in only one data phase. The currently-addressed target may be either a 32 or 64-bit target. If it turns out to be a 64-bit target, then it can accept all of the data in one data phase. On the other hand, if it turns out to be a 32-bit target, it's only capable of accepting 32-bits per data phase. This means that two data phases must be performed by the initiator when a 32-bit target claims the transaction.

The initiator does not know the size (32 or 64-bit) of the target until the target has decoded the address and command and asserted DEVSEL#. The initiator then samples ACK64# to make the size determination. When attempting the transfer of a single 64-bit data item, the initiator must defer the deassertion of FRAME# until it determines whether one (for a 64-bit target) or two phases (for a 32-bit target) will be necessary. Since the protocol dictates that FRAME# must be deasserted when the initiator is ready to complete the final data phase, this situation affects the timing of IRDY# as well. The initiator cannot assert IRDY# during the first data phase until it determines whether or not this is the final data phase (and therefore whether to deassert FRAME# or not).

In summary, if the designer uses 64-bit capability to transfer a single eight byte object, it requires additional design complexity to handle the atypical IRDY#/FRAME# timing. In addition, it would not result in a faster transfer than could be accomplished using normal, 32-bit transfers. In fact, using 32-bit transfer capability would be equally efficient and less complex.

## With 64-bit Target

Figure 13-4 illustrates the case where the 64-bit initiator attempts the transfer of a 64-bit data item using 64-bit transfer capability (REQ64# is asserted) and a 64-bit target claims the transaction. The initiator cannot assert IRDY# during clock two because it hasn't yet determined if this is the only data phase or the first of two. It therefore has not yet determined whether or not to deassert FRAME# with the assertion of IRDY#.

At the rising-edge of clock three, it samples DEVSEL# and ACK64# asserted, indicating that a 64-bit target has claimed the transaction. Since this means that only one data phase is necessary, the initiator can deassert FRAME# and assert IRDY# during clock three, indicating that it is ready to complete the final (and only) data phase of the transaction.

The data transfer occurs on the rising-edge of clock four when IRDY# and TRDY# are sampled asserted. The transaction takes three clocks to complete and requires atypical IRDY#/FRAME# timing.

## With 32-bit Target

Figure 13-5 illustrates the case where the 64-bit initiator attempts the transfer of a 64-bit data item using 64-bit transfer capability (REQ64# is asserted) and a 32-bit target claims the transaction. During clock two, the initiator can't assert IRDY# yet because it hasn't yet determined whether this is the only or the first of two data phases.

At the rising-edge of clock three, the initiator samples DEVSEL# asserted and ACK64# deasserted, indicating that a 32-bit target has claimed the transaction. Since this means that this is the first of two data phases, the initiator asserts IRDY# during clock three, but doesn't deassert FRAME#. IRDY# asserted indicates the presence of the lower 32-bits of write data on AD[31:0]. The first transfer of the first 32-bits occurs on the rising-edge of clock four when IRDY# and TRDY# are sampled asserted. This completes the first data phase and the second data phase then begins.

The initiator then copies the bytes from the upper four data paths, AD[63:32], to the lower four data paths and the upper byte enables, C/BE#[7:4], to the lower byte enables, C/BE#[3:0]. It keeps IRDY# asserted to indicate the presence of the data and also deasserts FRAME#, indicating its readiness to complete the last data phase. The second data transfer occurs on the rising-edge of clock five when IRDY# and TRDY# are sampled asserted. The transaction takes four clocks to complete and requires the atypical IRDY#/FRAME# timing.

## Simpler and Just as Fast: Use 32-bit Transfers

When performed without asserting REQ64#, the same transaction can be accomplished in three clocks using normal IRDY#/FRAME# timing. The transaction would consist of the address phase plus one clock for the transfer of each of the two 32-bit objects.

## With Known 64-bit Target

If the 64-bit master knows that the target it's addressing is a 64-bit target (via a device-specific configuration register or some other mechanism), it doesn't need to wait for DEVSEL# and ACK64# to assert IRDY# and deassert FRAME#. It can assert IRDY# and deassert FRAME# immediately upon entering the first data phase. When dealing with 0-wait state memory, the transfer could then be accomplished in two clocks (one for the address phase and one for the data phase).

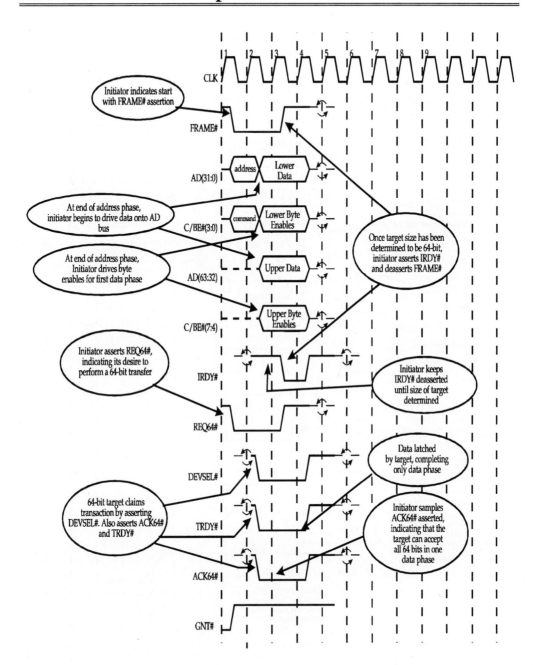

*Figure 13-4. Single Data Phase 64-bit Transfer With a 64-bit Target*

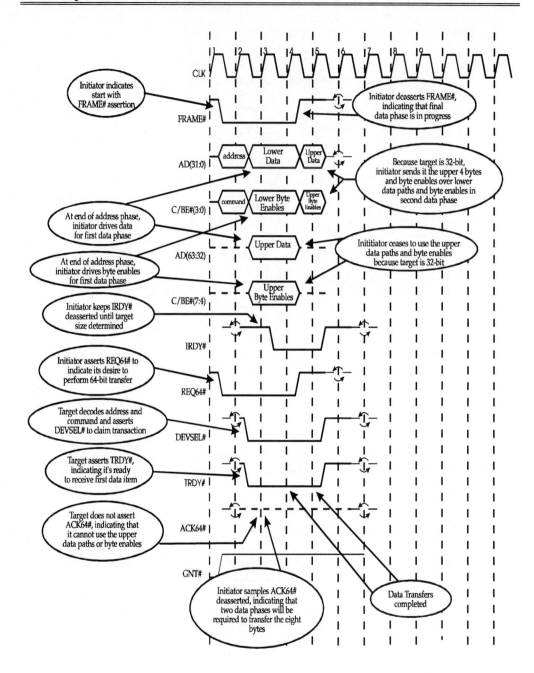

*Figure 13-5. Dual-Data Phase 64-bit Transfer With a 32-bit Target*

## Disconnect on Initial Data Phase

Assume that a master starts a multiple-data phase read transaction and asserts REQ64#. The quadword-aligned start address is 00000100h and all eight byte enables are asserted during the first data phase. Also assume that the target is a 32-bit target and is not capable of handling a multiple-data phase transaction. This has the following effects:

1. The target does not assert ACK64#.
2. The target only transfers locations 00000100h through 00000103h during the first data phase and terminates the transaction by asserting STOP# along with TRDY#.
3. The master accepts the four bytes and ends the transaction.
4. The master re-arbitrates for the bus and then initiates the read again. It asserts FRAME# and REQ64# again. This time, the quadword-aligned start address is once again 00000100h, but only the upper four byte enables are asserted during the first data phase (because 00000100h through 00000103h have already been transferred).
5. The 32-bit target doesn't assert ACK64# and doesn't transfer any data (because the lower four byte enables are deasserted) and terminates the transaction with a disconnect (TRDY# and STOP# asserted).
6. Recognizing that the upper four bytes in the quadword still haven't been transferred, the master re-arbitrates for the bus and tries it again. It will never be successful in transferring the upper four bytes.

The solution to this dilemma is as follows: when the master was disconnected after the first doubleword transfer, it should restart the transaction as a 32-bit transfer (i.e., do not assert REQ64# and output the doubleword-aligned address of the next four bytes to be transferred: 00000104h).

# 64-bit Addressing

## Used to Address Memory Above 4GB

Bus masters are only permitted to use 64-bit addressing when communicating with memory that resides above the 4GB address boundary. Standard 32-bit addressing must be used if the start address resides below this boundary (i.e., the upper 32 bits of the address are all zero).

## Introduction

Using the basic command set, the PCI address bus, AD[31:0], permits the initiator to address devices that reside within the first 4GB of address space (using a single address phase; any command that uses a single address phase is referred to as a single address command, or SAC).

Without the addition of any signals, the PCI specification also provides support for addressing memory devices that reside above the 4GB boundary. The dual address command, or DAC, is used by an initiator to inform the community of targets that it is broadcasting a 64-bit memory address. 64-bit addressing capability is not restricted to 64-bit initiators. Initiators fall into two categories:

- Those that are capable of generating only 32-bit addresses over AD[31:0] using a single address phase.
- Those that are capable of generating 32 and 64-bit addresses.

The sections that follow discuss the methods used by both 32-bit and 64-bit initiators in presenting a 64-bit address to the community of targets. Targets fall into two categories:

- Those that recognize the 64-bit addressing protocol (i.e., they have memory that resides above the 4GB address boundary).
- Those that only recognize the 32-bit addressing protocol (i.e., they do not have any memory that resides above the 4GB address boundary).

## 64-bit Addressing Protocol

### 64-bit Addressing by 32-bit Initiator

Figure 13-6 illustrates a 32-bit initiator performing a burst read access from above the 4GB boundary. The target in this example is a 32-bit target, although a 64-bit target would respond exactly the same way to a 64-bit address generated by a 32-bit initiator (because it would not see REQ64# asserted).

1. The initiator begins the transaction on the rising-edge of clock one by asserting FRAME#, placing the lower 32 bits of the address on AD[31:0], and placing the dual-address command, or DAC, on C/BE#[3:0]. All targets that support 64-bit addressing (in other words, memory targets that reside above 4GB) recognize the DAC and expect a second address phase to deliver the upper 32 bits of the address. All non-memory targets (i.e., I/O targets, configuration space and the interrupt controller) ignore the transaction after detecting the

dual-address command. In this example, the initiator is not a 64-bit device, so it doesn't assert REQ64#.

2.  On the rising edge of clock two, all targets latch the lower 32 bits of the address and the dual address command. A second address phase is begun during clock two. The initiator drives the upper 32 bits of the address onto AD[31:0]. In addition, the initiator drives the memory read command onto C/BE#[3:0].

3.  On the rising-edge of clock three, the memory targets that reside above 4GB latch the upper 32 bits of the address from AD[31:0], the memory read command from C/BE#[3:0], and begin the address decode process.

4.  The first data phase begins during clock three. The initiator ceases to drive the upper part of the address onto AD[31:0] (in preparation for the target driving the requested data onto the AD bus). The initiator asserts IRDY# to indicate that it is ready to receive the requested data and also sets the byte enables to indicate the bytes to be transferred and the data paths to be used. FRAME# is not deasserted when IRDY# is asserted, indicating that this is not the final data phase. The target has a fast address decoder and asserts DEVSEL# during clock three, but not ACK64# (because it's a 32-bit target).

5.  On the rising-edge of clock four, TRDY# is sampled deasserted. The target has kept TRDY# deasserted to enforce the turn-around cycle necessary between the address phase and the first data phase of a read. The target then asserts TRDY# during clock four (a wait state), indicating the presence of the first data item on the bus.

6.  On the rising-edge of clock five, the requested data is transferred (because TRDY# and IRDY# are sampled asserted). This completes the first data phase.

7.  During clock five, the initiator changes the setting on the byte enables to request the next set of bytes, but deasserts IRDY# to indicate that it will not be ready to accept the requested data on the next rising-edge of the clock (a wait state must be inserted). The target keeps TRDY# asserted and begins to drive the second data item onto the AD bus.

8.  On the rising-edge of clock six, IRDY# is sampled deasserted, so no data transfer takes place. The next clock (clock six) is a wait state. The target continues to drive the requested data onto the AD bus. During the wait state, the initiator asserts IRDY# to indicate that it will be ready to transfer the data on the next rising-edge of the clock. The initiator also deasserts FRAME# to indicate that the last data phase is in progress.

9.  On the rising-edge of clock seven, IRDY# and TRDY# are sampled asserted and the last data phase completes. The initiator then deasserts IRDY#, returning the bus to the idle state. It also ceases to drive the C/BE# bus. The target ceases to drive the data onto the AD bus and deasserts TRDY# and DEVSEL#.

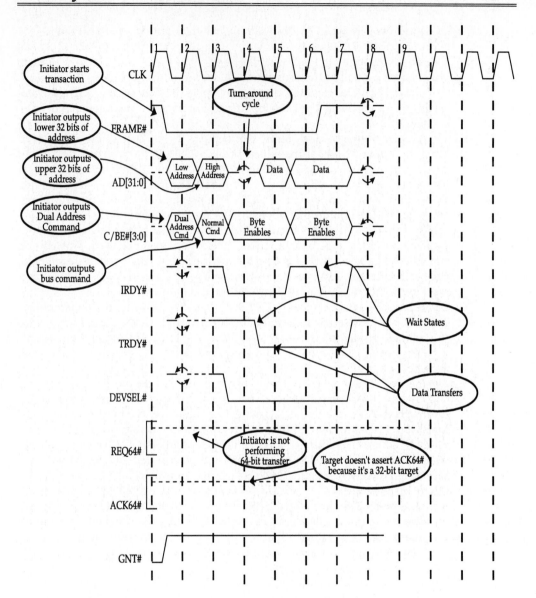

Figure 13-6. 32-bit Initiator Reading From Address at or Above 4GB

# Chapter 13: The 64-bit PCI Extension

## 64-bit Addressing by 64-bit Initiator

Figure 13-7 illustrates a 64-bit initiator performing a burst read access from an address above the 4GB boundary. In addition to using 64-bit addressing, the initiator asserts REQ64# to indicate that it wishes to perform 64-bit data transfers. The target of this transaction is a 64-bit target. If the target were a 32-bit device, it would not assert ACK64#, indicating that it could not handle 64-bit data transfers. The initiator would then reorder the byte enables from the upper lines, C/BE#[7:4], to the lower lines, C/BE#[3:0]. This subject is covered in the earlier part of this chapter. Since the target would only have visibility to AD[31:0] and C/BE#[3:0], it would handle the 64-bit address as discussed in the section preceding this one.

1. The initiator starts the transaction on the rising-edge of clock one by asserting FRAME# and REQ64#, and driving the dual-address command onto C/BE#[3:0]. It also drives the lower 32-bits of the address onto AD[31:0], the upper 32-bits of the address onto AD[63:32], and the memory read command onto C/BE#[7:4]. It continues to drive the upper part of the address onto AD[63:32] and the memory read command onto C/BE#[7:4] for the duration of both address phases. REQ64# is asserted, indicating that the initiator is using the entire 64-bit bus for address output (during the first address phase) and that the initiator wishes to perform 64-bit data transfers (if the addressed target is a 64-bit device).

2. On the rising-edge of clock two, the community of 32-bit targets latch the dual-address command from C/BE#[3:0] and the lower 32 bits of the address from AD[31:0]. The community of 64-bit memory targets that reside above the 4GB boundary latch the entire 64-bit address from AD[63:0] and the memory read command from C/BE#[7:4].

3. During clock two, all 32-bit targets other than memory targets that reside above the 4GB address boundary quit listening to the transaction. All 64-bit memory targets that reside below the 4GB boundary also quit listening.

4. During clock two, the initiator starts the second address phase by driving the upper part of the address onto AD[31:0] (in case the currently-addressed target is not a 64-bit device) and the memory read command onto C/BE#[3:0].

5. On the rising-edge of clock three, all 32-bit memory targets that reside above the 4GB address boundary latch the upper 32 bits of the address from AD[31:0] and the memory read command from C/BE#[3:0]. They begin the address decode during clock three.

6. During clock three, the initiator asserts IRDY# to indicate that it is ready to receive the requested data. It does not deassert FRAME#, indicating that this is not the final data phase. The initiator ceases to drive address information onto both halves of the AD bus so the bus is free to be driven by the target during the data phase. The initiator sets C/BE#[7:0] to indicate which bytes to transfer during the first data phase.

7. During clock three, the target asserts DEVSEL# to claim the transaction and ACK64# to indicate that it is capable of performing 64-bit data transfers.
8. On the rising-edge of clock four, TRDY# is sampled deasserted, enforcing the insertion of the turn-around cycle. During clock four, the target starts to drive the requested data onto the AD bus and asserts TRDY# to indicate its presence on the bus.
9. On the rising-edge of clock five, IRDY# and TRDY# are sampled asserted and the first data item is transferred. This completes the first data phase.
10. During clock five, the initiator sets C/BE#[7:0] to indicate which bytes to transfer during the second data phase and deasserts IRDY# to indicate that it will not be ready to accept the requested data on the next rising-edge of the clock.
11. During clock five, the target keeps TRDY# asserted and begins to drive the second data item onto the AD bus.
12. On the rising-edge of clock six, IRDY# is sampled deasserted and the data is not transferred. During the inserted wait state (clock six) the initiator asserts IRDY# to indicate that it will be ready to transfer the data on the next rising-edge of the clock. It also deasserts FRAME# and REQ64# to indicate that the last data transfer is in progress.
13. On the rising-edge of clock seven, IRDY# and TRDY# are sampled asserted and the final data item is transferred. The initiator then deasserts IRDY#, returning the bus to the idle state and ceases to drive C/BE#[7:0]. The target ceases to drive the final data item onto the AD bus and deasserts TRDY#, DEVSEL# and ACK64#.

A 64-bit target with a fast address decoder could assert DEVSEL# during clock two, but must insert two wait states to account for the second address phase and the turn-around cycle (on a read).

A 64-bit target with a medium-speed address decoder could assert DEVSEL# during clock three, but must insert one wait state to account for the turn-around cycle (on a read).

A 64-bit target with a slow address decoder could assert DEVSEL# during clock four. The address decode latency accounts for the second address phase and the turn-around cycle (on a read), so the target need not insert wait states to account for them.

The only advantage that a 64-bit target has (over a 32-bit target) during 64-bit addressing is a one clock jump on address decode.

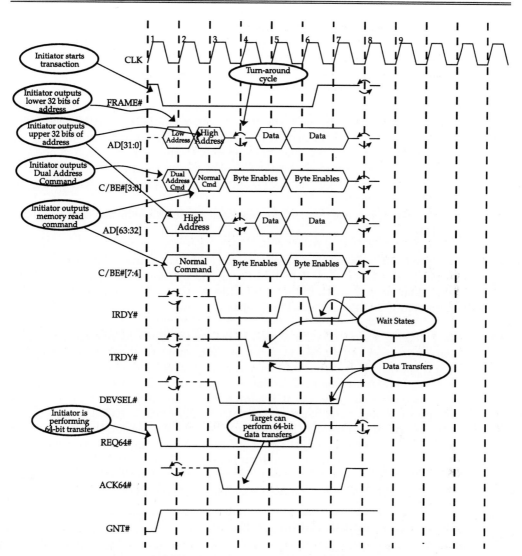

*Figure 13-7. 64-bit Initiator Reading From Address*
*Above 4GB With 64-Bit Data Transfers*

## 32-bit Initiator Addressing Above 4GB

An initiator that is only connected to AD[31:0] can communicate with memory above 4GB in two ways:

- The 64-bit memory target can alias all or some of its memory above 4GB into an address range in the lower 4GB. In other words, the configuration programmer could set up two address decoders (base address registers) for the same block of memory: one that responds to addresses above 4GB and one that recognizes addresses below 4GB. The master can then use SAC memory commands to transfer data into/out of the memory above 4GB (using the window below 4GB).
- The master can use the DAC to communicate directly with the memory above 4GB.

The specification also contains the following statement: "Another alternative is for the master to support only 32-bit addressing and the device driver moves the data from 32-bit address space to the 64-bit address space." This statement is open to interpretation and the author's interpretation follows.

The operating system issues a request to the device driver associated with a particular bus master to move a block of data into memory above 4GB. The device driver, knowing that its related bus master is incapable of performing 64-bit addressing, reprograms the memory target's memory base address register to map the memory buffer below the 4GB address boundary. It then instructs the 32-bit bus master to move the block of data into memory below 4GB. Upon receiving notice of completion (usually by interrupt) from the bus master, the device driver reprograms the memory target's memory base address register to map the memory buffer back above the 4GB address boundary. This scenario implies that the device driver has specific knowledge of the memory target (in order to issue requests to the BIOS or HAL to access its configuration registers).

## Subtractive Decode Timing Affected

If an expansion bus bridge located on the PCI bus employs subtractive decode, the expansion bus on the other side of the bridge either supports 64-bit addressing or it doesn't. As two examples, the ISA bus does not support 64-bit addressing, while the 64-bit Micro Channel does.

An ISA bridge that incorporates subtractive decode capability (virtually all implementations do) ignores any PCI transaction that uses 64-bit addressing (because there are no memory targets on the ISA bus that reside above 4GB).

# Chapter 13: The 64-bit PCI Extension

A bridge to an expansion bus that supports 64-bit addressing and that incorporates a subtractive decoder operates in the following manner: starting one clock after the end of the second address phase, it samples DEVSEL# on three successive rising-edges of the clock to determine that the transaction isn't claimed by any PCI memory targets. If none claim it (by asserting DEVSEL#), the bridge's subtractive decoder asserts DEVSEL# during the next clock to claim the transaction. It then initiates the memory transaction on the expansion bus to make it visible to all memory targets that reside above the 4GB address boundary on the expansion bus.

During a single address phase transaction, starting one clock after the end of the one and only address phase, a subtractive decoder samples DEVSEL# on three successive rising-edges of the clock to determine that the transaction isn't claimed by any PCI memory targets.

## Master Abort Timing Affected

Normally, a bus master samples DEVSEL# at the end of the second, third, fourth and fifth clocks of the transaction and then master aborts if DEVSEL# was not sampled asserted. When the master is using 64-bit addressing, it samples DEVSEL# at the end of the third, fourth, fifth and sixth clocks of the transaction and then aborts if DEVSEL# was not sampled asserted.

## Address Stepping

A bus master that uses stepping to gradually place the full address on the bus keeps FRAME# deasserted until the full address is present and stable on the bus. When the targets sample FRAME# asserted, the address is decoded.

The specification says that stepping cannot be used for 64-bit addressing. Although the master could keep FRAME# deasserted until the lower 32 bits of the address is present and stable on AD[31:0], 32-bit memory targets then expect the upper 32 bits of the address to be present and stable on AD[31:0] on the next rising-edge of the clock. The upper 32 bits of the address therefore cannot be stepped onto AD[31:0]. It must be presented in one clock.

Although the specification specifically states that stepping cannot be used for 64-bit addressing, the author should note that it's technically possible to step the lower 32-bit of the address onto AD[31:0] and then present the upper 32-bits in one clock. The author cannot think of any side effects stemming from this approach, but would also question the value in it.

## FRAME# Timing in Single Data Phase Transaction

If the initiator were using 64-bit addressing to perform a single data phase transaction, FRAME# is asserted at the start of the first address phase and must be kept asserted until IRDY# is asserted in the data phase. It cannot be removed during the second address phase.

# 64-bit Parity

## Address Phase Parity

### PAR64 Not Used for Single Address Phase

When the initiator is not using 64-bit addressing, there is a single address phase and a 32-bit address is generated by the initiator. In this case, address phase parity is supplied solely over the PAR signal. The 64-bit extension, consisting of AD[63:32], PAR64, and C/BE#[7:4], is not in use during the address phase of the transaction.

### PAR64 Not Used for Dual-Address Phases by 32-bit Master

When a 32-bit bus master is performing 64-bit addressing, it is only using AD[31:0] and C/BE#[3:0]. The 64-bit extension is not in use. The PAR64 signal is therefore not used to supply parity on the upper half of the bus.

### PAR64 Used for Dual-Address Phase by 64-bit Master
### (when requesting 64-bit data transfers)

When a 64-bit bus master is performing 64-bit addressing and has asserted REQ64#, it is required to drive the upper 32 bits of the address onto AD[63:32] and the memory command onto C/BE#[7:4] during the first address phase. It is also required to supply even parity for this information on the PAR64 signal on the next rising-edge of the clock. During the second address phase, the initiator is required to continue driving the same information on AD[63:32], C/BE#[7:4]. Although the specification doesn't cover this, it is the author's opinion that the initiator must once again supply even parity on PAR64 on the rising-edge of the clock that follows completion of the second address phase. A 64-bit target may be designed to latch the entire address and command and begin the decode at the end of either the first or the second address phase. The target then latches the state of PAR64 on the rising-edge of the clock that follows.

# Chapter 13: The 64-bit PCI Extension

## Data Phase Parity

Parity works the same for 32 and 64-bit transfers. For a detailed discussion of 32-bit parity, refer to the chapter entitled, "Error Detection and Handling." In a 64-bit implementation, an additional parity signal, PAR64, is added. It's timing and function are identical to that of the PAR signal. PAR64 must be implemented by all 64-bit agents.

PAR64 must be set to the appropriate state (to force even parity) one clock after the completion of each data phase. Usage of PAR64 is qualified by the assertion of REQ64# (indicating that the initiator wants to perform 64-bit data transfers) and ACK64# (the target supports 64-bit data transfers). If either REQ64# or ACK64# is deasserted, only the lower half of the bus is in use and PAR64 is not used.

# Chapter 14

## The Previous Chapter

The previous chapter provided a detailed discussion of the PCI 64-bit extension.

## In This Chapter

This chapter provides an introduction to the PCI expansion card and connector definition. It covers card and connector types, 5V and 3.3V operability, shared slots, and pinout definition. For a detailed description of electrical and mechanical issues, refer to the latest version of the PCI specification (as of this printing, revision 2.1). This chapter concludes part II of the book, "Revision 2.1 Essentials."

## The Next Chapter

The next chapter begins part III of the book, "Device Configuration In Single PCI Bus System."

## Expansion Connectors

### 32 and 64-bit Connectors

The PCI add-in card connector is derived from the Micro Channel connector. There are two basic types of connectors: the 32 and the 64-bit connector. A basic representation can be found in figure 14-1. Table 14-1 illustrates the pinout of the 32-bit and the 64-bit card (note that the 64-bit connector is a superset of the 32-bit connector). The table shows the card pinout for three types of cards: 5V, 3.3V, and universal (the three card types are defined later in this chapter). The system board designer must leave all reserved pins unconnected. The table illustrates the pinouts and keying for 3.3V and 5V connectors. In addition, a universal card can be installed in either a 3.3V or a 5V connector. Additional information regarding 3V, 5V and universal cards can be found in this chapter in the section entitled "3.3V and 5V Connectors."

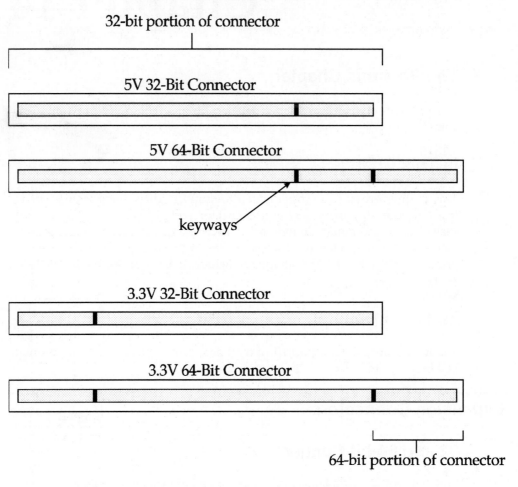

Figure 14-1. 32 and 64-bit Connectors

*Table 14-1. PCI Add-In Card Pinouts*

| Pin | 5V Card Side B | 5V Card Side A | Universal Card Side B | Universal Card Side A | 3.3V Card Side B | 3.3V Card Side A | Comment |
|-----|------|------|------|------|------|------|---------|
| 1  | -12V *(63)* | TRST# *(1)* | -12V | TRST# | -12V | TRST# | 32-bit connector start |
| 2  | TCK | +12V *(2)* | TCK | +12V | TCK | +12V | |
| 3  | Ground | TMS | Ground | TMS | Ground | TMS | |
| 4  | TDO | TDI | TDO | TDI | TDO | TDI | |
| 5  | +5V | +5V | +5V | +5V | +5V | +5V | |
| 6  | +5V | INTA# | +5V | INTA# | +5V | INTA# | |
| 7  | INTB# | INTC# | INTB# | INTC# | INTB# | INTC# | |
| 8  | INTD# | +5V | INTD# | +5V | INTD# | +5V | |
| 9  | PRSNT1# | Reserved | PRSNT1# | Reserved | PRSNT1# | Reserved | |
| 10 | Reserved | +5V | Reserved | +Vi/o | Reserved | +3.3V | |
| 11 | PRSNT2# | Reserved | PRSNT2# | Reserved | PRSNT2# | Reserved | |
| 12 | Ground | Ground | key | key | key | key | 3.3V key |
| 13 | Ground | Ground | key | key | key | key | 3.3V key |
| 14 | Reserved | Reserved | Reserved | Reserved | Reserved | Reserved | |
| 15 | Ground | RST# | Ground | RST# | Ground | RST# | |
| 16 | CLK | +5V | CLK | +Vi/o | CLK | +3.3V | |
| 17 | Ground | GNT# | Ground | GNT# | Ground | GNT# | |
| 18 | REQ# | Ground | REQ# | Ground | REQ# | Ground | |
| 19 | +5V | Reserved | +Vi/o | Reserved | +3.3V | Reserved | |
| 20 | AD[31] | AD[30] | AD[31] | AD[30] | AD[31] | AD[30] | |
| 21 | AD[29] | +3.3V | AD[29] | +3.3V | AD[29] | +3.3V | |
| 22 | Ground | AD[28] | Ground | AD[28] | Ground | AD[28] | |
| 23 | AD[27] | AD[26] | AD[27] | AD[26] | AD[27] | AD[26] | |
| 24 | AD[25] | Ground | AD[25] | Ground | AD[25] | Ground | |
| 25 | +3.3V | AD[24] | +3.3V | AD[24] | +3.3V | AD[24] | |
| 26 | C/BE#[3] | IDSEL | C/BE#[3] | IDSEL | C/BE#[3] | IDSEL | |
| 27 | AD[23] | +3.3V | AD[23] | +3.3V | AD[23] | +3.3V | |
| 28 | Ground | AD[22] | Ground | AD[22] | Ground | AD[22] | |
| 29 | AD[21] | AD[20] | AD[21] | AD[20] | AD[21] | AD[20] | |
| 30 | AD[19] | Ground | AD[19] | Ground | AD[19] | Ground | |
| 31 | +3.3V | AD[18] | +3.3V | AD[18] | +3.3V | AD[18] | |
| 32 | AD[17] | AD[16] | AD[17] | AD[16] | AD[17] | AD[16] | |
| 33 | C/BE#[2] | +3.3V | C/BE#[2] | +3.3V | C/BE#[2] | +3.3V | |
| 34 | Ground | FRAME# | Ground | FRAME# | Ground | FRAME# | |
| 35 | IRDY# | Ground | IRDY# | Ground | IRDY# | Ground | |
| 36 | +3.3V | TRDY# | +3.3V | TRDY# | +3.3V | TRDY# | |
| 37 | DEVSEL# | Ground | DEVSEL# | Ground | DEVSEL# | Ground | |
| 38 | Ground | STOP# | Ground | STOP# | Ground | STOP# | |
| 39 | LOCK# | +3.3V | LOCK# | +3.3V | LOCK# | +3.3V | |
| 40 | PERR# | SDONE | PERR# | SDONE | PERR# | SDONE | |
| 41 | +3.3V | SBO# | +3.3V | SBO# | +3.3V | SBO# | |
| 42 | SERR# | Ground | SERR# | Ground | SERR# | Ground | |
| 43 | +3.3V | PAR | +3.3V | PAR | +3.3V | PAR | |
| 44 | C/BE[1]# | AD[15} | C/BE[1]# | AD[15] | C/BE[1]# | AD[15} | |
| 45 | AD[14] | +3.3V | AD[14] | +3.3V | AD[14] | +3.3V | |

| Pin | 5V Card Side B | 5V Card Side A | Universal Card Side B | Universal Card Side A | 3.3V Card Side B | 3.3V Card Side A | Comment |
|---|---|---|---|---|---|---|---|
| 46 | Ground | AD[13] | Ground | AD[13] | Ground | AD[13] | |
| 47 | AD[12] | AD[11] | AD[12] | AD[11] | AD[12] | AD[11] | |
| 48 | AD[10] | Ground | AD[10] | Ground | AD[10] | Ground | |
| 49 | Ground | AD[09] | Ground | AD[09] | Ground ** | AD[09] | ** see note |
| 50 | Keyway | | Keyway | | Ground | Ground | 5V key |
| 51 | Keyway | | Keyway | | Ground | Ground | 5V key |
| 52 | AD[08] | C/BE#[0] | AD[08] | C/BE#[0] | AD[08] | C/BE#[0] | |
| 53 | AD[07] | +3.3V | AD[07] | +3.3V | AD[07] | +3.3V | |
| 54 | +3.3V | AD[06] | +3.3V | AD[06] | +3.3V | AD[06] | |
| 55 | AD[05] | AD[04] | AD[05] | AD[04] | AD[05] | AD[04] | |
| 56 | AD[03] | Ground | AD[03] | Ground | AD[03] | Ground | |
| 57 | Ground | AD[02] | Ground | AD[02] | Ground | AD[02] | |
| 58 | AD[01] | AD[00] | AD[01] | AD[00] | AD[01] | AD[00] | |
| 59 | +5V | +5V | +Vi/o | +Vi/o | +3.3V | +3.3V | |
| 60 | ACK64# | REQ64# | ACK64# | REQ64# | ACK64# | REQ64# | |
| 61 | +5V | +5V | +5V | +5V | +5V | +5V | |
| 62 | +5V | +5V | +5V | +5V | +5V | +5V | 32-bit connector end |
| | keyway | | keyway | | keyway | | 64-bit spacer |
| | keyway | | keyway | | keyway | | 64-bit spacer |
| 63 | Reserved | Ground | Reserved | Ground | Reserved | Ground | 64-bit start |
| 64 | Ground | C/BE#[7] | Ground | C/BE#[7] | Ground | C/BE#[7] | |
| 65 | C/BE#[6] | C/BE#[5] | C/BE#[6] | C/BE#[5] | C/BE#[6] | C/BE#[5] | |
| 66 | C/BE#[4] | +5V | C/BE#[4] | +Vi/o | C/BE#[4] | +3.3V | |
| 67 | Ground | PAR64 | Ground | PAR64 | Ground | PAR64 | |
| 68 | AD[63] | AD[62] | AD[63] | AD[62] | AD[63] | AD[62] | |
| 69 | AD[61] | Ground | AD[61] | Ground | AD[61] | Ground | |
| 70 | +5V | AD[60] | +Vi/o | AD[60] | +3.3V | AD[60] | |
| 71 | AD[59] | AD[58] | AD[59] | AD[58] | AD[59] | AD[58] | |
| 72 | AD[57] | Ground | AD[57] | Ground | AD[57] | Ground | |
| 73 | Ground | AD[56] | Ground | AD[56] | Ground | AD[56] | |
| 74 | AD[55] | AD[54] | AD[55] | AD[54] | AD[55] | AD[54] | |
| 75 | AD[53] | +5V | AD[53] | +Vi/o | AD[53] | +3.3V | |
| 76 | Ground | AD[52] | Ground | AD[52] | Ground | AD[52] | |
| 77 | AD[51] | AD[50] | AD[51] | AD[50] | AD[51] | AD[50] | |
| 78 | AD[49] | Ground | AD[49] | Ground | AD[49] | Ground | |
| 79 | +5V | AD[48] | +Vi/o | AD[48] | +3.3V | AD[48] | |
| 80 | AD[47] | AD[46] | AD[47] | AD[46] | AD[47] | AD[46] | |
| 81 | AD[45] | Ground | AD[45] | Ground | AD[45] | Ground | |
| 82 | Ground | AD[44] | Ground | AD[44] | Ground | AD[44] | |

| | 5V Card | | Universal Card | | 3.3V Card | | |
| Pin | Side B | Side A | Side B | Side A | Side B | Side A | Comment |
|---|---|---|---|---|---|---|---|
| 83 | AD[43] | AD[42] | AD[43] | AD[42] | AD[43] | AD[42] | |
| 84 | AD[41] | +5V | AD[41] | +Vi/o | AD[41] | +3.3V | |
| 85 | Ground | AD[40] | Ground | AD[40] | Ground | AD[40] | |
| 86 | AD[39] | AD[38] | AD[39] | AD[38] | AD[39] | AD[38] | |
| 87 | AD[37] | Ground | AD[37] | Ground | AD[37] | Ground | |
| 88 | +5V | AD[36] | +Vi/o | AD[36] | +3.3V | AD[36] | |
| 89 | AD[35] | AD[34] | AD[35] | AD[34] | AD[35] | AD[34] | |
| 90 | AD[33] | Ground | AD[33] | Ground | AD[33] | Ground | |
| 91 | Ground | AD[32] | Ground | AD[32] | Ground | AD[32] | |
| 92 | Reserved | Reserved | Reserved | Reserved | Reserved | Reserved | |
| 93 | Reserved | Ground | Reserved | Ground | Reserved | Ground | |
| 94 | Ground | Reserved | Ground | Reserved | Ground | Reserved | 64-bit end |

Note: pin B49 on 3.3V connectors is ground on a 33MHz PCI bus, but is called M66EN on a 66MHz PCI bus. For more information, refer to the chapter entitled "66MHz PCI Implementation."

## 32-bit Connector

The 32-bit connector contains all of the PCI signals for the implementation of 32-bit PCI. In addition, it contains two of the 64-bit extension signals, REQ64# and ACK64#, and the two card present signals, PRSNT1# and PRSNT2#.

### Card Present Signals

The card present signals are required for add-in cards, but optional for the system board. The system board designer must decouple both of the card present pins to ground through a 0.01µF high-speed capacitor because one or both of these pins also provide an AC return path. These two card pins must not be bussed together or otherwise connected to each other on the system board. In addition to following these implementation rules, the system board designer may optionally permit software to access the state of the card present signals through a machine-readable port. If they are used in this manner, the system board designer must place a separate pullup resistor on each of these signal lines.

The PCI card designer encodes the maximum power requirements of the card on the card present signals. When the card is installed in a PCI connector, it grounds one, the other, or both of the card present signals. At a minimum, the add-in card must ground one of these two pins.

Table 14-2 defines the value encoded on these two signals. The encoded value must indicate the total maximum consumption of the card when it is fully-configured and fully-operational. When interrogating this value to determine if the system's power supply and cooling will support the card, the system software should assume that the indicated power could be drawn from either the 3.3V or the 5V power rail.

*Table 14-2. Card Power Requirement Indication On Card Present Signals*

| Description | PRSNT1# | PRSNT2# |
|---|---|---|
| Slot empty | 1 | 1 |
| Card present; 25W max | 0 | 1 |
| Card present; 15W max | 1 | 0 |
| Card present; 7.5W max | 0 | 0 |

### REQ64# and ACK64#

The REQ64# and ACK64# signals are located on the 32-bit portion of the connector in order to support 64-bit cards installed in 32-bit slots. On 32-bit connectors (that do not implement the 64-bit extension), the system board designer must implement a separate pullup resistor on each connector's REQ64# and ACK64# pins (separate pullup on each). Nothing else should be connected to these pins.

If a 64-bit bus master is installed in a 32-bit card slot and it initiates a transaction, its assertion of REQ64# is not visible to any of the targets. In addition, its ACK64# input is always sampled deasserted. This forces the bus master to use only the lower part of the bus during the transfer. Furthermore, if the target addressed in the transaction is a 64-bit target, it samples REQ64# deasserted, forcing it to only utilize the lower half of the bus during the transaction.

As just explained, a 64-bit card installed in a 32-bit connector cannot use the upper half of the bus. This means that the signals related to the upper half of the bus will float unless some special action is taken by the on-card logic. This subject is covered in the chapter entitled "The 64-Bit PCI Extension" in the section entitled "Pullups Prevent 64-Bit Extension From Floating When Not In Use."

## 64-bit Connector

A 64-bit PCI connector consists of the 32-bit connector plus a 64-bit extension to the connector (refer to figure 14-1). The extension contains all of the 64-bit extension signals (with the exception of REQ64# and ACK64#). For a discussion of 64-bit extension operation, refer to the chapter entitled "The 64-Bit PCI Extension."

## 3.3V and 5V Connectors

A PCI system board is implemented around a PCI chip set. The buffer/driver logic that the chip set uses to interface to the PCI bus is implemented as either 5V or 3.3V logic. The chip set design therefore defines the PCI bus signaling environment as either 3.3V or 5V. In order for an add-in PCI card to operate correctly, its buffer/driver logic must match the system board's PCI signaling environment.

As illustrated in figure 14-1, 3.3V and 5V card connectors are keyed 180 degrees out from each other. A card that implements its buffer/driver logic using purely 5V logic is keyed to plug only into a 5V connector, while a card with 3.3V buffer/driver logic is keyed so as to install only in a 3.3V connector. It should be noted that a 5V card can incorporate a mix of 3.3V and 5V logic residing behind its buffer/drivers. Likewise, a 3.3V card can also incorporate a logic mix behind its front-end logic.

A card that implements its buffer/drivers with logic that can operate at either 3.3V or 5V is referred to as a universal card. It is keyed so as to install in either a 3.3V or a 5V card connector. Its buffer/driver logic receives power from a special set of pins referred to as Vio pins (see table 14-1). The system board designer connects the Vio pins to the voltage rail corresponding to the PCI chip set signaling environment. Figure 14-2 illustrates the relationship of the 3.3V, 5V and universal cards to the 5V and 3.3V connectors.

System boards implemented with 3.3V chip set buffer/driver logic must supply all four operating voltages to the card connectors. The four voltages are 5V, 3.3V, +12V and -12V.

System boards implemented with 5V chip set buffer/driver logic must supply 5V, +12V and -12V to the connectors. It is strongly recommended that 3.3V be supplied as well. The system board designer may supply a method for field upgrade for 3.3V power sourcing by the system board. In 5V systems that do not provide a 3.3V power source, an add-in card that requires 3.3V must derive it from the 5V or 12V supplies via an on-card regulator.

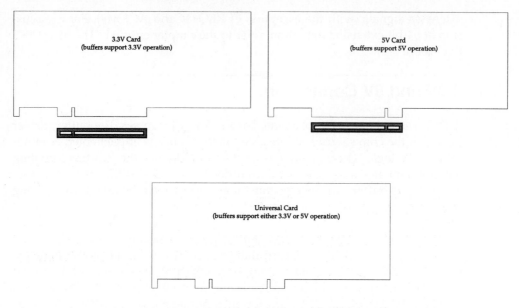

*Figure 14-2. 3.3V, 5V and Universal Cards*

## Shared Slot

It's important to note that the component side of a PCI add-in card is the op-posite of that for ISA, EISA and Micro Channel add-in cards. One of the slots can be implemented as a shared slot because it is shared by a standard EISA, ISA or Micro Channel connector and a PCI connector. Only one of these two slots may be populated, however. Standard card spacing of .8 inches for E/ISA cards and .85 inches for Micro Channel cards permits only one of the shared slots to be occupied. It will be the last slot in the series of E/ISA or Mi-cro Channel slots. Figure 14-3 illustrates a machine with PCI expansion slots and either ISA or EISA expansion slots. Figure 14-4 illustrates a unit with PCI and Micro Channel expansion slots. The purpose of the shared slot is to maximize usage of system board real estate.

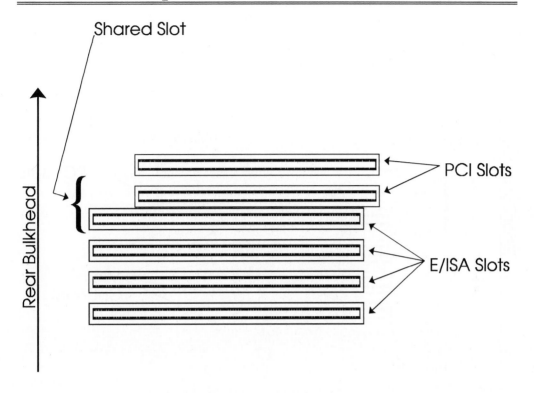

*Figure 14-3. ISA/EISA Unit Expansion Slots*

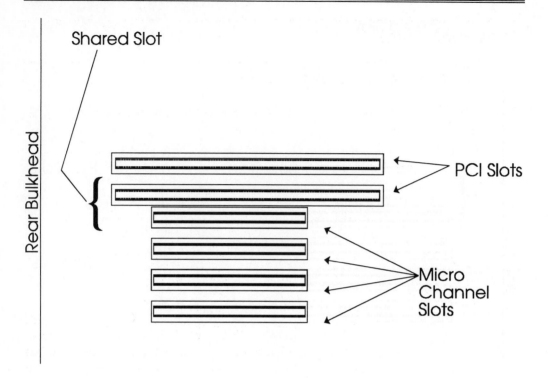

*Figure 14-4. Micro Channel Unit Expansion Slots*

## Riser Card

Although the specification only provides illustrations of systems with the PCI expansion connectors located on the system board itself, it is permitted to implement the PCI expansion connectors on a riser card. The designer must ensure that the PCI elctrical specification is not violated.

## Snoop Result Signals on Add-in Connector

The specification recommends that systems that do not support cacheable memory on the PCI bus should supply pullups on the SDONE and SBO# pins at each add-in connector. If a PCI memory card checks the snoop result signals before permitting access, it will then always detect a clean snoop immediately.

# Chapter 14: Add-in Cards and Connectors

## Expansion Cards

### 3.3V, 5V and Universal Cards

The section entitled "3.3V and 5V Connectors," found earlier in this chapter, provides a description of 3.3V, 5V and universal cards.

### Long and Short Form Cards

In addition to defining the 32 and 64-bit card types, the specification also defines three physical card sizes. They are described in the specification as:

- the standard, or long, cards.
- fixed-height short cards.
- variable-height short cards.

The standard card measures 12.283" by 4.2". The fixed-height short card measures 4.2" by 6.875". The variable-height short card can be anywhere from 1.42" to 4.2" in height. The fixed and variable-height short card provide less surface area but that are well-suited for small-footprint machines. The reader should refer to the 2.1 specification for a detailed description of the mechanical design.

### Component Layout

In order to meet the PCI signal propagation delay specification, it is critical that the length of PCI signal lines be kept as short as possible. Towards this end, the PCI specification strongly recommends that the pinout of PCI components be exactly aligned with the PCI edge connector ordering (as illustrated in figure 14-5). If implemented, the 64-bit extension signals should continue wrapping around the component in a counter-clockwise direction in the same order as they appear on the 64-bit connector.

The placement of IDSEL in close physical proximity to the upper AD lines facilitates resistively-coupling IDSEL to one of them. This subject is covered in the chapter entitled "Device Configuration In Single PCI Bus System."

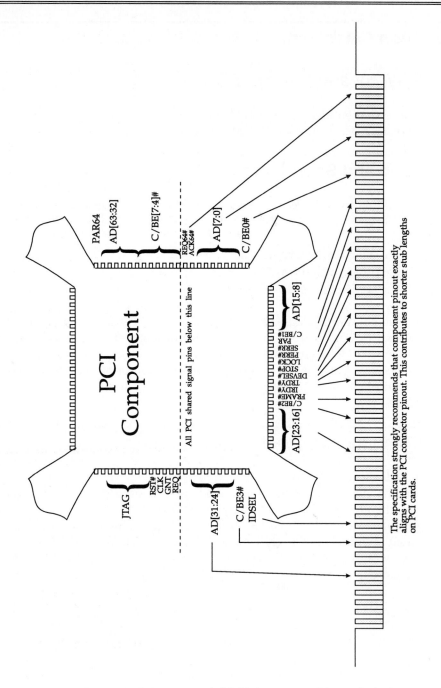

*Figure 14-5. Recommended PCI Component Pinout Ordering*

# Chapter 14: Add-in Cards and Connectors

## Maintain Integrity of Boundary Scan Chain

Some system board designers may choose to include the PCI expansion connectors in the boundary scan test chain. To ensure that the integrity of the TDI/TDO chain remains intact, cards designed without boundary scan capability must bus the TDI and TDO edge connector pins together. For the reader who isn't familiar with boundary scan testing, TDI and TDO are the serial test data in and test data out pins. Using the TCK, or test clock, signal, commands and requests can be shifted to or from the device in a serial fashion. The TDO from one device is connected to the TDI on the next device in the boundary scan test chain. A discussion of boundary scan is outside the scope of this book. The major audience for boundary scan, test engineers, already know this subject. Any who don't had better not let their boss find out.

## Card Power Requirement

As stated earlier in this chapter, system boards with a 3.3V PCI signaling environment are required to provide all four supply voltages to the PCI connectors. System boards with a 5V PCI signaling environment are required to provide 5V, -12V and +12V, and may optionally provide 3.3V as well. Table 14-3 defines the required current sourcing capability for the four power rails (on a per-connector basis).

*Table 14-3. Required Power Supply Current Sourcing Capability (per connector)*

| Power Rail | Tolerance | Current Sourcing Capability |
|:---:|:---:|:---|
| 5V | +/- 5% | 5A maximum per connector (system design-dependent). |
| 3.3V | +/- 0.3V | 7.6A maximum per connector (system design-dependent). |
| 12V | +/- 5% | 500mA per connector. |
| -12V | +/- 10% | 100mA per connector. |

The maximum power requirement per card is specified at 25 Watts. This value includes the summary power consumption on all four rails. PCI cards that consume more than 10 watts should power up and reset to a state that consumes 10 watts or less (if possible). While in this state, the card must permit access to its configuration registers. If the card is required for the raw boot process (POST and operating system boot), it must be capable of performing its bootstrap functions (e.g., text mode video) while in diminished power mode. After configuration, the card can be placed in full-power mode.

## Maximum Card Trace Lengths

The list that follows defines the maximum trace length for PCI signal lines on PCI add-in cards:

- All signals that comprise the 32 bit portion of the PCI bus must be limited to a maximum trace length of 1.5 inches.
- All signals that comprise the 64-bit extension signals must be limited to a maximum trace length of 2 inches.
- The PCI CLK signal trace length must be limited to a maximum trace length of 2.5 inches and it must be connected to only one load on the card.

## One Load per Shared Signal

The PCI specification contains a strict rule that each PCI device (embedded or on an add-in card) may place only one load on each shared (i.e., bussed) PCI signal line. The following list illustrates PCI add-in card design scenarios that would violate this rule:

- A device ROM attached directly to the PCI bus signals.
- Two or more PCI devices connected to the shared signals. In this case, a PCI-to-PCI bridge should be the only device connected to the system board PCI bus signals. The on-card PCI devices can then be connected to the PCI bus on the card itself.
- Two or more devices that snoop the same PCI signal(s) (in other words, two or more devices with a PCI signal connected to their input buffers).
- On-card chipsets that place more than one load on each pin.
- A card that has more than 10pF capacitance per pin.
- A card that places pullups or other discrete devices on shared PCI signals. Any system board shared PCI bus signals that require pullups already have them on the system board. Placing pullups on these signal lines on an expansion card would result in pullup current overload.

# Part III

# Device Configuration In a System With a Single PCI Bus

# Chapter 15

## The Previous Chapter

The previous chapter provided a discussion of the PCI expansion connectors and cards. It also concluded part II of the book, "Revision 2.1 PCI Essentials."

## This Chapter

As the chapter title states, this chapter provides an introduction to PCI configuration address space. The concept of single and multi-function devices is described. The configuration space available to the designer of a PCI designer is defined, including the device's configuration header space and its device-specific configuration register area.

## The Next Chapter

The next chapter provides a detailed discussion of three methods utilized to access PCI configuration registers. These three methods are referred to as the type one and type two configuration mechanisms, and the usage of memory-mapped configuration registers (as implemented in the PowerPC PREP platforms). The type zero configuration read and write configuration transactions are described in detail.

## Introduction

When the machine is first powered on, the configuration software must scan the PCI bus, or buses, to determine what PCI devices exist and what configuration requirements they have. This process is commonly referred to as scanning, walking or probing the bus. It also sometimes referred to as the discovery process. The program that performs the bus scan is frequently referred to as the PCI bus enumerator.

In order to facilitate this process, all PCI devices must implement a base set of configuration registers defined by the PCI specification. Depending on its operational characteristics, a device may also implement other required or optional configuration registers defined by the specification. In addition, the specification sets aside a number of additional configuration locations for the implementation of device-specific configuration registers.

The configuration software reads a subset of a device's configuration registers in order to determine the presence of the device and its type. Having determined the presence of the device, the software then accesses the device's other configuration registers to determine how many blocks of memory and/or IO space the device requires. It then programs the device's memory and/or IO address decoders to respond to memory and/or IO address ranges that are guaranteed to be mutually-exclusive from those assigned to other system devices.

If the device indicates usage of a PCI interrupt request line (via one of its configuration registers), the configuration software programs it with routing information indicating what system interrupt request (IRQ) line the device's PCI interrupt request line is routed to by the system.

If the device has bus mastering capability, the configuration software can read two of its configuration registers to determine how quickly it requires access to the PCI bus when it asserts REQ# and the average duration of its transfer when it has acquired ownership of the bus. The system configuration software can utilize this information to program the bus master's latency timer (or timeslice) register and the PCI bus arbiter to provide the optimal PCI bus utilization.

## PCI Package vs. PCI Function

A physical PCI package (e.g., a PCI component or a PCI expansion board) may contain one or more (up to eight) separate functional (i.e., logical) PCI devices. This is not a new concept. Multi-function boards have been used in PCs for years.

This means that a physical PCI package needs to know that it is the target of a configuration read or write, the identity of the target function within it, and the exact configuration register within that function. The method used to identify the target physical PCI package, PCI function and configuration register is discussed in the chapter entitled "Configuration Transactions."

A PCI package that contains only one function is referred to as a single-function PCI device. A PCI package that contains more than one function is referred to as a multi-function PCI device. A bit in one of a device's configuration registers defines whether the package contains one or more than one function. For the configuration process, a device's PCI functions are identified as functions zero through seven. The function contained in a single-function device must be designed as function zero. In a multi-function device, the first logical device must be designed to respond as function zero, while additional logical devices may be designed to respond as any function between one and seven. There is no requirement for multiple functions to be implemented sequentially. As an example, a card may be sold with minimal functionality and the customer may purchase additional functions as upgrades at a later time. These functions could be installed into any of several daughter-card connectors (on the PCI card) or may be installed as snap-in modules. As an example, a card could have functions zero, three and six populated, but not the others.

## Three Address Spaces: I/O, Memory and Configuration

Intel x86 and PowerPC™ 60x processors possess the ability to address two distinct address spaces: I/O and memory. PCI bus masters (including the host/PCI bridge) use PCI I/O and memory transactions to access PCI I/O and memory devices, respectively. In addition, a third access type, the configuration access, is used to access a device's configuration registers. A device's configuration registers must be initialized at startup time to configure the device to respond to memory and/or IO address ranges assigned to it by the configuration software.

The PCI memory space is either 4GB or $2^{64}$ locations in size (if 64-bit addressing is utilized). PCI I/O space is 4GB in size. PCI configuration space is divided into a separate configuration address space for each functional device contained within a physical device (i.e., in a chip or card). Figure 15-1 illustrates the basic format of a PCI functional device's configuration space. The first 16 doublewords of a device's space is referred to as the device's configuration header space. The format and usage of this area is defined by the specification. Two header formats are currently defined: header type zero for all devices other than PCI-to-PCI bridges; and header type one for PCI-to-PCI bridges. A detailed description of the header space can be found in the chapter entitled "Configuration Registers."

The system designer must provide some mechanism for converting predefined memory or I/O accesses initiated by the host processor into configuration accesses on the PCI bus. The mechanisms defined in the specification are described in the chapter entitled "Configuration Transactions."

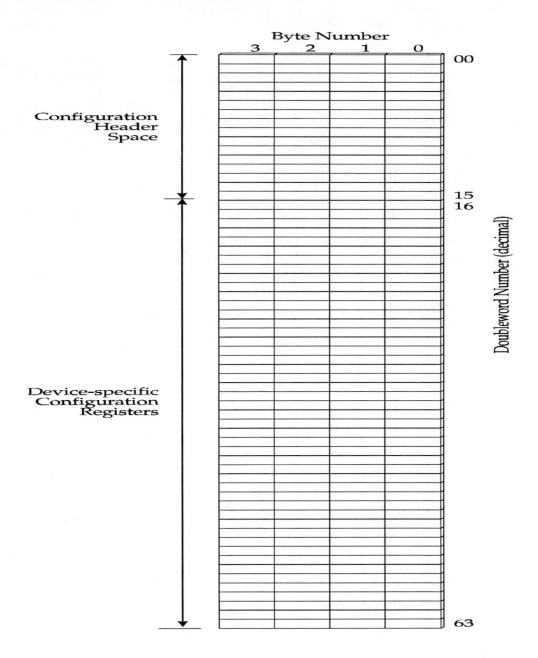

*Figure 15-1. PCI Functional Device's Basic Configuration Address Space Format*

# Chapter 15: Intro To Configuration Address Space

## System with Single PCI Bus

Figure 15-2 illustrates a typical system incorporating a single PCI bus. The interface between the host bus and the PCI bus is referred to as the host/PCI bridge. The bus closest to the host processor is the bridge's primary bus. If one of the devices on the PCI bus is a PCI-to-PCI bridge, the two PCI buses connected to the bridge are referred to as the bridge's primary (the PCI bus closer to the host processor) and secondary buses (the bus further away from the host processor). The next chapter, "Configuration Transactions", provides a detailed description of configuration read and write transactions targeting devices residing on the PCI bus connected to the host/PCI bridge. The chapter entitled "PCI-to-PCI Bridge" describes how the host processor accesses configuration registers for devices residing on subordinate PCI buses (PCI buses residing beneath the PCI bus closest to the host processor).

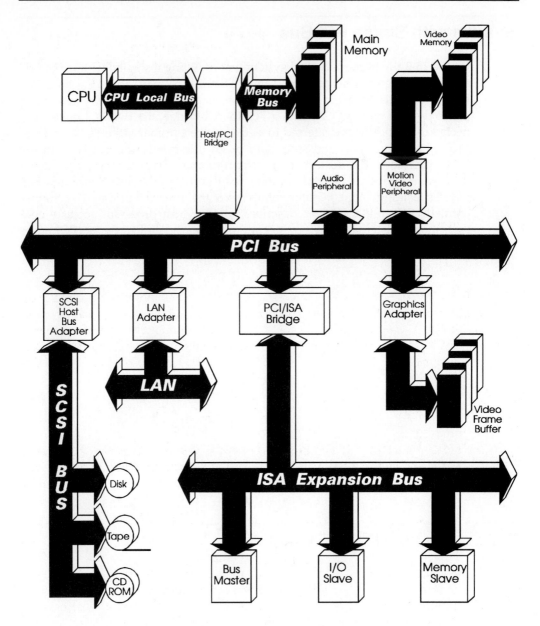

*Figure 15-2. System With a Single PCI Bus*

# Chapter 16

## The Previous Chapter

The previous chapter provided an introduction to PCI configuration address space. The concept of single and multi-function devices was described. The configuration space available to the designer of a PCI designer was defined, including the device's configuration header space and its device-specific configuration register area.

## This Chapter

This chapter provides a detailed discussion of three methods utilized to access PCI configuration registers. These three methods are referred to as the type one and type two configuration mechanisms, and the usage of memory-mapped configuration registers (e.g., as implemented in the PowerPC PReP platforms). The type zero configuration read and write transactions are described in detail.

## The Next Chapter

Now that this chapter has described how the registers are accessed, the next chapter provides a detailed description of the configuration register format and usage. A detailed description of the PCI-to-PCI bridge's configuration registers can be found in the chapter entitled "PCI-to-PCI Bridge."

## Which "Type" Are We Talking About?

The author added this section because, in teaching PCI for the past two years, a fair amount of confusion arises regarding the terms defined below. Throughout this part of the book, there are many references to this type vs that type. We are forced to utilize the nomenclature found in the specification, and, as with any specification, some terms can lead to confusion. The list that follows defines terms related to PCI configuration that have similar names:

- **Type zero configuration read and write transactions**. Used to access configuration registers located within PCI devices that reside on the PCI bus the transaction is performed on.
- **Type one configuration read and write transactions**. Used to instruct normal devices residing on a PCI bus that the transaction isn't for any of them. Rather, it is to be cascaded through a PCI-to-PCI bridge onto a subordinate PCI bus. When the transaction has arrived at the target bus, it is converted into a type zero configuration read or write on the target bus.
- **Type one configuration mechanism**. One of the two mechanisms defined in the specification for the host/PCI bridge to convert an Intel x86 I/O transaction into a PCI configuration transaction.
- **Type two configuration mechanism**. The other mechanism defined for the x86 platform.
- **Configuration header type zero**. Defines the format and usage of the first 16 doublewords of a normal PCI device's (i.e., not a PCI-to-PCI bridge) configuration address space.
- **Configuration header type one**. Defines the format and usage of the first 16 doublewords of a PCI-to-PCI bridge's configuration address space.

## Who Performs Configuration?

The configuration software executed by the host processor performs system configuration. This means that the host processor must have some way to instruct the host/PCI bridge to perform configuration read and write transactions on the PCI bus.

## Bus Hierarchy

This chapter focuses on the configuration of systems with one PCI bus. Assuming that the system has one or more PCI expansion connectors, however, a card may be installed at any time (perhaps more than one card) that incorporates a PCI-to-PCI bridge. The card has another PCI bus on it and one or more PCI devices reside on that PCI bus. The configuration software executing on the host processor must be able to perform configuration reads and writes with the devices on all PCI buses that live beyond the host/PCI bridge.

This highlights the fact that the programmer must indicate the following to the host/PCI bridge when performing a configuration read or write:

- target PCI bus.
- target physical package on the bus.
- target PCI functional device within the package.
- target doubleword within the device's configuration space.
- target byte(s) within the doubleword.

These parameters must be supplied to the host/PCI bridge. The bridge must then determine if the target PCI bus is:

- the bus immediately on the other side of the host/PCI bridge.
- a bus further out in the bus hierarchy.
- none of the buses behind the bridge.

This implies that the host/PCI bridge has some way of identifying its PCI bus and the range of PCI buses residing beyond its bus. The bus on the other side of the host/PCI bridge is always bus zero. The bridge also incorporates a subordinate bus number register that it uses to identify the bus furthest away from the host processor beyond this bridge. The bridge compares the target bus number specified by the programmer to the range of buses that exists beyond the bridge. There are three possible cases:

- the target bus is bus zero.
- the target bus isn't bus zero, but is less than or equal to the value in the subordinate bus number register. In other words, the transaction targets a device on a subordinate bus.
- the target bus doesn't fall within the range of buses that exists beyond this bridge.

In the third case, the bridge doesn't respond to the configuration transaction at all (because the target bus doesn't exist behind it).

In either the first or the second case, the host/PCI bridge must initiate a PCI configuration read or write transaction on its PCI bus. If the target bus is its PCI bus (the first case), the bridge must in some way indicate to the devices on its bus that one of them is the target of this configuration transaction. This is accomplished by setting AD[1:0] to 00b during the address phase of the configuration transaction. This identifies the transaction as a type zero configuration transaction targeting one of the devices on this bus.

If, on the other hand, the target bus is a bus that is subordinate to its PCI bus (the second case), the bridge must initiate the configuration transaction on its bus, but must indicate that none of the devices on this bus is the target of the transaction. Rather, only PCI-to-PCI bridges residing on the bus should pay attention to the transaction. This is accomplished by setting AD[1:0] to 01b during the address phase of the configuration transaction. This pattern instructs all devices other than PCI-to-PCI bridges that the transaction is not for any of them. This is referred to as a type one configuration transaction. Any PCI-to-PCI bridges on the bus, however, must compare the target bus number (supplied on the AD bus during the address phase) to the range of buses that reside beyond the PCI-to-PCI bridge. If the target bus isn't within the range of buses behind a PCI-to-PCI bridge, the bridge ignores the transaction. If the target bus is the bus immediately on the other side of a PCI-to-PCI bridge, the bridge passes the transaction through and converts it to a type zero configuration transaction (because the target device resides on its bus). If the target bus isn't its bus but is within the range of subordinate buses that live beyond the bridge, the bridge passes the transaction through as a type one configuration transaction to be submitted to the next tier of PCI-to-PCI bridges.

This implies that PCI-to-PCI bridges must incorporate a bus number and a subordinate bus number register. PCI-to-PCI bridges on the base PCI bus (bus zero) are discovered and numbered during the configuration process. This procedure is covered in the chapter entitled "PCI-to-PCI Bridge."

## Intro to Configuration Mechanisms

This section describes the methods used to stimulate the host/PCI bridge to generate PCI configuration transactions. A subsequent section in this chapter provides a detailed description of the type zero configuration transactions. The chapter entitled "PCI-to-PCI Bridge" provides a detailed description of the type one configuration transactions.

As mentioned earlier in this book, Intel x86 and PowerPC processors (as two processor family examples) do not possess the ability to perform configuration read and write transactions. They use memory and I/O read and write transactions to communicate with external devices. This means that the host/PCI bridge must be designed to recognize certain I/O or memory accesses initiated by the host processor as configuration accesses.

For PC-AT compatible systems (other than PREP-compliant PowerPC-based systems), the specification defines two designs that utilize processor-initiated I/O accesses to instruct the host/PCI bridge to perform configuration accesses. These two mechanisms are designated as configuration mechanism one and configuration mechanism two.

Configuration mechanism two is only defined in the specification for backward compatibility. This was the mechanism defined in the revision 1.0 specification. The revision 2.0 and 2.1 specifications both contain the following text:

> **Configuration mechanism #1 is the preferred implementation** and must be provided by all future host bridges (and existing bridges should convert if possible). Configuration mechanism #2 is defined for backward compatibility and must not be used by new designs. Host bridges implemented in PC-AT compatible systems must implement at least one of these mechanisms.

That about says it all.

The specification does not define the configuration mechanism to be used in systems other than PC-AT compatible systems.

Although PowerPC 60x processors are capable of performing I/O transactions, the PowerPC PReP specification forbids the generation of I/O transactions by the processor. Instead, all I/O and configuration registers are accessed via memory-mapped locations defined by the PReP specification. The section in this chapter entitled "PowerPC PReP Memory-Mapped Configuration" provides a basic description of this mechanism.

## Configuration Mechanism One

### Background

The x86 processor family is capable of addressing up to, but no more than, 64KB of I/O address space. In the EISA PC environment, the usage of this I/O space is defined as indicated in table 16-1. The only I/O address ranges available for the implementation of the PCI configuration mechanism (without conflicting with an ISA or EISA device) are 0400h - 04FFh, 0800h - 08FFh, and 0C00h - 0CFFh. Many EISA system board controllers already reside within the 0400h - 04FFh address range, making it unavailable.

Consider the following:

- As with any other PCI device, a host/PCI bridge requires the implementation of up to 64 doublewords of configuration registers.

- Each PCI function on each PCI bus requires an additional 64 doublewords of configuration locations.

Due to the lack of available I/O real estate within the 64KB of I/O space, it's not feasible to map each configuration register directly into host processor I/O address space. The designer could implement the configuration registers within the processor's memory space. This approach may consume a considerable amount of memory space (for example, twenty-five PCI functional devices would require 6KB of space). The amount of memory space consumed aside, the address range utilized would be unavailable for allocation to regular memory. This would limit the system's flexibility regarding the mapping of real memory.

*Table 16-1. EISA PC I/O Space Usage*

| I/O Address Range | Reserved For |
|---|---|
| 0000h - 00FFh | PC/AT-compatible system board I/O devices |
| 0100h - 03FFh | ISA-compatible I/O cards |
| 0400h - 04FFh | EISA system board I/O devices |
| 0500h - 07FFh | unusable due to conflict with ISA I/O cards |
| 0800h - 08FFh | EISA system board I/O devices |
| 0900h - 0BFFh | unusable due to conflict with ISA I/O cards |
| 0C00h - 0CFFh | EISA system board I/O devices |
| 0D00h - 0FFFh | unusable due to conflict with ISA I/O cards |
| 1000h - 1FFFh | EISA I/O card installed in EISA slot 1 |
| 2000h - 2FFFFh | EISA I/O card installed in EISA slot 2 |
| 3000h - 3FFFh | EISA I/O card installed in EISA slot 3 |
| 4000h - 4FFFh | EISA I/O card installed in EISA slot 4 |
| 5000h - 5FFFh | EISA I/O card installed in EISA slot 5 |
| 6000h - 6FFFh | EISA I/O card installed in EISA slot 6 |
| 7000h - 7FFFh | EISA I/O card installed in EISA slot 7 |
| 8000h - 8FFFh | EISA I/O card installed in EISA slot 8 |
| 9000h - 9FFFh | EISA I/O card installed in EISA slot 9 |
| A000h - AFFFh | EISA I/O card installed in EISA slot 10 |
| B000h - BFFFh | EISA I/O card installed in EISA slot 11 |
| C000h - CFFFh | EISA I/O card installed in EISA slot 12 |
| D000h - DFFFh | EISA I/O card installed in EISA slot 13 |
| E000h - EFFFh | EISA I/O card installed in EISA slot 14 |
| F000h - FFFFh | EISA I/O card installed in EISA slot 15 |

# Chapter 16: Configuration Transactions

## Configuration Mechanism One Description

### General

Configuration mechanism one utilizes two 32-bit I/O ports located at addresses 0CF8h and 0CFCh. These two ports are:

- 32-bit configuration address port, occupying I/O addresses 0CF8h through 0CFBh.
- 32-bit configuration data port, occupying I/O addresses 0CFCh through 0CFFh.

Accessing a PCI function's configuration port is a two step process:

- Write the target bus number, physical device number, function number and doubleword number to the configuration address port.
- Perform an I/O read from or an write to the configuration data port.

### Configuration Address Port

The configuration address port only latches information when the host processor performs a full 32-bit write to the port. A 32-bit read from the port returns its contents. The assertion of reset clears the port to all zeros. Any 8 or 16 bit access within this I/O doubleword is passed directly onto the PCI bus as an 8 or 16 bit PCI I/O access. The 32-bits of information written to the configuration address port must adhere to the following template (illustrated in figure 16-1):

- bits [1:0] are reserved and must be zeros.
- bits [7:2] identify the target doubleword (one of 64) within the target function's configuration space.
- bits [10:8] identify the target function number (one of eight) within the target physical PCI device.
- bits [15:11] identify the target physical PCI device number (one of thirty-two).
- bits [23:16] identifies the target PCI bus number (one of 256).
- bits [30:24] are reserved and must be zero.
- bit 31 must be set to a one, enabling the translation of a subsequent host bus I/O access to the configuration data port into a configuration access on the PCI bus. If bit 31 is zero and the processor initiates an I/O read

from or write to the configuration data port, the transaction is passed through to the PCI bus as a PCI I/O transaction.

## Bus Compare and Data Port Usage

Each host/PCI bridge implements a bus number (may be hardwired or implicit) and a subordinate bus number register. If bit 31 in the configuration address port (see figure 16-1) is enabled (set to one), the bridge compares the target bus number to the range of buses that exists beyond the bridge. If the target bus is the same as the value in the bus number register, the programmer wishes to perform a configuration transaction on the host/PCI bridge's PCI bus. A subsequent I/O read or write to the bridge's configuration data port at 0CFCh causes the bridge to generate a type zero configuration read or write transaction. When devices that reside on a PCI bus detect a type zero configuration transaction in progress, this informs them that one of them is the target device.

If the target bus specified in the configuration address port does not compare with the value in the bridge's bus number register, but is equal to or less than the value in the bridge's subordinate bus number register, the bridge converts the subsequent host processor I/O access to its configuration data port into a type one configuration transaction on its PCI bus. When devices that reside on a PCI bus detect a type one configuration access in progress, they ignore the transaction. The only devices on a PCI bus that pay attention to the transaction are PCI-to-PCI bridges. Each of them must determine if the target bus number is within the range of PCI buses that reside beneath them. If the target bus is not within range, then a PCI-to-PCI bridge ignores the type one access. If it's in range, the access is passed through the PCI-to-PCI bridge as either a type zero (if the target bus compares to the bridge's bus number register) or a type one (the target bus number is equal to or less than the value in the bridge's subordinate bus number register) transaction.

The subject of type zero configuration accesses is covered in detail in subsequent sections in this chapter. The subject of type one configuration accesses is covered in detail in the chapter entitled "PCI-to-PCI Bridge."

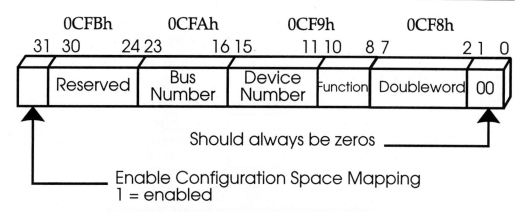

*Figure 16-1. The Configuration Address Register at 0CF8h*

## Multiple Host/PCI Bridges

If there are multiple host/PCI bridges present on the host bus (refer to figure 16-2), the configuration address and data ports are duplicated at the same I/O addresses in each of them. In order to prevent contention on the host processor's ready line, only one of the bridges controls the host processor's ready line to end the transfer. Each of the bridges compares the target bus number to the bus number of its PCI bus and to the number of the most subordinate PCI bus within its hierarchy. If the target bus doesn't reside behind a particular host/PCI bridge, that bridge doesn't convert the subsequent access to its configuration data port into a PCI configuration access on its PCI bus.

A subsequent read or write access to the configuration data port is only accepted by the host/PCI bridge that provides the gateway to the target bus. This bridge controls the processor's ready line to end the bus cycle. When an access is made to the data register, the bridge with a bus compare tests the state of the enable bit in its configuration address port. If enabled, the bridge converts the host bus I/O access into a PCI configuration access. If the target bus is the PCI bus immediately on the other side of the host/PCI bridge, the bridge converts the access to a type zero configuration access on its PCI bus. Otherwise, it converts it into a type one configuration access.

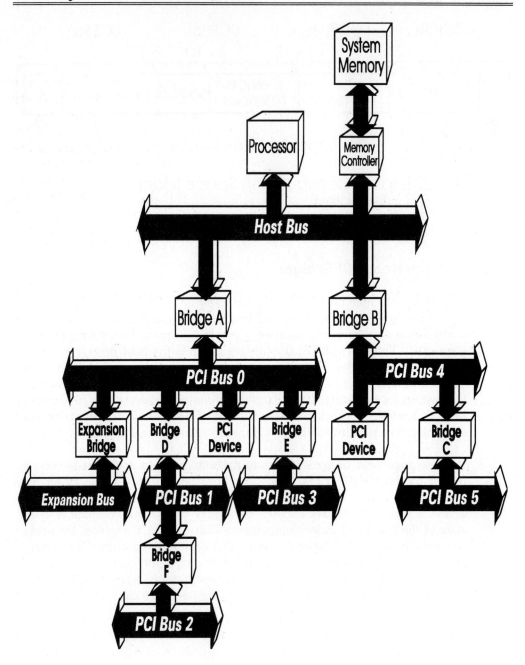

*Figure 16-2. Peer Host/PCI Bridges*

# Chapter 16: Configuration Transactions

## Single Host/PCI Bridge

The information written to the configuration address port is latched by the host/PCI bridge. If bit 31 is set to one and the target bus number compares to the bridge's PCI bus number (or is equal to or less than the value in the bridge's subordinate bus number register), the bridge is enabled to convert a subsequent host access targeting its configuration data port into a PCI configuration access. The host processor then initiates an I/O read or write transaction to the configuration data port at 0CFCh. This is either a one byte, two byte, or a four byte access (indicated by the processor's byte enable signals; or, if a PowerPC 60x processor, by A[29:31] and TSIZ[0:2]). This stimulates the bridge to arbitrate for ownership of the PCI bus and then to perform a configuration read (if the processor is reading from the configuration data port) or a configuration write (if the processor is writing to the configuration data port).

A section later in this chapter provides a detailed description of the type zero configuration read and write transactions.

## Generation of Special Cycles

Host/PCI bridges are not required to provide a means that allows software to initiate special cycles. If this capability is provided by the bridge, however, this section describes how it must be implemented when using configuration mechanism one.

To prime the host/PCI bridge to generate a special, or message, cycle, the host processor must write a 32-bit value with the following format to the configuration address port at I/O address 0CF8h:

- The target PCI bus should be set in the bus number field.
- The device number field must be set to all ones (31d, or 1Fh).
- The function number field must be set to all ones (7d).
- The configuration register number field must be set to all zeros.

After this has been accomplished, the next write to the configuration data port at I/O port 0CFCh causes the target bus's bridge to generate a special cycle on its PCI bus. The write data is driven onto AD[31:0] during the special cycle's data phase.

If the bridge's bus number does not match the specified target bus number, it passes the transaction through the bridge as a type one configuration write (so that it can be submitted to any PCI-to-PCI bridges further out in the hierarchy).

If the host/PCI bridge has been primed for a special cycle (by a write to the configuration address port) and an I/O read is performed from the configuration data port, the result is undefined. The bridge may pass it through as a type zero configuration read (which will result in a master-abort with all ones returned as data).

## Configuration Mechanism Two

The following quote from the specification was cited earlier in this chapter:

"Configuration mechanism #1 is the preferred implementation and must be provided by all future host bridges (and existing bridges should convert if possible). **Configuration mechanism #2 is defined for backward compatibility and must not be used by new designs.** Host bridges implemented in PC-AT compatible systems must implement at least one of these mechanisms."

Earlier PCI chipsets implement this configuration mechnism. The following sections describe configuration mechanism two.

## Basic Configuration Mechanism

The bridge implements the following two single-byte I/O ports:

- **Configuration space enable, or CSE, register** at I/O port 0CF8h.
- **Forward register** at I/O port 0CFAh.

To cause the host/PCI bridge to generate a PCI configuration transaction, the programmer performs the following actions:

- Write the target bus number (00h through FFh) into the forward register.
- Write a one byte value to the CSE register at 0CF8h. The bit pattern written to this register has three effects: disables the generation of special cycles; enables the generation of configuration transactions; specifies the target PCI functional device.

- Perform a one, two or four byte I/O read or write transaction within the I/O range C000h through CFFFh.

The 4KB I/O address range from C000h through CFFFh is divided into sub-ranges as indicated in table 16-2. The upper digit of the I/O address set to Ch maps the access into PCI configuration space. The third digit of the I/O address, $x$ in C$xyz$h, identifies the target physical package and is used by the bridge to select an IDSEL signal line to activate. The upper six bits of the first two digits in the I/O address, $yz$ in C$xyz$h, identifies the target configuration doubleword. The least-significant two bits of the first digit in the I/O address are not used by the bridge.

To summarize, the target bus is specified in the forward register. The target physical device is specified by the third digit of the I/O address. The target functional PCI device within the target physical device is specified by the function field in the CSE register. The target configuration doubleword within the target functional device's configuration space is specified by the upper six bits of the least-significant two digits of the I/O address. As the following list indicates, the bridge uses this information to determine what type of PCI configuration access to perform.

- The target bus in the forward register selects whether the bridge performs a type zero or a type one configuration access.
- The third digit of the I/O address selects which IDSEL to assert (if it's a type zero access).
- During a type zero access, the function number from the CSE register and the doubleword number from the least-significant two digits of the I/O address are placed on the AD bus.
- The setting on the host processor's byte enables during the access within the CXXXh range is used as the byte enable setting during the data phase of the configuration access.
- An I/O read (within the CXXXh range) by the host processor is converted into a configuration read and an I/O write into a configuration write.

Table 16-2. Sub-Ranges Within C000h through CFFFh I/O Range

| I/O Sub-Range | Targets Physical PCI Package |
|---|---|
| C000h - C0FFh | 0d |
| C100h - C1FFh | 1d |
| C200h - C2FFh | 2d |
| C300h - C3FFh | 3d |
| C400h - C4FFh | 4d |
| C500h - C5FFh | 5d |
| C600h - C6FFh | 6d |
| C700h - C7FFh | 7d |
| C800h - C8FFh | 8d |
| C900h - C9FFh | 9d |
| CA00h - CAFFh | 10d |
| CB00h - CBFFh | 11d |
| CC00h - CCFFh | 12d |
| CD00h - CDFFh | 13d |
| CE00h - CEFFh | 14d |
| CF00h - CFFFh | 15d |

## Configuration Space Enable, or CSE, Register

Figure 16-3 illustrates the format of the configuration space enable register. As stated earlier, the CSE register is an 8-bit register residing at I/O port 0CF8h. The assertion of reset clears this register to all zeros. A read from this register returns the last value written to it. When the SCE (SPECIAL CYCLE ENABLE) bit is cleared to zero, the host/PCI bridge cannot generate special cycles on the PCI bus. A section later in this chapter describes the generation of special cycles using configuration mechanism two.

The programmer writes the target function number into bits [3:1] of the CSE register. Setting the key field to a non-zero value enables (turns the key, if you will) the bridge's ability to convert host processor I/O accesses within the C000h through CFFFh range into PCI configuration accesses. The fact that reset clears the CSE register to zeros disables the bridge's ability to generate PCI configuration (key field cleared to zero) or special cycle (SCE bit cleared to zero) transactions.

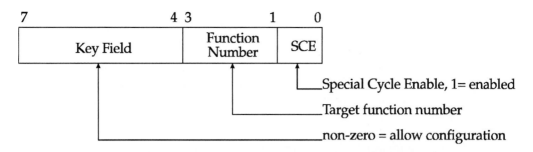

*Figure 16-3. Configuration Space Enable, or CSE, Register*

## Forward Register

The forward register is a read/write register located at I/O port 0CFAh. Reset clears it to zero and a read returns the last value written to it. It is an 8-bit register, permitting the specification of one of 256 possible PCI buses.

It is used to specify the target bus prior to enabling PCI configuration accesses via the CSE register.

## Support for Peer Bridges on Host Bus

Configuration mechanism two does not support peer bridges on the host bus.

## Generation of Special Cycles

Provision of the mechanism that permits software to generate special cycles is optional. The text that follows describes how it is implemented. The host/PCI bridge is enabled to generate special cycles in the following manner:

- The SCE bit in the CSE register is set to one.
- The function field is set to all ones.
- The key field is set a non-zero value.

This pattern in the CSE register also permits the programmer to instruct the host/PCI bridge to generate type one configuration accesses. The following text describes how to force the bridge to generate special cycle and type one configuration accesses.

Clearing the forward register to zero (and setting the CSE register to the pattern described earlier) permits the bridge to generate special cycles. When the processor performs an I/O write to port CF00h, the bridge acquires PCI bus ownership and initiates a special cycle. A dummy pattern is driven onto the AD bus during the address phase. During the data phase the data written to I/O port CF00h is driven onto the AD bus as the message (two or four byte message).

Setting the forward register to a non-zero value (and setting the CSE register to the pattern described earlier) permits the bridge to generate type one configuration accesses. AD[1:0] are set to 01b during the address phase and the bus number specified in the forward register is driven onto AD[23:16]. The physical device number and function number fields (AD[15:11] and AD[10:8], respectively) are set to all ones, while the configuration doubleword field, AD[7:2], is cleared to zeros.

Host processor reads from I/O addresses in the range C000h through CFFFh have undefined results. With the exception of I/O address CF00h, write accesses within this range also have undefined results. Setting the SCE bit in the CSE register to one and the function number field to zero has undefined results.

## PowerPC PReP Memory-Mapped Configuration

Figure 16-4 illustrates the PowerPC PReP specification memory map. Memory accesses within the 8MB memory address range from 80800000h through 80FFFFFFh are converted to PCI configuration accesses by the host/PCI bridge. Not all addresses within this range are used. The range is subdivided into nine sub-ranges. An access within one these ranges is converted to a PCI configuration access. The PREP host/PCI bridge uses the sub-range to select one AD line to set to one. AD[19:11] are resistively-coupled to the IDSEL pins on specific physical PCI device positions on the PCI bus. Bits [7:2]of the memory address supply the target configuration doubleword address. Bits [10:8] of the memory address supply the target function within the physical device. One bit in [19:11] of the memory address is set to one and supplies the IDSEL from the corresponding AD line ([19:11]. Table 16-3 defines the memory to configuration mapping.

# Chapter 16: Configuration Transactions

*Table 16-3. PREP Memory - to - Configuration Mapping*

| Memory Range | Maps to Device | Function | AD asserted |
|---|---|---|---|
| 80800800h – 808008FFh | 0 | 0 | 11 |
| 80800900h – 808009FFh | 0 | 1 | 11 |
| 80800A00h – 80800AFFh | 0 | 2 | 11 |
| 80800B00h – 80800BFFh | 0 | 3 | 11 |
| 80800C00h – 80800CFFh | 0 | 4 | 11 |
| 80800D00h – 80800DFFh | 0 | 5 | 11 |
| 80800E00h – 80800EFFh | 0 | 6 | 11 |
| 80800F00h – 80800FFFh | 0 | 7 | 11 |
| 80801000h – 808010FFh | 1 | 0 | 12 |
| 80801100h – 808011FFh | 1 | 1 | 12 |
| 80801200h – 808012FFh | 1 | 2 | 12 |
| 80801300h – 808013FFh | 1 | 3 | 12 |
| 80801400h – 808014FFh | 1 | 4 | 12 |
| 80801500h – 808015FFh | 1 | 5 | 12 |
| 80801600h – 808016FFh | 1 | 6 | 12 |
| 80801700h – 808017FFh | 1 | 7 | 12 |
| 80802000h – 808020FFh | 2 | 0 | 13 |
| . . . | ... | ... | ... |
| 80802700h – 808027FFh | 2 | 7 | 13 |
| 80804000h – 808040FFh | 3 | 0 | 14 |
| . . . | ... | ... | ... |
| 80804700h – 808047FFh | 3 | 7 | 14 |
| 80808000h – 808080FFh | 4 | 0 | 15 |
| . . . | ... | ... | ... |
| 80808700h – 808087FFh | 4 | 7 | 15 |
| 80810000h – 808100FFh | 5 | 0 | 16 |
| ... | ... | ... | ... |
| 80810700h – 808107FFh | 5 | 7 | 16 |
| 80820000h – 808200FFh | 6 | 0 | 17 |
| . . . | ... | ... | ... |
| 80820700h – 808207FFh | 6 | 7 | 17 |
| 80840000h – 808400FFh | 7 | 0 | 18 |
| . . . | ... | ... | ... |
| 80840700h – 808407FFh | 7 | 7 | 18 |
| 80880000h – 808800FFh | 8 | 0 | 19 |
| . . . | ... | ... | ... |
| 80880700h – 808807FFh | 8 | 7 | 19 |

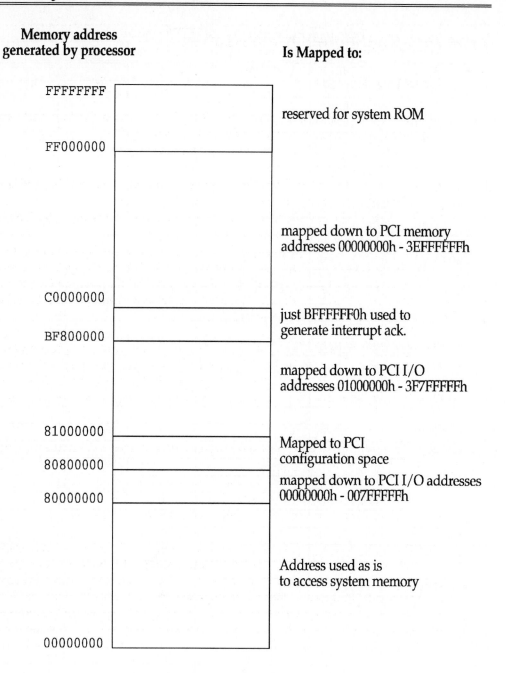

**Memory address generated by processor**

**Is Mapped to:**

FFFFFFFF

reserved for system ROM

FF000000

mapped down to PCI memory addresses 00000000h - 3EFFFFFFh

C0000000

just BFFFFFF0h used to generate interrupt ack.

BF800000

mapped down to PCI I/O addresses 01000000h - 3F7FFFFFh

81000000

Mapped to PCI configuration space

80800000

mapped down to PCI I/O addresses 00000000h - 007FFFFFh

80000000

Address used as is to access system memory

00000000

*Figure 16-4. PowerPC PReP Memory Map*

# Chapter 16: Configuration Transactions

## Type Zero Configuration Transaction

### Address Phase

During a PCI configuration transaction, all PCI devices on the bus latch the following information at the end of the address phase:

- The contents of the AD bus.
- The state of the FRAME# signal (asserted, indicating that a valid address and command have been latched from the bus).
- The state of the IDSEL signal. The physical device that samples its IDSEL asserted is the target physical device.
- The command on C/BE#[3:0] indicates that this is a configuration read or write transaction. The command type is derived from the type of access the host processor is performing with the host/PCI bridge's configuration data port. An I/O read converts to a configuration read and an I/O write converts to a configuration write.

00b on AD[1:0] indicates that this is a type zero configuration transaction targeting one of the devices on this PCI bus. If this is the case, the physical device that samples its IDSEL asserted is the target physical package. The AD bus information presented during a type zero configuration transaction indicates the following:

- AD[1:0] are 00b, indicating that this is a type zero transaction targeting one of the devices on this bus.
- AD[7:2] indicates the target configuration doubleword.
- AD[10:8] indicates the target function within the physical package.
- AD[31:11] are reserved and are not interpreted by any devices.

The target physical device number specified in bits [15:11] in the configuration address port are decoded and used to assert one of the bridge's IDSEL output signal lines. The bridge implements a separate IDSEL output for each physical package on the PCI bus, including one for each PCI expansion connector. Assertion of a specific IDSEL during the address phase of a type zero configuration access is used to select the physical package that is the target of the configuration access.

## Implementation of IDSEL

The IDSEL outputs can be implemented in one of two ways by the bridge designer:

1. The upper twenty-one address lines, AD[31:11], are not used during the address phase of a type zero configuration access. The system board designer is therefore free to use these signal lines as IDSEL signals to the various physical PCI packages (up to twenty-one of them). Internally, the bridge decodes the target physical number contained in configuration address port bits [15:11] to select which AD line to set to one. Each of these address lines is connected to the IDSEL input of a separate physical PCI package. Because of the rule that there can only be one load placed on each signal line by a PCI device, the package's IDSEL pin is resistively-coupled to the appropriate AD pin at the package. As an example, AD11 would be set to one if the target physical device is device zero (the first PCI device); AD12 set to one if the target physical device is device one, etc. This method saves pins on the bridge and traces on the system board. There isn't a danger of a device misinterpreting the information on the upper part of the address (AD[31:11) because no devices look at those address bits during a type zero configuration access.

2. The bridge designer can decode bits [15:11] (target physical device number) in the configuration address port and assert the target physical package's IDSEL output signal line. This method requires the implementation of a separate IDSEL output pin on the bridge for each physical package on the PCI bus and a separate point-to-point IDSEL trace on the system board between the bridge and each physical PCI package or connector.

As an example implementation approach, the specification suggests the following. The bridge internally decodes the device number field in the configuration address port and selects an IDSEL signal to assert. Rather than implementing IDSEL output pins, the IDSEL signals internal to the bridge be directed to AD[31:16] in the following manner:

- The IDSEL associated with device 0 is connected to AD16.
- The IDSEL associated with device 1 is connected to AD17.
- The IDSEL associated with device 2 is connected to AD18, etc.
- The IDSEL associated with device 15 is connected to AD31.
- For devices 16 through 31, none of the upper AD lines should be asserted when the type 0 configuration transaction is performed. Since no device

detects its IDSEL asserted, none respond, resulting in a master abort by the bridge.

This approach supports the implementation of 16 devices on a PCI bus.

## Data Phase

As the data phase is entered, the state of the host processor's byte enables (assuming that it's an x86 processor) is copied onto the PCI C/BE bus. The host processor byte enables are set to one of the following patterns:

- BE0# asserted indicates a one byte transfer over the lower data path with byte zero in the selected configuration doubleword.
- BE0# and BE1# asserted indicates a two byte transfer over the lower two data paths with bytes zero and one in the selected configuration doubleword.
- BE0#, BE1#, BE2# and BE3# asserted indicates a four byte transfer over all four data paths with bytes zero through three in the selected doubleword.

As the data phase is entered, the PCI devices are performing the address decode to determine which of them is the target of the transaction (00b on AD[1:0] indicates it is for one of them). Devices that sampled their IDSEL inputs deasserted at the end of the address phase ignore the transaction. The physical device that sampled its IDSEL asserted decodes the target function number presented on AD[10:8] to determine if the target function exists within the package. Assuming that it does, the package asserts DEVSEL# to claim the transaction. The remainder of the transaction is no different from a memory or an I/O read or write transaction.

## Type Zero Configuration Transaction Examples

The type zero configuration access is used to configure a PCI device on the same PCI bus on which the access is performed.

During the address phase of the transaction, the bridge places the configuration address information on the AD bus and the configuration command on the C/BE bus. Figure 16-5 illustrates the contents of the AD bus during the address phase of the type zero configuration access. Figures 16-6 and 16-7 are timing diagrams of type zero read and write configuration accesses.

Target configuration doubleword number

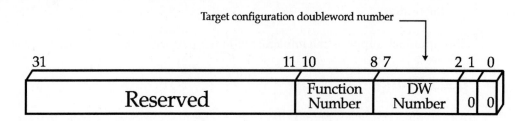

*Figure 16-5. Contents of the AD Bus During Address Phase of a Type Zero Configuration Access*

To be selected as the target of a configuration access, a PCI device must sample its device-specific IDSEL input asserted by the bridge during the address phase and it must be a type zero configuration access (AD[1:0] set to 00b). If its IDSEL is not asserted or if AD[1:0] are not set to 00b, the device should ignore the access.

Assuming both of these conditions are met, address bits AD[10:8] are used to select one of eight functions within the physical device. If the target function is implemented in the device, it asserts DEVSEL# (during the data phase) to claim the transaction. Address bits AD[7:2] are used to select one of sixty-four configuration doublewords within the target function's configuration space. The command on the C/BE bus during the address phase identifies it as a configuration read or write. During the data phase, the four byte enables, C/BE#[3:0], are used to select the bytes within the currently-addressed configuration doubleword. Assuming that the host processor is an x86, the byte enables are copied from the byte enables placed on the host bus by the processor when it initiated its read or write transaction. The data to be transferred between the bridge and the target configuration location(s) is transferred during the data phase.

# Chapter 16: Configuration Transactions

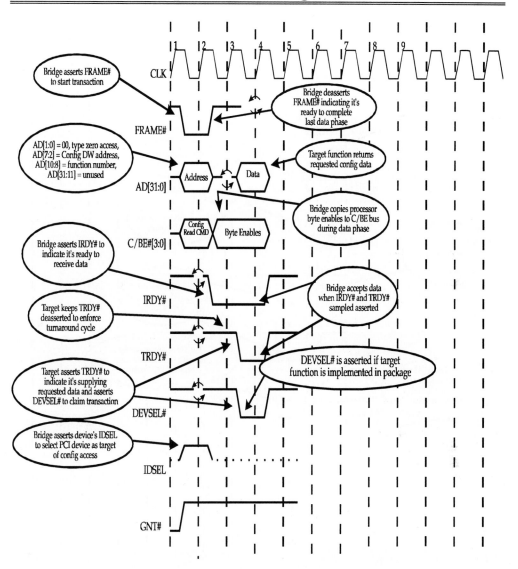

*Figure 16-6. The Type Zero Configuration Read Access*

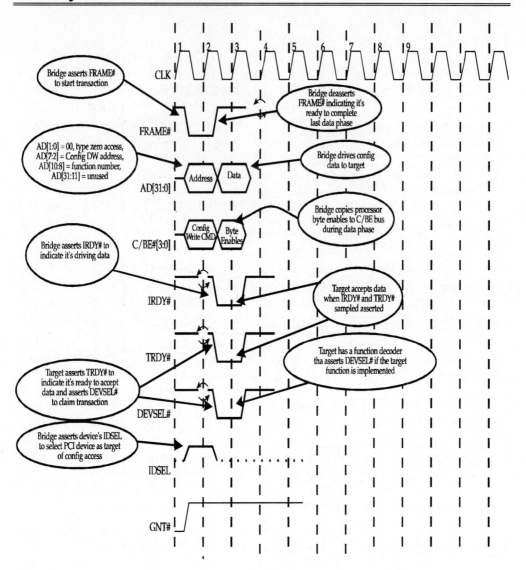

*Figure 16-7. The Type Zero Configuration Write Access*

# Chapter 16: Configuration Transactions

## Target Device Doesn't Exist

If the target of a configuration read transaction doesn't exist, DEVSEL# isn't asserted by any PCI device. Note that the subtractive decoder in the expansion bus bridge does not claim unclaimed PCI configuration transactions. When DEVSEL# remains deasserted, the host/PCI bridge aborts the transaction. The bridge sets the MASTER ABORT DETECTED bit in its configuration status register. On a read the bridge returns all ones to the host processor as the read data. The way that software determines that a PCI device doesn't exist is to read the device's vendor ID configuration register and check for all ones returned. If this is the case, a master abort occurred and the bridge returned all ones. The vendor ID of all ones (FFFFh) is reserved for this reason and is not assigned to any vendor by the SIG.

In the event that a configuration write attempt master aborts (due to no assertion of DEVSEL#), the bridge acts as if the configuration write completed normally (but sets the MASTER ABORT DETECTED bit in its configuration status register) and permits the processor to terminate the transaction normally.

## Configuration Burst Transactions

Although virtually all configuration transactions today are single data phase transactions, the specification permits burst configuration transactions. Linear addressing is implied in a multiple data phase configuration burst transaction. As each data phase completes and the next begins, the target device increments the configuration doubleword address in its address counter by four and then examines the byte enables to determine which bytes within the currently-addressed configuration doubleword are to be transferred.

## 64-Bit Configuration Transactions Not Permitted

The specification states "The bandwidth requirements for I/O and configuration commands cannot justify the added complexity and, therefore, only memory commands support 64-bit data transfers."

## Resistively-Coupled IDSEL is Slow

When the bridge asserts a device's IDSEL by placing a one on a specific upper address line (within the otherwise unused bit field consisting of AD[31:11]), the respective AD line is resistively-coupled (at the physical device position on the system board) to the device's IDSEL pin. The resistive coupling has the effect of a very slow transition on the IDSEL pin. When using this method, therefore, the bridge designer must drive the address onto the AD bus (including a one onto the respective upper AD line that is coupled to the target device's IDSEL pin). Because it takes more than one clock for a valid one to be seen on the device's IDSEL pin, the bridge must defer assertion of FRAME# until a sufficient number of clocks has gone by to permit propagation of the one from the respective apper AD line to the device's IDSEL pin.

# Chapter 17

## The Previous Chapter

The previous chapter provided a detailed discussion of the mechanisms used to generate configuration transactions as well as a detailed discussion of the type zero configuration read and write transactions themselves.

## This Chapter

This chapter provides a detailed description of the configuration register format and usage for PCI devices other than PCI-to-PCI bridges.

## The Next Chapter

The next chapter provides a detailed description of device ROMs associated with PCI devices. This includes the following topics:

- device ROM detection.
- internal code/data format.
- shadowing.
- initialization code execution.
- interrupt hooking.

## Intro to Configuration Header Region

Each functional (i.e., logical) PCI device possesses a block of 64 configuration doublewords reserved for the implementation of its configuration registers. The format, or usage, of the first 16 doublewords is predefined by the PCI specification. This area is referred to as the device's configuration header region. The specification currently defines two header formats, referred to as header types zero and one. Header type one is defined for PCI-to-PCI bridges, while header type zero is used for all other devices. This chapter defines header type zero. A full description of header type one can be found in the chapter entitled "PCI-to-PCI Bridge."

# PCI System Architecture

Figure 17-1 illustrates the format of a functional device's (other than a PCI-to-PCI bridge) header region. The registers marked in black are always mandatory. Note that although many of the configuration registers in the figure are not marked mandatory, a register may be mandatory for a particular type of device. The subsequent sections define each register and any circumstances where it may be mandatory.

As noted earlier, this format is referred to as header type zero. The registers within this range are used to identify the device, to control its PCI functions, and to sense its PCI status in a generic manner. The usage of the device's remaining 48 doublewords of configuration space is device-specific.

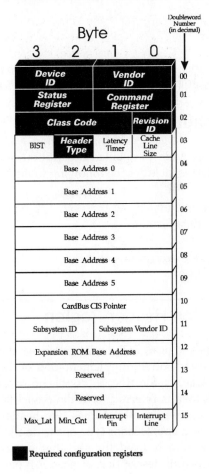

Figure 17-1. Format of a PCI Device's Configuration Header

## Mandatory Header Registers

### Introduction

The following sections describe the mandatory configuration registers that must be implemented in every PCI device, including bridges. The registers are illustrated (in black) in figure 17-1.

### Vendor ID Register

*Always mandatory.* This 16-bit register identifies the manufacturer of the device. The value hardwired in this read-only register is assigned by a central authority (the PCI SIG) that controls issuance of the numbers. The value FFFFh is reserved and must be returned by the host/PCI bridge when an attempt is made to perform a configuration read from a non-existent device's vendor ID configuration register. The read attempt results in a master-abort and the bridge must respond with a vendor ID of FFFFh. The master abort is not considered to be an error.

### Device ID Register

*Always mandatory.* This 16-bit value is assigned by the device manufacturer and identifies the type of device.

### Command Register

#### General

*Always mandatory.* This register provides basic control over the device's ability to respond to and/or perform PCI accesses. It's a 16-bit register, but only bits [9:0] are currently defined. Bits [15:10] are reserved for future use and must return zero. The bits are described in table 17-1 and the register is illustrated in figure 17-2. The designer only implements the bits that make sense for the device. As an example, a device with I/O but no memory requires bit zero, but not bit one.

After reset, bits [2:0] in this register are cleared to zero (except for a device that must be enabled at startup time because it's used during the raw boot process). This effectively disables the device (the exception being it remains responsive to configuration accesses) until it is configured and enabled by the configuration software. Devices that must be accessible at boot time through fixed addresses must provide an enable/disable bit to control the recognition of its fixed address ranges. This would permit the configuration software to turn off the recognition of the fixed ranges after boot up and to reconfigure the address range(s) the device responds to.

*Table 17-1. The Command Register*

| Bit | Function |
|-----|----------|
| 0 | **I/O Access Enable.** When this bit is set to a one, the device's I/O address decoder(s) (if any are implemented) responds to PCI I/O accesses. Zero disables it. Default setting is zero. |
| 1 | **Memory Access Enable.** When this bit is set to a one, the device responds to PCI memory accesses (if it implements any memory address decoders). Zero disables it. Default setting is zero. |
| 2 | **Master Enable.** When set to a one, enables the device to act as a bus master (if it has bus master capability). Zero disables it. Default setting is zero. |
| 3 | **Special Cycle Recognition.** When set to a one, the device is enabled to monitor for PCI special cycles (if it's designed to monitor special cycles). Zero causes it to ignore special cycles. Default setting is zero. |
| 4 | **Memory Write and Invalidate Enable.** When set to a one, the device can generate the memory write and invalidate command. When set to zero, the device uses memory write commands instead. This bit must be implemented by bus masters that are capable of generating the memory write and invalidate command. Software should not enable this bit until the device's cache line size configuration register is initialized with the system cache line size. Reset clears this bit. |
| 5 | **VGA Palette Snoop Enable.** Set to a one, this bit instructs its VGA-compatible device to perform palette snooping. This function is described in this chapter and in the chapter entitled "PCI-to-PCI Bridge." In a non-VGA graphics device, reset sets this bit to one, enabling palette snooping. Reset clears this bit in a VGA-compatible controller. |
| 6 | **Parity Error Response.** This bit is required for all devices (as noted in the chapter entitled "Error Detection and Handling", there are two exceptions). When set to a one, the device can report parity errors (PERR#). When set to a zero, the device ignores parity errors. This bit is cleared by reset. |

| Bit | Function |
|-----|----------|
| 7 | **Wait Cycle Enable**. Controls whether the device does address/data stepping. Devices that never use stepping must hardwire this bit to a zero. Devices that always use stepping must hardwire this bit to a one. Devices that can work both ways must implement this bit as read/writable and initialize it to one after reset. Additional information regarding stepping can be found in the chapter entitled "The Read and Write Transfers." |
| 8 | **System Error Enable**. When set a one, the device can drive the SERR# line. A zero disables the device's SERR# output driver. State after a reset is a zero. All devices that use SERR# must implement this bit. This bit and bit six must be set when reporting address parity errors. |
| 9 | **Fast Back-to-Back Enable**. Optional bit for bus masters. If a bus master is capable of performing fast back-to-back transactions to different targets, this bit is used to enable or disable this functionality. If all targets on the PCI bus that the master resides on are fast back-to-back capable, configuration software can use this bit to enable this master's ability to perform fast back-to-back transactions to different targets. A complete description of fast back-to-back transactions can be found in the chapter entitled "PCI Bus Arbitration." State after reset is zero. |
| 15:10 | Reserved |

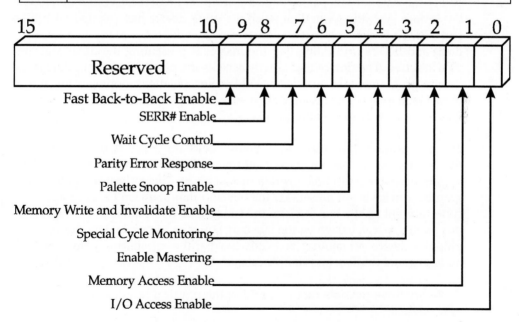

*Figure 17-2. The Command Register Bit Assignment*

## VGA Color Palette Snooping

*Mandatory for display adapters that implement the VGA palette registers and not required for other devices.* A system may have two display devices present in the system: a VGA-compatible interface and another graphics controller. In this case, both devices implement a set of color palette registers. Whenever the host processor performs an I/O write to update the palette registers, the palette in both devices must be updated. This presents a problem. Both devices implement the color palette registers at the same I/O addresses. If a write is performed to the palette registers, both will recognize the address and assert DEVSEL# and TRDY# (resulting in a collision on the DEVSEL# and TRDY# signals). In this case, the configuration software must program one of the devices to participate as the target, while the other device is programmed to quietly "snarf" the write data from the bus as it flies by on its way to the other device.

The VGA always responds to reads (asserts TRDY# and supplies the data) from its color palette registers. Either the VGA or the other graphics device is configured to respond to palette register writes (by asserting DEVSEL# and TRDY# and accepting the data), while the other one is configured to quietly accept the data into its palette register. It doesn't assert DEVSEL# or TRDY#, but it does latch the write data when the other device has asserted DEVSEL# and TRDY# (indicating that the other display adapter is ready to accept the data) and IRDY# (indicating that the master is presenting the data) are sampled asserted. The device that quietly accepts the palette register update is the device programmed to perform VGA color palette snooping (the author thinks of it as snarfing, because the device "snarfs" the data from the bus as it flies by on its way to the other display device).

The specification states that the snooping device must also snarf the data from the bus (to keep its palette register set updated) if it observes the color palette update transaction terminate with a master abort. This indicates that the other graphics device is not present on the bus and that there isn't a subtractive decoder present on the bus to claim the transaction and pass it to the expansion bus. In this case, a bridge on the bus may still pass the write data through to a graphics device on another bus (this is what the specification says, but the author cannot think of an example case).

There are three possible cases regarding the physical location of the two display devices:

1. When both devices are present on the same PCI bus, the configuration software programs one to snoop (by setting the VGA COLOR PALETTE SNOOP bit in its configuration command register) and the other to actively participate (snoop bit turned off) in color palette register set updates.

2. The two PCI display controllers reside on different PCI buses along the same path. In this case, the device on the PCI bus closer to the host processor is set to snoop the update. The device on the PCI bus further from the processor may be set to either actively respond to the update or to snoop. In either case, both devices will latch the data and update their palette register set.

3. When one device is on a PCI bus and the other is on the other side of an expansion bus bridge that uses subtractive decode, the PCI device is programmed to snoop. The subtractive decoder will claim any palette updates and pass them through to the expansion bus to update the expansion bus display device's palette register set.

In a system that only contains a VGA interface or where the graphics device is integrated into the VGA device, the VGA's snoop bit is turned off and it actively participates in palette register updates.

It should be evident that snooping only works if the two display controllers reside along the same bus path.

Additional information regarding VGA color palette register snooping can be found in the chapter entitled "PCI-to-PCI Bridge."

## Status Register

*Always mandatory*. The status register tracks the status of PCI bus-related events. A device must implement the bits that relate to its functionality. This register can be read from, but writes are handled differently than the norm. On a write, bits can be cleared, but not set. A bit is cleared by writing a one to it. This method was selected to simplify the programmer's job. After reading the state and ascertaining the error bits that are set, the programmer clears the bits by writing the value that was read back to the register.

Table 17-2 describes the status register bits and figure 17-3 illustrates its bit assignment.

*Table 17-2. The Status Register Bits*

| Bit | Function |
| --- | --- |
| 4:0 | **Reserved.** Hardwired to zero. |
| 5 | **66MHz-Capable.** 1 = device is capable of running at 66MHz. 0 = capable of running at 33MHz. Value hardwired by designer. For more information, refer to the chapter entitled "66MHz PCI Implementation." |
| 6 | **UDF Supported.** 1 = device supports user definable features. 0 = device does not support UDFs. Value hardwired by designer. For more information, refer to the section in this chapter entitled "User-Definable Features." |
| 7 | **Fast Back-to-Back Capable.** This read-only bit indicates whether or not the target device supports fast back-to-back transactions with different targets. It must be hardwired to zero if the device does not support this feature and to a one if it does. A complete description of fast back-to-back transactions can be found in the chapter entitled "PCI Bus Arbitration." Also refer to the description of the FAST BACK-TO-BACK ENABLE bit in the command register (in the previous section). |
| 8 | **Data Parity Reported.** This bit is only implemented by bus masters and is set only if the following conditions are met: the reporting bus master was the initiator and set PERR# itself (during a read) or detected it asserted by the target (during a write); and the PARITY ERROR RESPONSE bit in the master's command configuration register is set to a one. |
| 10:9 | **Device Select (DEVSEL#) Timing.** These bits are read-only and define the slowest DEVSEL# timing for a target device (except configuration accesses).<br>00b = fast<br>01b = medium<br>10b = slow<br>11b = reserved |
| 11 | **Signaled Target Abort.** Set by the target device whenever it terminates a transaction with a target-abort. A device that is incapable of signaling target-abort does not need to implement this bit. |
| 12 | **Received Target Abort.** This bit is set by a bus master whenever its transaction is terminated by a target-abort from the currently-addressed target. All bus masters must implement this bit. |
| 13 | **Received Master Abort.** This bit should be set by a master whenever its transaction (except for a special cycle) is terminated due to a master-abort. All bus masters must implement this bit. |
| 14 | **Signaled System Error** (SERR#). This bit should be set whenever a device generates a System Error on the SERR# line. If incapable of generating SERR#, it need not implement this bit. |

| Bit | Function |
|---|---|
| 15 | **Detected Parity Error.** This bit should be set by a device whenever it detects a parity error (even if parity error reporting is disabled by bit six of its command register). |

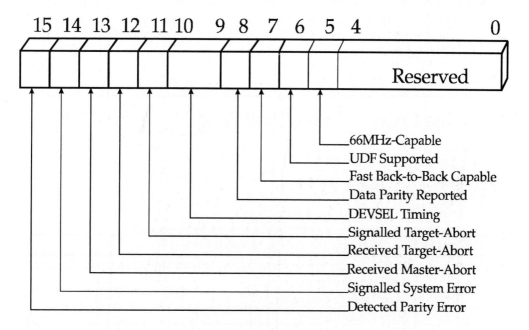

*Figure 17-3. Status Register Bit Assignment*

## Revision ID Register

*Always mandatory.* This 8-bit value is assigned by the device manufacturer and identifies the revision number of the device.

## Class Code Register

*Always mandatory.* The class code register is pictured in figure 17-4. It is a 24-bit, read-only register divided into three sub-registers: base class, sub-class, and programming interface. It identifies the basic function of the device (e.g., a mass storage controller), a more specific device sub-class (e.g., IDE controller), and, in some cases, a register-specific programming interface (such as the

VGA register set). The upper byte defines the basic class type, the middle byte a sub-class within the basic class, and the lower byte defines the programming interface. The values defined for the basic class code register are listed in table 17-3. Tables 17-4 through 17-16 define the sub-classes within each base class. With the advent of revision 2.0 of the specification, the programming interface byte is almost always hardwired to return zeros. The exceptions are VGA-compatible devices and IDE controllers. As seen in table 17-4, a revision 1.0-compliant VGA device has a 01h hardwired into this register and all other revision 1.0 device types are hardwired to zeros.

| 23 | 16 | 15 | 8 | 7 | 0 |
|---|---|---|---|---|---|
| Class Code | | Sub-Class Code | | Prog. I/F | |

*Figure 17-4. Class Code Register*

*Table 17-3. Defined Class Codes*

| Class | Description |
|---|---|
| 00h | Devices built before class codes defined (in other words: before rev 2.0 of the spec). |
| 01h | Mass storage controller. |
| 02h | Network controller. |
| 03h | Display controller. |
| 04h | Multimedia device. |
| 05h | Memory controller. |
| 06h | Bridge device. |
| 07h | Simple communications controllers. |
| 08h | Base system peripherals. |
| 09h | Input devices. |
| 0Ah | Docking stations. |
| 0Bh | Processors. |
| 0Ch | Serial bus controllers. |
| 0Dh-FEh | Reserved. |
| FFh | Device does not fit any of the defined classed codes. |

# Chapter 17: Configuration Registers

Table 17-4. Class Code 0 (pre rev 2.0)

| Sub-Class | Prog. I/F | Description |
|-----------|-----------|-------------|
| 00h | 00h | All devices other than VGA. |
| 01h | 01h | VGA-compatible device. |

Table 17-5. Class Code 1: Mass Storage Controllers

| Sub-Class | Prog. I/F | Description |
|-----------|-----------|-------------|
| 00h | 00h | SCSI controller. |
| 01h | XXh | IDE controller. See table 17-17 for definition of programmer's interface byte. |
| 02h | 00h | Floppy disk controller. |
| 03h | 00h | IPI controller. |
| 04h | 00h | RAID controller. |
| 80h | 00h | Other mass storage controller. |

Table 17-6. Class Code 2: Network Controllers

| Sub-Class | Prog. I/F | Description |
|-----------|-----------|-------------|
| 00h | 00h | Ethernet controller. |
| 01h | 00h | Token ring controller. |
| 02h | 00h | FDDI controller. |
| 03h | 00h | ATM controller. |
| 80h | 00h | Other network controller. |

Table 17-7. Class Code 3: Display Controllers

| Sub-Class | Prog. I/F | Description |
|-----------|-----------|-------------|
| 00h | 00h | VGA-compatible controller, responding to memory addresses 000A0000h through 000BFFFFh, and I/O addresses 03B0h through 3BBh and all aliases of these addresses. |
| | 01h | 8514-compatible controller, responding to I/O address 02E8h, and its aliases, 02EAh and 02EFh. |
| 01h | 00h | XGA controller. |
| 80h | 00h | Other display controller. |

*Table 17-8. Class Code 4: Multimedia Devices*

| Sub-Class | Prog. I/F | Description |
|-----------|-----------|-------------|
| 00h | 00h | Video device. |
| 01h | 00h | Audio device. |
| 80h | 00h | Other multimedia device. |

*Table 17-9. Class Code 5: Memory Controllers*

| Sub-Class | Prog. I/F | Description |
|-----------|-----------|-------------|
| 00h | 00h | RAM memory controller. |
| 01h | 00h | Flash memory controller. |
| 80h | 00h | Other memory controller. |

*Table 17-10. Class Code 6: Bridge Devices*

| Sub-Class | Prog. I/F | Description |
|-----------|-----------|-------------|
| 00h | 00h | Host/PCI bridge. |
| 01h | 00h | PCI/ISA bridge. |
| 02h | 00h | PCI/EISA bridge. |
| 03h | 00h | PCI/Micro Channel bridge. |
| 04h | 00h | PCI/PCI bridge. |
| 05h | 00h | PCI/PCMCIA bridge. |
| 06h | 00h | PCI/NuBus bridge. |
| 07h | 00h | PCI/CardBus bridge. |
| 80h | 00h | Other bridge type. |

*Table 17-11. Class Code 7: Simple Communications Controllers*

| Sub-Class | Prog. I/F | Description |
|-----------|-----------|-------------|
| 00h | 00h | Generic XT-compatible serial controller. |
|  | 01h | 16450-compatible serial controller. |
|  | 02h | 16550-compatible serial controller. |
| 01h | 00h | Parallel port. |
|  | 01h | Bi-directional parallel port. |
|  | 02h | ECP 1.X-compliant parallel port. |
| 80h | 00h | Other communications device. |

*Table 17-12. Class Code 8: Base System Peripherals*

| Sub-Class | Prog. I/F | Description |
|---|---|---|
| 00h | 00h | Generic 8259 programmable interrupt controller (PIC). |
| | 01h | ISA PIC. |
| | 02h | EISA PIC. |
| 01h | 00h | Generic 8237 DMA controller. |
| | 01h | ISA DMA controller. |
| | 02h | EISA DMA controller. |
| 02h | 00h | Generic 8254 timer. |
| | 01h | ISA system timers. |
| | 02h | EISA system timers. |
| 03h | 00h | Generic RTC controller. |
| | 01h | ISA RTC controller. |
| 80h | 00h | Other system peripheral. |

*Table 17-13. Class Code 9: Input Devices*

| Sub-Class | Prog. I/F | Description |
|---|---|---|
| 00h | 00h | Keyboard controller. |
| 01h | 00h | Digitizer (pen). |
| 02h | 00h | Mouse controller. |
| 80h | 00h | Other input controller. |

*Table 17-14. Class Code A: Docking Stations*

| Sub-Class | Prog. I/F | Description |
|---|---|---|
| 00h | 00h | Generic docking station. |
| 80h | 00h | Other type of docking station. |

*Table 17-15. Class Code B: Processors*

| Sub-Class | Prog. I/F | Description |
|---|---|---|
| 00h | 00h | 386. |
| 01h | 00h | 486. |
| 02h | 00h | Pentium. |
| 10h | 00h | Alpha. |
| 20h | 00h | PowerPC. |
| 40h | 00h | Co-processor. |

*Table 17-16. Class Code C: Serial Bus Controllers*

| Sub-Class | Prog. I/F | Description |
|-----------|-----------|-------------|
| 00h | 00h | Firewire (IEEE 1394). |
| 01h | 00h | ACCESS.bus. |
| 02h | 00h | SSA (Serial Storage Architecture). |
| 03h | 00h | USB (Universal Serial Bus). |
| 04h | 00h | Fibre Channel (its copper, not fiber!). |

*Table 17-17. Definition of IDE Programmer's Interface Byte Encoding*

| Bit(s) | Description |
|--------|-------------|
| 0 | Operating mode (primary). |
| 1 | Programmable indicator (primary). |
| 2 | Operating mode (secondary). |
| 3 | Programmable indicator (secondary). |
| 6:4 | Reserved. Hardwired to zero. |
| 7 | Master IDE device. |

Note: Two additional documents available from the PCI SIG contains a complete description of these fields. The two documents are: *PCI IDE Controller Specification* and *Programming Interface for Bus Master IDE Controller*. As of this writing, the author has not yet seen these documents, but the 2.1 specification syas they are available by calling (408) 741-1600 and requesting document 8038.

## Header Type Register

*Always mandatory.* Figure 17-5 illustrates the format of the header type register. Bits [6:0] of this one byte register define the format of doublewords 4d through 15d of the device's configuration header. In addition, bit seven defines the device as a single (bit seven = 0) or multi-function (bit seven = 1) device. During configuration, the programmer determines if there are any other functions in this package that require configuration by testing the state of bit seven.

Currently, the only header format defined other than the one pictured in figure 17-1 (header type 00h) is header type one (PCI-to-PCI bridge header format; description can be found in the chapter entitled "PCI-to-PCI Bridge"). Future versions of the specification may define other formats.

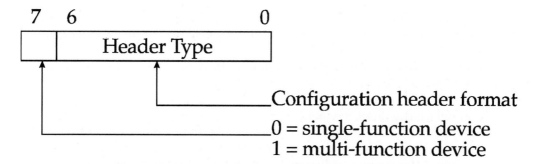

*Figure 17-5. Header Type Register Format*

## Other Header Registers

### Introduction

The configuration registers described in the following paragraphs may be optional or mandatory depending on the device type. They only need to be implemented if a device supports the affected function.

### Cache Line Size Register

*Mandatory for a master that uses memory write and invalidate command. Also mandatory for memory targets that support cacheline wrap addressing, and for memory targets that the processor may cache from.* This read/write configuration register specifies the system cache line size in doubleword increments (e.g., a 486-based system would store the value 04h, indicating a cache line size of four doublewords). The register must be implemented by bus masters that implement the memory write and invalidate command. Because it must know the cache line size in order to write a line into memory, the bus master may not use the memory write and invalidate command when this register is set to zero. In this case, the master should only use memory write transactions to update memory.

When a memory target is configured into memory space that the host processor does not cache from, the configuration software must set its cache line size to zero. The target can then ignore its snoop result inputs (SDONE and SBO#) when participating in a transaction. A memory target that is mapped into cacheable memory address space must have its cache line size register set to the proper line size by the configuration software. This permits the target to detect when a burst transfer is crossing a line boundary. The target can then issue a retry to the master, forcing it to terminate the current burst, rearbitrate for the bus and then re-initiate the transaction at the start address of the next line. This ensures that the new line address is snooped by the host/PCI bridge. The register is cleared when reset.

A device may limit the number of cache line sizes that it supports. If an unsupported value is written to the register by the configuration software, the device behaves as if the value zero was written (i.e., the memory does not monitor the snoop result signals and does not issue a retry when a burst transaction crosses a cache line boundary).

A detailed discussion of cache-related issues can be found in the chapter entitled "PCI Cache Support."

## Latency Timer: "Timeslice" Register

*Mandatory (read/writable) for masters that are capable of performing a burst consisting of more than two data phases.* The latency timer defines the minimum amount of time, in PCI clock cycles, that the bus master can retain ownership of the bus. The bus master decrements its latency timer by one on the rising-edge of each clock after it initiates a transaction. It may continue its transaction until either:

- it has completed the overall burst transfer, or
- it has exhausted its timeslice (LT value) and it has been preempted (lost its GNT# to another PCI master),

whichever comes first.

Every bus master that performs bursts of more than two data phases some of the time or all of the time must implement the latency timer, or LT, register as a read/writable register. It *may be implemented as a hardwired, read-only register by masters that can burst two or less data phases, but the hardwired value returned must not exceed sixteen.* Be aware that a hardwired value of zero is only permitted if the master never performs more than two data phases and that the zero means the master has a null timeslice. The net effect would be that the master would have to yield the bus after the first data phase if it immediately lost its GNT# to another master. Target devices do not implement this bit.

# Chapter 17: Configuration Registers

In a typical implementation of a programmable LT register, the low-order three bits are hardwired to zero and the programmer can program any value into the high-order five bits. This permits the programmer to specify the timeslice with a granularity of eight PCI clocks. If the register is programmable, reset clears it. More information on the latency timer can be found in the chapter entitled "PCI Bus Arbitration."

Optimally, every bus master should implement this as a read/writable register. This permits the configuration software maximum flexibility when it divides up the available bus time between the community of bus masters. The configuration software determines the bus master's desired timeslice by reading from the device's Min_Gnt (minimum grant) register. The designer indicates the desired timeslice by hardwiring the value, in increments of 250ns, into this register. When calculating this value, the designer assumes a bus speed of 33MHz. If the bus master has no stringent requirement regarding its timeslice, the designer hardwires zero into this register.

## BIST Register

*Optional.* This register may be implemented by both master and target devices. If a device implements a built-in self-test, or BIST, it must implement this register as illustrated in figure 17-6. Table 17-18 describes each bit's function. If the device doesn't support a BIST, this register must return zeros when read. The device's BIST is invoked by setting bit six to one. The device resets bit six upon completion of the BIST. Configuration software must fail the device if it doesn't reset bit six within two seconds. At the conclusion of the BIST, the test result is indicated in the lower four bits of the register. A completion code of zero indicates successful completion. A non-zero value represents a device-specific error code.

*Table 17- 18. The BIST Register Bit Assignment*

| Bit | Function |
|-----|----------|
| 3:0 | **Completion Code.** A value of zero indicates successful completion, while a non-zero result indicates a device-specific error. |
| 5:4 | Reserved. |
| 6 | **Start BIST.** A one in this bit starts the device's BIST. The device resets this bit automatically upon completion. Software should fail the device if the BIST does not complete within two seconds. |
| 7 | **BIST Capable.** Should return a one if the device implements a BIST, a zero if it doesn't. |

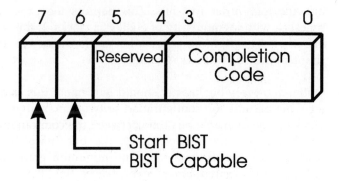

*Figure 17-6. The BIST Register*

## Base Address Registers

*Required if a device implements decoders.* Virtually all devices utilize some memory address space, I/O address space or both. Some examples follow:

- A parallel port's status, command and data registers would typically reside in I/O address space.
- A network interface's control registers (command/status, etc.) would reside in I/O address space. The interface may also incorporate RAM memory that must be mapped into the system's memory space. In addition, a device ROM containing the device's BIOS and interrupt service routines may be present.

On power-up, the system must be automatically configured so that each device's I/O and memory functions occupy mutually-exclusive address ranges. In order to accomplish this, the system must be able to detect how many memory and I/O address ranges a device requires and the size of each. In addition, the system must have the capability of programming a device's address decoders in order to assign its I/O and memory non-conflicting address ranges.

The base address configuration registers located in doublewords four through nine of the device's configuration header space permit this relocatibility. Each register is 32 bits in size (64 bits if the memory block it describes can be located anywhere within 64-bit address space) and is used to implement a programmable memory or I/O address decoder. Figures 17-7 and 17-8 illustrate the two possible formats of a base address configuration register. If bit zero is returned as a zero, the register is a memory address decoder. A one indicates an I/O address decoder. If one decoder is implemented, it must be implemented as base address register zero. If two decoders are implemented, they must be implemented as base address registers zero and one, etc. During configuration, the configuration software will stop looking for base address registers in a device's header when it detects an unimplemented base address register.

## Memory-Mapping Recommended

In a PC environment, I/O space is densely populated and will only become more so in the future. For this reason and because some processors are only capable of performing memory transactions, the specification strongly recommends that the device designer provide a memory base address register to map a device's register set into memory space. Optionally, an I/O base address register may also be included.

This gives the configuration software the flexibility to map the device's register set at least into memory space and, if an I/O base address register is also provided, into I/O space as well. The device driver associated with the device can choose whether to communicate with its device's register set through memory or I/O space.

## Memory Base Address Register

In a memory base address register (see figure 17-7), bits [2:1] define where the block of memory can be located (in the first meg, the first 4GB, or anywhere in 64-bit memory space). If this bit field indicates that the memory is 64-bit addressable, than this base address register occupies two doublewords of configuration space, not one. The first doubleword is used to set the lower 32 bits of the memory's base address and the second doubleword is used to set the upper 32 bits of the base address.

Bit three defines the block of memory as prefetchable or not. A block of memory space may be marked as prefetchable only if it can guarantee that:

- there are no side effects from reads (i.e., the read doesn't alter the contents of the location).
- on a read, it always returns all bytes irrespective of the byte enable settings.
- permitting bridges to post writes for the address range doesn't cause errors.
- permitting bridges to merge writes within this range doesn't cause errors.
- the memory is not cached from by the host processor.

As an example, the address decoder for a block of memory-mapped I/O ports would hardwire the PREFETCHABLE bit to zero, while the address decoder for regular memory (that is non-cacheable) would hardwire it to one. The configuration software uses this bit to determine the memory address ranges that the host/bridge can safely utilize prefetching in during reads and posting during writes.

Bits [31:4] (or [63:4], if the memory block it describes can be located anywhere within 64-bit address space) make up the base address field and are used to determine the size of the memory block and to set its start address. Programming of an example memory base address register is provided in a subsequent section.

If a memory device requires up to 4KB of memory space, the specification suggests that the memory range be set at 4KB (to minimize the number of bits to be resolved by the address decoder).

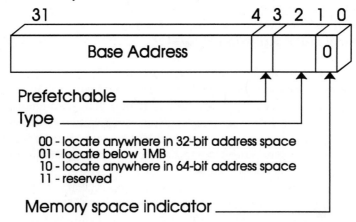

*Figure 17-7. Memory Base Address Register Format*

# Chapter 17: Configuration Registers

## I/O Base Address Register

In an I/O base address register, bit zero returns a one to indicate that I/O space is required. Bit one is reserved and should always return zero. Bits [31:2] make up the base address field and are used to determine the size of the I/O block and to set its start address. The specification requires that a device that maps its control register set into I/O space must not consume more than 256 locations per I/O base address register.

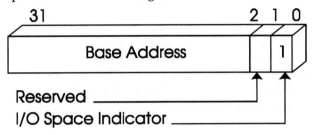

*Figure 17-8. I/O Base Address Register Format*

## Determining Block Size and Assigning Address Range

When the configuration programmer probes a base address register, he or she is attempting to discover the following:

- Is the base address register implemented?
- Is it a memory or an I/O address decoder?
- How much memory or address space does it require and with what alignment?

After discovering this information, the programmer then uses the base address register to assign a start address to the address decoder. All of this information can be ascertained simply by writing all ones to the doubleword and then reading it back. A return value of zero indicates that the base address register isn't implemented. Since the base address registers must be implemented sequentially, discovery of the first un-implemented register indicates the device has no more decoders to be programmed. By scanning the returned value (assuming its non-zero) upwards from bit four of a memory base address register or from bit two of an I/O base address register, the programmer can determine the size of the required address space. The binary-weighted value of the first one bit found indicates the required amount of space.

As an example, assume that FFFFFFFFh is written to a device's base address configuration register at configuration doubleword 04d and the value read back is FFF00000h. The fact that ones can be written into any bits indicates that the base address register is implemented.

- Bit 0 is a zero, indicating that this is a memory address decoder.
- Bits [2:1] are 00b, indicating that the memory can be located anywhere within the lower 4GB of memory space.
- Bit 3 is zero, indicating that the memory does not support prefetching.
- Scanning upwards starting at bit 4, bit 20 is the first one bit found. The binary-weighted value of this bit is 1,048,576, indicating that this is an address decoder for 1MB of memory space.

As a second example, assume that FFFFFFFFh is written to a device's base address configuration register at configuration doubleword address 05d and the value read back is FFFFFF01h. Bit 0 is a one, indicating that this is an I/O address decoder. Scanning upwards starting at bit 2, bit 8 is the first one bit found. The binary-weighted value of this bit is 256, indicating that this is an I/O address decoder for 256 bytes of I/O space.

After determining the size and type of address space the device requires, the programmer can specify the start address by writing the appropriate value to the register. Going back to the first example, assume that the programmer writes 00000000h to configuration doubleword 04d. The bits that were successfully written with ones earlier represent the programmable bit field that is used to set the start address of the decoder. Writing all zeros into this register sets up the device's memory address decoder to recognize a 1MB memory address space starting at memory address 00000000h. Writing a value of 00100000h would locate the device's memory at the start of the second megabyte of memory space, 00100000h. This highlights a PCI constraint: **all address spaces assigned are a power of two in size and are naturally aligned**. As an example, it is possible to program the memory address decoder for a 1MB block of memory to start on the one, two, or three meg boundary. As an example, it is not possible to set its start address at the 1.5, 2.3, 3.7 meg boundary.

The smallest memory address decoder would be implemented as a base address register that permitted bits [31:4] to be programmed. Since the binary-weighted value of bit four is 16, 16 bytes is the smallest memory block a PCI memory decoder can be designed for. The smallest I/O decoder would be implemented as a base address register that permitted bits [31:2] to be programmed. Since the binary-weighted value of bit four is 4, 4 bytes is the smallest memory block a PCI memory decoder can be designed for.

The first base address register implemented must occupy doubleword 04d and any additional base address registers must occupy sequential doublewords afterwards. When the programmer detects an unimplemented base address register, he or she knows that there are no more.

A device that requires the mapping of control registers into both memory and I/O space must implement two base address registers: one describing its memory block requirement and the other describing its I/O space requirement. The device driver may only use one of these two control blocks and leave the other unused. Because some processors are only capable of accessing memory locations (e.g., Motorola 68000 series processors), devices should always allow control registers to be mapped into memory space.

## Expansion ROM Base Address Register

*Required if a device incorporates a device ROM.* Many PCI devices incorporate a device ROM that contains the device's power-on self-test (POST), BIOS and interrupt service routines. The expansion ROM start memory address and size is specified in the expansion ROM base address register at configuration doubleword 12d in the configuration header region. As previously described in the section entitled "Base Address Registers", on power-up the system must be automatically configured so that each device's I/O and memory functions occupy mutually-exclusive address ranges. In order to allow this, the system must be able to detect how much memory space an expansion ROM requires. In addition, the system must have the capability of programming a ROM's address decoder in order to locate its ROM in a non-conflicting address range.

When the start-up configuration program detects that a device has an expansion ROM base address register implemented, it must check for an expansion ROM signature to determine if a ROM is actually installed (i.e., there may be an empty ROM socket). If installed, the configuration program must shadow the ROM and execute its initialization code. This process is described in the chapter entitled "Expansion ROMs."

The format of the expansion ROM base address register is illustrated in figure 17-9. A one in bit zero enables the device's ROM address decoder (assuming command register bit one is set to one). Bits [10:1] are reserved. Bits [31:11] are used to specify the ROM's start address (starting on an address divisible by the ROM's size).

As an example, assume that the programmer writes FFFFFFFEh to the ROM's base address register (bit 0, the ROM ENABLE bit, is kept cleared so as not to enable the ROM address decoder until a start memory address has been assigned). A subsequent read from the register yields FFFE0000h. This indicates the following:

- Bit 0 is a zero, indicating that the ROM address decoder is currently disabled.
- Bits [10:1] are reserved.
- In the [31:11] bit field, bit 17 is the least-significant bit that the programmer was able to set to one. It has a binary-weighted value of 128K, indicating that the ROM requires 128KB of memory space. Using bits [31:11], the programmer can initialize the ROM's base address register to assign the ROM start address on any 128K address boundary.

It's important to note that the designer should allocate a memory block slightly larger than that required by the current revision ROM to be installed. This permits the installation of subsequent ROM revisions that occupy more space without requiring a redesign of the logic associated with the device's expansion ROM base address register. The specification sets a limit of 16MB as the maximum expansion ROM size.

The MEMORY ENABLE bit in the command register has precedence over the EXPANSION ROM ENABLE bit. The device's expansion ROM should respond to memory accesses only if both its MEMORY ENABLE bit (in its command register) and the EXPANSION ROM ENABLE bit (in its expansion ROM register) are both set to one.

In order to minimize the number of address decoders that a device must implement, one address decoder can be shared between the expansion ROM base address register and one of the device's memory base address registers. The two base address registers must be able to hold different values at the same time, but the address decoder will not decode ROM accesses unless the enable bit is set in the expansion ROM base address register.

# Chapter 17: Configuration Registers

A more detailed description of expansion ROM detection, shadowing and usage can be found in the chapter entitled "Expansion ROMs."

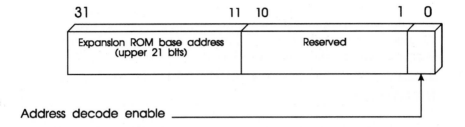

*Figure 17-9. Expansion ROM Register Format*

## CardBus CIS Pointer

*Optional.* This optional register is implemented by devices that share silicon between cardbus and PCI. This field points to the card information structure, or CIS, for the CardBus card. The register is read-only and contains the offset of the CIS in one of the following places:

- Offset within the device's device-specific configuration space (after doubleword 15 in the device's configuration space).
- Offset from the start address indicated in one of the device's memory base address registers.
- Offset within a code image in the device's expansion ROM.

The format of the CardBus CIS Pointer register is defined in the revision 3.0 PC Card specification.

A detailed description of the CIS can be found in the revision 3.0 PC Card specification and in the MindShare architecture series book entitled *PCMCIA System Architecture*.

## Subsystem Vendor ID and Subsystem ID Registers

*Optional.* **This register pair was added in revision 2.1 of the specification.** A PCI functional device may be contained on a card or be embedded within a subsystem. Two cards or subsystems that use the same PCI functional device core logic would have the same vendor and device IDs. These two optional registers are used to uniquely identify the add-in card or subsystem that the functional device resides within. Software can distinguish the difference between cards or subsystems manufactured by different vendors but with the same PCI functional device on the card or subsystem. The subsystem vendor ID is obtained from the SIG, while the vendor supplies its own subsystem ID. A value of zero in these registers indicates there isn't a subsystem vendor and subsystem ID associated with the device.

## Interrupt Pin Register

*Required if a PCI device generates interrupt requests.* The read-only interrupt pin register defines which of the four PCI interrupt request pins, INTA# through INTD#, a PCI functional device is connected, or bonded, to. The values one through four correspond to PCI interrupt request lines INTA# through INTD#. A return value of zero indicates that the device doesn't use interrupts. For additional information, refer to the chapter entitled "Interrupt-Related Issues."

## Interrupt Line Register

*Required if a PCI device generates interrupt requests.* The read/writable interrupt line register is used to identify which of the system interrupt request lines on the interrupt controller the device's PCI interrupt request pin (as specified in its interrupt pin register) is routed to. In a PC environment, for example, the values zero (00h) through fifteen (0Fh) in this register correspond to IRQ0 through IRQ15. The value 255, or FFh, indicates "unknown" or "no connection." The values from sixteen through 254, inclusive, are reserved. Although it doesn't state this in the specification, it is the author's opinion that RST# should initialize the interrupt line register to a value of FFh, thereby indicating that a system IRQ line has not yet been assigned to the device's interrupt pin.

The operating system or device driver can examine a device's interrupt line register to determine which system interrupt request line the device will use to issue requests for service (and, therefore, which entry in the interrupt table to "hook").

In a non-PC environment, the value written to this register is architecture-specific and therefore outside the scope of the specification. For additional information, refer to the chapter entitled "Interrupt-Related Issues."

## Min_Gnt Register: Timeslice Request

*Optional for a bus master and not applicable to non-master devices.* This read-only register is implemented by bus master devices and not by target devices. This register indicates how long the master would like to retain PCI bus ownership (in order to attain good performance) whenever it initiates a transaction. The value hardwired into this register indicates how long a burst period the device needs (in increments of 1/4 of a microsecond, or 250ns). A value of zero indicates the device has no stringent requirement in this area.

This register and the Max_Lat register are information-only registers used by the configuration software to determine how often a bus master typically requires access to the PCI bus and the duration of a typical transfer when it does acquire the bus. This information is useful in determining the values to be programmed into bus master latency timers and in programming the algorithm to be used by the PCI bus arbiter (if it is programmable).

## Max_Lat Register: Priority-Level Request

*Optional for a bus master and not applicable to non-master devices.* The specification states that this read-only register specifies "how often" the device needs access to the PCI bus (in increments of 1/4 of a microsecond, or 250ns). A value of zero indicates the device has no stringent requirement in this area.

In the author's opinion, this description (i.e., "how often") is a little unclear. The name of the register, Max_Lat, indicates to the author that it defines how quickly the master would like access to the bus (i.e., its GNT# asserted by the arbiter) after it asserts its REQ#. If this is the case, then the value hardwired into this register would be used by the configuration software to determine the priority-level the bus arbiter assigns to the master.

# Add-In Memory

A future release of the specification (not revision 2.1) will define a mechanism for handling the automatic detection, sizing and configuration of add-in memory. A new header type will be described, as well as a new set of configuration registers to handle automatic detection, sizing, and configuration of the add-in memory devices.

## User-Definable Features

One of the major goals of PCI is to provide automatic detection and configuration of any new subsystem installed in the system. The configuration software has no problem detecting a device and in allocating system resources to it (memory space, I/O space, interrupt line, latency timer, arbitration priority level, etc.). However, some configurable aspects of certain subsystems cannot be automatically configured when the subsystem is first detected. It is necessary to provide the end user with a list of questions to be answered by the end user. An example would be a network controller card that must be assigned a network node ID. Another would be a token ring card that must be told what the token ring speed is. When the subsystem is first installed in the system, the end user must be provided with a menu of these selectable options and the user choices must then be saved in non-volatile memory to be used at startup time. Each time the machine is restarted, the configuration software reads the selections from non-volatile memory and writes them into device-specific configuration registers associated with the function.

The user choices are supplied in a file stored in the root directory of a 1.44MB DOS-formatted diskette. The file is referred to as a PCI configuration file, or PCF. The file name takes the form XXXXYYYY.PCF and adheres to the following format:

- **XXXX** is either the subsystem vendor ID from the function's subsystem vendor ID configuration register, or, if the subsystem vendor ID register isn't implemented, the vendor ID from the vendor ID configuration register.
- **YYYY** is either the subsystem ID from the function's subsystem ID configuration register, or, if the subsystem ID register isn't implemented, the device ID from the device ID configuration register.

The PCI function indicates to the configuration software that it has a PCF by hardwiring the UDF SUPPORTED bit in its PCI configuration status register to one. When the configuration software detects the new subsystem and recognizes that PCF has been supplied on diskette, it prompts the end user to insert the diskette into the system. The PCF is then read by the system-specific configuration utility (e.g., the EISA configuration utility). The end user is presented with a series of one or more menus related to the user definable features listed in the file. After the user has made the appropriate selections, the selections are stored in non-volatile memory along with the device-specific configuration registers they must be written to each time the system is powered up.

The specification recommends that the system designer supply sufficient non-volatile memory to store 32 bytes of user-defined configuration bytes for each function that could be added to the system. The number of bytes of storage is calculated by multiplying the number of add-in card connectors (system-dependent) times the maximum number of functions per card (eight) times 32 bytes of configuration information per function. Conversely, subsystem designers should design a function so as to require no more than 32 bytes of user-definable configuration data.

The PCF is in ASCII text. The format of the information in the PCF is defined in the 2.1 specification and bears a striking resemblance to the macro language used to write EISA configuration files (the author hasn't compared all aspects of the language, but at first glance it looks identical). The specification contains a definition of the language and the author will not duplicate this information here. It would be a gratuitous use of white space to fatten a book I'm only too glad to finish.

The specification contains the following rules/guidelines regarding the PCF:

- All selections cited in the PCF must target device-specific configuration registers, not registers in the device's configuration header.
- The PCF cannot be used to select system resources (e.g., interrupt line, memory or I/O assignments, expansion ROM assignments).
- The device can use the information written to its device-specific configuration registers directly, or may require that the device driver associated with the function copy the contents of the device-specific configuration registers into I/O or memory-mapped I/O registers associated with the device.
- The device can alias its device-specific configuration registers into its I/O or memory-mapped I/O registers.
- If any of the configuration information must be accessible after configuration completes, the information must be available through a mechanism other than the configuration registers (e.g., from I/O or memory-mapped I/O registers).

# Chapter 18

## The Previous Chapter

The previous chapter provided a detailed description of the header type zero configuration register format and usage for PCI devices other than PCI-to-PCI bridges.

## This Chapter

This chapter provides a detailed description of device ROMs associated with PCI devices. This includes the following topics:

- device ROM detection.
- internal code/data format.
- shadowing.
- initialization code execution.
- interrupt hooking.

This chapter concludes part III of the book, "Device Configuration In Single PCI Bus System."

## The Next Chapter

The next chapter comprises part IV of the book, "PCI-TO-PCI Bridge", and provides a detailed discussion of PCI-to-PCI bridge implementation.

# ROM Purpose

The designer of a PCI functional device may choose to incorporate an expansion ROM (also referred to as a device or option ROM) within the device. Expansion ROMs are nothing new in the PC environment. They are found on ISA, EISA and Micro Channel cards.

The device designer typically places the following type of information within the device's associated ROM:

- device-specific power-on self-test code.
- device-specific initialization code.
- device-specific interrupt service routine.
- device-specific BIOS routine.
- device-specific code to be executed during the system boot process.

## ROM Detection

When the configuration software is configuring a PCI device, it determines if a device-specific ROM exists by checking to see if the designer has implemented an expansion ROM base address register (refer to figure 18-2).

As described in the previous chapter, the programmer writes all ones (with the exception of bit zero, to prevent the enabling of the ROM address decoder; see figure 18-1) to the expansion ROM base address register and then reads it back. If unable to change any bits to ones, then the register has not been implemented and there isn't an expansion ROM associated with the device.

On the other hand, the ability to set any bits to ones indicates the presence of the expansion ROM base address register. This may or may not indicate the presence of a device ROM. Although the address decoder and a socket may exist for a device ROM, the socket may not be occupied at present. The programmer determines the presence of the device ROM by mapping the ROM into system memory space, enabling its decoder, and reading the first two locations. If the first two locations contain 55AAh, then the ROM is present.

Figure 18-1 illustrates the format of the expansion ROM base address register. Assume that the register returns a value of FFFE0000h when read back. Bit 17 is the least-significant bit that was successfully changed to a one. This bit has a binary-weighted value of 128K. This indicates that it is a 128KB ROM and the programmable bit field within the register that is used to set its start address is [31:17]. The programmer now writes a 128KB-aligned start address into the register and sets bit zero to one to enable its ROM address decoder. To permit accesses to the ROM, in addition to setting this bit to one, the programmer must also set the MEMORY ACCESS ENABLE bit in the device's configuration command register to a one. The device's ROM address decoder is then enabled and the ROM can be accessed. The maximum ROM size permitted by the specification is 16MB.

The programmer then performs a read from the first two locations of the ROM and checks for a return value of 55AAh. If this pattern is not received, the ROM is not present. The programmer disables the ROM address decoder (clears bit zero of the expansion ROM base address register to zero). If 55AAh is received, the ROM exists and a code image must be copied into system DRAM and its initialization code must be executed. This topic is covered in the sections that follow.

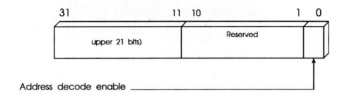

*Figure 18-1. Format of Expansion ROM Base Address Register*

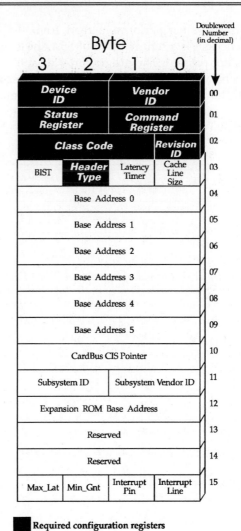

*Figure 18-2. Header Type Zero Configuration Register Format*

## ROM Shadowing Required

The PCI specification requires that device ROM code never be executed in place. This requirement exists for two reasons:

- ROM access time is typically quite slow, resulting in poor performance whenever the ROM code is executed.
- Once the initialization code has been executed, it can be discarded and the code image in DRAM memory can be shortened to include only the run-time code. The memory allocated to hold the initialization portion of the code can be freed up, allowing more efficient use of memory space.

Creating a copy of ROM code in system DRAM memory and only using the copy is referred to as shadowing the ROM.

Once the presence of the device ROM has been established (see the previous section), the configuration software must copy a code image into system DRAM and then disable the ROM address decoder (by clearing bit zero of the expansion ROM base address register to zero). In a non-PCI environment, the area of memory the code image is copied to could be anywhere in the 4GB space. The specification for that environment may define a particular area.

In a PC environment, the ROM code image must be copied into RAM memory into the range of addresses associated with device ROMs: 000C0000h through 000DFFFFh. If the class code indicates that this is the VGA's device ROM, its code image must be copied into memory starting at location 000C0000h.

The next section defines the format of the information in the ROM and how the configuration software determines which code image to load into system memory.

## ROM Content

### Multiple Code Images

The PCI specification permits the inclusion of more than one code image in a PCI device ROM. The configuration software can then scan through the images in the ROM and select the one that will result in the best performance when executed by the host processor. Another selection criterion that must be met is the vendor ID and device ID in the code image must match the vendor and device IDs from the device's configuration registers (because the ROM may contain drivers for a number of devices).

Figure 18-3 illustrates the concept of multiple code images embedded within a device ROM. Each image must start on an address divisible by 512. Each image consists of an information data structure, a run-time code image and an initialization code image. The configuration software interrogates the data structure in order to determine if this is the image it will copy to system memory and use. If it is, the configuration software copies the image to system memory, executes the initialization code, and then shortens the image kept in system memory to include only the data structure and the run-time code. The RAM containing the image is then write-protected. The remaining RAM is deallocated. The sections that follow provide a detailed discussion of the code image format and the initialization process.

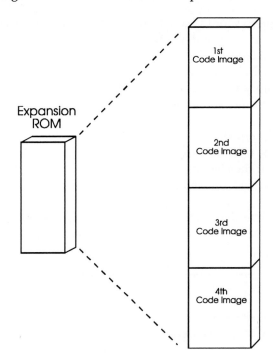

*Figure 18-3. Multiple Code Images Contained In One Device ROM*

## Format of a Code Image

### General

Figure 18-4 illustrates the format of a single code image. The image consists of the following components:

- **ROM header.** Described later in this section. Contains a 16-bit pointer to the ROM data structure.
- **ROM data structure.** Described later in this section, contains information about the device and the image.
- **Run-time code.** Code that is kept in system memory after the operating system loads and that remains available for execution on an on-going basis.
- **Initialization code.** Must always reside at the end of the image so it can be abbreviated or discarded after its initial execution at system startup.

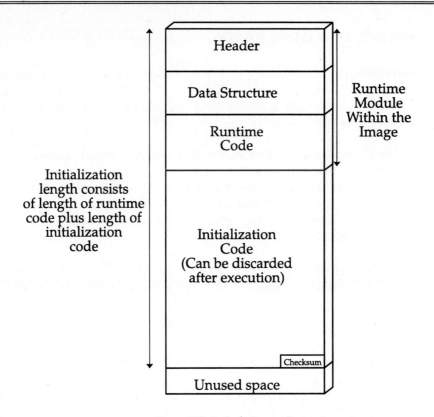

*Figure 18-4. Code Image Format*

## ROM Header Format

The ROM header must be located at the very start of each image within the ROM. Table 18-1 defines the format of the header and the purpose of each field is further defined in the paragraphs that follow. The offset specified in the table is the offset from the first location in this ROM code image.

# Chapter 18: Expansion ROMs

*Table 18-1. PCI Expansion ROM Header Format*

| Offset | Length (bytes) | Value | Description |
|--------|--------|-------|-------------|
| 00h | 1d | 55h | ROM signature byte one. |
| 01h | 1d | AAh | ROM signature byte two. |
| 02h - 17h | 22d | n | Reserved for processor architecture unique data. See table 18-2. |
| 18h - 19h | 2d | n | Pointer to PCI data structure. Since this is a 16-bit pointer, the data structure can be anywhere within 64K forward of the first location in this code image. |

### ROM Signature

The first two bytes should contain 55AAh, identifying this as a device ROM. This is the same signature used for a device ROM in any PC-compatible machine.

### Processor/Architecture Unique Data

This block of 22 locations is reserved for processor/architecture unique data. For PC-compatible environments and images that identify the code as Intel x86-compatible in the code type field of the ROM data structure, the revision 2.1 specification provides a definition of the structure of the processor/architecture unique data area in the image header. For non-PC compatible environments, the content of this structure is architecture-specific. Table 18-2 defines the fields that must be supplied for PC-compatibility. The offset specified in the table is the offset from the first location of this ROM code image.

*Table 18-2. PC-Compatible Usage of Processor/Architecture Unique Data Area In ROM Header*

| Offset | Length (in bytes) | Description |
|--------|-------------------|-------------|
| 02h | 1 | Overall size of the image (in 512 byte increments). |
| 03h-05h | 3 | Entry point for the initialization code. Contains three-byte short jump to the initiator code entry point. The POST performs a far call to this location to initialize the device. |
| 06h-17h | 18d | Reserved (for application-unique data, such as the copyright notice). |

### Pointer to ROM Data Structure

This is the 16-bit offset (in little-endian format) to the ROM data structure within this code image. It is an offset from the start address of this code image. Because this is only a 16-bit offset from the first location of this code image, the data structure must reside within 64KB forward of the first location of this code image.

## ROM Data Structure Format

As stated earlier, the data structure associated with each code image must reside within the first 64KB of each code image. The data structure must reside within the run-time code (assuming there is one). If there isn't a run-time code module, the data structure must reside within the initialization code. The data structure's format is defined in table 18-3 and the purpose of each field is further defined in the paragraphs that follow the table.

*Table 18-3. PCI Expansion ROM Data Structure Format*

| Offset | Length | Description |
|--------|--------|-------------|
| 00h | 4 | **Signature** consisting of the ASCII string "PCIR" (PCI ROM). |
| 04h | 2 | **Vendor ID**. The configuration software does not select a code image unless the vendor and device IDs in the image's data structure match the device's vendor and device IDs. |
| 06h | 2 | **Device ID**. Refer to the previous row in this table. |
| 08h | 2 | **Pointer to vital product data**. Offset from the start location of the code image. |
| 0Ah | 2 | PCI **data structure length** in bytes, little-endian format. |
| 0Ch | 1 | PCI **data structure revision**. The format shown here is revision zero (in both revision 2.0 and 2.1). |
| 0Dh | 3 | **Class code**. This is a duplication of the class code found in the device's configuration class code register. |
| 10h | 2 | **Image length**. Code image length in increments of 512 bytes (little-endian format). |
| 12h | 2 | **Revision level of code/data** in this code image. |

| Offset | Length | Description |
|--------|--------|-------------|
| 14h | 1 | **Code type**. See text. |
| 15h | 1 | **Indicator byte**. Bit 7 indicates whether this is the last code image in the ROM (1 = last image). Bits [6:0] are reserved and must be zero. |
| 16h | 2 | **Reserved**. |

### ROM Signature

This unique signature identifies the start of the PCI data structure. The **P** is stored at offset 00h, the **C** at offset 01h, etc. **PCIR** stands for PCI ROM.

### Vendor ID

As stated in the table, the configuration software does not select a code image to load into system memory unless the vendor and device IDs in the image's data structure match the device's vendor and device IDs. The ROM may contain code images for variations on the device, either from the same vendor or supplied by different vendors.

### Device ID

Refer to the description of the vendor ID field in the previous section..

### Pointer to Vital Product Data (VPD)

The offset (from the start of the image) of the vital product data area. The offset is stored in little-endian format. Because the offset is only 16-bits in size, the vital product data area must reside within the first 64KB of the image. A value of zero indicates that the image contains no vital product data. The revision 2.0 specification said that the pointer is required, but the 2.1 specification has removed that requirement. If no device ROM is present on a device other than the one containing the VPD, there is only one image and it contains the VPD. If multiple code images are present, each image will contain VPD for that device. The VPD data describes the device may be duplicated in each code image, but the VPD that pertains to software may be different for each code image.

A detailed description of the VPD can be found later in this chapter.

### PCI Data Structure Length

This 16-bit value is stored in the little-endian format. It defines the length (in bytes) of the PCI data structure for this image.

### PCI Data Structure Revision

This 8-bit field reflects the revision of the image's data structure. The currently-defined (as of revision 2.1 of the specification) data structure format is revision zero.

### Class Code

The 24-bit class code field contains the same information as the class code field within the device's configuration header. The configuration software examines this field to determine if this is a VGA-compatible interface. If it is, the ROM code image must be copied into system memory starting at location 000C0000h (for compatibility).

### Image Length

This two-byte field indicates the length of the entire code image (refer to figure 18-4) in increments of 512 bytes. It is stored in little-endian format.

### Revision Level of Code/Data

This two-byte field reflects the revision level of the code within the image.

### Code Type

This one-byte field identifies the type of code contained in this image as either executable machine language for a particular processor/architecture or as interpretive code. A value of 00h indicates Intel ix86 (IBM PC-AT compatible) executable code, while 01h indicates interpretive code. The Open Firmware standard (reference IEEE standard 1275-1994) is used for interpretive code. The values from 02h through FFh are reserved. A basic description of the Open Firmware standard can be found at the end of this chapter.

### Indicator Byte

Only bit seven is currently defined. A one indicates that this is the last image in the ROM, while a zero indicates other images follow this one. Bits [6:0] are reserved.

## Execution of Initialization Code

Prior to discovery of the device's ROM, the configuration software has assigned memory space and/or I/O space to the device by programming its base address registers. If the device is interrupt-driven, the interrupt routing information has been programmed into the device's interrupt line register. In addition, if the UDF bit was set in the device 's configuration status register, the user has been prompted to insert the PCI configuration file, or PCF, and the user selected any configuration options available from the file. Finally, the configuration software copied a code image from the ROM into RAM memory.

After the appropriate code image has been copied into system memory, the device ROM's address decoder is disabled. The configuration software must keep the area of RAM (the image resides in) read/writable. The configuration software then executes the following sequence:

1. The software then calls the initialization module within the image (through the pointer stored in the ROM image header), supplying it with three parameters: the bus number, device number and function number of the device associated with the ROM. The 8-bit bus number is supplied in AH, the device number is supplied in the upper five bits of AL, and the function number in the lower three bits of AL. It's necessary to supply the initialization code with this information so that it can determine what IO and/or memory address range the configuration software has allocated to the device (via its base address registers).
2. The initialization code then issues a call to the system BIOS (or the HAL: hardware abstraction layer), supplying these three input parameters and requesting the contents of the device's base address registers. Armed with this information, the initialization code can now communicate with the device's I/O register set to initialize the device.
3. If the ROM image has a device-specific interrupt service routine embedded within the run-time module, it reads from the device's interrupt line configuration register to determine which system interrupt request line the device's PCI interrupt pin has been routed to by the configuration

software. Using this routing information, the initialization code knows which entry in the interrupt table must be hooked. It reads and saves the pointer currently stored in that interrupt table entry and then stores the pointer to the interrupt service routine embedded within the run-time module of the code image. In this way, it maintains the integrity of the interrupt chain.

4. The ROM image may also have a device-specific BIOS routine embedded within the run-time module of the code image. In this case, it needs to hook another interrupt entry to this BIOS routine. Once again, it reads and saves the pointer currently stored in that interrupt table entry and then stores the pointer to the BIOS routine embedded within the run-time module of the code image. In this way, it maintains the integrity of the interrupt chain.

5. Since the area of system memory it resides in has been kept read/writable, the initialization code can alter the code image: embed static data in it (e.g., a pointer to another device's interrupt service routine), adjust its length, etc. If this is the case, the initialization software is responsible for re-computing the new length and updating the image length field in the image's data structure and in the ROM header.

6. In addition, the new checksum must be computed and stored at the end of the adjusted image. If upon completion the initialization code sets the image length to zero, it doesn't need to recompute the image checksum and update it.

7. Once the initialization code has completed execution, it executes a return to the system software that called it.

The system software then takes two actions:

1. Interrogates the image size to determine if it has changed. If it has, the system software adjust the amount of memory allocated to the image to make more efficient use of memory. The image is typically shorter than it was.

2. Write-protect the area of system memory the image resides in.

The Plug and Play specification now refers to the PCI method of writing device ROM code and handling its detection, shadowing, and initialization, as the DDIM (device driver initialization model). That specification stresses that this is model that all new device ROMs for other buses (e.g., ISA, EISA, Micro Channel, etc.) should adhere to.

# Chapter 18: Expansion ROMs

## Introduction to Open Firmware

Historically, all of the PC-compatible machines marketed in the past have been based on Intel x86 processors. When writing ROM code for an add-in subsystem on an ISA, EISA or Micro Channel card, it was a simple decision to create an x86 machine language image to be stored in the ROM. Two factors drove the decision to permit code images other than x86-compatible in the PCI environment:

- A number of system vendors are creating PCs based on processors other than the x86 processor family. These machines would take a substantial performance hit when executing expansion ROM code that isn't written in the processor's native machine language (i.e., x86 code is "foreign" to PowerPC and other types of non-Intel compatible processors). They would be forced to emulate the x86 code, an inherently inefficient solution.
- The PCI bus is being designed into many non-PC compatible systems based on host processors other than the x86 processor family. Examples would be embedded applications such as scanners, laser printers, etc., and mini and mainframe computer systems. These host processors would also be forced to emulate the x86 code, once again resulting in performance degradation.

Rather than writing an add-in device's ROM code in machine language native to a particular processor, the subsystem designer can write the ROM code in Fcode based on the Open Firmware specification, IEEE 1275-1994.

The Open Firmware would consist of two main components:

- The system board's Open Firmware contains the Fcode interpreter and possibly an individual Fcode ROM program associated with each of the embedded subsystems that the system Open Firmware is already cognizant of.
- Each add-in subsystem would hopefully contain an Open Firmware Fcode image.

The Open Firmware language is based on the Forth programming language. The ROM code would be written in Forth source code (in ASCII text). The ASCII-based source code is then supplied as input to a "tokenizer" program. The tokenizer processes the ASCII source code into a series of byte commands, known as Fcode. As an example, an entire line of ASCII source code might be reduced to a single byte that represents the Forth command, only in a much more compact form.

The system firmware that "discovered" the ROM (as described earlier in this chapter), incorporates an interpreter that converts the Fcode byte stream read from the ROM into machine language instructions specific to the system's host processor.

Typically, the goal is that the Fcode is only used at system startup to initialize the I/O device. If the device is required to boot the operating system into memory, the Fcode would handle that as well. Upon completion of the operating system load, the operating system would take over.

There's a lot more to it than has been covered here: the standard is approximately 300 pages in length, 8.5" x 11" in size. A detailed discussion of Open Firmware is outside the scope of this book.

The 2.1 specification refers the reader to another document, *PCI Bus Binding to IEEE 1275-1994*, for PCI specific to the implementation of Open Firmware in a PCI-based machine. This document is available using anonymous FTP to the machine playground.sun.com with the file name

/pub/p1275/bindings/postscript/PCI.ps.

## Vital Product Data (VPD)

### General

If present, the VPD is a data structure that identifies items such as hardware, software, and microcode within a system. It provides the configuration software and/or operating system with information on field replaceable units (FRUs), such as part number, serial number, etc. The VPD also provides a method for storing performance and failure data related to a device that is being monitored. Although the VPD is optional, designers are urged to implement it. The presence of the VPD permits a system vendor to implement processes to verify the completeness of a hardware order (in a build-to-order manufacturing environment). The presence of the VPD also permits the device vendor to obtain performance and failure analysis data on their product in the field. VPD also enhances the ability of technical support to ascertain the products that populate a machine.

There are three types of fields within the VPD: recommended, conditionally recommended, and additional fields. If VPD is included, the recommended fields should be included. The conditionally recommended and additional fields may be present (based on the type of device).

## Data Structure

The VPD consist of large and small resource descriptors as defined in the version 1.0a PLug and Play specification (refer to the MindShare book entitled *Plug and Play System Architecture*). The VPD therefore consists of a series of tagged data structures (i.e., descriptors).

The Plug and Play descriptor types that are used in the VPD are:

- small Compatible Device ID descriptor
- small Vendor-Defined descriptor
- small End descriptor
- large Identifier String descriptor
- large Vendor-Defined descriptor

The 2.1 PCI specification defines a new large descriptor type for the VPD and it is called the VPD descriptor. It has the format defined in table 18 - 4:

*Table 18 - 4. VPD Descriptor Format*

| Byte | Description |
|------|-------------|
| 0 | 90h (bit 7=1 indicates large descriptor type, 10h in [6:0] indicates start of the VPD). |
| 0-1 | Overall length of the VPD in bytes. |
| 2-n | Body of the VPD. Consists of one or more VPD keyword fields, such as part number, serial number, etc. The recommended, conditionally recommended, and additional fields are defined in tables 18-5, 18-6, and 18-7. |
| n + 1 | checksum on entire VPD structure |

*Table 18 - 5. Recommended Fields*

| ASCII Name | Description |
|------------|-------------|
| PN | **Part number.** |
| FN | **FRU part number.** |
| EC | **Engineering change** level of assembly. |
| MN | **Manufacturer** ID. |
| SN | **Serial number.** |

*Table 18 - 6. Conditionally Recommended Fields*

| ASCII Name | Description |
|------------|-------------|
| LI | **Load ID.** This is a part of the name of the software download code module that may be required by a device to make it a functional. |
| RL | **ROM level.** Revision level of any non-alterable (as opposed to flash-programmable) ROM code on the device. |
| RM | **Alterable ROM level.** Revision level of any alterable ROM code (flash-programmable ROM) on the device. |
| NA | **Network Address.** Needed by network adapters that require a unique network address (e.g., toekn ring, Basband, or Ethernet). |
| DD | **Device driver level.** The minimum device driver level required for proper operation of the device. |
| DG | **Diagnostic level.** The minimum diagnostic software level required for testing the device. |
| LL | **Loadable microcode level.** If not present, level zero is implied. If a device uses loadable microcode (firmware), indicates the microcode level required for proper device operation. This field is associated with card ID, rather than the part number or EC level. As changes are made to a card, a new level of microcode may be required. |
| VI | **Vendor ID/Device ID.** Same as that found in the device's configuration header space. |
| FU | **Function number.** Indicates the function in a multifunction device that the VPD is associated with. Only one FU field is permitted within the extent of each VPD descriptor. |
| SI | **Subsystem Vendor ID/Subsystem ID.** Same as that found in the device's configuration header space. |

*Table 18 - 7. Additional Fields*

| ASCII Name | Description |
|------------|-------------|
| ZO-ZZ | **User/Product-specific fields**. Available for device-specific data for which no keyword has been defined. |

The following is the example VPD supplied in the specification. It actually consists of two VPDs: one for the device and one for its associated diagnostic software.

| Offset | Value | Item/Description |
|---|---|---|
| 0 | 82h | Identification String descriptor. |
| 1 | 0021h | descriptor length |
| 3 | "ABC Super-Fast Widget Controller" | Identification string |
| 36 | 90h | VPD start |
| 37 | 0033h | length |
| 39 | "PN" | part number field |
| 41 | 08h | length |
| 42 | "6181682A" | part number |
| 50 | "EC" | engineering change (EC) field |
| 52 | 0Ah | length |
| 53 | "4950262536" | EC number |
| 63 | "SN" | serial number field |
| 65 | 08h | length |
| 66 | "00000194" | serial number |
| 74 | "FN" | FRU number field |
| 76 | 06h | length |
| 77 | "135722" | FRU number |
| 83 | "MN" | manufacturer number field |
| 85 | 04h | length |
| 86 | "1037" | manufacturer number |
| 90 | 90h | VPD start |
| 91 | 000Ah | length |
| 93 | "DG" | diagnostic level field |
| 95 | 02h | length |
| 96 | "01" | diagnostic level |
| 98 | "DD" | device driver level field |
| 100 | 02h | length |
| 101 | "01" | device driver level |
| 103 | 79h | End tag |
| 104 | Checksum | checksum of entire VPD (the checksum is correct if the sum of all bytes, including checksum, equal zero). |

# Part IV

# The PCI-to-PCI Bridge

# Chapter 19

## Prior To This Chapter

The previous chapter provided a detailed description of device ROMs associated with PCI devices. This included the following topics:

- device ROM detection.
- internal code/data format.
- shadowing.
- initialization code execution.
- interrupt hooking.

This chapter concluded part III of the book, "Device Configuration In Single PCI Bus System."

## In This Chapter

This chapter comprises part IV of the book, "PCI-TO-PCI Bridge", providing a detailed discussion of PCI-to-PCI bridge implementation. This information is drawn from the revision 1.0 PCI-to-PCI bridge architecture specification, dated April 5, 1994.

## The Next Chapter

The next chapter discusses the PCI BIOS specification.

## Scaleable Bus Architecture

A machine that incorporates one PCI bus has some obvious limitations. Some examples follow:

- If too many electrical loads (i.e., devices) are placed on a PCI bus, it ceases to function correctly.

- The devices that populate a particular PCI bus may not co-exist together too well. A master that requires a lot of bus time in order to achieve good performance must share the bus with other masters. Demands for bus time by these other masters may degrade the performance of this bus master subsystem.
- One PCI bus only supports a limited number of PCI expansion connectors (due to the electrical loading constraints mentioned earlier).

These problems could be solved by adding one or more additional PCI buses into the system and re-distributing the device population. How can a customer (or a system designer) add another PCI bus into the system? The specification provides a complete definition of a PCI-to-PCI bridge device. This device can either be embedded on a PCI bus or may be on an add-in card installed in a PCI expansion connector. The PCI-to-PCI bridge provides a bridge from one PCI bus to another, but it only places one electrical load on its host PCI bus. The new PCI bus can then support a number of additional devices and/or PCI expansion connectors. The electrical loading constraint is on a per bus basis, not a system basis. Of course, the power supply in the host system must be capable of supplying sufficient power for the load imposed by the additional devices residing on the new bus. Alternately, the system designer could include more than one host/PCI bridge.

## Terminology

Before proceeding, it's important to define some basic terms associated with PCI-to-PCI bridges. Each PCI-to-PCI bridge is connected to two PCI buses, referred to as its primary and secondary buses.

- **Primary bus**. PCI bus closest to the host processor.
- **Secondary bus**. PCI bus that resides behind a PCI-to-PCI bridge.
- **Subordinate bus**. PCI bus furthest from the host processor.
- **Downstream**. When a transaction is initiated and is passed through one or more PCI-to-PCI bridges flowing away from the host processor, it is said to be moving downstream.
- **Upstream**. When a transaction is initiated and is passed through one or more PCI-to-PCI bridges flowing towards the host processor, it is said to be moving upstream.

## Example Systems

Figures 19-1 and 19-2 illustrate two examples of systems with more than one PCI bus.

## Example One

The system in figure 19-1 has two PCI buses. Bus number one is subordinate to, or beneath, bus number zero. The bus on the other side of the host/PCI bridge is guaranteed present in every PCI system and is always assigned a bus number of zero. Since the host/PCI bridge "knows" its bus number, the bridge designer may or may not implement a bus number register in the bridge. If the bus number register is present, the value it contains would be hardwired to zero.

It is a rule that each PCI-to-PCI bridge must implement three bus number registers in pre-defined locations within its configuration space. All three registers are read/writable and reset forces them to zero. They are assigned numbers during the configuration process. Those three registers are:

- **Primary bus number register.** Initialized by software with the number of the bridge's PCI bus that is closer to the processor. The host/PCI bridge is only connected to one PCI bus, so that is its primary bus. The host/PCI bridge doesn't have to implement a secondary bus number register (because it is irrelevant).
- **Secondary bus number register.** Initialized by software with the number of the bridge's PCI bus that is further from the processor.
- **Subordinate bus number register.** Initialized by software with the highest numbered PCI bus that exists behind the bridge (on the secondary side). If the only bus behind the bridge is the bridge's secondary bus, then the secondary and subordinate bus number registers would be initialized with the number of the secondary bus.

The host/PCI bridge only has to implement the primary and subordinate bus number registers. In figure 19-1, the host/PCI bridge's bus number registers are initialized (during configuration) as follows:

- **Primary bus = 0.** The host/PCI bridge's PCI bus is always numbered zero.
- **Subordinate bus = 1**, the number of the highest numbered PCI bus that exists behind the bridge. The host/PCI bridge is therefore supposed to

pass through all configuration read and write transactions initiated by the host processor specifying a bus number in the range zero through one.

PCI-to-PCI bridge number one has its bus registers initialized as follows:

- **Primary bus = 0**. This is the number of the PCI bus closer to the host processor.
- **Secondary bus = 1**. This is the number of the PCI bus further from the processor.
- **Subordinate bus = 1**. This is the number of the highest-numbered bus that exists behind the bridge.

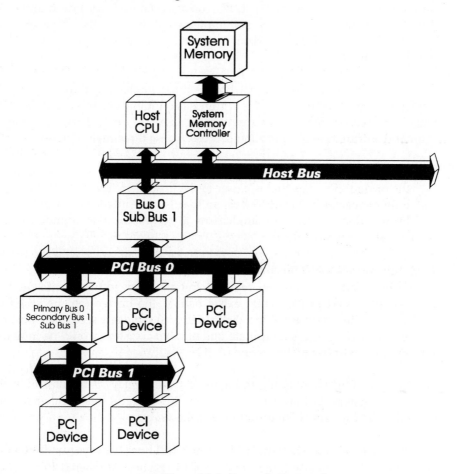

*Figure 19-1. Example System One*

## Example Two

Figure 19-2 has four PCI buses. During configuration, the host/PCI bridge's bus number registers are initialized as follows:

- **Primary bus = 0**. The host/PCI bridge's PCI bus is always numbered zero.
- **Subordinate bus = 3**. This is the number of the highest-numbered bus that exists behind the host/PCI bridge. The host/PCI bridge must therefore pass through all configuration read and write transactions initiated by the host processor specifying a target bus number in the range zero through three.

Bridge one's bus number registers are initialized as follows:

- **Primary bus = 0**. This is the number of its PCI bus that is closer to the host processor.
- **Secondary bus = 1**. This is the number of its PCI bus that is further from the host processor.
- **Subordinate bus = 1**. This is the number of highest-numbered PCI bus that exists behind the bridge (in this case, it's the same as the secondary bus number).

Bridge two's bus number registers are initialized as follows:

- **Primary bus = 0**. This is the number of its PCI bus that is closer to the processor.
- **Secondary bus = 2**. This is the number of its PCI bus that is further from the processor.
- **Subordinate bus = 3**. This the is number of the highest-numbered bus that exists behind the bridge (bus 3 is subordinate to bus 2).

Bridge three's bus number registers are initialized as follows:

- **Primary bus = 2**. This is the number of its PCI bus that is closer to the processor.
- **Secondary bus = 3**. This is the number of its PCI bus that is further from the processor.
- **Subordinate bus = 3**. This the is number of the highest-numbered bus that exists behind the bridge (in this case, the same as secondary bus number).

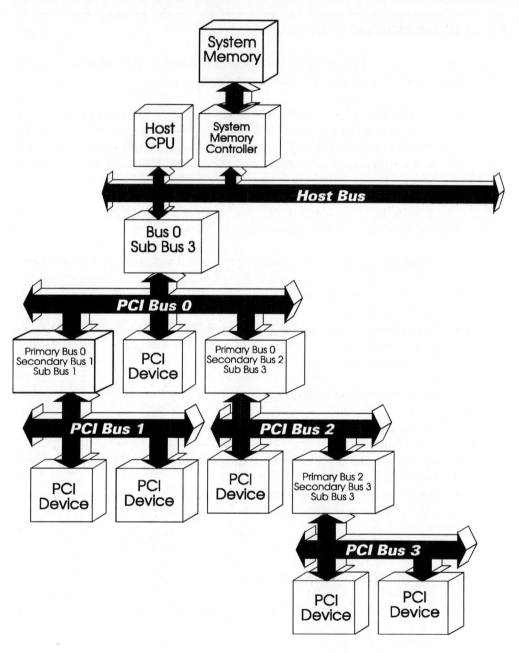

*Figure 19-2. Example System Two*

## PCI-to-PCI Bridge: Traffic Director

The PCI-to-PCI bridge functions as a traffic coordinator between two PCI buses. Its job is to monitor each transaction that is initiated on the two PCI buses and to decide whether or not to pass the transaction through to the opposite PCI bus. When the bridge determines that a transaction on one bus needs to be passed to the other bus, the bridge must act as the target of the transaction on the originating bus and as the initiator of the new transaction on the destination bus. The fact that the bridge resides between the transaction initiator and the target is invisible to the initiator (as well as to the target).

In addition to determining if a transaction initiated on one bus must be passed through to the other, the bridge also supplies the following functions:

- The bridge monitors SERR# on the secondary bus and passes it to SERR# on its primary bus if it is sampled asserted.
- A bridge may incorporate a device ROM associated with itself. In this case, it must recognize and permit accesses to the ROM memory.
- A bridge may incorporate a set of device-specific, memory-mapped registers that control its own functionality. In this case, it must recognize and permit accesses to these registers.
- A bridge may incorporate a set of device-specific, IO-mapped registers that control its own functionality. In this case, it must recognize and permit accesses to these registers.

Table 19-1 defines the types of transactions that may be detected on a PCI bus and how the bridge handles each of them. The section in this chapter entitled "Configuration Registers" provides a detailed description of the address decode mechanisms implemented in a PCI-to-PCI bridge.

*Table 19-1. Transaction Types That the Bridge Must Detect and Handle*

| Transaction Type | Bus Detected On | Action by Bridge |
|---|---|---|
| Memory read | Primary or secondary | There are five cases:<br>1. Within memory range to pass through: claim and pass through.<br>2. Within memory range of bridge's device ROM: claim and permit access to internal ROM; do not pass through.<br>3. Within memory-mapped I/O range to pass through: claim and pass through.<br>4. Within memory range of bridge's device-specific memory-mapped internal registers: claim and permit access to internal register(s); do not pass through.<br>5. None of the above: do not pass through and do not claim for internal access. |
| Memory read line | Primary or secondary | Same as memory read. |
| Memory read multiple | Primary or secondary | Same as memory read. |
| Memory write | Primary or secondary | Same as memory read. |
| Memory write and invalidate | Primary or secondary | Same as memory read. |
| I/O read | Primary or secondary | There are three cases:<br>1. Within I/O range to pass through: claim and pass through.<br>2. Within I/O range of bridge's device-specific I/O-mapped internal registers: claim and permit access to internal register(s); do not pass through.<br>3. None of the above: do not pass through and do not claim for internal access. |
| I/O write | Primary or secondary | Same as I/O read. |

| Transaction Type | Bus Detected On | Action by Bridge |
|---|---|---|
| Type 0 configuration read | Primary | If the bridge's IDSEL# input is asserted, perform function decode and claim if target function implemented, otherwise ignore. If claimed, permit access to target function's configuration registers. Do not pass through under any circumstances. |
| | Secondary | Ignore. |
| Type 0 configuration write | Primary | Same as configuration read. |
| | Secondary | Ignore. |
| Type 1 configuration read | Primary | There are three cases: 1. Target bus is the bridge's secondary bus: claim and pass through as a type zero configuration read. 2. Target bus is in the range of subordinate buses that exists behind the bridge (but not equal to the secondary bus): claim and pass through as type one configuration read. 3. None of the above: ignore. |
| | Secondary | Ignore. |
| Type 1 configuration write (not a special cycle request) | Primary | There are three cases: 1. Target bus is the bridge's secondary bus: claim and pass through as a type zero configuration write. 2. Target bus is in the range of subordinate buses that exists behind the bridge (but not equal to the secondary bus): claim and pass through unchanged as type one configuration write. 3. None of the above: ignore. |
| | Secondary | Ignore. |

| Transaction Type | Bus Detected On | Action by Bridge |
|---|---|---|
| Type 1 configuration write as special cycle request (device = 1Fh, function = 7h and doubleword = 0) | Primary | There are three cases:<br>1. Target bus is the bridge's secondary bus: claim and pass through as a special cycle.<br>2. Target bus is in the range of subordinate buses that exists behind the bridge (but not equal to the secondary bus): claim and pass through unchanged as type one configuration write.<br>3. None of the above: ignore. |
| | Secondary | There are three cases:<br>1. Target bus is the bridge's primary bus: claim and pass through as a special cycle.<br>2. Target bus is neither the bridge's primary bus nor is it in the range of buses defined by the bridge's secondary and subordinate bus registers: claim and pass through unchanged as type one configuration write.<br>3. Target bus is not the bridge's primary bus, but it is within the range of buses defined by the bridge's secondary and subordinate bus registers: ignore. |
| Special cycle | Primary or secondary | Do not claim. Ignore. Special cycles are meaningless to PCI-to-PCI bridges. |
| Interrupt acknowledge | Primary or secondary | Ignore. |

| Transaction Type | Bus Detected On | Action by Bridge |
|---|---|---|
| Dual-address cycle (DAC) | Primary | There are three cases:<br>1. The bridge does not support memory above the 4GB address boundary behind the bridge: in this case, the bridge ignores the access.<br>2. The bridge supports memory above the 4GB address boundary behind the bridge, but the system may not have any there: in this case, the bridge ignores the access.<br>3. The bridge supports memory above the 4GB address boundary behind the bridge and the system has programmed the bridge to recognize addresses above 4GB: in this case, the bridge latches the two address packets delivered during the two address phases and decodes. If the address is in range, transaction is claimed and passed through. If out of range, it is ignored. |

| Transaction Type | Bus Detected On | Action by Bridge |
|---|---|---|
|  | Secondary | There are three cases:<br>1. The bridge supports memory above the 4GB boundary behind the bridge and is programmed to recognize that range on the primary side: a DAC detected on the secondary side where the address is outside the range defined is claimed and passed through to the primary bus.<br>2. Same as case 1, but address is within range defined as memory above 4GB that exists on secondary side of the bridge: bridge ignores it.<br>3. Bridge does not support memory above the 4GB address boundary behind the bridge: when a DAC is detected on the secondary side, the bridge can claim the transaction and pass it through to the primary bus. The theory is that a master on the secondary side is attempting access system memory above 4GB, so the bridge forwards the transaction upstream towards system memory. |

# Configuration Registers

## General

The chapter entitled "Configuration Registers" provided a detailed discussion of the configuration registers defined by the specification for inclusion in all PCI devices other than PCI-to-PCI bridges. These configuration registers were defined as configuration header type zero. This section provides a detailed description of the configuration registers defined by the specification for implementation in PCI-to-PCI bridges. This is referred to as configuration header type one, illustrated in figure 19-3. It consists of the first 16 of the 64 doublewords of configuration space associated with the bridge.

# Chapter 19: PCI-to-PCI Bridge

This chapter also provides a detailed description of the methods utilized by the bridge to decide what memory and I/O transactions to accept and which to ignore.

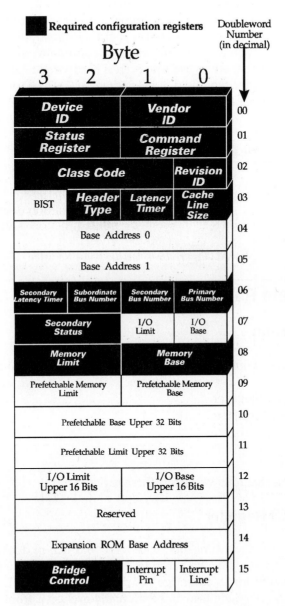

*Figure 19-3. PCI-to-PCI Bridge's Configuration Registers*

## Header Type Register

*Mandatory.* Location in header: byte two (the least-significant byte in the doubleword is zero and the most-significant is three) within doubleword three of the bridge's configuration space. The register is illustrated in figure 19-4. If the bridge device contains other functions in addition to the bridge function, bit seven is set to one; otherwise, bit seven is hardwired to zero. For a PCI-to-PCI bridge, the header type field is hardwired to 000001b, or 01h. This indicates that doublewords 4 through 15 are structured according to header type one.

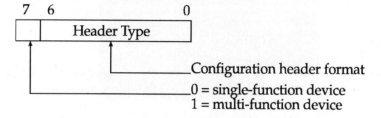

*Figure 19-4. Header Type Register*

# Registers Related to Device ID

## Introduction

There are four registers associated with device identification. They are:

- Vendor ID register.
- Device ID register.
- Revision ID register.
- Class code register.

The sections that follow describe these registers.

## Vendor ID Register

*Mandatory.* Location in header: bytes zero and one in doubleword zero. This 16-bit register contains the hardwired vendor ID and is implemented exactly the same as it is for a non-bridge PCI device. The vendor ID is assigned by the PCI SIG and is guaranteed to be mutually-exclusive from the IDs issued to other vendors. In combination with the device and revision ID, the vendor ID register can be used by a device driver to "discover" an instance of its associated device. The vendor ID of FFFFh is reserved and is not used. This is the value returned during a configuration read from a non-existent PCI device (returned to the host processor when the host/PCI bridge experiences a master abort due to no reply).

### Device ID Register

*Mandatory.* Location in header: bytes two and three in doubleword zero. The 16-bit device ID register is hardwired with the device ID chosen by the device vendor.

### Revision ID Register

*Mandatory.* Location in header: byte zero in doubleword two. The 8-bit revision ID register contains the device's hardwired revision number.

### Class Code Register

*Mandatory.* Location in header: bytes one, two and three in doubleword two. The three byte class code register is implemented in the same manner as it is for a PCI device other than a PCI-to-PCI bridge. Figure 19-5 illustrates the class code register. For a PCI-to-PCI bridge, the class code is 06h (bridge), sub-class is 04h (PCI-to-PCI bridge), and the programmer's interface byte is 00h.

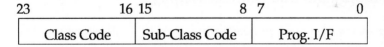

*Figure 19-5. Class Code Register*

## Bus Number Registers

### Introduction

Each PCI-to-PCI bridge must implement three mandatory bus number registers. All of them are read/writable and are cleared to zero by reset. During configuration, the configuration software initializes these three registers to assign bus numbers. They are:

- Primary bus number register.
- Secondary bus number register.
- Subordinate bus number register.

The combination of the secondary and the subordinate bus number registers defines the range of buses that exists behind the bridge. This information is used by the bridge to determine whether or not to pass through:

1. Type one configuration reads and writes.
2. Type one configuration writes that are to be converted to special cycles on the specified target bus.

## Primary Bus Number Register

*Mandatory.* Location in header: byte zero in doubleword six. The primary bus number register is initialized by software with the number of the bridge's bus that is closer to the host processor.

## Secondary Bus Number Register

*Mandatory.* Location in header: byte one in doubleword six. The secondary bus number register is initialized by software with the number of the bridge's bus that is further from the host processor.

## Subordinate Bus Number Register

*Mandatory.* Location in header: byte two in doubleword six. The subordinate bus number register is initialized by software with the number of the highest-numbered bus that exists behind the bridge. If there are no PCI-to-PCI bridges on the secondary bus, the subordinate bus number register is initialized with the same value as the secondary bus number.

# Address Decode-Related Registers

## Basic Transaction Filtering Mechanism

The devices that reside behind a PCI-to-PCI bridge may consist of only memory, only I/O, or a combination of memory and I/O devices. Furthermore, some of the I/O devices may be mapped into memory space while others are mapped into I/O space. The configuration program automatically detects the presence, type and address space requirements of these devices and allocates space to them by programming their address decoders to recognize the address ranges it assigns to them.

The configuration program assigns all I/O devices that reside behind a PCI-to-PCI bridge mutually-exclusive address ranges within a common overall range of I/O locations. The PCI-to-PCI bridge is then programmed to pass any I/O transactions detected on the primary side of the bridge to the secondary side if the target address is within the range associated with the community of I/O devices that reside behind the bridge. Conversely, any I/O transactions detected on the secondary side of the bridge are passed to the primary side if the target address is outside the range associated with the community of I/O devices that reside on the secondary side (because the target device doesn't reside on the secondary side, but may reside on the primary side).

All memory-mapped I/O devices that reside behind a PCI-to-PCI bridge are assigned mutually-exclusive memory address ranges within a common block of memory locations. The PCI-to-PCI bridge is then programmed to pass any memory transactions detected on the primary side of the bridge to the secondary side if the target address is within the range associated with the community of memory-mapped I/O devices that reside behind the bridge. Conversely, any memory transactions detected on the secondary side of the bridge are passed to the primary side if the target address is outside the range associated with the community of memory-mapped I/O devices that reside on the secondary side (because the target device doesn't reside on the secondary side, but may reside on the primary side).

All memory devices (i.e., regular memory, not memory-mapped I/O) that reside behind a PCI-to-PCI bridge are assigned mutually-exclusive memory address ranges within a common overall range of memory locations. The PCI-to-PCI bridge is then programmed to pass any memory transactions detected on the primary side of the bridge to the secondary side if the target address is within the range associated with the community of memory devices that reside behind the bridge. Conversely, any memory transactions detected on the secondary side of the bridge are passed to the primary side if the target address is outside the range associated with the community of memory devices that reside on the secondary side (because the target device doesn't reside on the secondary side, but may reside on the primary side).

The bridge may also incorporate some memory and/or IO locations within the bridge itself that are utilized as registers, as well as a device-specific device ROM that contains bridge-specific initialization code. The bridge must incorporate programmable address decoders for these devices.

## Bridge Support for Internal Registers and ROM

### Introduction

A PCI-to-PCI bridge designer may choose to incorporate the following entities within the bridge:

1. A set of internal, device-specific registers that are used to select operational characteristics or check status that is outside the scope of the PCI specification.
2. A device ROM that contains device-specific initialization code for the bridge.

In the first case, the register set must be mapped into memory or I/O address space, or both. The designer implements one or two base address registers (programmable address decoders) for this purpose.

In the second case, the designer must implement an expansion ROM base address register used by configuration software to map the ROM into memory space.

### Base Address Registers

*Optional. Only necessary if the bridge implements a device-specific register set which can be mapped into I/O, memory, or both spaces.* Location in the header: doublewords four and five. It should be obvious that the two base address registers are optional. If the designer doesn't implement any internal, device-specific I/O or memory registers, than these address decoders aren't necessary. These base address registers are used in the same manner as those described in the chapter entitled "Configuration Registers." If implemented, both may be implemented as memory decoders, both as I/O decoders, one as memory and one as I/O, or only one may be implemented as either I/O or memory.

### Expansion ROM Base Address Register

*Optional. Only necessary if the bridge implements a bridge-specific device ROM.* Location in the header: doubleword 14. This register is optional (because there may not be a device ROM incorporated within the bridge). The format and usage of this register is precisely the same as that described in the chapter entitled "Configuration Registers."

## Bridge's I/O Filter

### Introduction

*Optional. There is no requirement for a bridge to support I/O within or behind the bridge.* When the bridge detects an I/O transaction initiated on either PCI bus, it must determine which of the following actions to take:

1. **Ignore the transaction** because the target I/O address isn't located on the other side of the bridge, nor is it targeting an I/O location embedded within the bridge itself.
2. **Claim the transaction** because the target I/O address is one of the bridge's internal I/O registers. The initiator is permitted to access the targeted internal register and the **transaction is not passed through the bridge**.
3. **Claim the transaction** because the target I/O location is located on the other side of the bridge. The **transaction is passed through the bridge** and is initiated on the opposite bus.

The configuration registers within the bridge that support this "filtering" capability are:

- **Base address registers**. If present, the base address register or registers can be designed as I/O decoders for an internal, device-specific register set.
- **I/O base and I/O limit registers**. If the bridge supports I/O space behind the bridge, the I/O base register defines the start address and the I/O limit register defines the end address of the range to recognize and pass through.
- **I/O base upper 16-bits and I/O limit upper 16-bits registers**. If the bridge supports a 4GB (rather than a 64KB) I/O address space behind the bridge (as indicated in the I/O base and limit registers), the combination of the I/O base plus I/O base upper 16 bits registers define the start address, and the combination of the I/O limit plus the I/O limit upper 16-bits registers define the end address of the range to recognize.

### Bridge Doesn't Support Any I/O Space Behind Bridge

Assume that a bridge doesn't support any I/O space behind the bridge. In other words, it doesn't recognize any I/O addresses as being implemented behind the bridge and therefore ignores all I/O transactions detected on its primary bus. In this case, the bridge designer does not implement the optional I/O base, I/O limit, I/O base upper 16-bits and I/O limit upper 16-bits registers.

The bridge ignores all I/O transactions detected on the primary bus (other than transactions that may target an optional set of device-specific I/O bridge registers contained within the bridge itself: see earlier discussion of base address registers).

Any I/O transactions detected on the bridge's secondary bus would be claimed and passed through to the primary bus in case the target I/O device is implemented somewhere upstream of the secondary bus.

### Bridge Supports 64KB I/O Space Behind Bridge

Assume that a bridge is designed to recognize I/O transactions initiated on the primary bus targeting locations within the first 64KB of I/O space (I/O locations 00000000h through 0000FFFFh). It ignores any I/O accesses over the 64KB address boundary. In other words, the bridge supports a 64KB, but does not support a 4GB I/O space behind the bridge.

In this case, the bridge designer must implement the I/O base and the I/O limit registers, but must not implement the I/O base upper 16-bits and the I/O limit upper 16-bits registers.

The I/O base and I/O limit register pair comprise an I/O address decoder. Before the registers are initialized by the configuration software, they are read from to determine if they are capable of supporting a 64KB or a 4GB I/O address range behind the bridge. In this case, a field within each of the registers is hardwired to indicate that only a 64KB space is supported. The configuration software than walks the secondary bus (and any subordinate buses it discovers) and assigns each I/O device it discovers an exclusive I/O address range within the first 64KB of I/O space. The sub-ranges assigned to the devices are assigned in sequential blocks to make efficient use of I/O space.

The I/O base and limit register pair are then initialized by the startup configuration software with the start and end address of the I/O range that all I/O devices that were discovered behind the bridge (on the secondary and on any subordinate buses) have been programmed to reside within. In this case, since the bridge only supports the first 64KB of I/O space, the defined range will be a subset of the first 64KB of I/O space. After they have been initialized, these two registers provide the bridge with the start and the end address of the I/O address range to recognize.

Since the bridge only supports the lower 64KB of I/O space, the I/O address decoder comprised of the I/O base and limit registers performs an I/O address decode within address bits [15:0] to determine whether or not to pass an I/O access on the primary bus to the secondary bus.

The format of the I/O base and I/O limit registers is illustrated in figures 19-6 and 19-7. Both registers have the same format: the upper hex digit, bits [7:4], defines the most-significant hex digit of an I/O address; the lower hex digit, bits [3:0], defines whether the bridge performs a 16-bit or 32-bit I/O address decode. In this case, the lower hex digit of both registers is hardwired with the value 0h, indicating that it performs a 16-bit I/O address decode and therefore only supports recognition within the first 64KB of I/O space.

Assume that the configuration software programs the upper digit of the I/O base register with the value 2h and the upper digit of the I/O limit register with the value 3h. This indicates that the start of the I/O range to recognize is 2000h and the end address is 3FFFh, an 8KB block. As another example, assume that the upper digit in the base and limit registers are both set to 3h. The I/O address range to recognize is then 3000h through 3FFFh, a 4KB block. In other words, this register pair defines the start address aligned on a 4KB address boundary, and the size, also referred to as the granularity, of the defined block is in increments of 4KB.

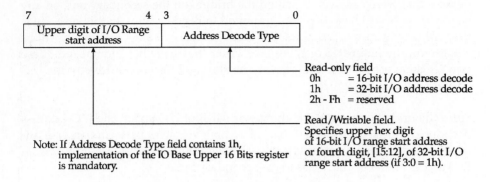

Note: If Address Decode Type field contains 1h,
implementation of the IO Base Upper 16 Bits register
is mandatory.

*Figure 19-6. I/O Base Register*

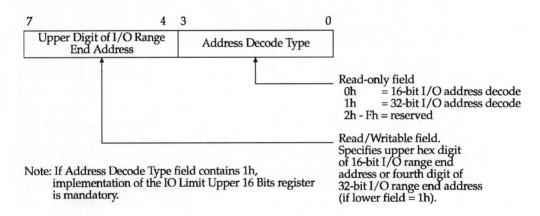

Note: If Address Decode Type field contains 1h,
implementation of the IO Limit Upper 16 Bits register
is mandatory.

*Figure 19-7. I/O Limit Register*

**Example**. Assume that the I/O base is set to 2h and the I/O limit is set to 3h. The bridge is now primed to recognize any I/O transaction on the primary bus that targets an I/O address within the range consisting of 2000h through 3FFFh. Refer to figure 19-8.

Anytime that the bridge detects an I/O transaction on the primary bus with an address inside the 2000h through 3FFFh range, it claims the transaction and passes it through (because it's within the range defined by the I/O base and limit registers and may therefore be for an I/O device that resides behind the bridge).

Anytime that the bridge detects an I/O transaction on the primary bus with an address outside the 2000h through 3FFFh range, it ignores the transaction (because the target I/O address is outside the range of addresses assigned to I/O devices that reside behind the bridge).

Anytime that the bridge detects an I/O transaction on the secondary bus with an address inside the 2000h through 3FFFh range, it ignores the transaction (because the target address falls within the range assigned to I/O devices that reside on the secondary side of the bridge).

Anytime that the bridge detects an I/O transaction on the secondary bus with an address outside the 2000h through 3FFFh range, it claims the transaction and passes it through to the primary side (because the target address falls outside the range assigned to I/O devices that reside on the secondary side of the bridge, but it may be for an I/O device on the primary side).

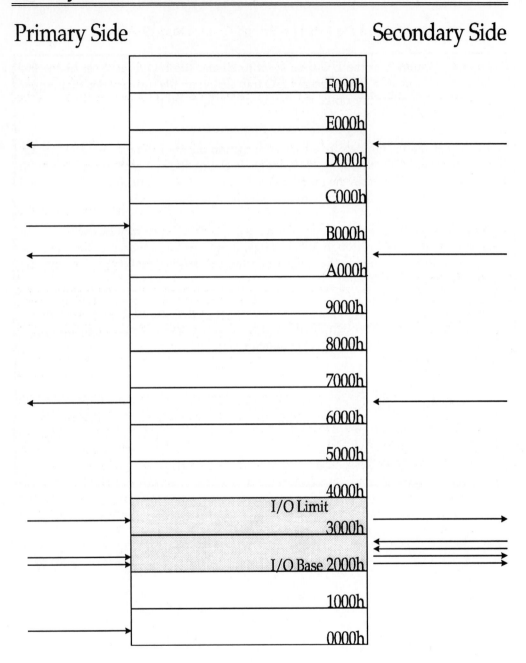

*Figure 19-8. Example of I/O Filtering Actions*

# Chapter 19: PCI-to-PCI Bridge

### Effect of ISA Mode Bit (in Bridge Control Register)

The bridge control configuration register contains a bit referred to as the ISA MODE bit. A better name for this bit would be the ISA I/O MASK bit. The previous discussion of I/O address decoder operation was predicated on the ISA MODE bit being cleared to zero.

If the ISA MODE bit is set to one, this alters the manner in which the I/O address decoder operates. Before proceeding, it would be valuable to define the problem that this feature addresses.

When the original IBM PC and XT were designed, IBM defined the use of the processor's 64KB I/O address space as shown in table 19-2.

*Table 19-2. IBM PC and XT I/O Address Space Usage*

| I/O Address Range | Reserved For |
|---|---|
| 0000h through 00FFh | 256 locations set aside for I/O devices integrated onto the system board. |
| 0100h through 03FFh | 768 locations set aside for I/O expansion cards. |
| 0400h through FFFFh | Not used. |

Initially, I/O addresses above 03FFh were not used due to the inadequate I/O address decode performed by many of the early I/O expansion cards (note, however, that a number of later I/O cards perform a full 16-bit I/O address decode). The card's I/O address decoder inspects A[9:5] to determine which of the 24, 32 location blocks of I/O space is currently being addressed. Figure 19-9 illustrates these 24 address ranges. If the currently addressed I/O location is within the block of 32 locations assigned to the I/O expansion card, the card's logic examines address bits A[4:0] to determine if one of up to 32 I/O ports on the addressed expansion card is being addressed.

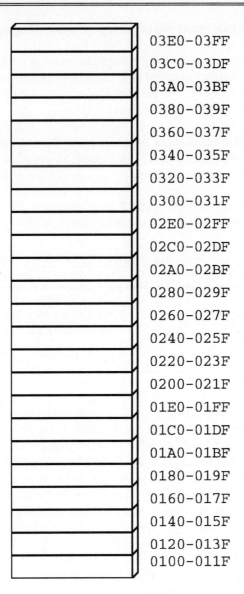

03E0-03FF
03C0-03DF
03A0-03BF
0380-039F
0360-037F
0340-035F
0320-033F
0300-031F
02E0-02FF
02C0-02DF
02A0-02BF
0280-029F
0260-027F
0240-025F
0220-023F
0200-021F
01E0-01FF
01C0-01DF
01A0-01BF
0180-019F
0160-017F
0140-015F
0120-013F
0100-011F

*Figure 19-9. ISA I/O Expansion I/O Ranges*

On I/O cards for the PC, XT and AT that perform the inadequate decode, the I/O address decoders only looked at address bits A[9:5], ignoring bits A[15:10]. The I/O address range used by these I/O cards is 0100h through 03FFh. Within the group of address bits used by expansion I/O address decoders, A[9:5], bits A9 and A8 would therefore be either 01b (0100h through 01FFh range), 10b (0200h through 02FFh range), or 11b (0300h through 03FFh range). When the microprocessor places any I/O address on the address bus with A[9:8] = 01b, 10b, or 11b, an ISA I/O expansion card may respond.

As an example, assume that a machine has two expansion cards installed. One of them performs an inadequate address decode using A[9:5] and has eight registers residing at I/O ports 0100h through 0107h. The other card performs a full decode using A[15:5] and has four registers residing at I/O ports 0500h through 0503h. Now assume that the microprocessor initiates a one byte I/O read from I/O port 0500h. The address placed on the bus is shown in table 19-3.

*Table 19-3. Example I/O Address*

| A15 | A14 | A13 | A12 | A11 | A10 | A9 | A8 | A7 | A6 | A5 | A4 | A3 | A2 | A1 | A0 |
|-----|-----|-----|-----|-----|-----|----|----|----|----|----|----|----|----|----|----|
| 0 | 0 | 0 | 0 | 0 | 1 | 0 | 1 | 0 | 0 | 0 | 0 | 0 | 0 | 0 | 0 |

The board that occupies the 0500h through 0503h range looks at A[15:5] and determines that the address is within the 0500h through 051Fh block. It then looks at A[1:0] and determines that location 0500h is being addressed. Since this is an I/O read bus cycle, the card places the contents of location 0500h on the lower data path (this is an even address).

At the same time, the board that occupies the 0100h through 0107h range looks at A[9:5], a subset of the address seen by the other card's address decoder, and determines that the address appears to be within the 0100h through 011Fh block. It then looks at A[2:0] and determines that location 0100h is apparently being addressed. Since this is an I/O read bus cycle, the card places the contents of location 0100h on the lower data path (this is an even address).

Since both cards are driving a byte of data onto the lower ISA data path, SD[7:0], data bus contention is occurring. This results in garbage data and possible hardware damage because two separate current sources are driving the lower data path. The problem occurs because the card residing in the 0100h through 0107h range looks at A[9:8] and thinks that this address is within the 0100h through 01FFh range. If the card were designed to perform a full address decode using A[15:5], the problem could have been avoided.

Addresses above 03FFh may be used as long as A[9:8] are always 00b, thus ensuring that the address does not appear to be in the 0100h through 01FFh,

0200h through 02FFh, or 0300h through 03FF ranges. Table 19-4 illustrates the usability or unusability of address ranges above 03FFh.

Table 19-4. Usable and Unusable I/O Address Ranges Above 03FFh

| I/O Address Range | Usable or Unusable |
|-------------------|--------------------|
| x000h – x0FFh | usable |
| x100h – x1FFh | Unusable. Appears to be 0100h - 01FFh |
| x200h – x2FFh | Unusable. Appears to be 0200h - 02FFh |
| x300h – x3FFh | Unusable. Appears to be 0300h - 03FFh |
| x400h – x4FFh | usable |
| x500h – x5FFh | Unusable. Appears to be 0100h - 01FFh |
| x600h – x6FFh | Unusable. Appears to be 0200h - 02FFh |
| x700h – x7FFh | Unusable. Appears to be 0300h - 03FFh |
| x800h – x8FFh | usable |
| x900h – x9FFh | Unusable. Appears to be 0100h - 01FFh |
| xA00h – xAFFh | Unusable. Appears to be 0200h - 02FFh |
| xB00h – xBFFh | Unusable. Appears to be 0300h - 03FFh |
| xC00h – xCFFh | usable |
| xD00h – xDFFh | Unusable. Appears to be 0100h - 01FFh |
| xE00h – xEFFh | Unusable. Appears to be 0200h - 02FFh |
| xF00h – xFFFh | Unusable. Appears to be 0300h - 03FFh |

Note: where x = any hex digit.

Now assume that the ISA MODE bit is set to one and that the I/O base and limit (possibly in conjunction with the base and limit extension registers) registers are defining an address range within the lower 64KB. Within the block of addresses defined by the base and limit, the bridge only passes I/O transactions on the primary to the secondary if the I/O address falls within one of the sub-ranges marked usable in the table. When the bridge is placed into ISA Mode, the I/O devices on the secondary side of the bridge are all programmed into the areas marked usable in the table.

When the bridge detects I/O transactions on the secondary bus and the target address is in the lower 64KB (specifically, in the sub-range defined by the I/O base and limit), the bridge passes the transaction to the primary bus only if the address is within the ranges that are designated unusable in the table. Any I/O transaction that targets an address outside these ranges is not for any of the I/O devices on the secondary or subordinate buses, but it may be for a device on the primary side.

# Chapter 19: PCI-to-PCI Bridge

## Bridge Supports 4GB I/O Space Behind Bridge

Assume that a bridge is designed to recognize I/O transactions initiated on the primary bus targeting locations anywhere within the 4GB of I/O space (I/O locations 00000000h through FFFFFFFFh).

In this case, the bridge designer must implement the I/O base and the I/O limit registers, and must also implement the I/O base upper 16-bits and the I/O limit upper 16-bits registers. As before, the I/O base register is initialized with the fourth digit of the start I/O address, while the I/O base upper 16 bits register is initialized with the fifth through the eight digits of the 32-bit start address of the range. In addition, the I/O limit register is initialized with the fourth digit of the end I/O address, while the I/O limit upper 16 bits register is initialized with the fifth through the eight digits of the 32-bit end address of the range.

The I/O base and I/O limit register pair comprise an I/O address decoder. Before the registers are initialized by the configuration software, they are read from to determine if they are capable of supporting a 64KB or a 4GB I/O address space behind the bridge. In this case, the Address Decode Type field within each of the registers is hardwired (with a value of 1h) to indicate that the entire 4GB space is supported. The configuration software than walks the secondary bus (and any subordinate buses it discovers) and assigns each I/O device that it discovers an exclusive I/O address range within the 4GB I/O space. The sub-ranges assigned to the devices are assigned in sequential blocks to make efficient use of I/O space.

The I/O base and I/O base upper 16-bits register pair is then initialized by the startup configuration software with the upper five digits of the 4KB-aligned start address of the I/O range that all I/O devices that were discovered behind the bridge (on the secondary and on any subordinate buses) have been programmed to reside within. The I/O limit and I/O limit upper 16 bits register pair is initialized with the 4KB-aligned end address of the range the devices occupy. In this case, since the bridge supports the entire 4GB I/O space, the defined range is a subset of the overall 4GB I/O space. After they have been initialized, these four registers provide the bridge with the start and the end address of the I/O address range to recognize.

Since the bridge supports the entire 4GB I/O space, the I/O address decoder comprised of the four registers (base and limit registers plus their extension registers) performs an I/O address decode within address bits [31:12] to determine whether or not to pass an I/O access detected on the primary bus through to the secondary bus.

The format of the I/O base and I/O limit registers was illustrated earlier in figures 19-6 and 19-7. In this case, the lower hex digit of the base and limit registers is hardwired with the value 1h, indicating a 32-bit I/O address decode, supporting recognition within the entire 4GB I/O space. Simply put, the I/O base and I/O limit upper 16-bits registers are used to hold the upper four digits of the start and end I/O address boundaries, respectively.

Assume that the configuration software programs the registers as follows:

- Upper digit of the I/O base register programmed with the value 2h in the upper digit.
- I/O base upper 16-bits register programmed with the value 1234h.
- Upper digit of the I/O limit register programmed with the value 3h.
- I/O limit upper 16-bits register programmed with the value 1235h.

This indicates that the start of the I/O range to recognize is 12342000h and the end address is 12353FFFh, a 72KB block. As another example, assume the following:

- Upper digit of the I/O base register programmed with the value 3h in the upper digit.
- I/O base upper 16-bits register programmed with the value 1234h.
- Upper digit of the I/O limit register programmed with the value 3h.
- I/O limit upper 16-bits register programmed with the value 1234h.

This indicates that the start of the I/O range to recognize is 12343000h and the end address is 12343FFFh, a 4KB block. In other words, the four registers define the start address aligned on a 4KB address boundary, and the size of the defined block is an increment of 4KB.

## Bridge's Memory Filter

### Introduction

*The memory base and limit registers are mandatory (to support memory-mapped I/O behind the bridge. The prefetchable memory base and limit registers (and their extensions) are optional (there is no requirement for a bridge to support prefetchable memory behind the bridge). The PCI-to-PCI bridge specification recognizes the fact* that although both groups are mapped into memory address space, memory devices and memory-mapped I/O devices have distinctly different operational characteristics.

A memory device always returns the same data from a location no matter how many times the location is read from. In other words, reading from a memory device doesn't in any way alter the contents of memory. Due to this operational characteristic, it is permissible for a bridge to perform a read-ahead when performing a memory read for a master on the other side of the bridge. Assume that a master initiates a memory read to read a doubleword from a memory device. The bridge could read the requested doubleword and go on to prefetch data that hasn't been requested yet (e.g., an entire line of information) into a read buffer in case the master should ask for that data as well. If the master does request that data, it can be delivered quickly, yielding better performance. If the master doesn't ask for it, no harm is done.

A bridge could incorporate a posted-write buffer that quickly absorbs data to be written to a memory device on the other side of the bridge. Since the initiating master doesn't have to delay until the write to the memory device has actually been completed, posting yields better performance during memory write operations. The bridge would ensure that, before any subsequent memory read is permitted to propagate through the bridge, the bridge would flush its posted-write buffer to the memory device.

To summarize, it is permissible to performs prefetches from and posted-writes to regular memory devices. The PCI-to-PCI bridge specification refers to areas of memory space occupied by regular memory as prefetchable memory areas. A set of registers are provided to permit the configuration software to define the start and end address of the prefetchable memory space that is occupied by regular memory devices behind the bridge.

Memory-mapped I/O devices present a different set of operational characteristics. Performing a memory read from a memory-mapped I/O location often has the effect of altering the contents of the location. As examples, one of the following may be true:

1.  The location may be occupied by a memory-mapped I/O status port. Reading from the location causes the I/O device to deassert any status bits that were set in the register (on the assumption that they've been read and will therefore be dealt with by the device driver). If the read was

caused by a prefetch and the prefetched data is never actually read by the device driver, then status information has just been discarded.

2. The location may be the front-end of a FIFO data buffer. Performing a read from the location causes the delivery of its current contents and the next data item is then automatically placed in the location by the I/O device. The device assumes that the first data item has just been read by the device driver and sets up the next data item in the FIFO location. If the read was caused by a prefetch and the prefetched data is never actually read by the device driver, then the data has just been discarded.

Reads within an area of memory space occupied by memory-mapped I/O devices must never cause prefetching to occur. Any writes to the memory-mapped I/O ports must not be posted in the bridge. A set of registers are provided to permit the configuration software to define the start and end address of the memory space that is occupied by memory-mapped I/O devices behind the bridge.

### Configuration Software Detection of Prefetchable Memory Target

The configuration software determines that a PCI memory target supports prefetching by testing the state of the PREFETCHABLE attribute bit in the memory target's base address register. This subject is covered in the chapter entitled "Configuration Registers." A one indicates that the memory is prefetchable. A zero indicates that it's not. In the latter case, the memory target must be mapped into memory-mapped I/O space (using the memory base and limit registers).

### Bridge Supports 4GB Prefetchable Memory Space Behind Bridge

Support for prefetchable memory is optional for a PCI-to-PCI bridge designer. If the designer chooses to support this capability, then the following registers must be implemented to define the start and end address of the memory range occupied by prefetchable memory devices behind the bridge:

- Prefetchable memory base register.
- Prefetchable memory limit register.

These two registers are used to defined the start (base) and end (limit) address of the memory range. Any address within the lower 4GB can be specified. The start address is 1MB-aligned and the size of the range can be any 1MB increment. If the bridge designer intends to support a $2^{64}$ prefetchable memory space behind the bridge, then the extensions to these two registers must also be implemented:

- Prefetchable memory base upper 32-bits register.
- Prefetchable memory limit upper 32-bits register.

A discussion of these two registers and $2^{64}$ prefetchable memory support can be found in the section immediately following this one. The prefetchable memory base and limit registers are illustrated in figures 19-10 and 19-11. Assuming that the bridge only supports a 4GB ($2^{32}$) prefetchable memory space, the lower hex digit of both the base and limit registers is hardwired with the value 0h to indicate this to the configuration software. The configuration software then walks the secondary and any buses subordinate to the bridge and assigns all prefetchable memory targets a sub-range within a common overall range within the lower 4GB of memory space. After completing the address assignment process, the software then writes the upper three hex digits of the range's start address into the upper three digits of the base register and the upper three hex digits of the end address into the upper three digits of the limit register.

As an example, assume that the upper three digits in the two registers are set as follows:

- 123h written into the upper three digits of the base register.
- 124h written into the upper three digits of the limit register.

This defines the prefetchable memory address range as the 2MB range from 12300000h through 124FFFFFh. As another example, assume they are programmed as follows:

- 222h written into the upper three digits of the base register.
- 222h written into the upper three digits of the limit register.

This defines the prefetchable memory address range as the 1MB range from 22200000h through 222FFFFFh.

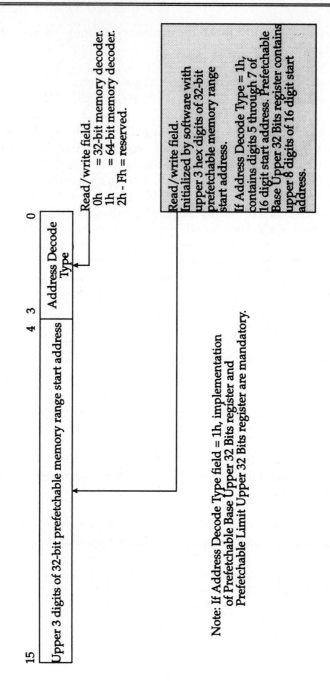

15

| | |
|---|---|
| Upper 3 digits of 32-bit prefetchable memory range start address | Address Decode Type |

4   3   0

Read/write field.
0h   = 32-bit memory decoder.
1h   = 64-bit memory decoder.
2h - Fh = reserved.

Read/write field. Initialized by software with upper 3 hex digits of 32-bit prefetchable memory range start address.

If Address Decode Type = 1h, contains digits 5 through 7 of 16 digit start address. Prefetchable Base Upper 32 Bits register contains upper 8 digits of 16 digit start address.

Note: If Address Decode Type field = 1h, implementation of Prefetchable Base Upper 32 Bits register and Prefetchable Limit Upper 32 Bits register are mandatory.

*Figure 19-10. Prefetchable Memory Base Register*

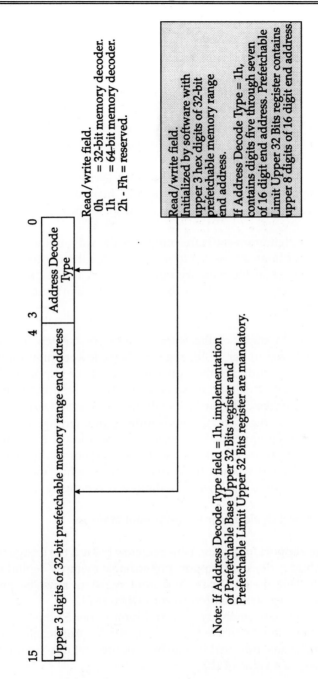

Read/write field.
0h = 32-bit memory decoder.
1h = 64-bit memory decoder.
2h - Fh = reserved.

Read/write field. Initialized by software with upper 3 hex digits of 32-bit prefetchable memory range end address.

If Address Decode Type = 1h, contains digits five through seven of 16 digit end address. Prefetchable Limit Upper 32 Bits register contains upper 8 digits of 16 digit end address.

| 15 | | 4 | 3 | | 0 |
|---|---|---|---|---|---|
| Upper 3 digits of 32-bit prefetchable memory range end address | | | Address Decode Type | | |

Note: If Address Decode Type field = 1h, implementation of Prefetchable Base Upper 32 Bits register and Prefetchable Limit Upper 32 Bits register are mandatory.

*Figure 19-11. Prefetchable Memory Limit Register*

## Bridge Supports $2^{64}$ Prefetchable Memory Space Behind Bridge

If the bridge designer wants the bridge to support $2^{64}$ prefetchable memory space behind the bridge, the prefetchable base and limit registers must be implemented as well as their extension registers:

- Prefetchable base upper 32-bits register.
- Prefetchable limit upper 32-bits register.

To inform the configuration software that the bridge can map prefetchable memory behind the bridge anywhere in $2^{64}$ memory space, the designer must hardwire the value 1h into the lower hex digit of the base and limit registers.

After the configuration software completes the walk of the bridge's secondary and any subordinate buses, the four registers are then initialized with the start and end address of the memory range assigned to the prefetchable memory targets that were found behind the bridge. The start and end addresses are assigned as follows:

- Upper eight digits of the start address are written to the prefetchable memory base upper 32-bit register. Next lower three digits of the start address are written to the upper three digits of the prefetchable memory base register. Together, these two registers define the upper 11 digits of the start address. The lower five digits are assumed to be 00000h.
- Upper eight digits of the end address are written to the prefetchable memory limit upper 32-bit register. The next lower three digits of the end address are written to the upper three digits of the prefetchable memory limit register. Together, these two registers define the upper 11 digits of the end address. The lower five digits are assumed to be FFFFFh.

### Rules and Options for Prefetchable Memory

1. Bridge support for prefetchable memory behind the bridge is optional.
2. If the bridge does not support prefetchable memory behind the bridge, the prefetchable memory base and limit registers must be implemented as read-only registers that return zero when read.
3. The prefetchable memory base and limit upper 32-bits registers only have to be implemented if the bridge supports $2^{64}$ prefetchable memory behind the bridge (as indicated by hardwiring the first digit in the base and limit registers to a value of 1h).

4. Bridge can prefetch read data when a memory read crosses the bridge within the address range defined by the prefetchable memory base and limit registers.

5. Memory transactions are forwarded from the primary to the secondary bus if the address is within the range defined by the prefetchable memory base and limit registers or that defined by the memory base and limit registers (for memory-mapped I/O).

6. Memory transactions are forwarded from the secondary to the primary bus when the address is outside the ranges defined by the prefetchable memory base and limit registers and the memory base and limit registers (for memory-mapped I/O).

7. When $2^{64}$ memory is supported, transactions targeting addresses within the address range specified by the prefetchable memory base and limit registers (and their extensions) are permitted to cross the 4GB boundary.

8. The bridge designer may choose to not support 64-bit addressing on either the primary or the secondary sides. In this case, all dual-address commands are ignored.

9. The bridge can be designed to not support 64-bit addressing on the primary side, but to forward all dual-address command detected on the secondary side to the primary side. The assumption is that the initiator is attempting to transfer data with system memory above the 4GB boundary. The transaction may therefore be permitted to flow upstream (towards system memory).

10. Assume that the bridge supports prefetchable memory anywhere in $2^{64}$ memory space behind the bridge, but the configuration software maps all prefetchable memory behind the bridge below the 4GB boundary. In this case, the upper extensions of the prefetchable base and limit registers must be set to zero and the bridge does not respond to dual-address memory commands initiated on the primary side. Those initiated on the secondary side would be passed to the primary side (in case the initiator is addressing main memory above the 4GB boundary).

11. Assume that the bridge supports prefetchable memory anywhere in $2^{64}$ memory space behind the bridge and that the configuration software maps all prefetchable memory behind the bridge above the 4GB boundary. In this case, the upper extensions of the prefetchable base and limit registers contain non-zero values and the bridge responds only to dual-address memory commands initiated on either side.

12. Assume that the bridge supports prefetchable memory anywhere in $2^{64}$ memory space behind the bridge and that the configuration software maps the prefetchable memory behind the bridge into a space that straddles the 4GB boundary. In this case, the upper extension of the prefetch-

able base register is set to zero and the extension to the limit register contains a non-zero value. When a single-address memory command is detected on either side, the bridge compares the address only to the prefetchable memory base register. If the address is equal to or greater than the start address specified in the register, the address is in range. When a dual-address command is detected on either side, the bridge compares the lower 32-bits of the address to the limit register and the upper 32-bits of the address to the limit upper 32-bits register. If the address is equal to or less than the end address specified in the two registers, the address is in range.

13. The bridge may safely prefetch data when the transaction uses the memory read line or the memory read multiple command.

14. The bridge may safely convert a memory read command to a memory read line or a memory read multiple command, or may turn a single data phase memory read into an extended read burst if the address is within the range specified by the prefetchable memory base and limit registers.

15. The bridge may safely prefetch data on the primary bus if the command detected on the secondary bus is a memory read line or a memory read multiple command.

16. The bridge may be designed to assume that all memory accesses detected on the secondary bus that are passed to the primary bus are prefetchable. This assumes that the destination of all memory reads traveling upstream is system memory (which is prefetchable). If a bridge makes this assumption and performs "blind" prefetches, it must implement a device-specific bit in its configuration space that allows this ability to be disabled (in case a problem results from blind prefetching).

17. Bridges that prefetch must ensure that they do not cross a 4KB address boundary when prefetching. If the bridge were to do so, it may cross the upper boundary (specified by the prefetchable limit register) into memory that does not support prefetching.

## Bridge's Memory-Mapped I/O Filter

*Mandatory.* The bridge designer is required to implement the base and limit registers used to define a memory-mapped I/O range. These two registers are used to define a range of memory occupied by memory-mapped I/O devices that exists behind the bridge. Figures 19-12 and 19-13 illustrate the base and limit registers used for this purpose. The lower digit of each register is hardwired to zero and the upper three digits are used to define the upper three hex digits of the eight-digit start and end addresses, respectively.

As an example, assume that the configuration software has written the following values to the base and limit registers:

- The upper three digits of the base register contain 555h.
- The upper three digits of the limit register contain 678h.

This defines a memory-mapped 12.4MB region behind the bridge starting at 55500000h and ending at 678FFFFFh.

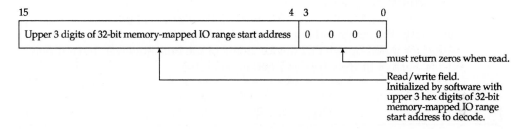

*Figure 19-12. Memory (mapped I/O) Base Register*

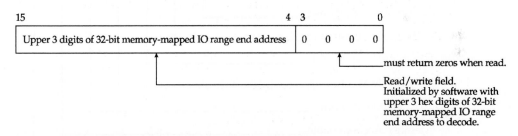

*Figure 19-13. Memory (mapped I/O) Limit Register*

## Command Registers

### Introduction

The PCI-to-PCI bridge designer must implement two required command registers in the bridge's configuration header region:

- The command register is the standard configuration command register defined by the specification for any PCI device. It is associated with the bridge's primary bus interface.
- The bridge control register is an extension to the standard command register. It is associated with the operation of both of the bus interfaces.

These two registers are defined in the next two sections.

## Command Register

*Mandatory.* The command register format, pictured in figure 19-14, is the same as that for a non-bridge PCI device. Some of the bits, however, have different effects. Each of the bits are described in table 19-5.

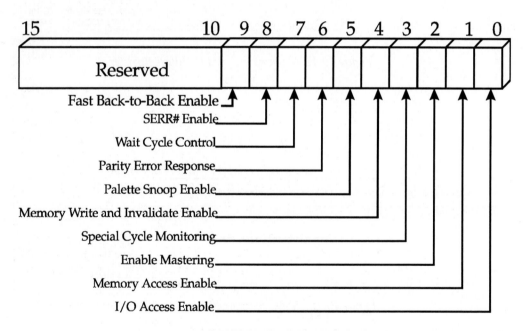

*Figure 19-14. Command Register*

*Table 19-5. Command Register Bit Assignment*

| Bit | Description |
|---|---|
| 0 | **I/O Space Enable.** When set, the bridge's I/O address decoders on its primary side are enabled. When cleared, they are disabled. If cleared, any I/O transactions detected on the secondary side are passed through to the primary side and all I/O transactions detected on the primary side are ignored. Reset clears this bit. |
| 1 | **Memory Space Enable.** When set, the bridge's memory and memory-mapped I/O address decoders on its primary side are enabled. When cleared, they are disabled. If cleared, any memory transactions detected on the secondary side are passed through to the primary side and all memory transactions on the primary side are ignored. Reset clears this bit. |
| 2 | **Bus Master Enable.** Control's the bridge's ability to act as a master on the primary side. However, the bridge is always enabled to forward and convert configuration transactions. When cleared, the bridge ignores all memory and I/O transactions detected on the secondary side (because it cannot pass the transactions through to the primary side). Reset clears this bit. |
| 3 | **Special Cycle Enable.** Hardwired to zero (because PCI-to-PCI bridges don't monitor special cycles). |
| 4 | **Memory Write and Invalidate Enable.** Hardwired to zero because this bit is irrelevant to the bridge. The initiating master decides what type of memory write transaction to use. The bridge only evaluates the address to determine whether to pass the transaction through to the other side. |
| 5 | **VGA Palette Snoop Enable.** Implementation of this bit is optional. If not implemented, must be hardwired to zero. Reset clears this bit. When set, I/O writes to 03C6h, 03C8h and 03C9h (including any I/O addresses that alias to these addresses) are positively decoded on the primary side and are passed through to the secondary side. If I/O writes to these addresses are detected on the secondary side, they are ignored. Also see description of the VGA ENABLE bit in the bridge control register. |
| 6 | **Parity Error Response.** When set, the bridge takes the normal actions defined by the specification when a parity error is detected on the primary side. When cleared, parity errors are ignored, but the bridge must generate proper parity. Reset clears this bit. |
| 7 | **Wait Cycle Control.** Bridges that never use stepping hardwire this bit to zero. Bridges that always use stepping hardwire this bit to one. Bridges that permit stepping to be turned on and off implement this as a read/writable bit. If the bit is read/writable, reset sets the bit to one. |

| Bit | Description |
|:---:|:---|
| 8 | **SERR# Enable.** Controls the SERR# output driver on the primary bus. When set, the bridge is enabled to generate SERR# on the primary side. When cleared it cannot generate SERR#. Reset clears this bit. |
| 9 | **Fast Back-to-Back Enable.** Controls the bridge's ability to utilize fast back-to-back transactions with different targets on the primary bus. A bridge that doesn't support this ability hardwires this bit to zero, otherwise it must be read/writable. Reset clears this bit. |
| 15:10 | **Reserved.** Read-only and must return zero when read. |

### Bridge Control Register

*Mandatory.* The bridge control register is a required extension to the bridge's command register and is associated with operation of the secondary side. Figure 19-15 illustrates this register and table 19-6 defines its bit assignment.

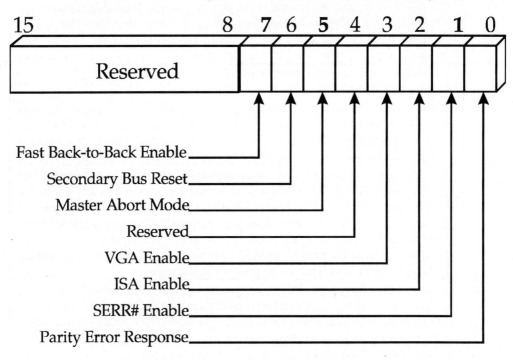

*Figure 19-15. Bridge Control Register*

*Table 19-6. Bridge Control Register Bit Assignment*

| Bit | Description |
| --- | --- |
| 0 | **Parity Error Response.** When set, the bridge takes the normal actions defined by the specification when a parity error is detected on the secondary side. When cleared, parity errors are ignored, but the bridge must generate proper parity. Reset clears this bit. |
| 1 | **SERR# Enable.** When set, detection of SERR# asserted on the secondary side causes the bridge to assert SERR# on the primary side (but only if the SERR# ENABLE bit in the device's configuration command register is set). When cleared, detection of SERR# on secondary side is ignored. Reset clears this bit. |
| 2 | **ISA Mode.** When set, bridge only recognizes I/O addresses within the usable ranges that do not alias to an ISA range. For information, refer to the section in this chapter entitled "Affect of ISA Mode Bit." Reset clears this bit. |
| 3 | **VGA Enable.** When set, bridge performs positive decode on memory accesses in the range from 000A0000h through 000BFFFFh (the address range of the video frame buffer), I/O addresses from 03B0h through 03BBh, and I/O addresses 03C0h through 03DFh (including addresses that alias into these two I/O ranges). This bit is qualified by bits zero and one in the command register. Reset clears this bit. |
| 4 | **Reserved.** Hardwired to zero. |
| 5 | **Master Abort Mode.** Controls the manner in which the bridge responds when it is mastering a transaction on either bus and experiences a master abort. When this bit is cleared, any reads that experience a master abort return all ones; any writes complete normally and the data is thrown away. When this bit is set and the bridge experiences a master abort, it issues a target abort to the initiating master (for all reads and non-posted writes). If the bridge experiences a master abort while performing a posted-write, it signals SERR# on the primary side (if the SERR# ENABLE bit in the command register is set). Reset clears this bit. |
| 6 | **Secondary Bus Reset.** When set, the bridge asserts RST# on the secondary bus. When cleared, the secondary bus RST# is deasserted. Irrespective of the state of this bit, secondary bus RST# follows primary bus RST#. The bridge's interface to the secondary bus and all buffers between the two buffers are initialized by the assertion of RST# on the secondary bus. Assertion of RST# on the secondary bus, however, does not affect the configuration registers nor the primary bus interface logic. Reset clears this bit. |
| 7 | **Fast Back-to-Back Enable.** Same as the FAST BACK-TO-BACK ENABLE bit in the command register only with respect to the secondary bus. |
| 15:8 | **Reserved.** Hardwire to zero. |

## Status Registers

### Introduction

The bridge contains two required status registers, each of which is associated with one of the buses.

### Status Register (Primary Bus)

*Mandatory.* This required register is completely compatible with the status register definition for a non-bridge PCI device and only reflects the status of the primary side.

### Secondary Status Register

*Mandatory.* With the exception of the RECEIVED SYSTEM ERROR bit, this required register is completely compatible with the status register definition for a non-bridge PCI device and only reflects the status of the secondary side.

Bit 14, the SIGNALED SYSTEM ERROR bit, has been redefined as the RECEIVED SYSTEM ERROR bit for the secondary side. When set, indicates that SERR# was detected asserted on the secondary side. Writing a one to it clears the bit, while a zero doesn't affect it. Reset clears this bit.

## Cache Line Size Register

*Mandatory.* The format and usage of this required register is completely compatible with its definition for non-bridge PCI devices. It defines the system cache line size for both sides of the bridge. The value in this register is used by the bridge:

- in determining when it has transferred an entire line when using the memory write and invalidate transaction.
- in determining the cache line size during performance of memory read line and memory read multiple transactions.

## Latency Timer Registers

### Introduction

The bridge includes an independent master latency (i.e., timeslice) timer for each of the two buses. The contents of each of these required registers defines the minimum period of time (in PCI clock cycles since FRAME# asserted) the bridge may continue a burst transaction even if it's preempted (loses its GNT#).

### Latency Timer Register (Primary Bus)

*Mandatory*. This required register defines the timeslice for the primary interface when the bridge is acting as the initiator.

### Secondary Latency Timer Register

*Mandatory*. This required register defines the timeslice for the secondary interface when the bridge is acting as the initiator.

## BIST Register

*Optional*. This optional register is fully-compatible with the BIST register definition for non-bridge PCI devices.

## Interrupt-Related Registers

*Only required if the bridge itself generates interrupts*. If the bridge is capable of generating an interrupt (to signal a bridge event) on any of the PCI interrupt request lines, then the designer must implement the interrupt pin and interrupt line registers. The format and usage of these registers are compatible with that of non-bridge PCI devices. It should be noted that the IRQ lines from devices on the secondary side do not go through the bridge.

## Configuration and Special Cycle Filter

### Introduction

In addition to memory and I/O transactions, the PCI-to-PCI bridge must also monitor both buses for configuration transactions. These transactions occur for the following reasons:

- Host/PCI bridge is performing a configuration read or write to access a specific device's configuration registers.
- Host/PCI bridge or another PCI master is performing a special form of the type 1 configuration write transaction in order to broadcast a message on a specific PCI bus in the system.

Table 19-7 defines the various types of configuration reads and writes that may be detected on the bridge's two interfaces and the action to be taken by the bridge. A complete description of the type 0 configuration transaction can be found in the chapter entitled "Configuration Transactions." A complete description of the type 1 configuration transaction can be found later in this chapter.

*Table 19-7. Configuration Transactions That May Be Detected On the Two Buses*

| Transaction | Bus Detected On | Description |
|---|---|---|
| Type 0 configuration read | primary | If the bridge's IDSEL# input is not asserted, ignore. If asserted, perform function decode to determine if target function implemented. If not, ignore. If implemented, assert DEVSEL# and permit access to internal configuration registers. |
| Type 0 configuration read | secondary | Ignore. |
| Type 0 configuration write | primary | Same as configuration read. |
| Type 0 configuration write | secondary | Ignore. |

| Transaction | Bus Detected On | Description |
|---|---|---|
| Type 1 configuration read | primary | Compare target bus to bridge's bus number registers. If not equal to secondary bus register and not in range defined by secondary and subordinate bus numbers, ignore. If equal to secondary bus number, claim and pass through as type 0 configuration read on secondary. If not equal to secondary, but in range defined by secondary and subordinate, claim and pass through to secondary as type 1 configuration read as is (no conversion). |
| Type 1 configuration read | secondary | Ignore. |
| Type 1 configuration write (not special cycle request) | primary | Same as type 1 configuration read. |
| Type 1 configuration write (not special cycle request) | secondary | Ignore. |
| Type 1 configuration write (special cycle request) | primary | If target bus matches secondary, claim and convert to special cycle on secondary. The write data supplies the message during the data phase. If target bus doesn't match secondary, but is in the range defined by secondary and subordinate, claim and pass through to secondary unchanged as type 1 special cycle request. If target bus not secondary and not in range defined by secondary and subordinate, ignore. |

| Transaction | Bus Detected On | Description |
|---|---|---|
| Type 1 configuration write (special cycle request) | secondary | If target bus matches primary, claim and pass through as special cycle with write data as message. If target bus is not primary and not in range of buses defined by secondary and subordinate, claim and pass through unchanged as type 1 special cycle request. If target bus is within range of buses subordinate to secondary, ignore. |

## Special Cycle Transactions

The special cycle transaction is defined in the chapter entitled "The Commands." The host/PCI bridge designer may or may not supply a method that permits the programmer to stimulate the host/PCI bridge to forward a special cycle request to a specific PCI bus in the system. Assuming that the host/PCI bridge designer implements configuration mechanism number one and includes support for software-generated special cycles, the following sequence causes the host/PCI bridge to generate a special cycle on a specific target bus.

1.  Programmer writes a 32-bit pattern to the configuration address port specifying the target bus number and setting the target device to 1Fh, function to 7h, and doubleword to 0. The enable bit (bit 31) is set to one.
2.  The programmer then performs either a 16 or a 32-bit write to the configuration data port.
3.  The host/PCI bridge compares the target bus to the number of its PCI bus (typically zero). If it matches, the bridge generates a special cycle on the PCI bus and supplies the write data as the message.
4.  If the target bus is not the bridge's PCI bus but is within the range of subordinate buses that exist behind the bridge, the bridge generates a special form of the type one configuration write that is recognized as a special cycle request by PCI-to-PCI bridges. During the address phase, it drives the contents of the configuration address port (except for bits 31 and [1:0]) onto the AD bus. AD[1:0] is set to 01b, indicating that this is a type one configuration write transaction. During the data phase it drives the data being written to the configuration data port onto the AD bus as the message.

The only devices on the PCI bus that pay attention to a type one configuration transaction are PCI-to-PCI bridges. They test the target bus to determine whether to ignore the transaction or to pass it through as:

- Type 0 configuration transaction for one of its devices.
- Type 1 configuration transaction for a device on a subordinate bus.
- Type 1 special cycle request for a subordinate bus.
- Special cycle transaction on the opposite bus.

When the specified bus matches the number of the bridge's opposite bus number, that bridge converts the special cycle request into a special cycle on the opposite bus. A bus master residing on any PCI bus can utilize this special form of the type 1 configuration write to force PCI bridges to forward a special cycle request upstream or downstream until it arrives on the target bus.

## Type One Configuration Transactions

Type one accesses (AD[1:0] set to 01b) are ignored by all PCI devices except PCI-to-PCI bridges residing on the PCI bus. If the target of a configuration access resides on a PCI bus subordinate to the bus upon which the configuration access is being run, the PCI-to-PCI bridge that connects the two PCI buses must pass the configuration access through to its secondary bus. When a PCI-to-PCI bridge recognizes a type one configuration access on its primary bus (with one of its PCI devices or one of its subordinate PCI buses as the target), it must pass the access through to its secondary bus in one of two forms:
- If the access is for a device residing on the bridge's secondary bus, it must pass it through as a **type zero configuration access**.
- If the access is for a device residing on a PCI bus that is subordinate to its secondary bus, it must pass the access through as a **type one configuration access**.

When a bridge initiates a configuration access on its PCI bus, it places the configuration address information on the AD bus and the configuration command on the C/BE bus. Figure 19-16 illustrates the contents of the AD bus during the address phase of the type one configuration access. Figures 19-17 and 19-18 are timing diagrams of type one configuration read and write accesses.

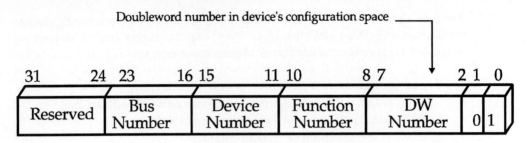

Doubleword number in device's configuration space

| 31      24 | 23      16 | 15      11 | 10      8 | 7      2 | 1 | 0 |

*Figure 19-16. Contents of the AD Bus During Address Phase of a
Type One Configuration Access*

During the address phase of a type one configuration access, the information on the AD bus is formatted as follows:

- AD[1:0] contain a 01b, identifying this as a type one configuration access.
- AD[7:2] identifies one of sixty-four configuration doublewords within the target device's configuration space.
- AD[10:8] identifies one of eight functions within the target physical device.
- AD[15:11] identifies one of thirty-two physical devices. This field is used by the bridge to select which device's IDSEL line to assert.
- AD[23:16] identifies one of two hundred and fifty-six PCI buses in the system.
- AD[31:24] are reserved and are cleared to zero.

The configuration read or write command is presented on the C/BE bus during the address phase. During a type one access, PCI devices ignore the state of their IDSEL inputs. When any PCI-to-PCI bridge on the bus detects a type one configuration access in progress (AD[1:0] = 01b) on its primary side, it must determine which of the following actions to take:

- If the bus number field on the AD bus doesn't match the number of its secondary bus and isn't within the range of its subordinate buses, the bridge should **ignore** the access.
- If the bus number field matches the bus number of its secondary bus, it should pass the configuration access onto its secondary bus as a **type zero configuration access**. AD[1:0] on the secondary bus are set to 00b (indicating a type zero access), AD[10:2] are passed directly from the bridge's primary to its secondary AD bus. The device number field on its primary AD bus is used to select one of the IDSEL lines to assert on the

secondary bus. The configuration command is passed from the primary to the secondary C/BE bus.

- If the bus number field isn't equal to its secondary bus, but is within the range of buses that are subordinate to the secondary bus, the bridge passes the access through as a **type one access**. AD[31:0] are passed directly from the primary to the secondary AD bus. Since AD[1:0] are passed directly through to the secondary AD bus and are set to 01b, this indicates that a type one access is in progress on the secondary bus. The configuration command is passed from the primary to the secondary C/BE bus.

When a type one configuration write is detected on the secondary side with a target device of 31d, function seven, doubleword zero, this is a special cycle request. If the specified target bus matches the bridge's primary bus number register, the transaction must be passed through as a special cycle. If the target bus is within the range of buses specified by the bridge's secondary and subordinate bus number registers, the transaction must be ignored. If the target bus is outside the range of buses specified by the bridge's primary, secondary, and subordinate bus number regsiters, the transaction must be passed through as a type one configuration write (i.e., unchanged).

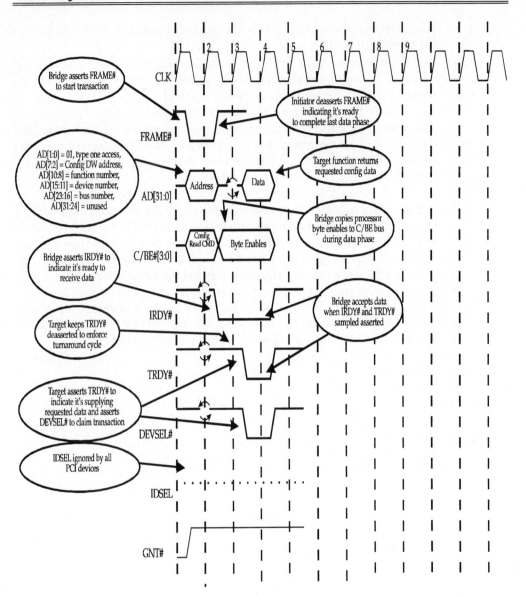

*Figure 19-17. The Type One Configuration Read Access*

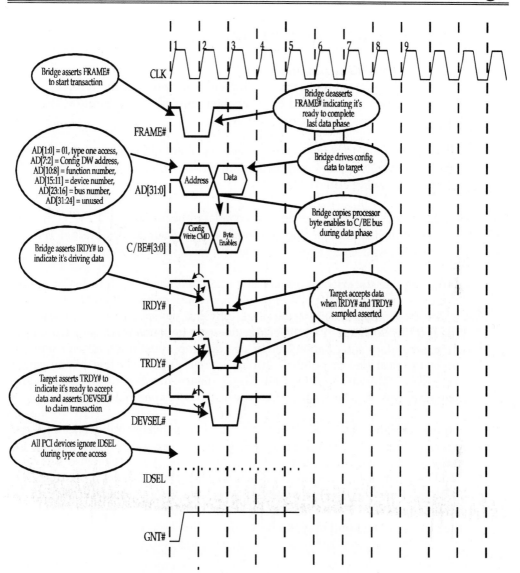

*Figure 19-18. The Type One Configuration Write Access*

## Type Zero Configuration Access

The type zero configuration read and write transactions are used to access a device's configuration registers. A complete description of the type zero configuration access can be found in the chapter entitled "Configuration Transactions."

When a PCI-to-PCI bridge detects a type one configuration access on its primary side, it converts the transaction into a type zero access on its secondary bus if the following criteria are met:

- Target bus matches the bridge's secondary bus number.
- Target device number, function number and doubleword are not 1Fh, 7h and 0h, respectively (this would be a special cycle request).

Assuming that the criteria are met, the bridge converts the transaction into a type zero configuration transaction on the secondary bus. When doing so, the bridge must assert IDSEL to the target physical device on its secondary bus. The specification states that the bridge does not implement IDSEL output pins on its secondary side. Rather, the bridge designer must internally decode the target physical device number and assert one upper AD line in the range AD[31:16]. Table 19-8 defines the target device number to AD signal line mapping. This imposes a limit of 16 physical devices per PCI bus.

On the secondary PCI bus, the designer must resistively-couple each of these upper AD lines (AD[31:16]) to an IDSEL pin at a separate physical device location on the bus. The designer of a device to be embedded or installed on a PCI bus must never internally couple one of these AD lines to the device's IDSEL pin. This would effectively "hardwire" the device's physical address. If everyone did this, there is the strong probability that two or more devices on the bus would respond to type zero configuration accesses.

Table 19-8. Target Device Number to AD Line Mapping (for IDSEL assertion)

| Target Device | AD Line to Assert in AD[31:16] Field |
|:---:|:---:|
| 0 | AD16 |
| 1 | AD17 |
| 2 | AD18 |
| 3 | AD19 |
| 4 | AD20 |
| 5 | AD21 |
| 6 | AD22 |
| 7 | AD23 |
| 8 | AD24 |
| 9 | AD25 |
| 10d | AD26 |
| 11d | AD27 |
| 12d | AD28 |
| 13d | AD29 |
| 14d | AD30 |
| 15d | AD31 |
| 16d - 31d | none |

## Interrupt Acknowledge Handling

A PCI-to-PCI bridge ignores all interrupt acknowledge transactions detected on either side (because the system interrupt controller is never placed on a subordinate PCI bus).

## Configuration Process

### Introduction

At startup time, the configuration software must (among other things) accomplish the following:

- The bus number registers in all PCI-to-PCI bridges and in the host/PCI bridge must be assigned.
- Detection of all I/O and memory devices and the assignment of mutually-exclusive address ranges to each of them.

- Detection of interrupt-driven PCI devices and programming the interrupt routing information into each of their interrupt line registers.
- Initialization of the display subsystem on the PCI bus.

## Bus Number Assignment

At startup time, the configuration software is only aware of the existence of PCI bus zero. It must build a picture of the bus "tree" that represents the overall system topology. The system startup configuration software must walk the base PCI bus (bus zero) and search for PCI-to-PCI bridges. When a bridge is discovered (using the class code register), the software walks the secondary bus in an attempt to discover other bridges. The software proceeds with this process until all PCI buses behind the first PCI-to-PCI bridge have been discovered. As each was discovered, the software assigns it a bus number and must also go back and update the subordinate bus number registers in each bridge that resides upstream of the bridge (including the host/PCI bridge).

When a complete picture of the tree branch that extends behind the first PCI-to-PCI bridge has been built, the software searches for other PCI-to-PCI bridges stemming from the first PCI bus and builds pictures of the branch behind each.

The specification does not define in what order bus numbers are assigned and when they are assigned. This is system-specific. It does, however, dictate that the bus number assigned to each bus that resides behind a PCI-to-PCI bridge must be a value greater than the bridge's secondary bus number and less then or equal to the value placed in its own subordinate bus number register.

## Address Space Allocation

Each PCI-to-PCI bridge contains three groups of registers that are used to define the address space allocated to devices residing behind the bridge:

- Base and limit for I/O space allocated to I/O devices that reside behind the bridge.
- Base and limit for memory-mapped I/O space allocated to memory-mapped I/O devices that reside behind the bridge.
- Base and limit for prefetchable memory space allocated to prefetchable memory devices that reside behind the bridge.

Since only one range can be defined for each device group (memory-mapped I/O, I/O, or prefetchable memory), each device within a given group must be assigned an address range that is contiguous with the address ranges assigned with one or two (the one assigned the range before it and the one assigned the range after it) other devices of the same type.

As an example, refer to figure 19-19. Assume that the device on PCI bus two is a prefetchable memory device that requires 4MB of space. Also assume that the two devices on bus three are also prefetchable memory, one requiring 2MB and the other 1MB of space. Assuming that the configuration software has already assigned the memory space from 00000000h through 00FFFFFFh to system memory and prefetchable memory on PCI bus zero, the configuration software would assign memory space to the three prefetchable memory devices on buses two and three as follows:

- Locations 01000000h through 013FFFFFh are assigned to the 4MB prefetchable memory device on bus two.
- Locations 01400000h through 015FFFFFh are assigned to the 2MB prefetchable memory device on bus three.
- Locations 01600000h through 016FFFFFh are assigned to the 1MB device on bus three.

The prefetchable base register and limit registers in bridges two and three are programmed as follows:

- The prefetchable base register in bridge two is set to the base address of the prefetchable memory device on bus two: 01000000h.
- The prefetchable limit register in bridge two is set to the end address of the range assigned to the last prefetchable memory device on bus three: 016FFFFFh.
- The prefetchable base register in bridge three is set to the base address assigned to the first prefetchable memory device on bus three: 01400000h.
- The prefetchable limit register in bridge three is set to the end address of the range assigned to the last prefetchable memory device on bus three: 016FFFFFh.

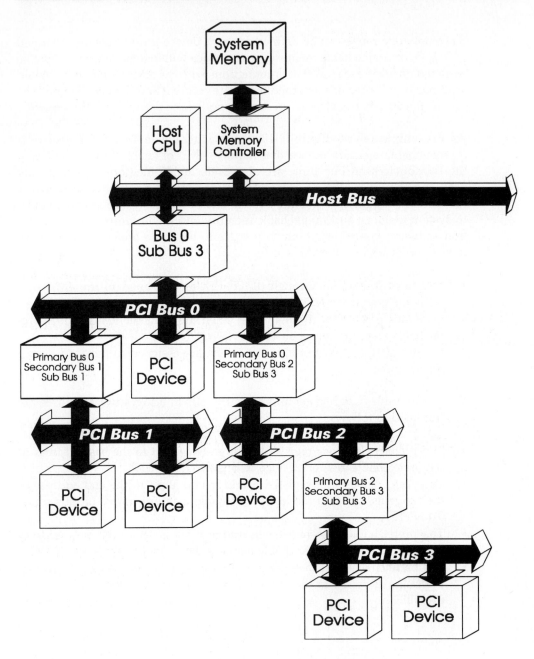

*Figure 19-19. Example System*

## IRQ Assignment

During the discovery process, the startup configuration software also determines which PCI devices are interrupt driven. Each device that indicates that it is interrupt-driven (a value between 01h and 04h hardwired into the device's interrupt pin register) also implements an interrupt line register. The startup software must write the interrupt routing information into each device's interrupt line register. This process is described later in this chapter in the section entitled "Interrupt Support."

## Display Configuration

At startup time, reset creates the following conditions:

- **PCI-to-PCI bridges ignore all VGA accesses** (because reset clears the bridge's VGA ENABLE bit and its VGA SNOOP ENABLE bit).
- Non-VGA graphics display controllers, referred to as **GFXs** in the specification, **snoop all VGA palette register writes** (because reset sets the VGA SNOOP ENABLE bit in their command registers to one).
- **VGA**-compatible display controllers **do not snoop VGA palette register writes** (because reset clears the VGA SNOOP ENABLE bit in their command registers).

The sequence that must be utilized to detect and set up all VGA-compatible controllers and non-VGA, GFX controllers is as follows:

1. Identify the VGA display device to be utilized during the boot process. This is accomplished by first scanning the standard expansion bus (i.e., ISA, EISA or Micro Channel). If the display device is found on the expansion bus, that display is used for the boot process and the initialization sequence has completed. Do not perform the steps that follow. If the device is not found on the expansion bus, scan the PCI bus(es). If found on a PCI bus, save the bus number for use during the remaining steps in the initialization sequence.
2. Set the I/O enable and memory enable bits in the device's command register so it can respond to VGA accesses.
3. Starting at the PCI bus number the boot display device is on, scan the PCI bus hierarchy upstream (towards bus zero). In each PCI-to-PCI bridge detected, set the VGA ENABLE bit in its bridge control register.

4.  Starting at the PCI bus the boot display device is on, scan the PCI buses downstream (all buses subordinate to this bus) looking for GFXs. Abort the scan when the first instance of a GFX is found. Set the GFX device's I/O enable and VGA snoop enable bits in its command register. If no GFXs were found, go to the next step.
5.  Scan back upstream from the bus the GFX is on towards the bus the boot display device resides on. At each PCI-to-PCI bridge encountered, set the VGA SNOOP ENABLE bit in the bridge's command register.
6.  Finally, set the VGA SNOOP ENABLE bit in the boot display device's command register.

The PCI-to-PCI bridge specification provides pseudo-code for two procedures that can be used to implement the sequence described above. The two procedures are:

*   DisplayInit(). This is the top-level procedure. It has no input parameters and it calls the GFXScanR procedure.
*   GFXScanR(BusNUM). This procedure scans the buses subordinate to the one the boot display was found on looking for the first instance of a GFX device.

The appendix of the PCI-to-PCI bridge specification also provides a more detailed discussion of issues related to VGA palette snooping.

## Reset

The RST# signal on the bridge's secondary side is asserted under two conditions (in other words, it's the logical OR of two conditions):

*   When RST# is detected asserted on the primary side, the bridge must assert RST# on the secondary side.
*   The bridge asserts RST# on the secondary side whenever software sets the SECONDARY BUS RESET bit in the bridge's bridge control register to one.

All PCI-to-PCI bridges are required to take ownership of the secondary bus's AD, C/BE and PAR signals whenever RST# is asserted on the secondary bus. The bridge must drive all of these signals low to keep them from floating during the reset period (otherwise, input buffers connected to the secondary bus would oscillate and draw excessive power). This requirement is independent of the location (inside or outside the bridge) of the secondary bus's arbiter. There isn't a danger of another PCI device on the secondary bus also driving the bus during reset, because reset causes all PCI devices other than the PCI-to-PCI bridge to float their AD, C/BE and PAR outputs.

## Arbitration

The PCI-to-PCI bridge designer is not required to provide a PCI bus arbiter for the bridge's secondary bus, but it is strongly recommended that the bridge include the arbiter (it makes sense to do so).

When transactions on opposite sides of the bridge occur simultaneously and both require a crossover to the opposite bus, the bridge must give precedence to the primary side.

When the bridge designer integrates the secondary bus arbiter into the bridge, the arbiter's operation must adhere to the revision 2.1 specification. These rules are covered in the chapter entitled "PCI Bus Arbitration."

The bridge specification states:

"The arbiter must drop into some type of fairness algorithm when LOCK# is active on the secondary bus to avoid deadlocks. Note that the interpretation of the requirement to drop into a fairness algorithm to avoid deadlocks is as follows: it is a requirement to avoid deadlocks which may be achieved by using fairness algorithms for arbitration (as an example method)."

The author is forced to admit that this statement defies his ability to fathom it. Perhaps this is due to exhaustion, lack of intellectual prowess, or perhaps it really is as murky as it appears to me.

## Interrupt Support

A PCI-to-PCI bridge is not required to route interrupt requests generated by devices on the secondary side through the bridge.

The revision 2.1 specification requires that either the system, the device-specific interrupt handler or the device itself (if it has bus master capability) ensure that all posted-write buffers between the device and host processor are flushed to memory before interrupts are delivered to the host processor. The author would like to stress at this point that the bridge specification uses the wording "between the device and its final destination." "Final destination" is quite vague. The author believes the specification is saying between the device and the device that services the interrupt. That would be the host processor. The device-specific interrupt handler within the device driver must take responsibility for ensuring that this rule is met if it does not "know" that flushing of posted-write buffers is handled by the system board logic or by the device itself.

All posted-write buffers can be flushed by the interrupt handler by performing a read from any location within the device that generated the request. The buffers can be flushed by the device itself (if it has bus master capability) by having the device perform a read from the last memory address it wrote to before generating the interrupt request. Either one of these actions causes all bridges between the device and the host processor to flush all outstanding posted-writes to memory.

The system configuration software has the responsibility of providing interrupt routing information to each interrupt-driven PCI device at startup time. This routing information consists of the system IRQ input the interrupt is routed to on the system interrupt controller. The routing information is used by a device's device driver to determine which entry in the memory-based interrupt table to "hook."

The system configuration software "knows" the signal routing between the interrupt pins on embedded devices and the system interrupt controller. The software writes the IRQ number into the device's interrupt line register. Each add-in card connector on a PCI bus must implement the four PCI interrupt pins: INTA# through INTD#. If a card implements a PCI-to-PCI bridge and a secondary PCI bus, the bridge specification dictates that the interrupt pins on the secondary bus's PCI devices must be connected to the add-in card's connector interrupt pins as indicated in table 19-9.

*Table 19-9. Interrupt Routing on Add-in Card With PCI-to-PCI Bridge*

| Device On Add-in Bus | Device's INT Pin | Wired To Connector INT Pin |
|---|---|---|
| 0, 4, 8, 12, 16, 20, 24, 28 | INTA# | INTA# |
| | INTB# | INTB# |
| | INTC# | INTC# |
| | INTD# | INTD# |
| 1, 5, 9, 13, 17, 21, 25, 29 | INTA# | INTB# |
| | INTB# | INTC# |
| | INTC# | INTD# |
| | INTD# | INTA# |
| 2, 6, 10, 14, 18, 22, 26, 30 | INTA# | INTC# |
| | INTB# | INTD# |
| | INTC# | INTA# |
| | INTD# | INTB# |
| 3, 7, 11, 15, 19, 23, 27, 31 | INTA# | INTD# |
| | INTB# | INTA# |
| | INTC# | INTB# |
| | INTD# | INTC# |

This table does not specify the physical interconnect to the add-in connector for the bridge's interrupt pin (if it implements one). The bridge specification states: "Assuming that the bridge is a single function device, its interrupt pin must be INTA#." While that's true, the 2.1 specification does not define the external interconnect of a device's pin to a trace. By this statement, the writers of the specification are apparently indicating that it should be routed to the INTA# pin on the connector.

# Buffer Management

## Ensuring Reads Return Correct Data

A PCI-to-PCI bridge deals with two streams of transactions: those occurring on the primary side and those occurring on the secondary side. As already described in this chapter, a transaction on either side falls into one of the following categories with reference to the bridge:

1. The bridge ignores it.
2. The bridge must claim it because the initiator is attempting to access one of the bridge's internal registers. The transaction is not passed to the other side.
3. The bridge must claim it and pass it through to the other side because the address falls within the I/O, memory-mapped I/O or prefetchable memory windows that the bridge has been configured to recognize.
4. The bridge must claim it and pass it through because it is a type one configuration access that targets the bridge's secondary bus or one of its subordinate buses.

Another aspect of bridge design that bears mentioning is that the designer may choose to implement posted memory write buffers on both sides of the bridge to increase the performance of bus masters writing through the bridge to memory.

If a read is detected on either side of the bridge and that read must be passed through the bridge, and assuming that the bridge has outstanding posted memory writes buffered up, the bridge must:

1. Issue a retry to the master attempting the read.
2. Flush the posted memory write buffers.
3. Permit the read (which is retried by the master) to pass through the bridge.

This policy ensures that the read will fetch the correct data from memory.

## Posted Memory Write Buffer

The bridge designer has the option of embedding posted memory write buffers in the bridge. Assuming that this feature is implemented, the posting of memory write data is permissible when servicing either a memory write or a memory write and invalidate transaction.

If the bridge currently has posted write data to be transferred to the other side and a memory write (or memory write and invalidate) is detected on the opposite side, the bridge must accept (i.e., post) the write data being presented by the master on the opposite side without first flushing the posted write(s) from the other side. The specification states that this policy is necessary or a deadlock could result.

Consider the following scenario (refer to figure 19-20):

1.  Bridge one accepts a memory write into its posted write buffer to be written towards bridge two.
2.  Bridge two accepts a memory write into its posted write buffer to be written towards bridge one.
3.  Bridge two starts a memory write to unload its posted write to bridge one.
4.  Bridge one issues a retry to bridge two because it wants to unload its posted write to bridge two before accepting the memory write from bridge two.
5.  Bridge one then starts the memory write to bridge two.
6.  Bridge two issues a retry to bridge one because it wants to unload its posted write buffer to bridge one before accepting the write data from bridge one.

Deadlock!

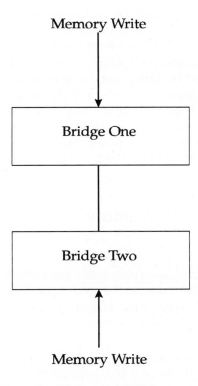

Figure 19-20. Posted-Write Scenario (refer to text)

## Handling of Memory Write and Invalidate Command

Assume that a PCI-to-PCI bridge accepts a memory write and invalidate command and initiates it on the opposite side of the bridge. If the memory target is non-cacheable, it may issue a disconnect before it has accepted the entire line from the bridge. In this case, assuming that the initiating master on the other side has not yet completed sending the write data to the bridge, the bridge can issue a disconnect to the master. The master that was disconnected will resume the transaction as a memory write and the bridge will then reinitiate the transaction as a memory write to the target and the entire line is written to the target. The specification says that no error is generated in this case (because, truly, everything worked just fine).

## Creating Burst Write from Separate Posted Writes

If the bridge posts sequential memory writes by a master to separate doubleword addresses where each doubleword address is higher than the one posted before it, the bridge can create a write burst transaction to offload the data rapidly. The doubleword addresses must be in ascending numerical order, but they needn't be contiguous. As an example, writes to doublewords 0, 1 and 3 could be turned into a burst with no byte enables asserted in the third doubleword. On the other hand, it is not permissible to create a single burst write transaction from writes to doublewords 0, 3, and 2. In this case, the bridge would have to perform this as three separate single-data phase write transactions. Combining of I/O and configuration writes into a burst is forbidden. Inclusion of the **combining feature** in a bridge **is optional**.

## Merging Separate Memory Writes into Single Data Phase Write

Separate single-data phase writes within prefetchable memory, each to different bytes within the same doubleword, may be merged into a single-data phase doubleword write to the memory target. As an example,  assume a master generates the following separate transactions:

1. A single byte write to prefetchable memory location 00000102h.
2. A single byte write to prefetchable memory location 00000100h.
3. A single byte write to prefetchable memory location 00000103h.

The bridge could merge these three transactions into a single-data phase write to doubleword 00000100h with byte enables 0, 2 and 3 asserted, but not byte enable 1.

Provision of the **merge feature is optional**. Merging may not be performed for I/O, configuration, or memory-mapped I/O write operations.

## Collapsing Writes: Don't Do It

Multiple writes to the same location(s) cannot be performed as a single write on the other side of the bridge. Two sequential writes to the same doubleword where at least one of the byte enables was asserted in both transactions must be performed as two separate transactions on the other bus. Collapsing of writes is forbidden for any type of write transactions.

## Bridge Support for Cacheable Memory on Secondary Bus

Support for cacheable memory on the secondary bus is optional. This means that implementation of the snoop result signals, SDONE and SBO#, on both sides of the bridge is also optional. The specification seriously questions the wisdom of supporting this feature. It adds a great deal of complexity to the overall system design and the rewards are highly questionable.

## Multiple-Data Phase Special Cycle Requests

The revision 2.1 specification permits the generation of special cycle transactions with multiple data phases. This subject is covered in the chapter entitled "The Commands." If the programmer instructs the host/PCI bridge to perform a multiple-data phase special cycle transaction on bus zero, it will work. If, however, the programmer instructs the host/PCI bridge to generate a type one configuration write to forward a multiple data phase special cycle to a subordinate bus, problems can occur.

It is permissible for a target to issue a disconnect during a multiple-data phase configuration write. Assuming that this were to occur, the transaction could arrive at the bridge that will perform the conversion to a special cycle as a series of single-data phase configuration accesses. This would result in the generation of a series of single-data phase special cycle transactions on the target bus, thereby sending the wrong message (no pun intended).

The bridge specification therefore dictates that is illegal to request a multiple-data phase special transaction on any bus other than bus zero.

## Potential Deadlock Condition

One of the primary rules that a PCI-to-PCI bridge must adhere to is that it cannot allow a read to be performed on one of its PCI buses while previously-posted writes for that bus have not yet been performed by the bridge. If it allowed the read to be performed on the target bus before the previously-posted writes, the read might return stale data (because one or more of the posted writes might target the area being read from).

Now assume the following:

1. The system has two PCI-to-PCI buses (as illustrated in figure 19-21).
2. Master A initiates an eight byte (64-bit) memory read from target C to get eight bytes of data.
3. The PCI-to-PCI bridge acts as the target of the transaction and passes it through to PCI bus 1 as a 32-bit transfer with two data phases. The bridge also issues a retry to master A (because it will take awhile to get the data from the target on the other bus). This is referred to as a delayed transaction and has the advantage of freeing up PCI bus 2 while the bridge accumulates the requested read data from target C.
4. Target C supplies the bridge with the first four bytes, asserting TRDY# to indicate the presence of the data. In addition, target C asserts STOP# (issues a disconnect) because it isn't designed to handle multiple data phases. At this point, the bridge has read partial data from target C.
5. Master B now acquires ownership of PCI bus 2 and initiates a memory write. The bridge absorbs the write into its posted write buffer.
6. The bridge still has to perform the second read from target C to get the remaining data, but permitting this read to occur on PCI bus 1 while the posted-write buffer has data posted is a violation of the specification (because one or more of the writes might be to the location(s) to be read).
7. The bridge must assume that the device being read from changes the contents of locations after a read (e.g., it could be a FIFO buffer or a memory-mapped I/O status port). For this reason, the bridge cannot just throw away the first data item it read and start the read over after it has accomplished the posted writes on PCI bus 1.

A strange scenario has been created wherein write data was posted in the midst of a fragmented read. A deadlock now exists. The second read cannot be performed on PCI bus 1 before the posted writes, and the posted writes never should have been accepted.

The solution is as follows: the bridge should asserted LOCK# on PCI bus 1 when it started the read. The bridge is not permitted to accepted posted writes destined for a locked PCI bus. It issues retry to the master attempting the write.

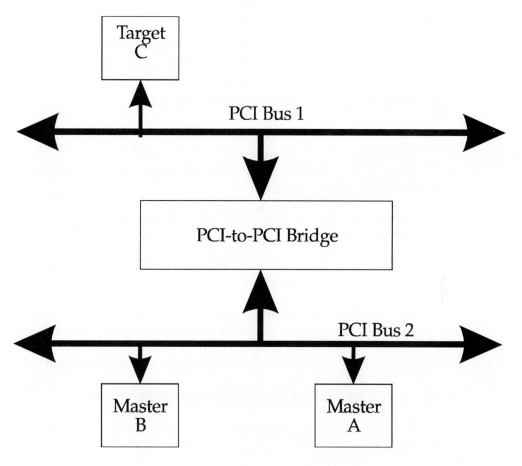

*Figure 19-21. Another Deadlock Scenario (refer to text)*

# Error Detection and Handling

## General

As required by the 2.1 specification for all PCI devices, the PCI-to-PCI bridge must generate parity, check parity and report parity errors (if enabled to do so) on both buses. The sections that follow describe how the bridge must behave, relative to parity operation, during both the address and data phases of the transaction.

In addition, behavior when handling master and target aborts is described, as well as the affect of SERR# assertion on the secondary bus.

## Handling Address Phase Parity Errors

The bridge acts as the target of transactions that must cross the bridge. The specification defines the manner in which any target can respond to detection of an address phase parity error. Any of the following reactions to an address phase parity error may be implemented:

1. The bridge may claim the transaction and complete it normally.
2. The bridge may claim the cycle and terminate the transaction with a target abort.
3. The bridge may choose not to claim the transaction, thereby letting it terminate with a master abort.

In all three cases, however, the bridge must report the address parity error by asserting SERR# (if enabled via the SERR# ENABLE bit in the command register). The following two sections define the exact response of the bridge to an address phase parity error detected on the primary and secondary sides.

### Address Phase Parity Error on Primary Side

When the bridge detects an address phase parity error on its primary side, it must take all of the following actions:

1. Assert SERR# on the primary side, but only if the SERR# ENABLE and the PARITY ERROR RESPONSE bits in the command register are set.
2. Set the SIGNALED SYSTEM ERROR bit in the status register (if SERR# was asserted).

3. Set the DETECTED PARITY ERROR bit in the status register.
4. If the bridge claimed the transaction and terminated it with a target abort, it must also set the SIGNALED TARGET ABORT bit in its status register.

## Address Phase Parity Error on Secondary Side

When the bridge detects an address phase parity error on its secondary side, it must take all of the following actions:

1. Assert SERR# on the primary side, but only if the SERR ENABLE and the PARITY ERROR RESPONSE bits in the bridge control register are set and the SERR# ENABLE bit is set in the command register.
2. Set the SIGNALED SYSTEM ERROR bit in the status register (if SERR# was asserted).
3. Set the DETECTED PARITY ERROR bit in the secondary status register.
4. If the bridge claimed the transaction and terminated it with a target abort, it must also set the SIGNALED TARGET ABORT bit in its secondary status register.

# Handling Data Phase Parity Errors

## General

Whenever the bridge detects bad data parity during a transaction that is passed through the bridge, the bad data and the bad parity must be passed to the other side if at all possible.

## Read Data Phase Parity Error

When the bridge detects bad data parity on the target bus during a read, it must assert PERR# on the target bus. The bridge must pass the bad data and parity to the initiating bus. The initiating master then detects the bad parity and also asserts PERR# on that bus. The bridge must set the DETECTED PARITY ERROR bit and the DATA PARITY REPORTED bits (if enabled to do so by the PARITY ERROR RESPONSE bit in the command or bridge control register; whichever corresponds to the target bus) in the status register corresponding to the target bus.

When the initiating master detects bad data parity delivered by the bridge during a read, it asserts PERR#.

## Write Data Phase Parity Error

### General

When the bridge accepts data from the initiator during a write, it must check the parity of the write data for correctness. If the parity is bad, the bridge must assert PERR# on the initiator's bus and must also set the DETECTED PARITY ERROR bit in the status register associated with the initiator's bus. In addition, the bridge must pass the bad data and parity to the target on the target bus when it performs the write on the target bus. There are two possible cases:

1. Immediately upon receipt of the data (TRDY# and IRDY# both asserted on initiator's bus), the bridge acquires ownership of the target bus and then starts the write on the target bus. The bad data and parity are delivered to the target at that time.
2. The bridge absorbs the bad data and bad parity into its posted-write buffer and performs the write to the target on the other bus at a later time.

### Write Data Phase Parity Error on Non-Posted Write

When the bridge immediately passes a write to the other side without posting it, the target of the write may detect a parity error and assert PERR#. The bridge, acting as master on the target bus, detects the assertion of PERR#. Depending on the timing relationship of IRDY# assertion by the initiator (on the initiating bus) and the target's assertion of TRDY# (on the target bus), the bridge uses one of two methods for reporting the parity error to the initiator.

1. In the first case, the write data transfer completes on the target bus before it completes on the initiator's bus. The bridge establishes a real-time relationship between the initiator and the target. It does not assert TRDY# to the initiator until the target asserts TRDY#, thereby indicating that it has accepted the data. The bridge doesn't assert IRDY# on the target bus until it has set up the write data on the target bus. When the target then asserts TRDY# and latches the data, the bridge then asserts TRDY# to the initiator, thereby permitting it to end the data phase. In this case, if a data parity error is reported to the bridge by the target (PERR# is asserted by the target), the bridge asserts PERR# to the initiator (if enabled to do so by software) and it also sets the DATA PARITY ERROR DETECTED bit in the status register corresponding to the target bus. The DATA PARITY ERROR DETECTED bit is not set in the status register corresponding to

the initiator's bus (because the bridge didn't detect a parity error on the initiating bus.

2. In the second case, the write transfer completes on the initiator's bus before it completes on the target bus. This can occur if the initiator inserts wait states by keeping IRDY# deasserted. If the initiator delays the assertion of IRDY# long enough so that the bridge detects TRDY# asserted by the target (indicating its readiness to accept the data), then the bridge knows that the target will accept the data (will not terminate with a retry). In this case, the bridge asserts TRDY# before the initiator asserts IRDY# to indicate the presence of the data on the bus. The bridge cannot assert IRDY# on the target bus until the initiator asserts IRDY# and the data is latched by the bridge and is then driven onto the target bus. When IRDY# is sampled asserted by the bridge, the data item is transferred on the initiating bus. Subsequently, the data is driven onto the target bus, IRDY# is asserted by the bridge, and the data transfer completes on the target bus. If the target asserts PERR# (if enabled to do so), the bridge cannot assert PERR# back to the initiator within two clocks (required by the specification; the initiator samples PERR# at that time) after the completion of the data phase. If the SERR# ENABLE bit in the command is set, the bridge asserts SERR# on the primary bus to propagate the error upstream (towards the host processor). If it asserts SERR#, the bridge must also set the SIGNALED SYSTEM ERROR bit in its status register. The bridge must also set the DATA PARITY ERROR DETECTED bit in the status register corresponding to the target bus.

### Write Data Phase Parity Error on Posted Write

There are two cases that can occur regarding data parity errors incurred during performance of a posted write:

1. The bridge receives bad data and parity from the initiator. In this case, the bridge retains the bad data and parity in the posted write buffer. It asserts PERR# (if enabled to do so) to the initiator and sets its DATA PARITY ERROR DETECTED bit in the status register. When the posted write is performed on the target bus, the bad data and parity are supplied to the target. If enabled to do so, the target asserts PERR# upon receipt of the bad data and parity and sets its DATA PARITY ERROR DETECTED bit in its status register. Upon receipt of the PERR#, the bridge sets its DATA PARITY ERROR DETECTED bit in the status register corresponding to the target bus.

2. The bridge receives good data and parity from the initiator, but the data is corrupted upon being delivered to the target. In this case, its too late to in-

form the original initiator of the write that a data parity error has occurred. Instead, assuming that the SERR# ENABLE bit in the command register is set, the bridge asserts SERR# on the primary side and sets the SIGNALED SYSTEM ERROR bit in the status register.

## Handling Master Abort

The manner in which the bridge handles master aborts is controlled by the state of the MASTER ABORT MODE bit in the bridge control register. When this bit is cleared (its default state after reset), master aborts are not reported to software. Rather, a read that is passed through the bridge and is terminated by a master abort (because no target asserted DEVSEL#), returns all ones as the read data and the transaction completes normally. When a write results in a master abort on the target bus, the bridge throws the data away and does not report an error. In both cases, the bridge must set the RECEIVED MASTER ABORT bit in the status register corresponding to the target bus.

When the MASTER ABORT MODE bit is set and the transaction passed through the bridge results in a master abort, the bridge terminates a read or a non-posted write by issuing a target abort to the initiator. The bridge must also set the RECEIVED MASTER ABORT bit in the status register corresponding to the target bus.

When a master abort occurs during performance of a posted write on the target bus, the specification recommends that the bridge terminate the transaction on the initiator's bus (assuming that a burst write is still in progress and is being paced by the bridge) as soon as possible after the detection of the master abort on the target bus.

## Handling Target Abort

For all transactions performed on the target bus other than posted writes, reception of a target abort on the target bus causes the bridge to respond to the initiator with a target abort. The bridge must set the RECEIVED TARGET ABORT bit in the status register corresponding to the target bus. It must also set the SIGNALED TARGET ABORT bit in the status register corresponding to the initiator's bus.

If a target abort is experienced while performing a posted write on the target bus, the bridge must signal a target abort to the initiator if the burst write is still in progress. The bridge must set the RECEIVED TARGET ABORT bit in the status register corresponding to the target bus. It must also set the SIGNALED TARGET ABORT bit in the status register corresponding to the initiator's bus. If the initiator that posted the write has already completed the transaction, then it's too late to issue it a target abort. Instead, the bridge asserts SERR# on the primary side (if enabled to do so by software). The bridge also sets the RECEIVED TARGET ABORT bit in the status register corresponding to the target bus and sets the SIGNALED SYSTEM ERROR bit in the status register.

## Handling SERR# on Secondary Side

When SERR# is asserted on the secondary side, the bridge must assert SERR# on the primary side (if enabled to do so). The bridge must also set the RECEIVED SYSTEM ERROR bit in the secondary status register.

# Part V

# The PCI BIOS

# Chapter 20

## Prior To This Chapter

The previous chapter comprised part IV of the book, "PCI-TO-PCI Bridge", and provided a detailed discussion of PCI-to-PCI bridge implementation. This information was drawn from the revision 1.0 PCI-to-PCI bridge architecture specification, dated April 5, 1994.

## In This Chapter

This chapter introduces the PCI BIOS specification, revision 21., dated August 26, 1994.

## The Next Chapter

The next chapter describes the issues related to the placement of cacheable memory on the PCI bus.

## Purpose of PCI BIOS

The operating system (except for the platform-specific micro-kernel), applications programs and device drivers must not directly access the PCI configuration registers, interrupt routing logic, or the special cycle generation logic. The hardware methods utilized to implement these capabilities are platform-specific. Any software that directly accesses these mechanisms is therefore, by definition, platform-specific. This will lead to compatibility problems (i.e., the software works on some platforms but not on others).

Instead, the request should be issued to the PCI BIOS. The BIOS is platform-specific. It is implemented in firmware and possibly in the operating system's hardware abstraction layer (HAL). The PCI BIOS supplies the following services:

- Permits determination of configuration mechanism(s) supported by the PCI chipset.
- Permits determination of the chipset's ability to generate special cycles and the mechanism(s) used to do so.
- Permits determination of the range of PCI buses present in system.
- Searches for all instances of a specific PCI device or a device that falls within a class.
- Permits generation of special cycles.
- Allows caller to get PCI interrupt routing options and then to assign one to a device.
- Permits read and write of a device's configuration registers.

## Operating System Environments Supported

### General

Different operating systems have different operational characteristics (such as the method for defining the usage of system memory and the method utilized to call BIOS services). In systems based on the x86 processor family, the operating system executing on a particular platform falls into one of the following three categories:

- Real-mode operating system (in other words, MS-DOS).
- 286 protected mode.
- 386 protected mode. There are two flavors of 386 protected mode: the segmented and the flat models.

The PCI BIOS specification defines the following rules regarding the implementation of the PCI BIOS and the software that calls it:

- The PCI BIOS must support all of these operating system environments.
- The BIOS must preserve all registers and flags with the exception of those used to return parameters.
- Caller will be returned to with the state of interrupt flag the same as it was on entry.
- Interrupts will not be enabled during the execution of the BIOS function call.
- The BIOS routines must be reentrant (i.e., they can be called from within themselves).

- The operating system must define a stack memory area at least 1KB in size for the BIOS.
- The stack segment and code segment defined by the operating system for the BIOS must have the same size (16 or 32-bit).
- Protected mode operating systems that call the INT 1Ah BIOS must set the CS register to F000h.
- The operating system must ensure that the privilege defined for the BIOS permits interrupt enable/disable and performance of I/O instructions.
- Implementers of the BIOS must assume that the CS for the BIOS defined by the operating system is execute-only and that the DS is read-only.

## Real-Mode

Real-mode operating systems, such as MS-DOS, are written to be executed on the 8088 processor. That processor is only capable of addressing up to 1MB of memory (00000h through FFFFFh). Using four 16-bit segment registers (CS, DS, SS, ES), the programmer defines four segments of memory, each with a fixed length of 64KB. When a program begins execution, each of the four segment registers is initialized with the upper four hex digits of the respective segment's start address in memory. The code segment contains the currently-executing program, the data segment defines the area of memory that contains the data the program operates upon, the stack segment defines the area of memory used to temporarily save values, and the extra data segment can be used to define another data segment associated with the currently-executing program.

MS-DOS makes calls to the BIOS by loading a subset of the processor's register set with request parameters and then executing a software interrupt instruction that specifies entry 1Ah in the interrupt table as containing the entry point to the BIOS. Upon execution of the INT 1Ah instruction, the processor pushes the address of the instruction that follows the INT 1Ah onto stack memory. Having saved this return address, the processor then reads the pointer from entry 1Ah in the interrupt table and starts executing at the indicated address. This is the entry point of the BIOS.

An alternative method for calling the BIOS is to make a call directly to the BIOS entry point at physical memory location 000FFE6Eh. Use of this method ensures that the caller doesn't have to worry about the 1Ah entry in the interrupt table having been "hooked" by someone else.

## 286 Protected Mode (16:16)

The BIOS specification refers to this as 16:16 mode because the 286 processor has 16-bit segment registers and the programmer specifies the address of an object in memory by defining the 16-bit offset of the object within the segment (code, data, stack or extra). Although the maximum size of each segment is still 64KB (as it is with the 8088 processor), the operating system programmer can set the segment length to any value from one to 64KB in length. When operating in real-mode, the 286 addresses memory just like the 8088 with the same fixed segment size of 64KB and the ability to only access locations within the first megabyte of memory space.

When operating in protected mode, the 286 addresses memory differently. Rather than containing the upper four hex digits of the segment's physical five-digit start address in memory, the value in the segment register is referred to as a segment selector. It points to an entry in a segment descriptor table in memory that is built and maintained by the operating system. Each entry in the segment descriptor table contains eight bytes of information defining:

* the 24-bit start physical address of the segment in memory. In other words, the segment start address can be specified anywhere in the first 16MB of memory space.
* the length of the segment (from one byte through 64KB).
* the manner in which the program is permitted to access the segment of memory (read-only, execute-only, read/write, or not at all).

Some operating systems (such as Windows 3.1 when operating in 286 mode) use the segment capability to assign separate code, data and stack segments within the 16MB total memory space to each program. Whenever the operating system performs a task switch, it must load the segment registers with the set of values defining the segments of memory "belonging" to the current application.

As in the real-mode operating system environment, the BIOS is called via execution of INT 1Ah or by directly calling the industry standard entry point of the BIOS.

## 16:32 Protected Mode

The 386 processor changed the maximum size of each segment from 64KB to 4GB in size. The 486 and Pentium processors have the same maximum segment size as the 386. In addition to increasing the maximum segment size to 4GB, the 386 also introduced a 32-bit register set, permitting the programmer to specify the 32-bit offset of an object within a segment. The segment registers are still 16-bits in size. Rather than containing the upper four hex digits of the segment's physical five-digit start address in memory, however, the value in the segment register is referred to as a segment selector (when the processor is operating in protected mode). It points to an entry in a segment descriptor table in memory that is built and maintained by the operating system. Each entry in the segment descriptor table contains eight bytes of information defining:

- the 32-bit start physical address of the segment in memory. In other words, the base address of the segment can be specified anywhere within the overall 4GB of memory space.
- the length of the segment (from one byte through 4GB).
- the manner in which the program is permitted to access the segment of memory (read-only, execute-only, read/write, or not at all).

Some operating systems (such as Windows 3.1 when operating in 386 enhanced mode) use the segment capability to assign separate code, data and stack segments within the 4GB total memory space to each program. Whenever the operating system performs a task switch, it must load the segment registers with the set of values defining the segments of memory "belonging" to the current application. This is referred to in the specification as 16:32 mode because the 16-bit segment register defines (indirectly) the segment start address and the programmer can use a 32-bit register to specify the offset of the object anywhere in the 4GB of total memory space.

In a 32-bit operating system environment, the BIOS is not called using INT 1Ah. Rather, the calling program executes a far call to the BIOS entry point. This implies that the entry point address is known. A subsequent section in this chapter defines how the BIOS entry point is discovered.

## Flat Mode (0:32)

A much simpler memory model is to set all of the segment registers to point to segment descriptors that define each segment as starting at physical memory location 00000000h and with a length of 4GB. This is referred as the flat memory model. The BIOS specification refers to this as 0:32 mode because all segments start at location 00000000h and have a 32-bit length of FFFFFFFFh, or 4GB. Since separate segments aren't defined for each program, the operating system has the responsibility of managing memory and making sure different programs don't play in each other's space.

As stated earlier, in a 32-bit operating system environment, the BIOS is not called using INT 1Ah. Rather, the calling program executes a far call to the BIOS entry point. This implies that the entry is known. A subsequent section in this chapter defines how the BIOS entry point is discovered.

## Determining if System Implements 32-bit BIOS

Before attempting a call to the 32-bit BIOS, the 32-bit operating system must first determine if a 32-bit BIOS is present and what its entry point is. The BIOS specification states that the operating system must scan the physical memory area from 000E0000h through 000FFFF0h looking for the 16-byte data structure defined in table 20-1. This data structure must be aligned on a 16-byte address boundary.

*Table 20-1. 32-Bit BIOS Data Structure*

| Offset | Size | Description |
|--------|------|-------------|
| 0 | 4 bytes | ASCII signature "_32_." The left-most underscore is stored at offset 0, while the right-most is stored at offset 3. |
| 4 | 4 bytes | 32-bit entry point of the 32-bit BIOS service directory program. The service directory program can be called to determine what services (such as PCI BIOS services) are offered by the 32-bit BIOS. |
| 8 | 1 bytes | Revision level of this data structure (currently 00h). |
| 9 | 1 bytes | Data structure length in 16-byte increments. As currently-defined, the data structure is 16 bytes long, so this field contains 01h. |
| Ah | 1 bytes | Checksum of all bytes in data structure. Sum must add up to 00h. |
| Bh | 5 bytes | Reserved and must be zero. |

## Determining Services 32-bit BIOS Supports

Now that the existence and entry point of the 32-bit service directory program has been established, the operating system may interrogate the service directory program to determine if the 32-bit BIOS implements the PCI BIOS. This is accomplished by calling the entry point and supplying the following as input parameters:

- The service directory program performs a lookup based on the four byte **service identifier** (see next section) supplied by the caller in the EAX register to determine if the indicated service (in this case, the PCI BIOS services) is supported by the 32-bit BIOS.
- The **service directory function identifier** supplied in the BL register. The only one currently defined is 00h, which directs the service directory to search for the service identifier provided in the EAX register. The upper three bytes of EBX are reserved and must be cleared to zero.

Upon return from the call to the service directory, the register set contains the following values:

- AL contains 00h if the specified service exists, 80h if the specified service isn't present, or 81h if the function identifier supplied in BL isn't implemented.
- EBX contains the physical start address of the indicated BIOS service.
- ECX contains the length of the indicated BIOS service.
- EDX contains the indicated BIOS service entry point. This is an offset from the start address returned in EBX.

## Determining if 32-bit BIOS Supports PCI BIOS Services

The service identifier for the PCI BIOS services consists of the ASCII string "$PCI", specified in EAX as 49435024h. Assuming that the service directory call indicates that the PCI BIOS exists, the PCI BIOS may be called by performing a far call to the entry point returned in the EDX register. Before calling the PCI BIOS, the operating system must define the BIOS's code and data segments as encompassing the physical address range returned in EBX and ECX. The code and data segments must have the same start address. The operating system must set up the BIOS's privilege level to permit I/O operations and it must define a stack area for the BIOS that is at least 1KB in size. BIOS writers must assume that the operating system defines the code segment as execute-only and the data segment as read-only.

## Calling PCI BIOS

As stated earlier in this chapter, the 16-bit PCI BIOS is called by either executing an INT 1Ah instruction or directly by calling the PCI BIOS at physical memory location 000FFE6Eh. The 32-bit BIOS is called by performing a far call.

In both cases, the caller must first load the required request parameters into the processor's register set. On entry, the AH register must contain the PCI function ID of B1h. The AL register must contain the PCI sub-function identifier. Table 20-2 identifies the input parameters for the various types of PCI function calls. On exit, the state of the carry flag indicates the general success or failure of the call.

## PCI BIOS Present Call

Prior to calling the PCI BIOS, AH is set to B1h and AL to 01h. On return, the register set contains the following values:

- EDX contains the ASCII character string " PCI", with DL = "P", DH = "C", the byte above DL = "I", and the upper byte of EDX set to the ASCII space character.
- AH = 00h.
- AL contains the information in figure 20 - 1.
- BH = BIOS major version in BCD.
- BL = BIOS minor version in BCD.
- CL = the number of the last PCI bus in the system.
- Carry bit is cleared if BIOS present, set if it's not.

The programmer is only assured that the PCI BIOS is present if EDX, AL and the carry flag contains the indicated information.

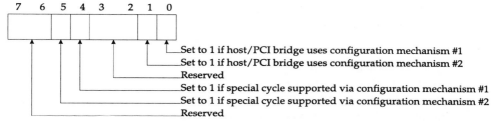

Figure 20 - 1. AL Contents After BIOS Present Call

Table 20-2. PCI BIOS Function Request Codes

| Function Request | AH Value | AL Value |
|---|---|---|
| PCI function ID. | B1h | |
| **Test for PCI BIOS present.** | | 01h |
| **Find PCI device.** Can find all instances of a device in the system using the device's vendor and device IDs as search criteria. If an instance of the device is found, the physical location is returned (bus, device and function numbers). These values can then be used as input parameters to the configuration read and write BIOS functions to access the device's configuration registers. | | 02h |
| **Find PCI class code.** Can find all instances of devices in the system with the indicated class code using the specified class code as search criteria. If an instance of the device is found, the physical location is returned (bus, device and function numbers). These values can then be used as input parameters to the configuration read and write BIOS functions to access the device's configuration registers. As an example of usage, this function would be used to scan for a VGA-compatible interface to be used as the boot display device. | | 03h |
| **Generate special cycle.** Used to generate a special cycle with the specified message on the indicated bus. | | 06h |
| **Read configuration byte.** | | 08h |
| **Read configuration word.** | | 09h |
| **Read configuration doubleword.** | | 0Ah |
| **Write configuration byte.** | | 0Bh |
| **Write configuration word.** | | 0Ch |
| **Write configuration doubleword.** | | 0Dh |
| **Get interrupt routing options.** Used to discover the | | 0Eh |

| Function Request | AH Value | AL Value |
|---|---|---|
| manner in which interrupts from PCI devices can be routed to system interrupt request lines. | | |
| **Set (assign) PCI interrupt**. Used to route a device's PCI interrupt request line to the specified system interrupt request line. | | 0Fh |

The BIOS specification contains a detailed description of each of these function calls. Since they are clearly described in the specification, duplication of that information is not contained in this chapter.

# Part VI

# PCI Cache Support

# Chapter 21

## The Previous Chapter

The previous chapter described the PCI BIOS.

## In This Chapter

This chapter provides a detailed description of issues related to caching from PCI memory targets. This subject has been segregated in the latter part of the book because most PCI systems currently on the market do not support cacheable memory on the PCI bus. It injects considerable complexity into system and component design and the rewards may not be justified (due to the resultant degradation in performance).

## The Next Chapter

The next chapter provides a description of 66MHz PCI bus implementation.

## Definition of Cacheable PCI Memory

A cacheable PCI memory target is a memory device residing on the PCI bus that the processor's L1 cache (and, if present, its L2 cache) caches information from.

## Why Specification Supports Cacheable Memory on PCI Bus

There are quite a few PCI design rules related to support for cacheable memory targets on the PCI bus. There are so many rules, in fact, that it makes one wonder why anyone would even consider caching from memory targets that reside on the PCI bus.

The specification includes support for cacheable memory on the PCI bus for system designs where the processor (and its internal L1 cache), main memory and all other major system devices reside directly on the PCI bus. In other words, there is no host/PCI bridge. The processor's front end logic has been redesigned to interface directly to the PCI bus. In this type of system, therefore, the cache and the memory that it caches from are located right on the PCI bus.

## Cache's Task

Relative to the native speed of the host processor, system DRAM memory is typically quite slow. Whenever the processor must access system memory, wait states are inserted in each bus cycle. This diminishes the performance of the processor in particular and the system as a whole.

The problem could be solved by populating all of system memory with high-speed static RAM rather than slow-access DRAM memory. This solution is impractical, however, due to the high-cost of static RAM.

A better solution is to position a relatively small amount of high-speed static RAM between the processor and DRAM memory. A device referred to as a cache controller attempts to keep copies of information that the processor may request in its static, or cache, memory. The controller maintains a directory to track information currently in the cache. Whenever the processor initiates a memory read, the controller performs a very quick search of the directory to determine if the requested information is already in the cache. If it is, this is referred to as a hit. If not, it is called a miss.

When a hit occurs, the controller accesses the cache memory to get the requested information, routes it to the processor and informs the processor of the presence of the data on the bus (via the BRDY# signal in an Intel-based system or TA# in a PowerPC™-based system). The quick directory search and fast-access time of the static RAM guarantees the processor fast access to the requested information.

If a miss occurs, the memory controller accesses DRAM to get the requested data and one or more wait states are inserted in the processor's bus cycle. Whenever the cache controller is forced to go to DRAM to get information, it always gets an object of a fixed size from memory. This is referred to as a line of information. The line size is defined by the cache controller design. As an example, the 486's internal cache has a line size of sixteen bytes (also referred to as a paragraph of information). When the controller gets the line from DRAM memory, it supplies the line containing the originally requested data item to the processor and also records the entire line in the external cache (if one is present). If the processor has an internal cache, as most do, the entire line is also supplied to the processor for storage in its internal cache.

## Intro to Write-Through vs. Write-Back Caches

A cache controller that resides between its associated processor and the rest of the world is referred to as a look-through cache controller. Look-through cache controllers are divided into two categories: write-through and write-back. The cache controller checks its directory for both memory reads and writes initiated by the host processor. The write-through cache controller handles processor-initiated memory writes as follows:

On a write hit, it updates the line in both cache and DRAM. This method ensures that the contents of the cache always mirrors the information in memory. This is referred to as coherency or consistency. On a write miss, it only updates the line in memory, not in the cache.

The **write-back cache controller** handles memory writes as follows:

On a write hit, it updates the line in cache, but not in DRAM. It then marks the line as **dirty**, or **modified**, in the cache directory. This means that the line no longer mirrors its associated line in DRAM memory. Of the two lines, the cache line is current and the memory line is **stale** (out-of-date). On a write miss, it typically only updates the line in memory. There is a variation on this method where, on a write miss, the processor reads the entire line from external memory, places it in its internal, L1 cache and then modifies it. The PowerPC 60x family of processors use this policy, referred to as allocate-on-write.

The write-back cache's handling of memory write hits allows the cache and memory contents to become de-synchronized, or inconsistent. This implies a more complex system design and is discussed in more detail later in this chapter.

## Integrated Cache/Bridge

Many systems that incorporate the PCI bus also incorporate a level-two (L2) cache associated with the host processor. These systems possess the following basic elements:

- The host processor (possibly with an integrated level-one cache).
- L2 cache controller and cache SRAM.
- System DRAM memory and controller.
- The host/PCI bridge.
- The PCI bus.
- PCI memory and I/O targets.
- PCI bus masters.
- Expansion bus (ISA, EISA or Micro Channel).

The L2 cache and the bridge may be implemented as separate elements or may be integrated into one element. In either case, the actions taken by each are the same. Figure 21-1 illustrates a system with an integrated L2 cache and bridge.

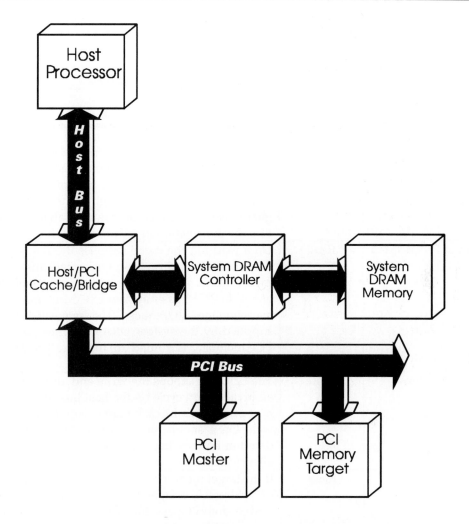

*Figure 21-1. The Integrated Cache/Bridge Element*

The L2 cache controller integrated with the bridge may use either a write-through or a write-back policy when handling memory writes initiated by the host processor. Table 21-1 defines the actions that must be taken by a write-through cache and/or the bridge when either the host processor or a PCI master initiates a memory access. Table 21-2 defines the actions that must be taken by a write-back cache and/or the bridge when either the host processor or a PCI master initiates a memory access. The term snoop means the cache latches the line address and looks it up in its cache to determine if it has a copy of the line being accessed.

*Table 21-1. Write-Through Cache Action Table*

| Initiator of Memory Access | Access Type | Cache/Bridge Action |
| --- | --- | --- |
| Host Processor | Write | The L2 cache performs a directory search and updates its line on a write hit. In addition, the memory write is routed to either system or PCI memory to update the target memory location. In this way, the write-through cache controller guarantees that the cache contents always mirrors the information in memory. |
| Host Processor | Read | On a read hit, the cache supplies the requested data to the host processor. On a read miss, the cache/bridge passes the transaction through to either the PCI bus or system DRAM memory as a cache line fill request. The requested line, supplied by the system DRAM memory or the PCI memory, is routed to the host processor and is also recorded in the L2 cache. |
| PCI Master | Write | The L2 cache snoops the write and also initiates an invalidation cycle on the host bus so that the host processor's L1 cache can snoop the write as well. On a snoop hit, the cache line is invalidated in both caches (because the bus master is altering some portion of the line in memory). |
| PCI Master | Read | If the target memory location is within the range of addresses assigned to PCI memory, the bridge doesn't pass the transaction to system memory. The data is supplied to the requesting PCI master by the PCI memory. If the target memory location is within system memory address space, the data is supplied to the PCI master by system memory. |

*Table 21-2. Write-Back Cache Action Table*

| Initiator of Memory Access | Access Type | Cache/Bridge Action |
|---|---|---|
| Host Processor | Write | The L2 cache performs a directory search and updates its copy of the line on a write hit. Unlike the write-through cache, the memory write is not routed to memory to update the line in memory. The L2 cache line is marked modified to indicate that it no longer matches memory. The line in memory is stale. On a miss, the write is performed in the target memory. |
| Host Processor | Read | On a read hit, the L2 cache supplies the requested data to the host processor. On a read miss, the cache/bridge passes the transaction through to either the PCI bus or the system DRAM memory as a cache line fill request. The requested line is routed to the host processor and is also recorded in the L2 cache. |
| PCI Master | Write | The L2 cache snoops the write and also initiates an invalidation cycle on the host bus so the host processor's L1 cache can snoop the write as well. If it's a snoop hit on a clean line in the L2 cache, the L2 cache invalidates its copy of the line (because the master is changing it in memory). If it results in a snoop hit on a clean line in L1, the L1 invalidates its copy as well. If it's a snoop hit on a modified line, the master is about to update one or more bytes within a stale line in memory. The bridge forces the master to retry the bus cycle. The cache (either L1 or L2, whichever has the latest copy) writes the modified line into memory and then both the L1 and L2 invalidate their cache copies. The master is then permitted to retry its bus cycle and updates the fresh line in memory. |

| Initiator of Memory Access | Access Type | Cache/Bridge Action |
|---|---|---|
| PCI Master | Read | If the target memory location is within the range of addresses assigned to PCI memory, the bridge does not pass the transaction to system memory. The data is supplied to the requesting PCI master by the PCI memory. If the target memory location is within the range associated with system memory and the snoop results in a hit on a modified line, the bridge issues a retry to the PCI master. The L1 or L2, whichever has the latest copy, then writes the modified cache line into memory so that it may subsequently be read by the PCI master when it retries the read. If the snoop results in a read miss, the bridge accesses system memory for the PCI master. |

## PCI Cache Support Protocol

### Basics

Whenever a memory access is initiated on the PCI bus by a bus master other than the host/PCI bridge, the bridge must ensure the following:

- If it implements a write-back cache controller, it must ensure that the current initiator isn't about to read data from or update data in a stale line in memory. It must also ensure that it (and the processor's L1 cache) invalidates its copy of a clean cache line in the event of a snoop hit on a write by a PCI bus master.
- If it implements a write-through cache controller, it must ensure that it (and the processor's L1 cache) invalidates its copy of a cache line in the event of a snoop hit on a write by a PCI bus master.

To prevent a PCI bus master from reading data from or updating data in a stale memory line, the bridge must have some way of informing the PCI memory target of the snoop result. Under some circumstances, the target memory must force the PCI initiator to retry the transaction later. Those circumstances were defined in table 21-2 and involved a snoop hit on a modified cache line.

The bridge implements two output signals, SDONE and SBO#, to inform the cacheable PCI memory target of the snoop result. **SDONE stands for Snoop Done** and is asserted by the bridge when it has completed snooping a PCI memory access. When SDONE is asserted, this indicates that the snoop result is available on the bridge's SBO# output signal. **SBO# stands for Snoop Back-Off** and is asserted by the bridge (in conjunction with SDONE) to force the addressed PCI memory target to issue a retry to the PCI initiator in the event of a snoop hit on a modified cache line.

## Simple Case: Clean Snoop

Figure 21-2 illustrates the bridge snooping a PCI bus master performing a memory write to a cacheable PCI memory target. This figure assumes that the cache is a write-back cache. All cacheable PCI memory targets must monitor SDONE and SBO# during memory accesses. The currently-addressed cacheable memory target must insert wait states in the data phase (by keeping TRDY# deasserted) until the snoop results are made available by the bridge. In this example, the result of the snoop indicates either a miss or a hit on a clean line (SDONE asserted and SBO# deasserted) and the bridge signals this to the memory target. This is referred to as a clean snoop. The target then asserts TRDY#, accepts the data from the initiator and the initiator ends the transaction. The following numbered list describes this process.

1. The bus master starts the transaction when it samples its GNT# asserted and bus idle (FRAME# and IRDY# deasserted). It asserts FRAME#, drives the address onto the AD bus and the memory write command onto the C/BE bus.
2. The memory target samples FRAME#, the address and the command on clock edge two and begins the address decode process (the assertion of FRAME# indicates a transaction has begun and that the sampled address and command are valid).
3. The address phase completes on the rising-edge of clock two and the initiator ceases to drive the address and command and begins to drive the write data onto the AD bus and the byte enables onto the C/BE bus. It asserts IRDY# to indicate the presence of the data to the target. It also deasserts FRAME#, indicating that it's ready to complete the last (and only) data phase. The currently-addressed target asserts DEVSEL# during clock two to claim the transaction (fast decode).
4. Because the memory target is cacheable memory, it must monitor SDONE and SBO# and is not permitted to accept the data from the initiator until the results of the snoop become available (until SDONE is asserted by the

bridge). The target keeps TRDY# deasserted until clock cell four because SDONE has not yet been asserted. On the rising-edge of clock five, SDONE is sampled asserted, indicating that the results of the snoop are available on SBO#. SBO# is sampled deasserted, indicating a clean snoop.

5. The target asserts TRDY# during clock cell five. The target and initiator sample IRDY# and TRDY# asserted on the rising-edge of clock six. The target accepts the data, completing the data phase. The initiator deasserts IRDY#, returning the bus to the idle state, and ceases to drive the write data and the byte enables. The target deasserts TRDY# and DEVSEL#.

6. The bridge deasserts SDONE in clock cell five, indicating that it is ready to receive another snoop address.

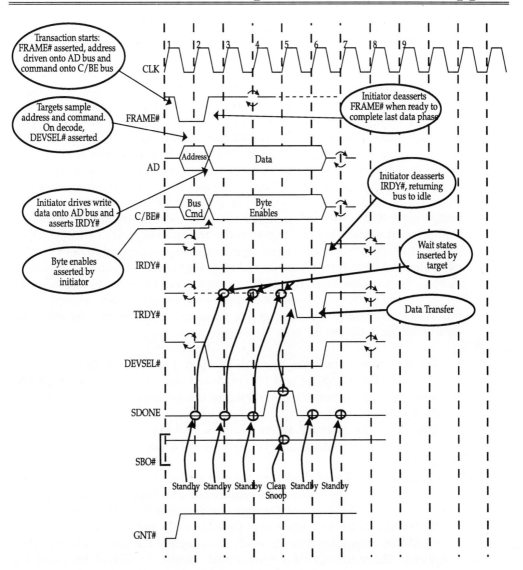

*Figure 21-2. A Simple Clean Snoop*

## Snoop Hit on Modified Line Followed by Write-Back

Assume that a PCI bus master starts a memory read or write transaction targeting a cacheable memory target on the PCI bus. The address is snooped by the bridge, resulting in a snoop hit on a modified line. Unless something is done to prevent it, the bus master is about to read data from or deposit data into a stale line in memory. To prevent this, the bridge instructs the memory target to issue a retry to the initiator. The bridge then arbitrates for bus ownership and initiates a write transaction (frequently referred to as a writeback, or as a snoop push-back transaction) to deposit the fresh line into memory before the bus master re-attempts the memory access. In order to ensure that the bridge receives bus ownership quickly, the specification recommends that the bridge assert a point-to-point signal to the arbiter along with its REQ#. Upon sensing this, the arbiter would grant bus ownership to the bridge next. Having deposited the fresh line into memory, the bridge marks its copy of the line as clean (if the writeback was caused by a memory read attempt by the bus master) or invalid (if the writeback was caused by a memory write attempt by the bus master). Figure 21-3 illustrates this sequence of events and the following numbered list describes it.

1.  The bus master starts the transaction when it samples its GNT# asserted and bus idle (FRAME# and IRDY# deasserted). It asserts FRAME# and drives the address onto the AD bus and the memory write command onto the C/BE bus.
2.  The cacheable memory target samples FRAME#, the address and the command on the rising-edge of clock two and begins the address decode process.
3.  On the rising-edge of clock two, the end of the address phase, the initiator ceases to drive the address and command and begins to drive the write data onto the AD bus and the byte enables onto the C/BE bus. It asserts IRDY# to indicate the presence of the data to the target and also deasserts FRAME#, indicating that it's ready to complete the last (and only) data phase. The currently-addressed target asserts DEVSEL# to claim the transaction.
4.  Because the memory target is a cacheable PCI memory device, it must monitor SDONE and SBO# and is not permitted to accept the write data from the initiator until the results of the snoop become available (until SDONE is asserted by the bridge). The target keeps TRDY# deasserted while it awaits the snoop result. On the rising-edge of clock four, SDONE is sampled asserted, indicating that the results of the snoop are available

on SBO#. SBO# is sampled asserted, indicating that it was a snoop hit on a modified line.

5. As a result, the target keeps TRDY# deasserted and asserts STOP# during clock four, instructing the initiator to stop the transaction on this data phase with no data transferred and to retry the transaction again later.

6. When the initiator samples STOP# and DEVSEL# asserted and TRDY# deasserted, it deasserts IRDY# on during clock cell five, returning the bus to the idle state. The bridge must leave SDONE and SBO# asserted until it accomplishes the writeback of the modified line to the cacheable memory target. As a result, any bus master that attempts to access any cacheable memory during this interim period is retried by the memory target because of the bridge's continued indication of a snoop hit on a modified line (the bridge has to complete the writeback before snooping any other transaction). Attempts to access non-cacheable memory or any non-memory transactions will complete (because only cacheable PCI memory targets are required to monitor the snoop signals).

7. The bridge then arbitrates for access to the bus so that it may deposit the fresh line into memory (i.e., to perform the writeback). After some period of time (based on the arbitration algorithm, etc.), the arbiter grants the bus to the bridge and the bridge starts the writeback (during clock cell A). During the address phase, the bridge changes the setting on SBO# to indicate a clean snoop (because it is now performing the writeback). This transition from an indication of a snoop hit on a modified line to a clean snoop indication instructs the memory to accept the entire line being deposited in memory by the bridge. If the memory target cannot immediately accept the entire line (because it is being refreshed at the moment), it must insert wait states (by keeping TRDY# deasserted) until it can accept the data.

8. During clock B, the bridge deasserts SDONE, returning the snoop signals to the standby state. The bridge performs the required number of data phases to deposit the entire line in memory and ends the transaction.

9. The bus master retries the transaction and it is snooped by the bridge again (not pictured in the illustration). This time, it results in a clean snoop (because the cache changes the state of its copy of the line either to clean (if the bus master is attempting a read) or invalid (if the bus master is attempting a write). The memory target asserts TRDY# and accepts the data being written to it or sources the data being requested from it (on a read).

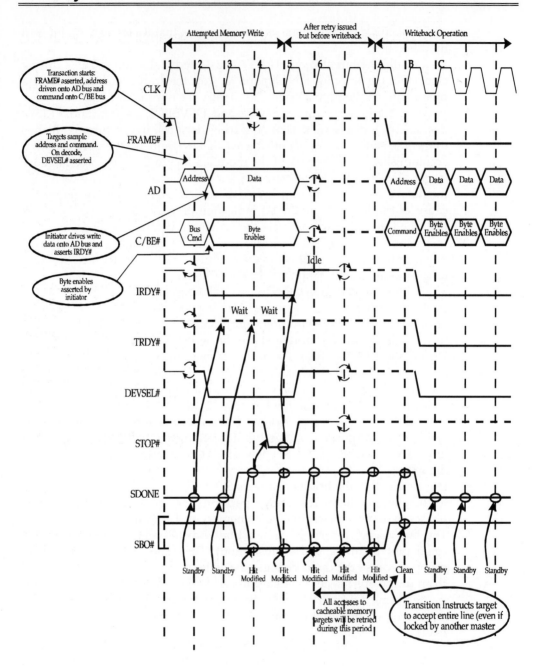

*Figure 21-3. Writeback Caused by a Snoop Hit on a Modified Line*

## Treatment of Memory Write and Invalidate Command

When a bus master initiates a memory write and invalidate transaction, it is guaranteeing that it is going to write the entire line (or multiple lines) into memory. When the bridge detects a memory write and invalidate command, it can take one of two actions.

1. In the event of a snoop miss or a snoop hit on a clean or modified line, the bridge can signal a clean snoop back to the memory target (SDONE asserted and SBO# deasserted), and the PCI memory target can assert TRDY# and start accepting the data. If the result is a snoop hit on a modified line, the bridge can invalidate the line and indicate a clean snoop (because the current bus master is guaranteeing that it will update the entire line in memory, rendering the cache's copy stale). From a performance standpoint, **this is the preferred approach**.
2. In the event of a snoop hit on a modified line, the cache could signal the result as a hit on a modified line (SDONE and SBO# asserted). As a result, the PCI memory target asserts STOP#, issuing a retry to the master (described earlier in figure 21-3). The bridge would then perform a writeback and invalidate its copy of the line, after which the bus master's memory write and invalidate transaction would be re-initiated and the entire memory line overwritten in memory. This approach is wasteful (because it results in an unnecessary writeback transaction), but it works.

## Non-Cacheable Access Followed Immediately by Cacheable Access

### Problem

Up to this point in the discussion, it has been assumed that the bridge and the cacheable memory target have the ability to latch one line address at a time. Continuing this assumption, consider the following scenario. It should be noted that all cacheable memory controllers that are not involved in the current memory access must monitor SDONE to recognize when the snoop for the transaction completes and what the snoop result is.

1. A bus master starts a single data phase memory transaction with a non-cacheable memory target. The bridge latches the address for snooping and the memory target latches it for decode. The bridge keeps SDONE deasserted while it performs the snoop, but, because the memory target is non-

cacheable, the target isn't connected to the snoop result signals and therefore permits the initiator to complete the transaction (i.e., it asserts TRDY#) while the snoop is still in progress.

2. A bus master starts another memory access to a cacheable memory target. This memory target's controller was monitoring SDONE's activity for the previous transaction and has not yet seen it asserted. This indicates that the bridge is not yet done snooping the line address submitted in the previous transaction. Because the bridge can only latch and snoop one address at a time in this scenario, the cacheable memory target must issue a retry to its initiator (because the bridge cannot yet latch the address to be snooped for the transaction targeting this memory target).

3. During the premature termination of this transaction, the snoop for the first access is completed and the result is presented on SDONE and SBO# for one clock (but nobody cares about it).

4. When the memory access to the cacheable memory target has been stopped (by the retry), a bus master initiates another single data phase access targeting a non-cacheable memory target. When this transaction is initiated, the bridge latches the address for this transaction and initiates a snoop. This transaction completes without awaiting snoop completion (the assertion of SDONE) because the target of the access is non-cacheable memory.

5. The transaction to the cacheable memory that was stopped (retried) earlier is now re-initiated and is retried again because the snoop for the previous access is still in progress.

In theory, an access to a cacheable memory target may never complete if the bus is experiencing interleaved single-data phase accesses to non-cacheable and cacheable memory targets. This problem exists because the bridge can only remember, or latch, one snoop address at a time. That's all the revision 1.0 PCI required it do to.

## Solution: Snoop Address Buffer with Two Entries

The revision 2.0 specification made it a requirement that the bridge and cacheable memory targets have the ability to latch two addresses: the first for the snoop-in-progress and the second for the transaction just initiated.

1. In the scenario described in the previous section, the bridge latched the snoop address for the first access (to a non-cacheable memory target).

2. When that access completes (without waiting for snoop completion), the access to the cacheable memory target starts. The bridge latches this ad-

dress to be snooped after completion of the first snoop. The cacheable memory target is required to insert wait states into the data phase (by keeping TRDY# deasserted) until the result of the first snoop is presented (SDONE asserted).

3. It then monitors SDONE again on each clock edge until the result of the second snoop (the one for the transaction in progress) becomes available (SDONE asserted again). When its snoop result is presented, it reacts accordingly (based on whether it results in a clean snoop or a snoop hit on a modified line).

4. If the target of the second transaction asserts TRDY# (indicating its readiness to complete a data transfer) or STOP# (due to a target-abort or disconnect) before or coincident with the presentation of result of the first snoop (SDONE assertion), this indicates that the target of the second access is non-cacheable and doesn't care about its snoop result. In response, the cache/bridge discards the second snoop address (it isn't snooped).

## Gambling Cacheable Memory Targets

It is permissible within the constraints of the specification to build a cacheable memory target that doesn't wait for the results of a snoop before allowing a memory write access to complete. The goal would be performance enhancement during burst writes to cacheable memory targets. This implies that data could be written to a stale line in memory. In order to implement this feature, the following steps would have to occur.

1. The cacheable memory target allows the memory write to complete without awaiting the result of the snoop (SDONE assertion). It must latch and remember the data written and the address it was written to (so that it can "fix" the situation later if necessary). After the memory write has completed, the target must continue to monitor the snoop result signals until the results of the bridge's snoop become available.

2. All cache memory targets that reside on the PCI bus are required to "watch" memory transactions even when they are not the target of the current transaction. This being the case, other cacheable memory targets on the bus are aware that the next snoop result that shows up on the snoop result signals is for a previously-completed transaction.

3. If no other access to a cacheable memory target occurs before the snoop result for the write is presented, the snoop result just falls on the floor (nobody cares).

4. If, however, an access is started to any cacheable memory target on the bus, that cacheable target can assert DEVSEL# and claim the transaction,

but it must insert wait states (by keeping TRDY# deasserted) until the snoop result for the previously-concluded transaction is presented by the bridge.

5. The first time that SDONE is asserted during this transaction, the snoop result is latched by both the target of the current transaction and by the target that accepted the write data earlier (the gambler).

6. If the snoop result is clean, the gambler breathes a sigh of relief and the target of the current transaction then continues to keep TRDY# deasserted until the result of its snoop is presented (on the second assertion of SDONE). If its snoop result is clean, it asserts TRDY# and permits its master to transfer data. If it's snoop result is a hit on a modified line, it issues a retry to its master so the bridge can get the bus and freshen the stale line memory.

7. If the result of the first snoop had been a hit on a modified line, the gambler has gambled and lost. The target of the current transaction issues a retry to its master. It realizes that the bridge cannot snoop its address because it is now devoted to performing the writeback of the modified line to memory. The gambler had accepted write data into a stale line in memory. It now realizes that the bridge will get the bus and burst write the fresh line into memory. It must accept the line and then make the changes that were made earlier by the bus master.

## Snoop Result

Table 21-3 defines the manner in which the PCI cacheable memory target should interpret the setting of the snoop result signals, SDONE and SBO#. Figure 21-4 illustrates the relationship of SDONE and SBO# to the host/PCI bridge and to cacheable PCI memory targets.

*Table 21-3. Memory Target Interpretation of Snoop Result Signals from Bridge*

| SDONE | SBO# | Description |
|:---:|:---:|:---|
| 0 | x | **Standby**; snoop results pending. Informs the addressed memory target that the bridge is snooping the transaction. Upon decoding its address, the memory target claims the transaction by asserting DEVSEL#, but it inserts wait states until the bridge indicates either a clean snoop, or a hit on a modified line. See the next two table entries for a description of these states. |
| 1 | 1 | **Clean snoop**; OK to proceed with data transfer. The bridge has determined that no intervention is necessary (i.e., the line has not been modified) and the transaction may proceed. In response, the memory target accepts the data from (on a memory write) or supplies the data to the bus master (on a memory read). |
| 1 | 0 | **Hit on a modified line**; issue a retry to the master. The addressed PCI memory target issues a retry to the master, causing it to abort the transaction with no data transferred. The cache writes the modified line into the PCI memory, invalidates the line (on snoop of write) or marks line clean (on snoop of read), and then permits the master to retry its memory access to the line in memory. |

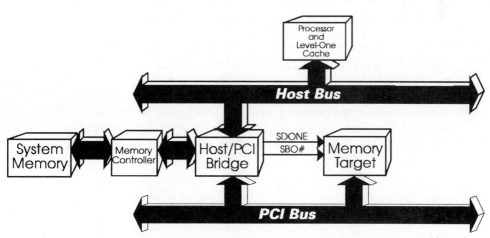

*Figure 21-4. The Snoop Protocol Signals*

## When Host/PCI Bridge Doesn't Incorporate Cache

When the bridge doesn't incorporate a cache and none of the PCI masters on the bus have caches, the SDONE and SBO# input pins on any PCI memory targets should be tied high. This instructs the memory target to reply to any memory accesses within its assigned memory address range (because all snoops result in clean snoops). If a PCI master has a cache, it would control the SDONE and SBO# lines to the memory targets. If a PCI memory target is designated as non-cacheable, it can tie SDONE and SBO# high or it can just ignore them (since its configuration information would indicate its memory is non-cacheable).

## When Host/PCI Bridge Incorporates Write-Through Cache

A write-through cache controller always propagates all host processor memory writes through to memory. This means that all lines contained in the cache are always the same as their respective lines in memory. By definition, all snoops result in clean snoops. The cache must be given the opportunity to snoop all memory writes performed by PCI masters so that it can invalidate a line when it determines that a master is changing data within that memory line. In addition, the bridge must initiate an invalidate cycle on the host bus so that the host processor's internal, L1 cache can snoop the write to determine whether to invalidate the L1 copy of the cache line. The bridge can ignore all memory reads because there is no danger that a master may read stale information from memory (as there is when the cache is a write-back cache).

When the bridge incorporates a write-through cache, the bridge need only implement SDONE. SBO# can be tied high. This gives the bridge the ability to signal STANDBY or CLEAN SNOOP  (see table 21-3) to the currently-addressed PCI memory target. Each time SDONE is asserted, a cacheable memory target can permit a memory transaction to complete. It is recommended that cache targets implement both SDONE and SBO# (so that they support operation in both write-through and write-back environments).

## When Host/PCI Bridge Incorporates Write-Back Cache

If the L2 cache uses a write-back policy, all PCI memory targets should connect to both SDONE and SBO#.

## When Burst Transfer Crosses Line Boundary

When a PCI master initiates a burst transfer, the master drives the start address onto the AD bus during the address phase of the multiple-data phase transaction. The cache latches this start address and snoops it in the cache. As the burst progresses, the memory target must monitor the address of the currently-addressed doubleword in order to determine if the burst transfer crosses over a cache line boundary. This is necessary because the master is not outputting addresses onto the AD bus for each data item transferred and the cache must receive the next cache line address in order to snoop it.

To determine when the burst is crossing over the line address boundary, the memory agent must know the cache line size. This information would be either hardwired (this approach limits the type of system the memory target can be used in) or programmed (preferred method) into the PCI memory target's cache line size configuration register. If the transfer crosses the boundary, the memory target must issue either a **disconnect** (on completion of the last transfer in current line) **or retry** (during transfer of first doubleword in next line) to the master. This forces the master to end the current transfer, re-arbitrate for the bus and then re-initiate the transfer, specifying the start address of the next line as the start address of the next transaction. The cache can then latch and snoop the new line address.

## Treatment of Snoop Result Signals on Add-in Connectors

The specification recommends that systems that do not support cacheable memory on the PCI bus should supply pullups on the SDONE and SBO# pins at each add-in connector.

## Treatment of Snoop Result Signals After Reset

In order to guarantee proper operation in systems that do not support cacheable memory on the PCI bus, cacheable PCI memory targets must ignore SDONE and SBO# after reset is deasserted. If the system supports cacheable PCI memory, the configuration software will write the system cache line size into the target's cache line size configuration register.

# Part VII

# 66MHz PCI Implementation

# Chapter 22

## Prior To This Chapter

The previous chapter provided a detailed description of issues related to caching from PCI memory targets. This subject was segregated in the latter part of the book because most PCI systems currently on the market do not support cacheable memory on the PCI bus. It injects considerable complexity into system and component design and the rewards may not be justified (due to the resultant degradation in performance).

## In This Chapter

This chapter describes the implementation of a 66MHz bus and components.

## The Next Chapter

The next chapter provides an overview of the VLSI Technology VL82C59x SuperCore PCI chipset.

## Introduction

The revision 2.1 PCI specification defines support for the implementation of buses and components that operate at speeds of up to 66MHz. This chapter covers the issues related to this topic. Note that all references to 66MHz in this chapter indicate a frequency within the range greater than 33MHz, but less than or equal to 66MHz.

## 66MHz Uses 3.3V Signaling Environment

66MHz components only operate correctly in a 3.3V signaling environment. The 5V environment is not supported. This means that 66MHz add-in cards are keyed to install in 3.3V or universal card connectors and cannot be installed in 5V card connectors.

## How Components Indicate 66MHz Support

The 66MHz PCI component or add-in card indicates its support in two fashions: programmatically and electrically. The 66MHz-CAPABLE bit has been added to the status register. The designer hardwires a one into this bit if the device support operation from 0 through 66MHz.

A 66MHz PCI bus includes a newly-defined signal, M66EN. This signal must be bussed to the M66EN pin on all 66MHz-capable devices embedded on the system board and to a redefined pin (referred to as M66EN) on any 3.3V connectors that reside on the bus. The system board designer must supply a single pullup on this trace. The redefined pin on the 3.3V connector is B49 and is used as a ground pin by 33MHz PCI devices. Unless grounded by a PCI device, the natural state of the M66EN signal is asserted (due to the pullup). 66MHz embedded devices and cards either use M66EN as an input or don't use it at all (this is discussed later in this chapter).

The designer must include a 0.01µF capacitor located within .25" of the M66EN pin on each add-in connector in order to provide an AC return path and to decouple the M66EN signal to ground.

The PCI devices embedded on a 66MHz PCI bus are all 66MHz devices. A card installed in a connector on the bus may be either a 66MHz or a 33MHz card. If the card connector(s) aren't populated, M66EN stays asserted (by virtue of the pullup). If any 33MHz component is installed in a connector, the ground plane on the 33MHz card is connected to the M66EN signal, deasserting it.

## How Clock Circuit Sets Its Frequency

The M66EN signal is provided as an input to the PCI clock circuit on the system board. If M66EN is sampled asserted by the clock circuit, it provides a 66MHz PCI clock to all PCI devices. If M66EN is sampled deasserted, the clock circuit supplies a 33MHz PCI clock. It should be fairly obvious that if any 33MHz components are installed on a 66MHz bus, the bus then operates at 33MHz.

# Chapter 22: 66MHz PCI Implementation

## Does Clock Have to be 66MHz?

As defined in revision 1.0 and 2.0 of the specification, the PCI bus does not have to be implemented at its top rated speed of 33MHz. Lower speeds are acceptable. The same is true of the 66MHz PCI bus description found in revision 2.1 of the specification. All 66MHz-rated components are required to support operation from 0 through 66MHz. The system designer may choose, however, to implement a 50MHz PCI bus, a 60MHz PCI bus, etc.

## Clock Signal Source and Routing

The specification recommends that the PCI clock be individually-sourced to each PCI component as a point-to-point signal from separate, low-skew clock drivers. This diminishes signal reflection effects and improves signal integrity. In addition, the system board and add-in card designer must adhere to the clock signal maximum trace length defined in revision 2.0 of the specification (2.5″).

## Stopping Clock and Changing Clock Frequency

The 66MHz specification states that the clock frequency may be changed at any time as long as the clock edges remain clean and the minimum high and low times are not violated. Unlike the 33MHz specification, however, the clock frequency may not be changed except in conjunction with assertion of the PCI RST# signal. Components designed to be integrated onto the system board may be designed to operate at a fixed frequency (up to 66MHz) and may require that no clock frequency changes occur.

The clock may be stopped, but only in the low state (to conserve power).

## How 66MHz Components Determine Bus Speed

When a 66MHz-capable device senses M66EN deasserted (at reset time), this automatically disables the device's ability to perform operations at speeds above 33MHz. If M66EN is sensed asserted, this indicates that no 33MHz devices are installed on the bus and the clock circuit is supplying a high-speed PCI clock.

A 66MHz device uses the M66EN signal in one of two fashions:

- The device is not connected to M66EN at all (because the device has no need to determine the bus speed in order to operate correctly).
- The device implements M66EN as an input (because the device requires knowledge of the bus speed in order to operate correctly).

## System Board with Separate Buses

The system board designer can partition the board into two or more PCI buses. A 66MHz bus can be populated with devices that demand low-latency and high throughput. A separate 33MHz PCI bus is populated only with 33MHz devices.

## Maximum Achievable Throughput

The theoretical maximum achievable throughput on a 66MHz PCI bus would be:

- 4 bytes per data phase * 66 million data phases per second = 264MB/second. This would be a 32-bit bus master bursting with a 32-bit target.
- 8 bytes per data phase * 66 million data phases per second = 528MB/second. This would be a 64-bit bus master bursting with a 64-bit target.

## Electrical Characteristics

To ensure compatibility when operating in a 33MHz PCI bus environment, 66MHz PCI drivers must meet the same DC characteristics and AC drive points as 33MHz bus drivers. However, 66MHz PCI bus operation requires faster timing parameters and redefined measurement conditions. Because of this, a 66MHz PCI bus may require less loading and shorter trace lengths than the 33MHz PCI bus environment.

Figure 22-1 illustrates the differences in timing between 33 and 66MHz component operation. The chapter entitled "Intro To Reflected-Wave Switching" provides detailed information regarding 33MHz bus timing and the various timing components (e.g., Tval, Tprop, etc.).

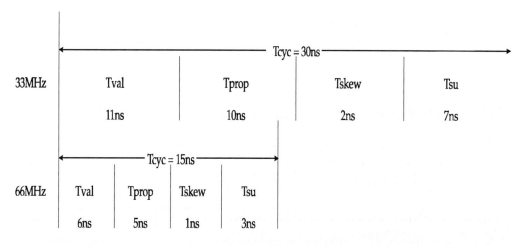

*Figure 22-1. 33 versus 66MHz Timing*

33MHz drivers are specified by their V/I curves, while 66MHz drivers are specified in terms of their AC and DC drive points, timing parameters, and slew rate. The specification defines the following parameters:

- The minimum AC drive point defines an acceptable first step voltage and must be reached within the maximum Tval time.
- The maximum AC drive point limits the amount of overshoot and under-shoot in the system.
- The DC drive point specifies steady-state conditions.
- The minimum slew rate and the timing parameters guarantee 66MHz operation.
- The maximum slew rate minimizes system noise.

66MHz PCI designers must design drivers that launch sufficient energy into a 25Ω transmission line so that correct input levels are guaranteed after the first reflection.

At 66MHz, the clock cycle time is 15ns (vs. 30ns at 33MHz), while the minimum clock high and low times are 6ns each (vs. 11ns at 33MHz). The clock slew rate has a minimum specification of 1.5 and a maximum of 4 volts/ns (same as 33MHz specification). Table 22-1 defines the 66MHz timing parameters and provides a side-by-side comparison with the 33MHz timing parameters. The following exception applies to the 66MHz values in the table: REQ# and GNT# are point-to-point signals and have different setup times than do bussed signals. They have a setup time of 5ns.

*Table 22-1. 66MHz Timing Parameters*

| Symbol | Description | 66MHz | | 33MHz | |
|---|---|---|---|---|---|
| | | Min | Max | Min | Max |
| Tval | CLK to signal valid delay, bussed signals | 2ns | 6ns | 2ns | 11ns |
| Tval (ptp) | CLK to signal valid delay, point-to-point signals | 2ns | 6ns | 2ns | 12ns |
| Ton | Float to active delay | 2ns | | 2ns | |
| Toff | Active to float delay | | 14ns | | 28ns |
| Tsu | Input setup time to CLK, bussed signals | 3ns | | 7ns | |
| Tsu (ptp) | Input setup time to CLK, point-to-point signals | | | | |
| Th | Input hold time from CLK | 0ns | | 0ns | |
| Trst | Reset active time after power stable | 1ms | | 1ms | |
| Trst-clk | Reset active time after CLK stable | 100µs | | 100µs | |
| Trst-off | Reset active to output float delay | | 40ns | | 40ns |
| Trrsu | REQ64# to RST# setup time | 10Tcyc | | 10Tcyc | |
| Trrh | RST# to REQ64# hold time | 0ns | 50ns | 0ns | 50ns |

When computing the 66MHz bus loading model, a maximum pin capacitance of 10pF must be assumed for add-in boards, whereas the actual pin capacitance may be used for devices embedded on the system board.

## Addition to Configuration Status Register

A 66MHz-capable device adds one additional bit to its configuration status register. Bit 5 is defined as the 66MHZ-CAPABLE bit. A 66MHz-capable device hardwires this bit to one. For all 33MHz devices, this bit is reserved and is hardwired to zero. Software can determine the speed capability of a PCI bus by checking the state of this bit in the status register of the bridge to the bus in question (host/PCI or PCI-to-PCI bridge). Software can also check this bit in the status register of each additional device discovered on the bus in question to determine if all of the devices on the bus are 66MHz-capable. If just one device returns a zero from this bit, the bus runs at 33MHz, not 66MHz. Table 22-2 defines the combinations of bus and device capability that may be detected.

*Table 22-2. Combinations of 66MHz-Capable Bit Settings*

| Bridge's 66MHz-Capable Bit | Device's 66MHz-Capable Bit | Description |
|:---:|:---:|:---|
| 0 | 0 | 33MHz device located on 33MHz bus. Bus and all devices operate at 33MHz. |
| 0 | 1 | 66MHz-capable device located on 33MHz bus. Bus and all devices operate at 33MHz. If the device is an add-in device and is only capable of proper operation when installed on a 66MHz bus, the configuration software may decide to prompt the user to install the card in an add-in connector on a different bus. |
| 1 | 0 | 33MHz device located on 66MHz-capable bus. Bus and all devices operate at 33MHz. |
| 1 | 1 | 66MHz-capable device located on 66MHz-capable bus. If status check of all other devices on the bus indicates that all of the devices are 66MHz capable, the bus and all devices operate at 66MHz. |

## Latency Rule

Devices residing on the 66MHz PCI bus are typically low-latency devices. The revision 2.1 specification requires that, on a read transaction, the time from assertion of FRAME# to the completion of the first data phase not exceed 16 PCI clocks. If it will, the target device must issue retry to the master. For multimedia applications, the majority of accesses are writes, not reads. Typically, a target device can accept write data faster than it may be able to supply read data. On a read, the device may need to access a slow medium. The device cannot be permitted to tie up the bus while fetching the requested data.

## 66MHz Component Recommended Pinout

The revision 2.0 specification suggested a recommended PCI component pinout wherein the signals wrapped around the component in the same order as the pin sequence on the add-in connector. The revision 2.1 specification states that "the designer may modify the suggested pinout...as required" to meet the 66MHz electrical specification.

## Adding More Loads and/or Lengthening Bus

Running the PCI bus at 66MHz imposes tighter constraints on trace length and the number of loads the bus supports. The system board designer may choose to run the bus at a lower speed (e.g., 50MHz), thereby permitting longer traces and/or additional loads.

## Number of Add-In Connectors

As a general rule, there is only one add-in connector on a 66MHz bus, but the specification does not preclude the inclusion of additional connectors (as long as the electrical integrity of the bus is maintained).

# Part VIII

# Overview of VLSI Technology VL82C59x SuperCore PCI Chipset

# Part VIII

## Overview of VLSI Technology, VLSI Chips, SuperChip C Chips

# Chapter 23

## Prior To This Chapter

The previous chapter described the implementation of a 66MHz bus and components.

## In This Chapter

The PCI specification supports many permutations of system and therefore chipset design. This chapter provides an overview of the VL82C59x Super-Core PCI chip set from VLSI Technology. This overview is provided to present an example of PCI chipset implementation. It is not intended to provide a detailed description of the chipset operation. The VLSI component specification should be consulted for that purpose. In addition, it is assumed that the reader already has an understanding of the ISA bus. For detailed information on the ISA bus operation and environment, refer to the Addison-Wesley publication entitled *ISA System Architecture*, also authored by MindShare. The author would like to thank VLSI Technology for providing access to the chipset specification.

## Chipset Features

The VLSI VL82C59x chipset provides the core logic necessary to design a Pentium-based system that incorporates both the PCI and ISA buses. It supports all 5V and 3.3V Pentium processors with host bus speeds of up to 66MHz. This includes the P5, P54C, P54CM and P54CT. It also supports dual-P54C processors. The chipset design includes the following features:

- Bridges the host and PCI buses.
- Bridges the PCI and ISA buses.
- Integrated L2 lookaside, direct mapped, write-through cache.
- Integrated system DRAM controller.
- Integrated PCI bus arbiter.

- Provision of posted-memory write buffers in both bridges.
- Supports Pentium processor's pipelined bus cycles.
- Self-configuring system DRAM banks.
- Shadow RAM support
- SMM support.
- Decoupled DRAM refresh.
- Supports synchronized or asynchronous processor and PCI clocks.
- Supports optional posting of I/O writes.
- Optional support for memory prefetching.
- PCI master reads from system DRAM memory can be serviced from processor's L2 cache or system memory.
- PCI master writes to system DRAM memory are absorbed by the bridge's posted-write buffer.
- Supports multiple-data phase PCI burst transactions.

## Intro to Chipset Members

Refer to figure 23-1. The VLSI VL82C59x SuperCore PCI chipset consists of the following entities:

- VL82C591 Pentium System Controller. In conjunction with two VL82C592 Data Buffers, the system controller comprises the bridge between the host processor's local bus and the PCI bus.
- VL82C592 Pentium Processor Data Buffer. Taken together, two data buffers provide a triple-ported data bus bridge between the host data bus, system DRAM data bus and the PCI data bus (AD bus).
- VL82C593 PCI/ISA Bridge. The '593 provides the bridge between the ISA and PCI buses. In addition, the '593 incorporates much of the ISA system support logic.

The sections that follow provide additional information about the capabilities of the chipset.

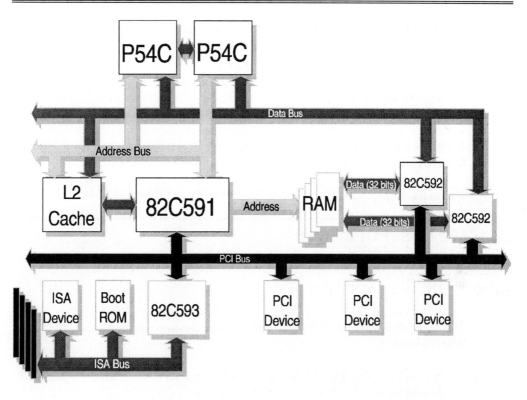

*Figure 23-1. System Design Using VLSI VL82C59x SuperCore Chipset*

## VL82C592 Pentium Processor Data Buffer

As illustrated in figure 23-1, the host/PCI bridging function consists of the VL82C591 Pentium system controller and two VL82C592 data buffers. The two data buffer chips are controlled by the '591. They provide the following basic capabilities:

- On host processor reads from system memory, the '591 reads the requested data from DRAM and instructs the '592 data buffers to pass it to the host data bus.
- On host processor writes to system memory, the '591 instructs the data buffers to accept the write data into the posted-write buffer. This permits the host processor to conclude the memory write quickly. The posted-write buffer then offloads the write data to DRAM memory.

- On PCI-initiated memory reads from system DRAM memory, the '591 reads the requested data from memory and instructs the '592 data buffers to pass it to the requester on the PCI data bus.
- On PCI-initiated memory writes to system DRAM memory, the '591 addresses memory and instructs the '592 data buffers to accept the data presented on the PCI data bus and route it into system DRAM.

A discussion of the data buffer posted write capability can be found later in this chapter.

The following section discusses the functionality of the host/PCI bridge.

## '591/'592 Host/PCI Bridge

### General

As stated earlier, the host/PCI bridge functionality is provided by the '591 in combination with two '592 data buffers. The bridge performs the following basic functions:

- Services system DRAM memory reads and writes initiated by the host processor.
- Permits host processor(s) L1 cache(s) to snoop system memory accesses initiated by PCI and ISA masters.
- Translates host processor-initiated memory and I/O accesses into PCI memory and I/O accesses.
- Services system memory accesses initiated by PCI and ISA masters.
- Translates specific host processor-initiated I/O operations into PCI configuration read or write operations.
- Translates specific host processor-initiated I/O operations into PCI special cycle transactions.
- Incorporates the PCI and host bus arbiters.
- Translates host processor-initiated interrupt acknowledge bus cycles into PCI interrupt acknowledge transaction.

### System DRAM Controller

The controller for system DRAM memory resides within the '591. Each memory bank (up to four) is either 64-bits (without parity) or 72-bits wide (with parity). Each bank may be up to 256MB in size, yielding a maximum possible memory population of 1GB. In addition, each bank may be populated with 32 or 36-bits memory modules, permitting less-costly memory upgrade. The DRAM configuration registers permit the DRAM controller to work with DRAMs of various speeds and different geometries.

The controller supports two-way interleaved, page-mode memory. One or two pages (one in each bank) can be kept open at a time. For page-mode DRAMs that have a page open timeout of less than 15µs, the controller automatically closes a page that has been open for a period of 10µs. When using DRAMs with a maximum page open timeout in excess of 15µs, the 10µs automatic page close feature may be disabled and the refresh cycles can take care of ensuring that a page does not remain open for an excessive period. Non-page mode DRAM is not supported.

Refresh cycles may be set to occur every 15.625µs, 62.5µs, 125µs or 250µs. DRAM refresh cycles are transparent to the processor. If the processor initiates a DRAM access request simultaneously with a refresh cycle, the processor is stalled (i.e., wait states are inserted in its bus cycle) until the refresh cycle completes.

When a system DRAM parity error is detected, it is reported by the assertion of the PCI SERR# signal (assuming that the SERR# enabled and parity error response bits are set in the bridge's configuration command register). SERR# is typically connected to the '593 which asserts NMI to the host processor when SERR# is asserted. An option permits bad parity to be deliberately written to system DRAM to facilitate test and diagnostics.

Host processor-initiated memory accesses that target locations above the top of installed system DRAM are passed to the PCI bus and are not cached in the L1 and L2 caches. In addition, memory address ranges defined by the bridge's segment attribute and programmed memory region registers are also passed to the PCI bus and are not cached from.

The chipset does not permit the L1 and L2 caches to cache information from memory beyond the host/PCI bridge (i.e., PCI and ISA memory). This being the case, the '591 does not implement the snoop result outputs (SDONE and SBO#).

## L2 Cache

The L2 cache controller is embedded within the '591 system controller. It is a direct-mapped, lookaside, buffered write-through cache. The L2 cache only caches information from system DRAM memory, never from PCI or ISA memory. The DRAM controller may be programmed to recognize sub-ranges within the overall memory address range assigned to system DRAM as PCI memory. When the processor initiates a memory transaction targeting an address in any of these programmed sub-ranges, the transaction is passed to the PCI bus and the data is not cached in L1 or L2.

The recommended L2 cache sizes are 256KB, 512KB and 1MB, but the L2 cache may be implemented as any desired size. The limitation is the amount of tag SRAM supplied by the system designer. The tag SRAM (i.e., the cache directory) is external to the '591 and can be of any size. Optionally, the L2 cache may be parity-protected.

The cache controller supports L2 cache line sizes of both 32 and 64 bytes. Additional SRAM is necessary to support the larger line size. When the 64 byte line size is implemented, a processor-initiated read miss in L2 results in the requested 32 byte line being read from DRAM. The line is sent back to the processor and a copy is also stored in the L2 cache. To the L2 cache, this is considered to be half of a line. The cache reads the next 32 bytes from DRAM and establishes it in the L2 as the second half of the 64 byte line.

A write-through cache usually extends the duration of a host processor-initiated memory write until the data has been written through to system memory. In this chipset design, the '591 instructs the '592 data buffers to accept the write data and permits the processor to complete its memory write immediately.

The cache controller supports both asynchronous and synchronous SRAMs. When using asynchronous SRAMs, burst read timing of 3-2-2-2 (three processor bus clocks to transfer the first quadword, and two clocks each for the transfer of each of the other three quadwords in the line) is achievable (at a bus speed of 66MHz). Burst write timing of 4-2-2-2 or 3-2-2-2 is achievable (depending on tag SRAM speed and signal loading). When using synchronous SRAMs, burst reads and write timing of 3-1-1-1 or 2-1-1-1 is achievable (depending on tag SRAM speed and SRAM type). When the processor performs back-to-back burst reads, pipelining reduces access time to 1-1-1-1.

Startup software can determine the following information related to the L2 cache:

- Cache SRAM type (asynchronous, synchronous type one or synchronous type two).
- Cache size.
- Line size.
- Cacheable memory range.
- Wait states imposed by cache SRAM type/speed.

## Posted-Write Buffer

### General

The posted-write buffer absorbs processor-initiated writes and permits the processor to end the write transaction quickly. The buffer logic then initiates the write to memory (or to PCI). While the buffer is engaged in the write, the processor can start and complete another memory write (assuming the buffer isn't full, it is absorbed by the posted-write buffer as well), a read hit on the L2 cache, or a write to the PCI bus (if the previously posted write was to system memory). The posted-write buffer that absorbs processor writes destined for system memory is eight quadwords deep (a quadword is 64-bits).

The posted-write buffer that absorbs memory writes destined for the PCI (or ISA) bus is one quadword deep. The bridge can only post writes to PCI/ISA memory within regions of memory programmed with the prefetchable attribute (in a '591 device-specific register). Optionally, the '591 can also be programmed to post PCI I/O writes initiated by the host processor. Any time the processor initiates a write to PCI/ISA memory in an area programmed to permit posting, the write is absorbed into the 64-bit PCI posted-write buffer. If the processor should initiate a subsequent memory write within the same quadword, the second write is merged into the bytes already in the buffer. This can result in non-contiguous byte enables asserted during the resulting PCI memory transaction, but this feature can be disabled. When disabled, the '591 uses a byte-reduction algorithm to generate two separate PCI memory writes utilizing only contiguous byte enables. Whenever the '591 has a PCI/ISA memory write posted in the buffer, it arbitrates for PCI bus ownership. When the bus has been acquired, it performs the memory write on the PCI bus. If the processor should initiate another PCI memory write prior to the conclusion of the one already in progress on the PCI bus, the processor is stalled until the write buffer becomes available at the completion of the current PCI memory write transaction. In addition, bus ownership requests from other PCI bus masters are ignored until the conclusion of the current transaction.

The '591 does not permit a processor-initiated PCI read transaction to be performed on the PCI bus if a processor write to PCI memory is currently-posted in the buffer. The buffer is first flushed to PCI memory before the read is performed on the PCI bus.

The processor initiates burst write operations during the castout of a modified line or a snoop push-back (write-back) operation). The posted-write buffer (located in the data buffers) can accept the burst data at full bus speed (0 wait states).

The write buffer permits posting of memory writes to PCI memory within regions of memory space defined as prefetchable by bridge configuration registers.

A status bit can be checked by software to determine if the write buffer is empty.

## Combining Writes Feature

The write buffer supports combining of writes. Assume that the processor performs a memory write to write two bytes into memory locations 00000100h and 00000101h. The processor outputs the following information:

- The quadword-aligned address placed on the host processor address bus is 00000100h.
- Byte enables [1:0] are asserted to indicate that the first two locations in the currently-addressed quadword are being addressed. Byte enables [7:2] are deasserted, indicating that the third through the eight locations in the quadword are not being addressed.
- The two bytes of data destined for memory locations 00000100h and 00000101h are driven onto data paths zero (D[7:0]) and one (D[15:8]).

The posted-write buffer latches the quadword address and the two bytes into the next available quadword location in its FIFO buffer. BRDY# is assert to the processor, permitting it to end the memory write transaction. Now assume that the processor initiates another memory write, this time to memory location 00000104h (before the buffer logic has written the previous two bytes into system DRAM memory). Assume that the processor outputs the following information:

- The quadword-aligned address placed on the host processor address bus is 00000100h.
- Byte enable [4] is asserted to indicate that the fifth location in the currently-addressed quadword is being addressed. Byte enables [7:5] and [3:0] are deasserted, indicating that the first through fourth and the sixth through the eight locations in the quadword are not being addressed.
- The byte of data destined for memory location 00000104h is driven onto data path four (D[39:32]).

The buffer recognizes that some portion of quadword 00000100h has already been posted to be written to memory. Instead of using up another quadword-wide buffer location for the new write, it combines the new data being supplied by the processor with the older data in the buffer location. The buffer location now contains three bytes to be written to quadword 00000100h in system DRAM. Although the processor performed two separate memory writes to system memory, the buffer logic only has to perform one write operation when it offloads the data to memory.

## Read-Around and Merge Features

If the processor initiates a read from system DRAM while one or more memory write operations reside within the posted-write buffer, the buffer logic performs the read from DRAM before flushing the writes to memory. If the read hits on a posted-write in the buffer, the bytes posted to be written to memory are merged with the data read from memory and the resulting data is supplied back to the processor.

## Write Buffer Prioritization

The '591 can be programmed to adjust the priority of posted-write buffer writes to memory relative to memory reads. The following settings are available:

- The write buffer can access memory whenever the DRAM is idle.
- The write buffer can access memory after a minimum of 2, 4, 8, 16, 32 or 64 CPU clocks from the completion of the last DRAM read. The count is restarted at the completion of each read. When any of these settings are selected, the write buffer is permitted to access memory when the proces-

sor generates an access that is not a read (e.g., another write or a PCI transaction).

- Write buffer access to system memory is permitted only when the processor generates a non-system memory read transaction.

## Configuration Mechanism

The '59x chipset implements PCI configuration mechanism number one (configuration address port at I/O location 0CF8h and configuration data port at I/O location 0CFCh).

## PCI Arbitration

The '591 incorporates the PCI bus arbiter. The arbiter supports the '591, the '593 and up to four additional PCI bus masters. The '591's REQ# and GNT# signals are internally connected to the arbiter. A single signal line is used by the '593 to request and be granted ownership of the PCI bus (refer to the section in this chapter entitled "'593 Characteristics When PCI Master." Optionally, the '593 may use one of the four REQ#/GNT# signal pairs for arbitration.

The '591 never generates fast back-to-back transactions because it doesn't know the address boundaries of different targets.

The priority scheme may be software selected as fixed or rotational. When fixed is selected, the '593's REQGNT# signal has highest priority. This guarantees DMA channels timely access to the bus. Then, in descending order of importance, the priorities of the other masters are master 3, master 2, master 1, master 0 and the processor. The processor has lowest priority. Whenever any of the PCI masters require access to the PCI bus, the '591 asserts HOLD to the processor and takes the bus away from it to grant to the most important PCI master.

When rotational priority is selected, the '593 has highest priority, with priority rotating between bus masters 0 through 3 and the host processor. Refer to figure 23-2.

The arbiter can be programmed to park the bus either on the '591 or on the last master that used the bus. The latter mode can only be selected when rotational priority has been selected.

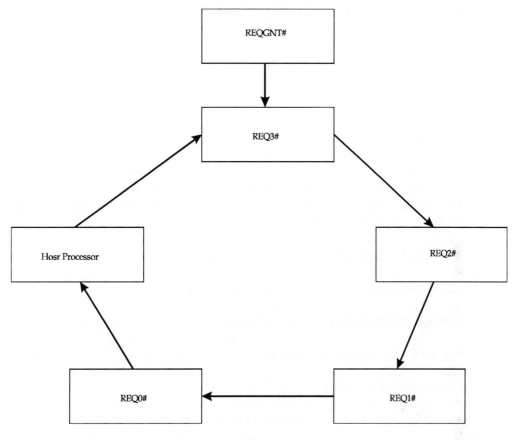

*Figure 23-2. Rotational Priority Scheme*

## Locking

The arbiter in the '591 implements a bus lock. It does not support target locking.

## Special Cycle Generation

Software can stimulate the host/PCI bridge to generate a PCI special cycle to PCI bus zero or to any of its subordinate PCI buses using the method defined for configuration mechanism number one; that is, the programmer performs a 32-bit write to the configuration address port specifying the target PCI bus, and sets the target device number, function number and doubleword number to 1Fh, 7h and 00h, respectively. The programmer then performs a two byte or four byte write to the configuration data port. The bridge performs a special cycle on the target PCI bus, supplying the data written to the configuration data port as the message during the data phase. If the target bus is a subordinate bus, the '591 generates a special cycle request using a type 1 configuration write transaction.

## '591 Configuration Registers

Figure 23-3 illustrates the '591's PCI configuration registers. The sections that follow define the manner in which the chipset implements each of these registers. For a description of the '591's device-specific configuration registers, refer to the chipset specification.

### Vendor ID Register

The vendor ID for VLSI Technology is 1004h.

### Device ID Register

The device ID for the '591 is 0005h.

### Command Register

Table 23-1 defines the '591's usage of its command register bits.

*Table 23-1. '591 Command Register Bit Assignment*

| Bit | Description |
|-----|-------------|
| 0 | **I/O enable bit**. Hardwired to zero because the '591 doesn't respond to any PCI I/O transactions. |
| 1 | **Memory enable bit**. When set to one, PCI bus masters can access system DRAM memory. Reset sets this bit to one. |
| 2 | **Master enable bit**. Hardwired to one because the '591 is always enabled to initiate PCI transactions. |
| 3 | **Special cycle monitor enable bit**. Hardwired to zero because the '591 does not monitor special cycles generated by other PCI masters. |
| 4 | **Memory write and invalidate enable bit**. Hardwired to zero because the '591 never generates the memory write and invalidate command. |
| 5 | **VGA color palette snoop enable bit**. Hardwired to zero. Only VGA-compatible devices and PCI-to-PCI bridges are required to implement this bit. |
| 6 | **Parity error response bit**. When set to one, the '591 asserts PERR# when a data parity error is detected. Also used to qualify the assertion of SERR# on address phase parity error. Reset clears this bit. |
| 7 | **Stepping enable bit**. Hardwired to zero because the '591 never uses address or data stepping. |
| 8 | **System error response bit**. When set to one, the '591 is enabled to assert SERR# (if the PARITY ERROR RESPONSE bit is also set to one) when address phase parity error detected or system DRAM parity error. Reset clears this bit. |
| 9 | **Fast back-to-back enable bit**. Hardwired to zero because the '591 never performs fast back-to-back transactions. |
| 15:10 | **Reserved** and hardwired to zero. |

## Status Register

Table 23-2 defines the '591's usage of its status register bits.

*Table 23-2. '591's Status Register Bit Assignment*

| Bit | Description |
|-----|-------------|
| 6:0 | **Reserved** and hardwired to zero. |
| 7 | **Fast back-to-back capable bit.** Hardwired to one, indicating that, when acting as a target, the '591 supports fast back-to-back transactions to different targets. |
| 8 | **Signaled parity error bit.** Set to one when the '591, acting as a master, samples PERR# asserted by the target during a write or the '591 asserts PERR# on a read. Reset clears this bit to zero. |
| 10:9 | **DEVSEL timing.** Hardwired to 01b, indicating that the '591 has a medium speed PCI address decoder. |
| 11 | **Signaled target abort.** Hardwired to zero because the '591 never signals a target abort. |
| 12 | **Received target abort.** Set to one when the '591 receives a target abort from a target when acting as master. Reset clears this bit to zero. |
| 13 | **Received master abort.** Set to one when the '591 experiences a master abort when acting as master. Reset clears this bit to zero. |
| 14 | **Signaled system error.** Set to one by the '591 when it assert SERR#. Reset clears this bit to zero. The SERR# ENABLE and PARITY ERROR RESPONSE bits in the '591's command register must be set to enable the '591 to generate SERR# and set this bit. |
| 15 | **Received parity error.** Set to one when the '591 detects an address or data phase parity error. Reset clears this bit to zero. |

## Revision ID Register

The revision ID register contains 00h in the first release of the '591.

## Class Code Register

The class code register contains 060000h. 06h specifies the bridge class. The middle byte, 00h, specifies that the sub-class is host/PCI bridge. The lower byte is always 00h for all revision 2.x-compliant devices.

## Cache Line Size Configuration Register

Not implemented. Since the '591 contains the cache controller, it "knows" the system cache line size.

## Latency Timer Register

Hardwired with a value of 10h (16d). When acting as a PCI bus master, the '591 never performs bursts of longer than two data phases. The specification states that any device that never performs more than two data phases may hardwire a value into its LT, but the value may not exceed 16d.

## Header Type Register

Hardwired with the value 00h. This indicates that the '591 is a single-function device (bit 7 = 0) and that the format of configuration doublewords 4 through 15 adheres to the header type zero definition.

## BIST Register

Hardwired to 00h. Bit 7 = 0 indicates that the '591 does not implement a built-in self test.

## Base Address Registers

None implemented. The '591 utilizes device-specific registers to set up its system DRAM address decoders. Regarding I/O, the '591 only implements two I/O ports: the configuration address port at I/O address 0CF8h and the configuration data port at I/O address 0CFCh. It has hardwired address decoders for these registers.

## Expansion ROM Base Address Register

Not implemented because the '591 does not incorporate a PCI device ROM.

## Interrupt Line Register

Not implemented because the '591 does not generate interrupt requests.

### Interrupt Pin Register

Hardwired with 00h, indicating that the '591 does not implement a PCI interrupt request output pin.

### Min_Gnt Register

The '591 incorporates the PCI bus arbiter and already knows its timeslice and intrinsically knows its own bus acquisition latency requirements.

### Max_Lat Register

See Min_Gnt register section (previous section).

### Bus Number Register

Hardwired to 00h, indicating that the PCI bus residing directly behind the '591 is PCI bus zero.

### Subordinate Bus Number Register

Hardwired to FFh. Any software requests to perform special cycles or configuration reads or writes on buses other than bus zero are therefore passed through the '591 as type one configuration accesses. If the target bus doesn't exist, the type one configuration access will terminate in a master abort.

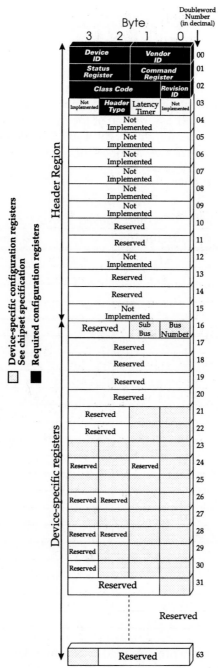

*Figure 23-3. '591 PCI Configuration Registers*

## PCI Device Selection (IDSEL)

When translating accesses to the configuration data port into PCI type zero configuration accesses, the '591 internally decodes the target device number specified in the configuration address port and selects an IDSEL to assert. Rather than implementing an IDSEL output for each physical device position on the PCI bus, the '591 asserts one of the upper AD lines during the address phase of the PCI configuration access. Table 23-3 defines the AD line asserted (set to one) for each device number that may be specified. On the system board, each physical device position resistively-couples one of the upper AD lines to the device's IDSEL input pin.

*Table 23-3. Device Number To AD Line Mapping*

| Device Number Specified (decimal) | AD Line Asserted |
|:---:|:---:|
| 0 | 11 * |
| 1 | 12 |
| 2 | 13 |
| 3 | 14 |
| 4 | 15 |
| 5 | 16 |
| 6 | 17 |
| 7 | 18 |
| 8 | 19 |
| 9 | 20 |
| 10 | 21 |
| 11 | 22 |
| 12 | 23 |
| 13 | 24 |
| 14 | 25 |
| 15 | 26 |
| 16 | 27 |
| 17 | 28 |
| 18 | 29 |
| 19 | 30 |
| 20 | 31 * |
| 21 - 31 | none |

* Note: the '591 may be programmed to be either device 0 or device 31.

# Chapter 23: Overview of VL82C59x PCI Chipset

## Handling of Host Processor-Initiated Transactions

### Memory Read

When the host processor initiates a memory (code or data) read transaction, one of the following is true:

- The target location is within the range of system DRAM memory.
- The target location falls within the range assigned to system DRAM memory, but is within a sub-range defined as PCI or ISA memory.
- The target location is above the top of installed system memory.

In the first case, the address is considered to be cacheable. The lookaside L2 cache performs a lookup to determine if the requested data is present in the cache. If present, the cache tells the DRAM controller to abort the access to system DRAM and the cache supplies the requested data to the processor. If the requested data isn't currently present in the L2 cache, the DRAM controller proceeds with the memory read to fetch the target line. If the read hits on any posted-writes currently outstanding in the posted-write buffer, the write data is merged with the data read from memory and the requested data is supplied to the processor. The L2 cache also latches a copy of the line of information. If the L2 cache line size is 64 bytes, the cache initiates a second line read from memory to load the second half of its line into the L2 cache.

In the second and third cases, the '591 arbitrates for ownership of the PCI bus and initiates a memory read transaction (note that if the processor already has a PCI memory write posted in the '591, the posted write will be flushed to PCI memory before the PCI memory read is initiated). Because the L2 and L1 caches are not permitted to cache from memory beyond the bridge, the resulting PCI memory read transaction does not fetch an entire line (32 bytes) from memory. Rather, the access consists of one or two data phases (at most, the processor is expecting to get back eight bytes of information). When the PCI memory read transaction is initiated, DEVSEL# is asserted if a memory target on the PCI bus recognizes that it is the target of the transaction. That target then supplies the requested data to the '591 and the '591 supplies it to the processor. If no PCI memory target asserts DEVSEL#, the subtractive decoder built into the '593 eventually asserts DEVSEL# and claims the transaction. The transaction is passed to the ISA bus. If an ISA memory target recognizes the address, that target supplies the data. If the address is not recognized by any ISA memory target, the ISA bus controller in the '593 latches all ones from the

ISA data bus (its quiescent state when not being driven) and that is sent back to the '591 and then to the processor.

Note that the '591 can be programmed to recognize that specific PCI memory regions support prefetching. In this case, when the '591 performs the PCI memory read, it asserts all four byte enables and fetches the entire double-word being addressed in the data phase (even if the processor had only requested a subset of the doubleword). The requested data is fed back to the processor and the prefetched bytes within the doubleword are stored in the '591's read-ahead buffer. This buffer can hold a quadword of data. If the processor should subsequently request any of the prefetched data, the data is supplied from the read-ahead buffer and the '591 does not perform a PCI memory read transaction.

## Memory Write

When the host processor initiates a memory write transaction, there are the same three cases:

- The target location is within the range of system DRAM memory.
- The target location falls within the range assigned to system DRAM memory, but is within a sub-range defined as PCI or ISA memory.
- The target location is above the top of installed system memory.

In the first case, the memory write is absorbed by the posted-write buffer (if the eight quadword FIFO isn't full). The processor can then initiate another transaction immediately. If the buffer is full, the processor's current memory write stalls.

In the second and third case, there are two possible cases:

- Memory write posting is enabled for the addressed area of PCI memory .
- Memory write posting is disabled for that area.

If write posting is enabled and the write buffer is currently-available, the memory write is absorbed by the buffer and the processor is permitted to end its transaction. The '591 then initiates the PCI memory write when it has acquired PCI bus ownership. If write posting is disabled in the target area, the processor is stalled until the PCI memory write has been completed on the PCI bus.

# Chapter 23: Overview of VL82C59x PCI Chipset

## I/O Read

When the processor initiates an I/O read transaction, the target device is one of the following:

- Configuration address port at I/O location 0CF8h.
- Configuration data port at I/O location 0CFCh.
- A PCI or an ISA I/O target device.

In the first two cases, the transaction is not passed through to the PCI bus. These two ports are integrated into the '591. The '591 therefore supplies the requested data directly to the host processor.

In the third case, the '591 stalls the processor until the PCI target (or the '593) supplies the requested data. The data is then routed to the processor, concluding the transaction.

## I/O Write

When the processor initiates an I/O write transaction, the target location is one of the following:

- Configuration address port at I/O location 0CF8h.
- Configuration data port at I/O location 0CFCh.
- A PCI or an ISA I/O target,

In the first two cases, the '591 accepts the write data into the target port and the transaction is not passed to the PCI bus.

In the third case, the transaction must be passed to the PCI bus. By default, the '591 does not post I/O writes, but it can be programmed to do so. Assuming I/O write posting is disabled, the processor is stalled until the '591 acquires ownership of the PCI bus and completes the PCI I/O write transaction.

## Interrupt Acknowledge

In response to an external interrupt from an 8259A interrupt controller, the processor generates two, back-to-back interrupt acknowledge transactions. The first one is generated to command the interrupt controller to prioritize its pending requests. The processor does not transfer data during this transaction. The processor generates the second interrupt acknowledge to request the interrupt vector associated with the highest-priority pending request. When the '591 detects the first interrupt acknowledge, it responds with BRDY# to permit the processor to end the transaction. This transaction is not passed through the bridge. When the '591 detects the initiation of the second interrupt acknowledge, it acquires ownership of the PCI bus and performs an interrupt acknowledge transaction. In response, the '593 internally generates two INTA (interrupt acknowledge) pulses to the two 8259A cores that reside inside the '593. During the second INTA, the interrupt controller gates the one byte vector onto PCI data path zero, AD[7:0], and asserts TRDY#. The '591 is already asserting IRDY# so the '591 latches the vector from the AD bus and terminates the transfer. During this period, the '591 has been stalling the processor by keeping BRDY# deasserted until the data is presented on the processor's data bus. The vector is placed on host data path zero, D[7:0], and BRDY# is asserted. The processor latches the vector, concluding the second interrupt acknowledge transaction.

## Special Cycle

The host processor is capable of generating the following types of special cycle transactions:

- Shutdown.
- Flush.
- Halt.
- Writeback.
- Flush Acknowledge.
- Branch Trace Message.
- Stop/Grant.

The '591 only passes shutdown, halt and stop/grant through the bridge to the PCI bus. The shutdown special cycle causes the '591 to generate a PCI special cycle transaction with the shutdown message sent during the data phase. The halt special cycle causes the '591 to generate a PCI special cycle transaction with the halt message sent during the data phase. The stop/grant special cycle causes the '591 to generate a PCI special cycle transaction with the halt message sent during the data phase. The stop/grant message is differentiated from a halt by AD4 set to one during the address phase (rather than low for a halt). The '593 is designed to test the state of AD4 during the address phase to determine if the message is a halt or a stop/grant. The other processor-initiated special cycles have the following effects:

- The flush special cycle transaction causes the '591 to invalidate the L2 cache.

- The writeback special cycle transaction has no effect (because the L2 cache is not a writeback cache and therefore does not have any modified lines to be written back to memory).

- The flush acknowledge special cycle transaction is generated by the processor in response to assertion of its FLUSH# input when it has completed writing back all modified lines to memory and has cleared the L1 cache. The author believes (but isn't certain) that the '591 ignores this transaction.

- If enabled to do so, the processor generates the branch trace message special cycle transaction whenever a branch instruction is taken. The '591 ignores this transaction.

## Handling of PCI-Initiated Transactions

### General

The following sections describe how the '591 responds to transactions initiated on the PCI bus by other masters. It's important to note that the '591 does not support concurrent operation of the host and PCI buses. In other words, when a PCI master other than the '591 has acquired ownership of the PCI bus, it has also acquired ownership of the host bus. The '591 accomplishes this by asserting HOLD to the processor and waiting until HLDA is asserted, indicating that the processor has released ownership of the host bus. The '591's PCI arbiter then grants ownership of both buses to the PCI master. The transaction initiated by the PCI master is passed through to the host bus so that the PCI master can access system DRAM memory (if this is a memory read or write transaction that targets system DRAM). If the transaction is not a memory transaction, or it is a memory transaction, but the target address is not system DRAM memory, then the DRAM controller, L2 cache and the processor (which is not told to snoop) ignore the transaction.

### PCI Master Accesses System DRAM

The '591 aliases all three of the PCI memory read transaction types (memory read, memory read line, memory read multiple) to the PCI memory read transaction. If it is a memory transaction and the target address is system DRAM, the following actions are taken:

- The processor's L1 cache is told to snoop the address (via AHOLD and EADS#) and report the snoop result (on HIT# and HITM#).
- The L2 cache performs a lookup.

If the L1 snoop results in a miss or a hit on a clean line (HITM# is not asserted), the PCI master is permitted to continue with the transaction.

1. If a read and the requested data is present in the L2 cache, the L2 cache supplies the data to the PCI master. This is a nice feature. If the PCI master is accessing a data structure that is shared by the host processor, the resulting L2 cache hits can result in remarkable performance for the PCI master.
2. If a read and the requested data is not present in the L2 cache, the DRAM controller accesses system DRAM and the data is supplied to the PCI master from system dram.
3. If a write, the posted-write buffer absorbs the write data from the PCI master. If the L2 and/or L1 caches have a hit, the cache copies of the line are invalidated. If the data isn't resident in either cache, the write has no effect on the caches. The memory write and invalidate command is treated as a memory write.

## PCI Master Accesses PCI or ISA Memory

Although the transaction is presented on the host bus, it has no effect on the L1 or L2 caches or on system memory.

## PCI Master Accesses Non-Existent Memory

In this case, the '593 asserts DEVSEL# (due to subtractive decode) and passes the transaction to the ISA bus. The '591 passes the transaction to the host bus, but it has no effect (because the target address is not within range of system DRAM memory).

## I/O Read or Write Initiated by PCI Master

Although passed to the host bus by the '591, have no effect.

## Special Cycle

The '591 ignores special cycle transactions generated by PCI masters.

## Type 0 Configuration Read or Write

A PCI master may access the '591's PCI configuration registers by directly generating the standard type 0 configuration read and write transactions. It cannot use the configuration address and data ports to stimulate the '591 to generate configuration transactions because the '591 would then have to use the PCI bus at the same time that the PCI master was using it.

## Type 1 Configuration Read or Write

A PCI master may use a type one configuration transaction to access the configuration registers in a device on another PCI bus or to cause the generation of a special cycle on a specified target PCI bus. The '591 is unaffected by these transaction types.

## Dual-Address Command (64-bit Addressing)

Because the system DRAM memory resides in the area up to but not above the 1GB address boundary, the detection of a PCI dual-address command has no effect on the '591.

## Support for Fast Back-to-Back Transactions

The '591 can act as the target of fast back-to-back transactions, but cannot initiate them when acting as a PCI master.

# '593 PCI/ISA Bridge

The '593 provides the following functionality:

- Bridges the PCI and ISA buses.
- Two 8259A interrupt controllers and the APIC I/O module.
- Two 8237A DMA controllers and their associated page registers.
- Real-Time Clock and CMOS RAM function (or, alternately, supports external RTC/CMOS).
- Port B logic.
- Tunable subtractive decoder (can be tuned to assert DEVSEL# in slow time slot).
- Programmable decoders for memory regions that exists on the ISA bus. This permits fast address decode of PCI accesses to the ISA bus. It also

permits memory accesses initiated by ISA bus masters or DMA channels to be contained on the ISA bus and not be passed to the PCI bus.

- Handles shutdown-to-processor INIT conversion. When a PCI special cycle transaction is detected with the shutdown message, the '593 toggles INIT to force a system reboot.
- A20 mask function.
- Processor self-test initiation.
- FERR# to IRQ13 conversion.
- NMI generation. The '593 generates NMI when CHCHK is asserted on the ISA bus, or when SERR# is asserted on the PCI bus.
- Hot reset generation.
- System Management Mode (SMM) interrupt logic.
- Monitors up to 27 different events related to power management.
- Includes watchdog timer for SMM usage.
- Supports software generation of the system management interrupt.
- Includes logic utilized to stop the processor clock.
- Positive decode for system ROM and keyboard controller, permitting fast address decode within these ranges.
- POWERGOOD/Reset logic.
- Speaker timer.
- Support for turbo mode. Can be used to periodically stop the processor's clock to make the processor appear to run slower.
- Integrated X-bus buffers.
- Can increase ISA BUSCLOCK speed up to 16MHZ within specified ISA memory regions.
- Decoupled ISA memory refresh. ISA memory refresh can occur on the ISA bus while PCI transactions are in progress.
- Supports disabling of internal DMA controllers (permitting implementation of an external DMA controller).

## '593 Handling of Transactions Initiated by PCI Masters

The '593 responds to PCI transactions as follows:

- When acting as the target of a multiple-data phase PCI transaction, the '593 always disconnects the master upon completion of the first data phase.

- The '593 treats the PCI memory read line and read multiple commands as a memory read.
- The '593 treats the PCI memory write and invalidate command as a memory write.
- The '593 ignores the PCI dual-address command.
- The '593 can respond as the target of fast back-to-back transactions, but cannot generate them.
- The '593 responds to the PCI interrupt acknowledge transaction by claiming the transaction and returning the interrupt vector on the lower data path.
- When the '593 detects a PCI special cycle transaction, it determines if the message delivered during the data phase is a shutdown or a halt (it ignores all other message types). If a shutdown, it issues INIT to the processor to reboot the system. If a halt, it examines the state of AD4 from the transaction's address phase. If AD4 = 0, the processor is halting. The SMM logic can be programmed to take action on this event. If AD4 = 1, the message is really a stop/grant message. This informs the SMM logic that the processor has stopped its clock in response to assertion of STPCLK# by the '593.
- The '593 ignores type one configuration read and writes. A type zero configuration read or write that asserts the '593's IDSEL is permitted to access the '593's PCI configuration registers.
- The '593 handles address and data phase parity errors according to the revision 2.x PCI specification.
- The posted-memory write buffer in the '593 can be enabled/disabled by software. When enabled, the buffer accepts up to 32-bits of write data being presented by a PCI master and then disconnects. It then performs the memory write on the ISA bus. If a PCI master attempts to access the ISA bus while the posted-write is being performed on the ISA bus, the '593 stalls it (by keeping TRDY# deasserted) until the write completes.

## Subtractive Decode Capability

The subtractive decoder in the '593 claims any unclaimed PCI memory access (even to addresses above 16MB). This means that areas of memory space above the top of system DRAM memory and above 16MB and not populated by PCI memory devices alias down into ISA's 16MB memory address space.

The subtractive decoder can be tuned to respond with slow DEVSEL#, rather than the normal subtractive DEVSEL# one clock after the slow time slot.

## '593 Characteristics When Acting as PCI Master

The '591 incorporates the PCI bus arbiter. When the '593 must pass an ISA bus master or DMA transaction onto the PCI bus, the '593 must issue a request to the '591 and await assertion of its grant. The '59x chipset can handle the arbitration between the '591 and the '593 in one of two ways (software-selectable):

1. The '593 normally drives its REQGNT# output high. When it requires access to the PCI bus, it drives REQGNT# low for one cycle of the processor's bus clock. One clock after that, the '591 takes ownership of the REQGNT# signal and drives it high. The '591 continues to drive REQGNT# high until the arbiter is going to grant the bus to the '593. The '591 then drives REQGNT# low for one cycle of the processor's bus clock. One clock after that, the '593 resumes ownership of the REQGNT# signal and continues to drive it low until it has completed using the PCI bus. When the '593 has concluded using the PCI bus, it drives REQGNT# high and leaves it high until it requires the PCI bus again.
2. Alternately, the '593 and '591 can use a normal PCI REQ#/GNT# signal pair for '593 bus arbitration.

When acting as the PCI master, the '593 cannot generate fast back-to-back transactions.

The '593 recognizes that the arbiter is parking the bus on it when it detects its GNT# asserted and the bus is idle. The '593 then takes ownership of the AD and C/BE buses and drives them low. One clock after driving them low, the '593 drives PAR low.

The '593 only initiates transactions on the PCI bus because:

- A DMA channel is performing a transfer to or from system memory.
- An ISA bus master is performing a system memory or an I/O read or write.

The only types of PCI transactions it generates are therefore memory and I/O read and write transactions.

## Interrupt Support

The '593 incorporates two 8259A interrupt controllers and an advanced programmable interrupt controller (APIC) I/O module. All of the system interrupt request signals, IRQ[15:0], are connected in parallel to the pair of 8259A's and to the APIC. This permits the programmer to set up the '593's interrupt logic to handle requests in an 8259A-compatible manner, or, in a multiprocessing environment, to route all interrupts from ISA and PCI to the APIC for delivery to the processors. A description of 8259A and APIC operation is outside the scope of this book. A complete description of the 8259A interrupt controller operation can be found in the Addison-Wesley publication (also authored by MindShare) entitled *ISA System Architecture*. A complete description of the APIC operation can be found in the Addison-Wesley publication (also authored by MindShare) entitled *Pentium Processor System Architecture*.

Eleven of the system IRQ inputs, IRQ[15:14], [12:9], and [7:3] may be individually programmed as either shareable or non-shareable interrupt request lines. Of these eleven, the '593's four PCI interrupt inputs may be routed to any of eight of them (IRQ[15:14], [12:9], [5], and [3]).

## DMA Support

The '593 incorporates two 8237A DMA controllers in a master/slave configuration. It also incorporates the page registers necessary to extend the start address registers to a full 32 bits. This enables the DMA controller to transfer data to or from memory anywhere within the 4GB memory address space. It is a constraint, however, that the specified DMA transfer in memory must reside fully with a 64KB-aligned block of memory space (because the 8237A DMA controller cannot issue a carry to the page register when incrementing over a 64KB address boundary).

## '593 Configuration Registers

Figure 23-4 illustrates the '593's usage of its PCI configuration space. The sections that follow define the manner in which the chipset implements each of these registers. For a description of the '593's device-specific configuration registers, refer to the chipset specification.

## Vendor ID Register

The vendor ID for VLSI Technology is 1004h.

## Device ID Register

The device ID for the '593 is 0006h.

## Command Register

Table 23-4 defines the '593's usage of its command register bits.

*Table 23-4. '593's Command Register Bit Assignment*

| Bit | Description |
|-----|-------------|
| 0 | **I/O enable bit**. When set one, the '593 is enabled to respond to PCI I/O transactions. Reset sets this bit to one. |
| 1 | **Memory enable bit**. When set to one, PCI bus masters can access ISA memory. Reset sets this bit to one. |
| 2 | **Master enable bit**. When set to one, the '593 is enabled to initiate PCI transactions. Reset sets this bit to one. |
| 3 | **Special cycle monitor enable bit**. When set to one, the '593 recognizes special cycles (only shutdown and halt) generated by other PCI masters (usually, the '591). Reset sets this bit to one. |
| 4 | **Memory write and invalidate enable bit**. Hardwired to zero because the '593 never generates the memory write and invalidate command. |
| 5 | **VGA color palette snoop enable bit**. Hardwired to zero. Only VGA-compatible devices and PCI-to-PCI bridges are required to implement this bit. |
| 6 | **Parity error response bit**. When set to one, the '593 asserts PERR# when a data parity error is detected. Also used to qualify the assertion of SERR# on address phase parity error. Reset clears this bit. |
| 7 | **Stepping enable bit**. Hardwired to zero because the '593 never uses address or data stepping. |
| 8 | **System error response bit**. When set to one, the '593 is enabled to assert SERR# (if the PARITY ERROR RESPONSE bit is also set to one) when address phase parity error detected. Reset clears this bit. |
| 9 | **Fast back-to-back enable bit**. Hardwired to zero because the '593 never performs fast back-to-back transactions. |
| 15:10 | **Reserved** and hardwired to zero. |

## Status Register

The '593's configuration status register bit assignment is defined in table 23-5.

*Table 23-5. '593's Status Register Bit Assignment*

| Bit | Description |
|-----|-------------|
| 6:0 | **Reserved** and hardwired to zero. |
| 7 | **Fast back-to-back capable bit.** Hardwired to one, indicating that, when acting as a target, the '593 supports fast back-to-back transactions to different targets. |
| 8 | **Signaled parity error bit.** Set to one when the '593, acting as a master, samples PERR# asserted by the target during a write or the '593 asserts PERR# on a read. Reset clears this bit to zero. |
| 10:9 | **DEVSEL timing.** Hardwired to 01b, indicating that the '593 has a medium speed PCI address decoder. |
| 11 | **Signaled target abort.** Set to one when the '593 has signaled a target abort to the initiator of a transaction. Reset clears this bit to zero. |
| 12 | **Received target abort.** Set to one when the '593 receives a target abort from a target when acting as master. Reset clears this bit to zero. |
| 13 | **Received master abort.** Set to one when the '593 experiences a master abort when acting as master. Reset clears this bit to zero. |
| 14 | **Signaled system error.** Set to one by the '593 when it assert SERR#. Reset clears this bit to zero. The SERR# ENABLE and PARITY ERROR RESPONSE bits in the '593's command register must be set to enable the '593 to generate SERR# and set this bit. |
| 15 | **Received parity error.** Set to one when the '593 detects an address or data phase parity error. Reset clears this bit to zero. |

## Revision ID Register

The revision ID register contains 00h in the first release of the '593.

## Class Code Register

The class code register contains 060100h. 06h specifies the bridge class. The middle byte, 01h, specifies that the sub-class is ISA/PCI bridge. The lower byte is always 00h for all revision 2.x-compliant devices.

### Cache Line Size Configuration Register

Not implemented.

### Latency Timer Register

Not implemented. When acting as a PCI master, the '593 only performs single data phase transactions initiated by ISA bus masters and DMA channels.

### Header Type Register

Hardwired with the value 00h. This indicates that the '593 is a single-function device (bit 7 = 0) and that the format of configuration doublewords four through 15 adheres to the header type zero definition.

### BIST Register

Hardwired to 00h. Bit 7 = 0 indicates that the '593 does not implement a built-in self test.

### Base Address Registers

None implemented. The '593 utilizes device-specific registers to set up its ISA, ROM and I/O address decoders.

### Expansion ROM Base Address Register

Not implemented because the '593 does not incorporate a PCI device ROM.

### Interrupt Line Register

Not implemented because the '593 does not generate interrupt requests for itself.

### Interrupt Pin Register

Hardwired with 00h, indicating that the '593 does not implement a PCI interrupt request output pin.

## Min_Gnt Register

Hardwired to 00h, indicating that the '593 has no specific requirements regarding the timeslice assigned to it. In addition, the '593 does not implement
the LT, so the Min_Gnt register is a moot point.

## Max_Lat Register

Hardwired to 00h, indicating that the '593 has no specific requirements regarding its arbitration priority level.

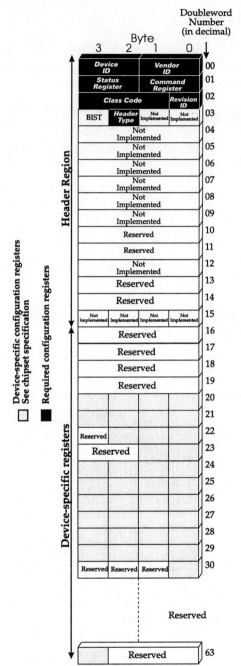

*Figure 23-4. VL82C593's Configuration Registers*

**Access Latency**. The amount of time that expires from the moment a bus master requests the use of the PCI bus until it completes the first data transfer of the transaction.

**AD Bus**. The PCI address/data bus carries address information during the address phase of a transaction and data during each data phase.

**Address Ordering**. During PCI burst memory transfers, the initiator must indicate whether the addressing sequence will be sequential (also referred to as linear) or will use cacheline wrap ordering of addresses. The initiator uses the state of AD[1:0] to indicate the addressing order. During I/O accesses, there is no explicit or implicit address ordering. It is the responsibility of the programmer to understand the I/O addressing characteristic of the target device.

**Address Phase**. During the first clock period of a PCI transaction, the initiator outputs the start address and the PCI command. This period is referred to as the address phase of the transaction. When 64-bit addressing is used, there are two address phases.

**Agents**. Each PCI device, whether a bus master (initiator) or a target is referred to as a PCI agent.

**Arbiter**. The arbiter is the device that evaluates the pending requests for access to the bus and grants the bus to a bus master based on a system-specific algorithm.

**Arbitration Latency**. The period of time from the bus master's assertion of REQ# until the bus arbiter asserts the bus master's GNT#. This period is a function of the arbitration algorithm, the master's priority and system utilization.

**Atomic Operation**. A series of two or more accesses to a device by the same initiator without intervening accesses by other bus masters.

**Base Address Registers**. Device configuration registers that define the start address, length and type of memory space required by a device. The type of space required will be either memory or I/O. The value written to this register during device configuration will program its memory or I/O address decoder to detect accesses within the indicated range.

**BIST**. Some integrated devices (such as the i486 microprocessor) implement a built-in self-test that can be invoked by external logic during system start up.

**Bridge**. The device that provides the bridge between two independent buses. Examples would be the bridge between the host processor bus and the PCI bus, the bridge between the PCI bus and a standard expansion bus (such as the ISA bus) and the bridge between two PCI buses.

**Bus Access Latency**. Defined as the amount of time that expires from the moment a bus master requests the use of the PCI bus until it completes the first data transfer of the transaction. In other words, it is the sum of arbitration, bus acquisition and target latency.

**Bus Acquisition Latency**. Defined as the period time from the reception of GNT# by the requesting bus master until the current bus master surrenders the bus and the requesting bus master can initiate its transaction by asserting FRAME#. The duration of this period is a function of how long the current bus master's transaction-in-progress will take to complete.

**Bus Concurrency**. Separate transfers occurring simultaneously on two or more separate buses. An example would be an EISA bus master transferring data to or from another EISA device while the host processor is transferring data to or from system memory.

**Bus Idle State.** A transaction is not currently in progress on the bus. On the PCI bus, this state is signalled when FRAME# and IRDY# are both deasserted.

**Bus Lock.** Gives a bus master sole access to the bus while it performs a series of two or more transfers. This can be implemented on the PCI bus, but the preferred method is resource locking. The EISA bus implements bus locking..

**Bus Master.** A device capable of initiating a data transfer with another device.

**Bus Parking.** An arbiter may grant the buses to a bus master when the bus is idle and no bus masters are generating a request for the bus. If the bus master that the bus is parked on subsequently issues a request for the bus, it has immediate access to the bus.

**Byte Enable.** I486, Pentium™ or PCI Bus control signal that indicates that a particular data path will be used during a transfer. Indirectly, the byte enable signal also indicates what byte within an addressed doubleword (or quadword, during 64-bit transfers) is being addressed.

**Cache.** A relatively small amount of high-speed Static RAM (SRAM) that is used to keep copies of information recently read from system DRAM memory. The cache controller maintains a directory that tracks the information currently resident within the cache. If the host processor should request any of the information currently resident in the cache, it will be returned to the processor quickly (due to the fast access time of the SRAM).

**Cache Controller.** See the definition of **Cache**.

**Cache Line Fill.** When a processor's internal cache, or its external second level cache has a miss on a read attempt by the processor, it will read a fixed amount (referred to as a line) of information from the external cache or system DRAM memory and record it in the cache. This is referred to as a cache line fill. The size of a line of information is cache controller design dependent.

**Cache Line Size.** See the definition of **Cache Line Fill**.

**CacheLine Wrap Mode.** At the start of each data phase of the burst read, the memory target increments the doubleword address in its address counter. When the end of the cache line is encountered and assuming that the transfer did not start at the first doubleword of the cache line, the target wraps to start address of the cacheline and continues incrementing the address in each data phase until the entire cache line has been transferred. If the burst continues past the point where the entire cache line has been transferred, the target starts the transfer of the next cache line at the same address that the transfer of the previous line started at.

**CAS Before RAS Refresh, or CBR Refresh.** Some DRAMs incorporate their own row counters to be used for DRAM refresh. The external DRAM refresh logic has only to activate the DRAM's CAS line and then its RAS line. The DRAM will automatically increment its internal row counter and refresh (recharge) the next row of storage.

**CBR Refresh.** See the definition of **CAS Before RAS Refresh**.

**Central Resource Functions.** Functions that are essential to operation of the PCI bus. Examples would be the PCI bus arbiter and "keeper" pullup resistors that return PCI control signals to their quiescent state or maintain them at the quiescent state once driven there by a PCI agent.

**Claiming the Transaction**. An initiator starts a PCI transaction by placing the target device's address on the AD bus and the command on the C/BE bus. All PCI targets latch the address on the next rising-edge of the PCI clock and begin to decode the address to determined if they are being addressed. The target that recognizes the address will "claim" the transaction by asserting DEVSEL#.

**Class Code**. Identifies the generic function of the device (for example, a display device) and, in some cases, a register-specific programming interface (such as the VGA register set). The upper byte defines a basic class type, the middle byte a sub-class within the basic class, and the lower byte may define the programming interface.

**Coherency**. If the information resident in a cache accurately reflects the original information in DRAM memory, the cache is said to be coherent or consistent.

**Commands**. During the address phase of a PCI transaction, the initiator broadcasts a command (such as the memory read command) on the C/BE bus.

**Compatibility Hole**. The DOS compatibility hole is defined as the memory address range from 80000h - FFFFFh. Depending on the function implemented within any of these memory address ranges, the area of memory will have to be defined in one of the following ways: Read-Only, Write-Only, Read/Writable, Inaccessible.

**Concurrent Bus Operation**. See the definition of **Bus Concurrency**.

**Configuration Access**. A PCI transaction to read or write the contents of one of a PCI device's configuration registers.

**Configuration Address Space**. x86 processors possess the ability to address two distinct address spaces: I/O and memory. The PCI bus uses I/O and memory accesses to access I/O and memory devices, respectively. In addition, a third access type, the configuration access, is used to access the configuration registers that must be implemented in all PCI devices.

**Configuration CMOS RAM**. The information used to configure devices each time an ISA, EISA or Micro Channel™ machine is powered up is stored in battery backed-up CMOS RAM.

**Configuration Header Region**. Each functional PCI device possesses a block of two hundred and fifty-six configuration addresses reserved for implementation of its configuration registers. The format, or usage, of the first sixty-four locations is predefined by the PCI specification. This area is referred to as the device's configuration header region.

**Consistency**. See the definition of **Coherency**.

**Data Packets**. In order to improve throughput, a PCI bridge may consolidate a series of single memory reads or writes into a single PCI memory burst transfer.

**Data Phase**. After the address phase of a PCI transaction, a data item will be transferred during each data phase of the transaction. The data is transferred when both TRDY# and IRDY# are sampled asserted.

**Deadlock**. A deadlock is a condition where two masters each require access to a target simultaneously, but the action taken by each will prevent the desired action of the other.

**Direct-Mapped Cache**. In a direct-mapped cache, the cache is the same size as a page in memory. When a line of information is fetched from a position within a page of DRAM memory, it is stored in the same relative position within the cache. If the processor should subsequently request a line of information from the same relative position within a different page of memory, the cache controller will fetch the new line from memory and must overwrite the line currently in the cache.

**Dirty Line**. A write-back cache controller has cached a line of information from memory. The processor subsequently performs a memory write to a location within the cache line. There is a hit on the cache and the cache line is updated with the new information, but the cache controller will not perform a memory write bus cycle to update the line in memory. The line in the cache no longer reflects the line in memory and now has the latest information. The cache line is said to be "dirty" and the memory line is "stale." Dirty is another way of saying "modified."

**Disconnect**. A very slow access target may force a disconnect between accesses to give other initiators a chance to use the bus. This is known as a disconnect. If the current access is quite long and will consume a lot of bus time, the target signals a disconnect, completes the current data phase, and the initiator terminates the transaction. The initiator then arbitrates for the bus again so that it may re-initiate the transaction, continuing the data transfer at the point of disconnection.

**DOS Compatibility Hole**. See the definition of **Compatibility Hole.**

**DRAM controller**. The DRAM controller converts memory read or write bus cycles on the host or PCI bus to the proper sequence of actions on the memory bus to access the target DRAM location.

**EISA**. Extension to Industry Standard Architecture. The EISA specification was developed to extend the capabilities of the ISA machine architecture to support more advanced features such as bus arbitration and faster types of bus transfers.

**Exclusive Access**. A series of accesses to a target by one bus master while other masters are prevented from accessing the device.

**Expansion ROM**. A device ROM related to a PCI function. This ROM typically contains the initialization code and possibly the BIOS and interrupt service routines for its associated device.

**Functional PCI Devices**. A PCI device that performs a single, self-contained function. Examples would be a video adapter or a serial port. A single, physical PCI component might actually contain from one to eight PCI functional devices.

**Hidden bus arbitration**. Unlike some arbitration schemes, the PCI scheme allows bus arbitration to take place at the same time that the current PCI bus master is performing a data transfer. No bus time is wasted on a dedicated period of time to perform an arbitration bus cycle. This is referred to as hidden arbitration.

**Hidden Refresh**. If a DRAM controller uses the memory bus to perform DRAM refresh when the system is currently accessing a device other than DRAM memory, this is referred to as hidden refresh. Refreshing DRAM in this fashion doesn't impact system performance.

**Hierarchical PCI Buses**. When one PCI bus is subordinate to another PCI bus, they are arranged in a hierarchical order. A PCI-to-PCI bridge would interconnect the two buses.

**Hit**. Refers to a hit on the cache. The processor initiates a memory read or write and the cache controller has a copy of the target line in its cache.

**Host/PCI Bridge**. A device that provides the bridge between the host processor's bus and a PCI bus. The bridge provides transaction translation in both directions. It may also provide data buffering and/or a second-level cache for the host processor.

**Idle State**. See the definition for the **Bus Idle State**.

**Incident-Wave Switching**. See the definition of **Class I Driver**.

**Initiator**. When a bus master has arbitrated for and won access to the PCI bus, it becomes the initiator of a transaction. It then starts a transaction, asserting FRAME# and driving the address and command onto the bus.

**Interrupt Acknowledge**. The host ix86 processor responds to an interrupt request on its INTR input by generating two, back-to-back interrupt acknowledge bus cycles. If the interrupt controller resides on the PCI bus, the host/PCI bridge translates the two cycles into a single PCI interrupt acknowledge bus cycle. In response to an interrupt acknowledge, the interrupt controller must send the interrupt vector corresponding to the highest priority device generating a request back to the processor.

**Interrupt Controller**. A device requiring service from the host processor generates a request to the interrupt controller. The interrupt controller, in turn, generates a request to the host processor on its INTR signal line. When the host processor responds with an interrupt acknowledge, the interrupt controller prioritizes the pending requests and returns the interrupt vector of the highest priority device to the processor.

**Level-Two, or L2, Cache**. The host processor's internal cache is frequently referred to as the primary, or level-one cache. An external cache that attempts to service misses on the internal cache is referred to as the level-two cache.

**Line**. See the definition of **Cache Line Fill**.

**Line Buffer**. If a device has a buffer that can hold an entire line of information previously fetched from memory, the buffer is frequently referred to as a line buffer.

**Linear Addressing**. If a PCI master initiates a burst memory transfer and sets AD[1:0] equal to a 00b, this indicates to the addressed target that the memory address should be incremented for each subsequent data phase of the transaction.

**Local Bus**. Generally, refers to the processor's local bus structure. An example would be the 486's bus structure.

**Look-Through Cache Controller**. A cache controller that resides between its associated processor and the rest of the world is referred to as a look-through cache controller. Look-through cache controllers are divided into two categories: write-through and write-back.

**Master Abort**. If an initiator starts a PCI transaction and the transaction isn't claimed by a target (DEVSEL# asserted) within five PCI clock periods, the initiator aborts the transaction with no data transfer.

**Master Latency Timer**. Each bus master must incorporate a Latency Timer, or LT. The LT benefits both the current bus master and any bus master that may request access to the PCI bus while the current bus master is performing a transaction. The LT ensures that the current bus master will not hog the bus if the PCI bus arbitrator indicates that another PCI master is requesting access to the bus. Looking at it from another point of view, it guarantees the current bus master a minimum amount of time on the bus before it must surrender it to another master.

**Master-Initiated Termination**. The LT count may have expired and the transaction continued without preemption by the arbitrator (removal of its grant) because no other PCI master required the bus. Another bus master may then request and be granted the bus while the current master still has a transaction in progress. Upon sensing the removal of its grant by the arbitrator, the current bus master must initiate transaction termination at the end of the current data transfer with the target. This is referred to as master-initiated termination.

**Memory Read Command**. The PCI memory read command should be used when reading less than a cache line from memory.
**Memory Read Line Command**. This PCI command should be used to fetch one complete cache line from memory.

**Memory Read Multiple Command**. This command should be used to fetch multiple memory cache lines from memory. When this command is used, the target memory device should fetch the requested cache line from memory. When the requested line has been fetched from memory, the memory controller should start fetching the next line from memory in anticipation of a request from the initiator. The memory controller should continue to prefetch lines from memory as long as the initiator keeps FRAME# asserted.

**Memory Write Command**. The initiator may use the PCI memory write or the memory write and invalidate command to update data in memory.

**Memory Write and Invalidate Command**. The memory write and invalidate command is identical to the memory write except that it transfers a complete cache line during the current transaction. The initiator's configuration registers must allow specification of the line size during system configuration. If, when snooping, the cache/bridge's write-back cache detects a memory write and invalidate issued by the initiator and has a snoop hit on a line marked as dirty, the cache can just invalidate the line and doesn't need to perform the flush to memory. This is possible because the initiator is updating the entire memory line and all of the data in the dirty cache line is therefor invalid. This increases performance by eliminating the requirement for the line flush.

**Message**. An initiator may broadcast a message to one or more PCI devices by using the PCI Special Cycle command. During the address phase, the AD bus is driven to random values and must be ignored. The initiator does, however, use the C/BE lines to broadcast the special cycle command. During the data phase, the initiator broadcasts the message type on AD[15:0] and an optional message-dependent data field over AD[31:16]. The message and data are only valid during the clock after IRDY# is asserted. The data contained in, and the timing of subsequent data phases is message dependent.

**Miss**. Refers to a miss on the cache. The processor initiates a memory read or write and the cache controller does not have a copy of the target line in its cache.

**Multi-Function Devices**. A physical PCI component may have one or more independent PCI functions integrated within the package. A component that incorporates more than one function is referred to as a Multi-Function Device.

**Non-Cacheable Memory**. Memory whose contents can be altered by a local processor without using the bus should be designated as non-cacheable. A cache somewhere else in the system would have no visibility to the change and could end up with stale data and not realize that it no longer accurately reflects the contents of memory.

**Packets**. See the definition of **Data Packets**.

**Page Register**. The upper portion of the start memory address for a DMA transfer is written to the respective DMA channel's Page register. The contents of this register is then driven onto the upper part of the address bus during a DMA data transfer.

**Parking**. See the definition of **Bus Parking**.

**PCI**. See the definition of **Peripheral Component Interconnect**.

**Peer PCI Buses**. PCI buses that occupy the same ranking in the PCI bus hierarchy (with respect to the host bus) are referred to as peer PCI buses.

**Peripheral Component Interconnect (or PCI)**. Specification that defines the PCI bus. This bus is intended to define the interconnect and bus transfer protocol between highly-integrated peripheral adapters that reside on a common local bus on the system board (or add-in expansion cards on the PCI bus).

**Physical PCI Device**. See the definition of **Functional PCI Devices**.

**Point-To-Point Signals**. Signals that provide a direct interconnect between two PCI agents. An example would be the REQ# and GNT# lines between a PCI bus master and the PCI bus arbiter.

**Posted-Write Capability**. The ability of a device to "memorize" or post a memory write transaction and signal immediate completion to the bus master. As long as there is room in the posted-write buffer, this permits the bus master to complete memory writes with no wait states. After posting the write and signalling completion to the bus master, the device will then perform the actual memory write.

**Preemption**. Preemption occurs when the arbitrator removes the grant from one master and gives it to another.

**Prefetching**. Fetching a line of information from memory before a bus master requests it. If the master should subsequently request the line, the target device can supply it immediately. This shields the master from the slow access time of the actual target memory.

**Primary Bus**. The bus closest to the host processor that is connected to one side of an inter-bus bridge.

**Reflected-Wave Switching**. The output drivers commonly implemented in highly-integrated components fall into the class II category. They take advantage of the reflected-wave switching characteristic common to high-speed transmission lines and printed circuit traces in order to achieve the input logic thresholds. When a class II output driver transitions a signal line from a logic low to a high, the low-to-high transition is rather weak and only achieves half of the voltage change required to cross the logic threshold. This transition wavefront is transmitted along the trace and is seen sequentially by the input of each device connected to the line. When the wavefront gets to the end of the transmission line, it is reflected back along the trace, effectively doubling the voltage change and thereby boosting the voltage change past the logic threshold. As the wave passes each device's input, the new valid logic level is detected.

**Reserved Bus Commands.** Several of the PCI bus command codes are reserved for future use. Targets should ignore reserved bus commands.

**Resource Lock.** The PCI bus implements a signal, LOCK#. It allows a master (a processor) to reserve a particular target for its sole use until it completes a series of accesses to the target. The master then indicates that it no longer requires exclusive access to the target. One of the nice features of the PCI bus is that it permits other masters to use the bus to access targets other than the locked target during the period that a master has locked access to a particular target.

**Retry.** If a target cannot respond to a transaction at the current time, it will signal "retry" to the initiator and terminate the transaction. The initiator will respond by ending the transaction and then retrying it later. No data transfer takes place during this transaction. An example of the need for a retry would be if the target is currently locked for exclusive access by another initiator.

**SCSI.** Small Computer System Interface. A bus designed to offload block data transfers from the host processor. The SCSI host bus adapter provides the interface between the host system's bus and the SCSI bus.

**Secondary Bus.** The bus further from the host processor that is connected to one side of an inter-bus bridge.

**Sideband Signals.** A sideband signal is defined as a signal that is not part of the PCI bus standard and interconnects two or more PCI agents. This signal only has meaning for the agents it interconnects.

**Single-Function Devices.** A physical PCI component may have one or more independent PCI functions integrated within the package. A component that incorporates only one function is referred to as a Single-Function Device.

**Slave.** Another name for the target being addressed during a transaction.

**Snooping.** When a memory access is performed by an agent other than the cache controller, the cache controller must snoop the transaction to determine if the current master is accessing information that is also resident within the cache. If a snoop hit occurs, the cache controller must take an appropriate action to ensure the continued consistency of its cached information.

**Soft-Encoded Messages.** The first two message codes, 0000h and 0001h, are defined as SHUTDOWN and HALT. Message code 0002h is reserved for Intel device-specific messages, while codes 0003h - through - FFFFh are reserved. Questions regarding the allocation of the reserved message codes should be forwarded to the PCI SIG. Also see the definition of **Message**.

**Special Cycle Command.** See the definition of **Message**.

**Special Interest Group, or SIG.** The PCI SIG manages the specification.

**Speedway.** Intel performed over 5000 hours of simulations in order to establish the best possible layout of the PCI bus on a high-frequency system board. The result is the Speedway (trademarked by Intel) definition. This layout may be used for up to ten physical PCI components operating at speeds up to 33MHz.

**Stale Information.** See the definition of **Dirty Line**.

**Standard Form Factor.** Also referred to as the long card form factor, the standard form factor defines a PCI expansion board that is designed to fit into existent desktop machines with ISA, EISA or Micro Channel™ card slots.

**Streaming Data Procedures.** Advanced bus cycle types implemented on the more advanced Micro Channel machines.

**Subordinate Bus Number.** The subordinate bus number configuration register in a PCI-to-PCI bridge (or a host/PCI bridge) defines the bus number of the highest-numbered PCI bus that exists behind the bridge.

**Subtractive Decode.** The PCI-to-expansion bus bridge is designed to claim many transactions not claimed by other devices on the PCI bus. If the bridge doesn't see DEVSEL# asserted by a PCI target within four PCI clock periods from the start of a transaction, the bridge may assert DEVSEL# to claim the transaction and then pass the transaction onto the standard expansion bus (such as ISA, EISA or the Micro Channel).

**Tag SRAM.** The high-speed static RAM used as a directory by a cache controller.

**Target.** The PCI device that is the target of a PCI transaction initiated by a PCI bus master.

**Target Latency.** Defined as the period of time until the currently-addressed target is ready to complete the first data phase of the transaction. This period is a function of the access time for the currently-addressed target device.

**Target-Abort.** If the target detects a fatal error or will never be able to respond to the transaction, it must signal a target-abort (using the STOP# signal). This will cause the initiator to end the transaction with no data transfer and no retry.

**Target-Initiated Termination.** Under some circumstances, the target may have to end a transfer prematurely. The following are some examples. A very slow access target may force a disconnect between accesses to give other initiators a chance to use the bus. This is known as a *disconnect*. If the current access is quite long and will consume a lot of bus time, the target signals a disconnect, completes the current data transfer, and the initiator terminates the transaction. The initiator then arbitrates for the bus again so that it may re-initiate the transaction, continuing the data transfer at the point of disconnection. If a target cannot respond to a transaction at the current time, it will signal *retry* to the initiator and terminate the transaction. The initiator will respond by ending the transaction and then retrying it. No data transfer takes place during this transaction. An example of the need for a retry would be if the target is currently locked for exclusive access by another initiator. If the target detects a fatal error or will never be able to respond to the transaction, it may signal a *target-abort*. This will cause the initiator to end the transaction with no data transfer and no retry.

**Turn-Around Cycle.** A turn-around cycle is required on all signals that may be driven by more than one PCI bus agent. This period is required to avoid contention when one agent stops driving a signal and another agent begins.

**Type One Configuration Access.** The type one access is used to configure a device on a lower-level PCI bus (in a system with hierarchical PCI buses).

**Type Zero Configuration Access**. The type zero access is used to configure a device on the PCI bus the configuration access is run on.

**Utility Bus**. The utility bus is located on the system board and is a buffered version of the standard expansion bus (ISA, EISA or the Micro Channel). Devices such as the keyboard controller, CMOS RAM, and floppy controller typically reside on the utility bus. This bus is also frequently referred to as the X-bus.

**Vendor ID**. Every PCI device must have a vendor ID configuration register that identifies the vendor of the device.

**VESA**. The Video Electronics Standards Association, or VESA, is a consortium of add-in card manufacturers tasked with developing standards for PC device interfacing.

**VESA VL Bus**. This is the local bus standard developed by the VESA consortium.

**Video Electronics Standards Association (VESA)**. See the definition of **VESA**.

**Video Memory**. Memory that is dedicated to the storage of the video image to be scanned out to the display device.

**VL bus**. See the definition of **VESA VL Bus**.

**VL Type A Local Bus**. This is the direct-connect version of the VESA VL bus. For more information, refer to chapter two.

**VL Type B Local Bus**. This is the buffered version of the VESA VL bus. For more information, refer to chapter two.

**Wait State**. A delay of one PCI clock period injected into a PCI data phase because either the initiator (IRDY# deasserted), the target (TRDY# deasserted), or both are not yet ready to complete the data transfer.

**Write Miss**. The processor initiates a memory write and the cache controller does not have a copy of the target memory location within its cache.

**Write-Back Cache**. The write-back cache controller is a variant of the look-through cache controller. When the processor initiates a memory write bus cycle, the cache controller determines whether or not is has a copy of the target memory location within its cache. If it does, this is a write hit. The cache controller updates the line of information in its cache, but does not initiate a memory write bus cycle to update the line in DRAM memory. This permits processor-initiated memory writes to complete with no wait states. The cache line is now dirty and the memory line is stale. The cache controller will not flush its dirty lines to memory until later. In the event of a miss, the data is written to memory.

**Write-Through Cache**. The write-through cache controller is a variant of the look-through cache controller. When the processor initiates a memory write bus cycle, the cache controller determines whether or not is has a copy of the target memory location within its cache. If it does, this is a write hit. The cache controller updates the line of information in its cache, and also writes it through to DRAM memory. This ensures that the cache and DRAM memory are always in sync. In the event of a miss, the data is written to memory.

**X-Bus**. See the definition of **Utility Bus**.

The following resources were utilized in the preparation of this book:

- The revision 2.1 PCI Local Bus specification.
- The revision 2.1 PCI BIOS specification.
- The revision 1.0 PCI-to-PCI bridge specification.
- The revision 2.10 PCI System Design Guide.
- The revision 1.0 PCI Mobile Design Guide.
- The IEEE Standard for Boot (Initialization Configuration) Firmware: Core Requirements and Practices. IEEE standard number 1275-1994.

The revision 1.0 PCI Multimedia Design Guide came into the authors' possession to late to be referenced in this book.

The PCI SIG has a Compuserve forum. To enter the forum, type GO PCVENH.

# Index

# Index

# MindShare, Inc.
# Technical Seminars

## MindShare Courses

- PCI System Architecture
- PCMCIA System Architecture
- 80486 System Architecture
- EISA System Architecture
- CardBus System Architecture

- Pentium System Architecture
- Plug and Play System Architecture
- ISA System Architecture
- PowerPC 60X Bus Architecture
- PowerPC Software Architecture

## On-Site Seminars

If you are interested in training at your location, please contact us with your requirements. We will tailor our courses to fit your specific needs and schedules.

## Contact MindShare at:

**Internet:** mindshar@interserv.com
**CompuServe:** 72507,1054

**Note:** New courses are constantly under development. Please contact MindShare for the latest course offerings.